Recovered Roots

COLLECTIVE MEMORY AND

Recovered

THE MAKING OF ISRAELI

Roots

NATIONAL TRADITION

YAEL ZERUBAVEL

THE UNIVERSITY OF CHICAGO PRESS
CHICAGO AND LONDON

Yael Zerubavel is associate professor of modern Hebrew literature and culture in the Department of Asian and Middle Eastern Studies at the University of Pennsylvania.

The University of Chicago Press, Chicago 60637
The University of Chicago Press, Ltd., London

04 03 02 01 00 99 98 97 96 95 1 2 3 4 5
ISBN 0-226-98157-6 (cloth)

Library of Congress Cataloging-in-Publication Data

Zerubavel, Yael.
Recovered roots : collective memory and the making of Israeli national tradition / Yael Zerubavel.
p. cm.
Includes bibliographical references and index.
1. Jews—Historiography. 2. Zionism—Philosophy. 3. Memory—Social aspects—Israel. 4. National characteristics, Israeli. 5. Masada Site (Israel)—Siege, 72–73. 6. Jews—History—Bar Kokhba Rebellion, 132–135. 7. Tel Ḥai (Israel)—History. I. Title.
DS115.5.Z47 1994
909′.04924′0072—dc20 94-9441
CIP

♾ The paper used in this publication meets the minimum requirements of the American National Standard for Information Sciences—Permance of Paper for Printed Library Materials, ANSI Z39.48-1984.

TO EVIATAR

Who has shared my journey to the past
with love and understanding

CONTENTS

ILLUSTRATIONS

Following page 200

1. Trumpeldor as an officer in the czarist army
2. Trumpeldor as the commander of the Zion Mule Corps in the British army
3. Central building and yard at Tel Ḥai in 1920
4. Monument of the Roaring Lion at Tel Ḥai
5. Tel Ḥai monument and Upper Galilee
6. Official ceremony at Tel Ḥai on the Eleventh of Adar
7. Aerial view of Masada
8. Youth raising flag at Masada during an early field trip
9. Volunteers and soldiers excavating at Masada
10. Yadin with Ben-Gurion at Masada
11. State burial of Masada defenders
12. Infantry unit of the Israel Defense Forces on the way to Masada
13. Israeli soldiers taking oath of allegiance at Masada
14. Bar mitzvah ceremony at the ancient synagogue of Masada
15. Bar Kokhba confronting a lion (drawing)
16. State burial of Bar Kokhba warriors
17. The Roaring Lion monument (cartoon)
18. Public school text on Yosef Trumpeldor (cartoon)
19. A "one-armed" T-shirt with a drawing of the Roaring Lion (cartoon)

PREFACE

This book is the product of more years of thinking about memory than I care to remember. But if I am to practice what I preach, I cannot but recount its origins. For the selection of a point of beginning, always arbitrary to a degree, sets the stage for the narrative as a whole. Like any reconstruction of the past, these few glimpses into the process of my writing create a story of their own.

The idea of studying the Israeli representations of the past first occurred to me in 1973. At that point I had been living in the United States for a year, enough to make me realize how different was my world of "tradition" from that of my new American Jewish acquaintances. As a second-generation Israeli-born, I was brought up in an exclusively Hebrew environment and raised by its secular national ethos. The distinct Israeli forms of celebrating holidays and commemorating the Jewish past were not only what I learned at school, but also part of my family's tradition. I assumed they were a centuries-long Jewish tradition. When I came to the United States, I realized this was only partly true.

My distinct secular Israeli brand of Jewishness made it quite difficult for me to meaningfully share holiday celebrations with American Jews. They knew the Hebrew prayers and the religious rituals. I, the native Hebrew speaker, had no idea what the prayers were and had to glance at others to find out what I should do during those rituals. Yet I, and other native Israelis, know scores of Hebrew songs for each holiday and share other rituals that are not part of the traditional Jewish script. When we invited American Jewish friends to our Israeli celebrations, they watched in amazement the "exotic folklore" of inexhaustible singing, dances, and performances, which was totally inaccessible to them.

Time has since passed. Closer contact during the last decades has made Israelis and American Jews less exotic to each other. Both cultures have undergone further changes. But what was true then is true now. Israeli Jews have developed a unique culture that, in spite of its Jewishness, is different from that of any other Jewish community. Moreover, the cultural gap between Israeli and American Jews is not an accidental by-product of the Israeli experience, but the result of a deliberate effort by the Jews who immigrated to Palestine to form a new nation with a distinct culture. In this book I explore how this drive to construct the new national Hebrew culture grew out of a certain interpretation of the Jewish past. I also analyze the cultural dynamics that have made it possible to develop a new tradition that is shared today by Israeli-born grandparents and children.

The Yom Kippur War of 1973 accounts in part for my decision to focus on historical events that emerged as heroic myths of the new Hebrew society in Palestine and are still central to Israel's understanding of its past. That wars should serve as both individual and collective temporal markers is, in itself, part of the Israeli experience, where life and history have been punctuated by repeated wars. My parents' generation reached adolescence within the context of rising tensions between Arabs and Jews and the development of Jewish undergrounds in Palestine. Their recruitment to military and paramilitary activities during World War II was soon to be followed by Israel's War of Independence of 1948–49.

I belong to the generation who came into the world during that first war of the State of Israel, who experienced the Suez Campaign of 1956 as young children, and whose rites of passage into adulthood were the 1967 Six-Day War and the prolonged War of Attrition that followed it. The seeds of my adult political consciousness were thus formed during those significant years. For Israeli society 1967 was a deep watershed. It was quite obvious that we were moving from a pre-1967 to a post-1967 Israel, for better or for worse.

In the early parts of my research I was particularly interested in finding out how historical events that had ended in death and defeat could be transformed in Israeli culture into heroic symbols. As my study evolved, I became increasingly intrigued by the various commemorative strategies that made such changes in collective memory possible. My further exploration of a wide variety of cultural expressions relating to the commemoration of these events has reinforced my belief that the study of history and memory touches a sensitive nerve of Israeli society that helps shed light on significant changes of its national culture.

The three cases I selected as the foci of my study—the fall of Masada (A.D. 73), the Bar Kokhba revolt (A.D. 132–35), and the defense of Tel Ḥai (1920)—all fit that mold. Although the first two events took place in Antiquity, they assumed their distinctive significance and prominence in the modern, national Hebrew culture. Although the three events revolve around the issues of death and survival, each has been subject to a somewhat different process of transformation in relation to traditional Jewish memory.

Focusing on the heroic defense of Tel Ḥai was almost self-evident, given its immediate emergence as a highly symbolic event in the secular national Hebrew culture. During the formative years of Israeli society, Tel Ḥai generated a pilgrimage tradition and other commemorative rituals and inspired a considerable body of literature. Pilgrimage to Tel Ḥai was also part of my family tradition. My mother's father is buried in Tel Ḥai, in a special lot for members of Ha-Shomer underground and their spouses. Every summer when we visited Tel Ḥai, I looked at the engraved tomb on my grandfather's grave and at the smooth-faced stone next to it, ready for my grandmother who was standing at my side. I do not recall anyone finding anything peculiar about that situation. But this early experience made me aware of the role of commemoration in establishing invisible ties between the communities of the living and the dead. My present work continues to explore this theme.

Three years ago, when I was already deeply immersed in the writing of this book, I had another unexpected personal encounter with the themes I have been exploring. My daughter had a school assignment to write about the history of her family. I pulled out a book entitled *Darko shel Adam* (A man's route), which was written in memory of my grandfather whom I mentioned above. To my great amazement I realized that my grandfather's life appears to have begun only when he immigrated as a young man to Palestine. Although the book contains photos, letters, notes, and colleagues' memories about his experiences after that, I could not find when and where he had been born. This literary monument thus obliterated his life as a child and adolescent in eastern Europe, constructing his symbolic rebirth as a Zionist pioneer for future generations.

Although I was writing about these very same themes on the national level, this encounter with my grandfather's memorial book was truly shocking: first, because it so powerfully shows the deliberate suppression of memory that any commemorative narrative involves; and second, because in all those times I had looked at the book as a child and a young adult I never thought that there was anything unusual about its beginning. Only when I returned to it as an adult and a mother, involved in the active transmission of a family memory, did I notice this gap.

Since I first conceived of this project, my interests in the dynamics of collective memory have broadened and deepened. Even when I put aside my research on Israeli commemorations of the past and pursued other studies, I came to realize that I was being drawn again to the issues of memory and the reconstruction of the past. I continue to be fascinated by our fundamental need to create meaningful narratives, ignore inconsistencies, silence some stories, and elaborate others; by our enormous capacity to forget and live on, and remember and live on, and take this dual process for granted; by our inexhaustible efforts to continuously reconstruct our memory of the past between words and silences, images and void.

This book is dedicated to Eviatar—my spouse, friend, and intellectual companion. He was the first enthusiastic reader of my work, the one who has trusted it all along, even when I had doubts about it. As his dubious reward, he read more versions of this study than he cared to, and I have benefited greatly from his comments. Without his love, patience, and moral support, as well as his readiness to shoulder more of his share in household activities, this book would never have been completed. My daughter, Noga, who has shared with me the ups and the downs of working on this book, and my son, Noam, who at times expressed his skepticism and personal reservations about the duration of this process, have been an enormous source of pleasure, fun, and pride. They were also there as a constant reminder to me that there are other important dimensions to life beyond the struggle to comprehend the pressures of the past and the working of memory. I am thankful to them for those times they were successful in so doing, and apologize for the times I may have failed to notice. I am passing this book on to them with love, in the hope that it will help them understand their parents' cultural heritage.

During the years I have been engaged in this study, many colleagues and friends have read different sections of this work. I am particularly indebted to Barry Schwartz, Charles Liebman, Mike Aronoff, Tamar Katriel, Ian Lustick, Dan Ben-Amos, Barbara Kirshenblatt-Gimblett, Michael Kammen, John Gillis, Elliott Oring, Peter Novick, Patrick Hutton, David Biale, Janet Theophano, and Jonathan Boyarin for their helpful comments on various parts of the manuscript. I would also like to thank my most immediate colleagues at Penn, Jeffrey Tigay, Barry Eichler, and David Stern, for their encouragement and support during these years, Berel Lang for his helpful suggestions in the final editing of the manuscript, and Etty Lassman for her help in preparing the index. I wish to thank Shulamit Laskov, Nakdimon Rogel, and Yehoshafat Harkabi for sharing with me material from their personal archive, and the University of Pennsylvania and its Research Foundation for giving me a semester of leave and a summer research grant that helped me get closer to the point of completing this book.

INTRODUCTION

This work grows out of the contemporary fascination with history and memory. Perhaps in no other period has the creation of an "archive of the present" turned into such a frenzy of popular activity. Once the exclusive domain of leaders and scholars, it is now conducted by individuals and families, communities and nations. Memory and commemoration have emerged as two major topics of scholarly concern. While psychologists and literary scholars tend to focus on the nature and dynamics of individuals' memory, anthropologists, folklorists, sociologists, social historians, and political scientists explore groups' memory and their social construction, and examine the history and politics of commemoration.

The present work on Israeli collective memory is interdisciplinary in its orientation. This is, to a large degree, a function of the topic itself. The construction of a new nation's memory is one facet of creating a new national culture, and cultures do not lend themselves well to academic disciplinary divisions. The advantage of this approach, I believe, is that it allows us to see the interplay among history, literature, folklore, and politics in the process of constructing a national memory.

In my research I used a wide variety of sources relating to the historical events that I study: public school textbooks, educational brochures produced by youth movements (i.e., youth organizations affiliated with Zionist parties), publications of the Israel Defense Forces' education headquarters, newspaper articles, television and radio programs, popular songs, jokes, plays, poems, children's stories, and novels. During the late 1970s I also conducted 120 in-depth interviews in which I asked twelve- to fourteen-year-old schoolchildren as well as their parents to give me their own accounts of the history and the meaning of the events I studied.[1] The analysis of these diverse sources reveals their intertextuality and makes it possible to identify broader themes within Israeli culture. Tracing these sources from the early formative years of Israeli society to the present provides the study with the historical perspective necessary for unravelling the intricate workings of collective memory.

The first part of the book begins with a general discussion of collective memory, which lays out the conceptual framework for the study as a whole. The first chapter explores the place of collective memory in relation to history and tradition and highlights the importance of commemoration for understanding the dynamic character of group memory. It examines the ways in which collective memory creates a particular periodization and evaluation of the past and turns certain events into political myths. The discussion addresses the emergence of countermemories and their impact on collective memory. The first chapter presents my conceptual approach and the terminology I use throughout the book.

Moving from this general discussion of collective memory to the particular Zionist reconstruction of Jewish history, the second chapter lays out the groundwork for understanding the centrality of the past to Zionist ideology. It explores how Zionism shaped its views in reaction to traditional Jewish memory in order to actively change the course of Jewish history. The Zionist periodization of Jewish history and its portrayal of symbolic continuities and discontinuities within it were designed to enhance its vision of a new national age, and conversely, the Zionist vision of the future was, to a great measure, shaped by its reconstruction of the past. It was within this context that the three events on which this study focuses—the fall of Masada, the Bar Kokhba revolt, and the defense of Tel Ḥai—evolved as major symbolic events in the Zionist Hebrew culture.

Part 2 explores the roots of the new Hebrew commemorations of those events. Chapters 3–5 examine the evolution of these events into central myths of the Jewish society in Palestine. These chapters explore the ways in which memory is transformed within the constraints of the historical records and highlight the selective attitude to tradition underlying the interpretation of this past. They examine how a historic battle in which several settlers die and the survivors evacuate the settlement can become a myth of successful defense and a symbol of "no retreat" (Tel Ḥai); how the leader of a revolt that ends with defeat is remembered as a legendary hero who led the people to freedom (Bar Kokhba); and how a historical episode that ends with a collective suicide is transformed into a myth of fighting to the bitter end and a symbol of national renewal (Masada).

The new commemorative lore that the Hebrew national culture generated is the subject of part 3. The literary reproduction of a national memory was a major part of the pioneering mission of creating a Hebrew national culture. The discussion addresses the role of Hebrew writers in educating the new Hebrew youth with literature that articulates and reinforces the Zionist view of the Jewish past. Many of those early works have indeed become part of the Israeli national lore. This commemorative literature was also supported by the emergence of new commemorative rituals. The linking of historical events to particular days within the Israeli calendar or particular geographical sites likewise helped reshape the meaning of the past. The discussion underscores the impact of the calendrical or geographical anchoring of each of these historical events on the development of its commemorative lore.

The commemoration of historical events is not only a powerful means of reinforcing social solidarity but also an arena of struggle over power and control. Part 4 explores the politics of commemoration and the use of past events as paradigms for understanding the present. In each case, different interpretations of those historical events presented competing claims on Israeli collective memory. While these controversies revolved around the appropriate commemoration of the past, their focus was clearly determined by present politics. The multiple commemorative narratives offered different interpretations of the past and presented opposing moral claims for using it. The disputes over each of the events examined here demonstrate how the past is invoked to promote present political agendas and the emergence of competing interpretations of "history" versus "memory" in Israeli discourse.

The construction of a countermemory not only occurs at the level of a formal political discourse but also is manifested in Israeli popular culture. This was clearly articulated in the rise of humor that targets the commemorative lore of the prestate and early state periods, creating a deliberate inversion of the myths. I collected these humorous texts from media sources, interviews, and informal conversations. The analysis of the oppositional character of this humorous lore and its relation to other kinds of Israeli humor reveals its function as a form of social and political protest.

The concluding chapter draws upon the specific case studies to offer broader observations concerning the study of collective memory and the invention of national traditions. It focuses on the nature and significance of collective memory in a modern society and its relations to history. It addresses the process of narrativization by which history is transformed into a story that defines the relevant "event" and shapes its symbolic meaning. The analysis of Israeli collective memory suggests that a society can have more than one vision of the past and that, as much as history can besiege memory, memory can also besiege history.

The translation of Hebrew texts quoted in the book is mine unless otherwise indicated. In translating I attempted to keep the quotations as close as possible to the original, sometimes perhaps at the expense of the flow of the English text. In order to have the sources I used for this study more easily identifiable, the notes and the bibliography provide Hebrew titles in transliteration, followed by an English translation. Where Hebrew publishers provided an English title, I followed their choice of translation. The transliteration follows the pronounciation of the Hebrew, using *ḥ* for the letter "ḥet," *kh* for "khaf," *ts* for the "tsadi." However, in particular cases where a conventional spelling differs from this rule, I chose to follow the convention (i.e., Eretz, kibbutz, Ben-Zvi, Menachem Begin).

Part One

HISTORY, COLLECTIVE MEMORY, AND COUNTERMEMORY

One

THE DYNAMICS OF COLLECTIVE REMEMBERING

Collective memory has recently emerged as a major focus of interdisciplinary research. This study is part of a growing body of literature exploring the social construction of collective memory, the relationship between history and memory, the role of commemorative narratives and rituals in contemporary social life, and their impact on the political sphere. It explores how a society of immigrants, engaged in constructing a distinct national identity and culture, recreated its roots in the past. These collective memories of recovered roots became a driving force for change and a means of articulating new values and ideas. In this process the new nation relied heavily on both history and tradition. By introducing a highly selective attitude to them, alternating between rejection and acceptance, suppression and elaboration, it has reconstructed a new national memory and tradition.

This book revolves around three historical events, yet it is not a historical study. Rather, it focuses on how members of society remember and interpret these events, how the meaning of the past is constructed, and how it is modified over time. My interest here is at that level of historical knowledge that, in the final analysis, is the most meaningful one in the context of everyday life. As Carl Becker observes:

> The kind of history that has most influence upon the life of the community and the course of events is *the history that common people carry around in their heads.* It won't do to say that history has no influence upon the course of events because people refuse to read history books. Whether the general run of people read history books or not, they inevitably picture the past in some fashion or other, and this picture, however little it corresponds to real past, helps to determine their ideas about politics and society. (Emphasis added)[1]

This book is thus concerned with that level of historical knowledge that Maurice Halbwachs calls collective memory.[2] As Halbwachs points out, every group develops the memory of its own past that highlights its unique identity vis-à-vis other groups. These reconstructed images provide the group with an account of its origin and development and thus allow it to recognize itself through time.[3] Although collective memory is carried by individuals, it expands beyond their autobiographical memory, as its relies on the transmission of knowledge from one generation to another.[4]

Halbwachs's seminal work made a major contribution to the study of collective memory by identifying it as a form of memory that is distinct from both the historical and the autobiographical. By highlighting the importance of understanding collective memory within its social frameworks (*cadres sociaux*), Halbwachs has inspired a growing body of research on the social and political dimensions of commemoration.[5] Yet Halbwachs's desire to highlight the unique qualities of collective memory appears to have led him to overstate its contrast to history. He therefore portrays them as two polar representations of the past. History, the product of a scholarly scrutiny of the records of the past, is essentially a "superorganic" science detached from the pressures of the immediate sociopolitical reality. Collective memory, on the other hand, is an organic part of social life that is continuously transformed in response to society's changing needs.[6]

This opposition is in part explained by Halbwachs's view of history and collective memory as historically situated modes of knowledge. When tradition weakens and social memory is fading, he argues, history emerges as the primary mode of knowledge about the past.[7] The scholarly study of the past is thus a typical expression of the modern era, which has discredited memory as a form of relating to the past. In that sense the contemporary French scholar Pierre Nora follows Halbwachs's approach. Like him he believes in the spontaneity and fluidity of collective memory, which is "in permanent evolution, open to the dialectic of remembering and forgetting, unconscious of its successive deformations, vulnerable to manipulation and appropriation, susceptible to being dormant and periodically revived."[8] Yet history, the critical discourse, has emerged in fundamental opposition to memory, wishing to suppress it. Thus, with the decline of the tradition of memory in modern society, Nora argues, we witness only archival forms of memory located in isolated "sites" (*les lieux de mémoire*). These sites are "fundamentally remains, the ultimate embodiments of a memorial consciousness that has barely survived in a historical age that calls out for memory because it has abandoned it."[9]

As Patrick Hutton points out, few historians today would embrace Halbwachs's view of history as expressed in his *Collective Memory*.[10] Historical writing is inevitably limited by its interpretive perspective, the choice and ordering of information, and narratological constraints.[11] Historians may indeed strive to become detached analysts, but they are also members of their own societies, and, as such, they often respond to prevalent social ideas about the past. In fact, historians may not only share the basic premises of collective memory but also help to shape them through their work, as the history of national movements has shown.[12]

On the other hand, in spite of its dynamic character, collective memory is not an entirely fluid knowledge nor is it totally detached from historical memory. As Barry Schwartz points out, Halbwachs's "presentist approach" undermines the notion of historical continuity by its overemphasis on the adaptability of collective memory. "Given the constraints of a recorded history," Schwartz argues, "the past cannot be literally construed; it can only be selectively exploited."[13] Collective memory continuously negotiates between available historical records and current social and political agendas. And in the process of referring back to these records, it shifts its interpretation, selectively emphasizing, suppressing, and elaborating different aspects of that record. History and memory, therefore, do not operate in totally detached, opposite directions. Their relationships are underlined by conflict as well as interdependence,[14] and this ambiguity provides the commemoration with the creative tension that makes it such a fascinating subject of study.

Collective memory, as this study demonstrates, has by no means disappeared, nor can it be confined to the status of mere "survival" from an older age. Modern societies continue to develop their shared memories of their past in spite of the upsurge of historical research and writing. And even today poets and writers, journalists and teachers often play a more decisive role than professional historians in shaping popular images of the past.[15] A wide range of formal and informal commemorations fuels the vitality of collective memory. Holiday celebrations, festivals, monuments, memorials, songs, stories, plays, and educational texts continue to compete with scholarly appraisals of the past in constructing collective memory.

Although Halbwachs points out the fluidity of collective memory, he does not address the question of *how* it is transformed. Within this context the concept of *commemoration* emerges as central to our understanding of the dynamics of memory change.[16] Collective memory is substantiated through multiple forms of commemoration: the celebration of a communal festival, the reading of a tale, the participation in a memorial service, or the observance of a holiday. Through these commemorative rituals, groups create, articulate, and negotiate their shared memories of particular events.[17] The performance of commemorative rituals allows participants not only to revive and affirm older memories of the past but also to modify them. Indeed, in the novel *Beloved*, Toni Morrison's expression "to rememory" articulates this idea, showing how the symbolic reexperiencing of the past reshapes its memory.[18] On the communal level each act of commemoration makes it possible to introduce new interpretations of the past, yet the recurrence of commemorative performances contributes to an overall sense of continuity of collective memory.

While scholars and intellectuals engage in a formal historical discourse, for most members of the society, knowledge of the past is first and foremost shaped by these multiple commemorations. Moreover, children's early socialization in collective memory precedes their introduction to the formal study of history and can exceed its influence. Schools play a prominent role in the socialization of national traditions. Early-childhood education in particular reinforces those shared images and stories that express and reinforce the group's memory. Children in nursery schools, kindergartens, and the first grades thus learn about major historical figures or events from stories, poems, school plays, and songs. These genres often blend facts with fiction, history with legend, for this colorful blend is believed to render the literature more appealing for the very young.[19] These commemorations contribute to the early formation of sentiments and ideas about the past that might persist even in the face of a later exposure to history.

Each act of commemoration reproduces a *commemorative narrative*, a story about a particular past that accounts for this ritualized remembrance and provides a moral message for the group members. In creating this narrative, collective memory clearly draws upon historical sources. Yet it does so selectively and creatively. Like the historical narrative, the commemorative narrative differs from the chronicle because it undergoes the process of narrativization. As Hayden White observes, the selection and organization of a vast array of chronicled facts into a narrative form requires a response to concerns that are essentially literary and poetic.[20] This fictional dimension, which he points out with regard to the historical narrative, is even more pronounced in the case of the commemorative narrative, which more easily blurs the line between the real and the imagined.[21] The creativity of the commemorative narrative within the constraints of the historical narrative, its manipulation of the historical record with deliberate suppressions and imaginative elaborations, is explored throughout this work.

Each commemoration reconstructs a specific segment of the past and is therefore fragmentary in nature. Yet these commemorations together contribute to the formation of a *master commemorative narrative* that structures collective memory. With this concept I refer to a broader view of history, a basic "story line" that is culturally constructed and provides the group members with a general notion of their shared past.[22]

To fully appreciate the meaning of individual commemorations, then, it is important to examine them within the framework of the master commemorative narrative. The study of the collective memory of a particular event thus calls for the examination of the history of its commemoration as well as its relation to other significant events in the group's past. As we shall see below, the formation of such analogies or contrasts between major historical periods and events is in itself a part of the construction of collective memory.

The master commemorative narrative focuses on the group's distinct social identity and highlights its historical development. In this sense it contributes to the formation of the nation, portraying it as a unified group moving through history.[23] This general thrust often implies a linear conception of time. Yet the master commemorative narrative occasionally suspends this linearity by the omission, regression, repetition, and the conflation of historical events. The holiday cycle, the annual calendar, and the liturgical cycle typically disrupt the flow of time by highlighting recurrent patterns in the group's experiences.[24] Indeed, the tension between the linear and cyclical perceptions of history often underlies the construction of collective memory.[25] As we shall see, the commemorative narratives of specific events often suggest their unique character, while their examination within the context of the master commemorative narrative indicates the recurrence of historical patterns in the group's experience.

Since collective memory highlights the group's distinct identity, the master commemorative narrative focuses on the event that marks the group's emergence as an independent social entity.[26] The commemoration of beginnings is clearly essential for demarcating the group's distinct identity vis-à-vis others. The emphasis on a "great divide"[27] between this group and others is used to dispel any denial of the group's legitimacy. The commemoration of beginnings justifies the group's claim as a distinct unit, often by demonstrating that its roots go back to a distant past. European national movements displayed keen interest in peasants' folklore since they believed that it provided evidence of a unique national past and traditions preserved by this folk.[28] Similarly, more modern nations attempted to recover or invent older traditions to display their common roots in a distant past.[29]

Pierre Nora comments that modern nations celebrate "birth" rather than "origins" to articulate a sense of historical discontinuity.[30] Indeed, birth symbolizes at one and the same time a point of separation from another group and the beginning of a new life as a collective entity with a future of its own. A shift in the commemoration of beginnings can also serve as a means of transforming a group's identity. The more recent emphasis by African Americans on their African origins is a case in point.

While the term "negro" is associated with their past as slaves in America, a greater desire to embrace their earlier African origins has contributed to the recasting of their identity as "African Americans."

Collective memory provides an overall sense of the group's development by offering a system of periodization that imposes a certain order on the past. Like other aspects of collective memory, this periodization involves a dialogue between the past and the present, as the group reconstructs its own history from a current ideological stance. Drawing upon selective criteria, collective memory divides the past into major stages, reducing complex historical events to basic plot structures. The power of collective memory does not lie in its accurate, systematic, or sophisticated mapping of the past, but in establishing basic images that articulate and reinforce a particular ideological stance.

The tendency to provide extreme images in the construction of collective memory accentuates the contrast between different periods and encourages the formation of unambiguous attitudes toward different stages of the group's development. Thus, it highlights certain periods as representing important developments for the group while defining others as historical setbacks. Nations typically portray eras of pioneering, conquest, or struggle for independence as "positive periods"; in contrast, they are likely to define those periods when they were part of a larger empire as essentially negative, denying the full realization of their legitimacy as separate political entities.

The mapping of the past through the construction of a master commemorative narrative also designates its *commemorative density*, which is the function of what Lévi-Strauss calls "the pressure of history."[31] Commemorative density thus indicates the importance that the society attributes to different periods in its past: while some periods enjoy multiple commemorations, others attract little attention, or fall into oblivion. The commemorative density thus ranges from periods or events that are central to the group's memory and commemorated in great detail and elaboration to ones that remain unmarked in the master commemorative narrative. Such periods or events that collective memory suppresses become subjects of *collective amnesia*.[32] Thus, the construction of the master commemorative narrative exposes the dynamics of remembering and forgetting that underlie the construction of any commemorative narrative: by focusing attention on certain aspects of the past, it necessarily covers up others that are deemed irrelevant or disruptive to the flow of the narrative and ideological message. Bernard Lewis points out the phenomenon of recovering a forgotten past. Yet it is no less important to note that such a recovery may lead to the covering up of other aspects of the past. Remembering and forgetting are thus closely interlinked in the construction of collective memory, and it is this duality of the process of recovering and re-covering roots that this book sets out to explore.

Through the restructuring of the past, the commemorative narrative creates its own version of historical time as it elaborates, condenses, omits, or conflates historical events. By using these and other discursive techniques, the narrative transforms historical time into *commemorative time.*[33] Thus, a highly elaborate reference to the past is likely to expand historical time, and conversely, a brief and generalized commemoration symbolically shrinks it within the framework of the narrative. Commemorative time is an important dimension in the analysis of the Zionist master commemorative narrative and the narratives relating to the specific events on which this study focuses.

Although historical changes usually occur over a period of time and as a result of a process rather than a single event, collective memory tends to select particular events and portrays them as symbolic markers of change. The choice of a single event clearly provides a better opportunity for ritualized remembrance than a gradual process of transition does.[34] The master commemorative narrative thus presents these events as *turning points* that changed the course of the group's historical development and hence are commemorated in great emphasis and elaboration. In turn, the selection of certain events as turning points highlights the ideological principles underlying the master commemorative narrative by dramatizing the transitions between periods.

The high commemorative density attributed to certain events not only serves to emphasize their historical significance. It may also elevate them beyond their immediate historical context into symbolic texts that serve as paradigms for understanding other developments in the group's experience. Thus, collective memory can transform historical events into *political myths*[35] that function as a lens through which group members perceive the present and prepare for the future. Because turning points often assume symbolic significance as markers of change, they are more likely to transform into myths. As such they not only reflect the social and political needs of the group that contributed to their formation but also become active agents in molding the group's needs.

Their highly symbolic function of representing historical transitions grants the turning points more ambiguity than events that the master commemorative narrative clearly locates within a particular period. Indeed, the ambiguity stems from their liminal location between periods, presenting a pattern of separation and reincorporation typical of rites of passage in general.[36] As Victor Turner observes: "Liminal entities are neither here nor there; there are betwixt and between the positions assigned and arrayed by law, custom, convention, and ceremonial. As such, their ambiguous and indeterminate attributes are expressed by a rich variety of symbols in the many societies that ritualize social and cultural transitions."[37]

Like other rites of passage, the commemoration of these turning points is imbued with sacredness but also with tensions. This symbolic state of liminality, of being between and betwixt historical periods, contributes to the ambiguity of turning points on the one hand, and to their ability to function as political myths, subject to different interpretations, on the other hand. The ambiguity may be less apparent within a single performance of commemoration that attempts to emphasize a certain meaning of the past and suppress other possible interpretations. But the comparative study of various commemorative performances relating to the same event makes it possible to observe these tensions and the amazing capacity of the myth to mediate between highly divergent readings of the past.

This capacity may help explain why certain events can continue to occupy a central place in the group's memory in spite of the tensions underlying their commemorations. The liminal position of the turning point allows for different interpretations, obscuring the tensions between them, and thereby protecting the sacredness of these events as well as their place within the master commemorative narrative. In some cases, however, a fragile coexistence between divergent interpretations breaks down, and the myth can no longer contain those tensions. At such points the past becomes openly contested, as rival parties engage in a conflict over its interpretation. The discussion of commemorations of specific turning points in Israel shows how myths can successfully contain, and be reinforced by, multiple interpretations and how they can become the subject of heated controversy when the political stakes associated with their mythical meaning become too high to ignore. In such situations the balance between the dominant commemorative narrative and alternative narratives can be upset then triggering a more profound change in the society's collective memory.

The alternative commemorative narrative that directly opposes the master commemorative narrative, operating under and against its hegemony, thus constitutes a *countermemory*. As the term implies, countermemory is essentially oppositional and stands in hostile and subversive relation to collective memory. If the master commemorative narrative attempts to suppress alternative views of the past, the countermemory in turn denies the validity of the narrative constructed by the collective memory and presents its own claim for a more accurate representation of history. This challenge not only addresses the symbolic realm, but obviously has direct political implications. The master commemorative narrative represents the political elite's construction of the past, which serves its special interests and promotes its political agenda. Countermemory challenges this hegemony by offering a divergent commemorative narrative representing the views of marginalized individuals or groups within the society. The commemoration of the past can thus become a contested territory in which groups engaging in a political conflict promote competing views of the past in order to gain control over the political center or to legitimize a separatist orientation.[38]

While this conception of countermemory shares Foucault's emphasis on its oppositional and subversive character, it departs from his insistence on the fragmentary nature of countermemory.[39] Countermemory is not necessarily limited to the construction of a single past event; it can be part of a different commemorative framework forming an alternative overview of the past that stands in opposition to the hegemonic one. In fact, even when countermemory challenges the commemoration of a single event, it is considered highly subversive precisely because the implications of this challenge tend to go beyond the memory of that particular event, targeting the master commemorative narrative.

Indeed, the subversive character of countermemory is acknowledged by regimes that prohibit minority groups from performing their distinctive commemorative rituals. The Bulgarians' efforts to suppress Turkish, Gypsy, Pomak, and Muslim folklore as "foreign" in order to support their construction of a distinct "Bulgarian" identity and past provide such an example.[40] Similarly, the Afrikaners, who had first used their constructions of the past to articulate their opposition to the British, later used them to reinforce the politics of apartheid on the black and colored population of South Africa.[41] But even in democratic societies the tensions between collective memory and countermemories can easily trigger intense public debates about the appropriate and more valid commemorative narrative. The controversy over Thanksgiving can illustrate this point. While the "traditional American" commemoration is constructed from the perspective of the European Pilgrims, a revisionist trend calls to include the Native Americans as active participants rather than as objects of commemoration. The issue is not limited to the specific holiday celebration; it implies a profound revision of the master commemorative narrative and its portrayal of origins. The demand to incorporate the Native Americans' countermemory in what was previously established as "American" collective memory requires the redefinition of the American collective identity and asserts a marginalized group's claim for greater representation.

The existence of such tensions ultimately forges change in collective memory and makes it a dynamic cultural force rather than a body of "survivals" that modern societies simply tolerate. Acts of commemoration recharge collective memory and allow for its transformation. The pressure of countermemory too can contribute to this vitality by encouraging further commemorative activity in response to its challenge. Collective memory can successfully suppress an oppositional memory or hold it in check; but countermemory may also gain momentum and, as it increases in popularity, lose its oppositional status. In such cases countermemory is transformed into a collective memory. The French and the Bolshevik revolutions provide examples of attempts to obliterate older commemorative systems by force, transforming what was previously a countermemory into an official memory, supporting those governments' new political, social, and economic orders.

This study focuses on the Zionist constructions of the past as they were formed in the Hebrew culture of Palestinian Jews and continued to evolve within Israeli culture following the foundation of the State of Israel in 1948. The Zionist views of the past first emerged as countermemory to traditional Jewish memory in Europe. As they developed, they constructed the master commemorative narrative of the society of Zionist settlers who immigrated to Palestine, inspired by the nationalist ideology that called for a revival of Jewish national culture and life in the ancient Jewish homeland.

Since the master commemorative narrative constructs the group's past by its periodization and delineation of major turning points, much can be learned about collective memory by studying these key events. This book therefore analyzes Israeli collective memory by focusing on events that did not occupy a major place in traditional Jewish memory yet emerged as major turning points in the master commemorative narrative of Israeli society. The themes raised in this general discussion will be further explored in the following chapters as we examine the Zionist reconstructions of the past and the development of the commemorations of the fall of Masada, the Bar Kokhba revolt, and the defense of Tel Ḥai within the national Hebrew culture.

Two

THE ZIONIST RECONSTRUCTION OF THE PAST

Although "Zionist" ideologies and immigration to Palestine predated the official establishment of the Zionist movement, the meeting of the first Zionist Congress at Basel in 1897 marked the emergence of Zionism as a major political force in modern Jewish history. Its central role in the revival of Jewish national life in the ancient homeland was ritually expressed in the ceremony in which the first Israeli prime minister, David Ben-Gurion, publicly proclaimed the establishment of the State of Israel in 1948: a picture of Theodor Herzl, the founder of the Zionist movement and the "Prophet of the Jewish State,"[1] was hanging above his head as a symbolic affirmation of his inspiration to Zionist resettlement of Palestine, culminating in the declaration of independence in that historical moment.

The Zionist movement was founded at the end of the nineteenth century in response to the immediate situation of European Jewry. Around that time earlier hopes that the emancipation of the Jews in the modern enlightened European state would solve the problem of Judaism and the Jews eroded. The threat of Jews' assimilation into western European society on the one hand, and the fear of modern antisemitism, dramatized by the 1894 Dreyfus trial in France, on the other hand, became major causes for concern in western Europe.[2]

But Zionism received its greatest impetus from the political and economic plight of the large Jewish communities of eastern Europe during the late nineteenth century and the beginning of the twentieth century. When a series of pogroms broke out in Russia in 1881, it led to a massive Jewish immigration to the United States and stimulated the first organized Jewish efforts to resettle Palestine.[3] The First Zionist Aliya (wave of immigration, literally "going up") followed these pogroms. When bloodshed recurred in 1903 in Kishinev, reports of the death and destruction that it inflicted alarmed the Jews in Russia and elsewhere in Europe. These reports, and the nationalist literature that they inspired,[4] contributed to the public awareness of the importance of an organized action to relieve the situation of Russian Jews and heightened the sense of urgency that marked the agenda of the newly founded Zionist movement.

The Zionist movement, whose members included residents of eastern and western Europe, secular and religious Jews, hard-core socialists and liberal bourgeois, encompassed a wide range of political, social, and religious views. In spite of this diversity, followers of Zionism shared some fundamental views about the Jewish past and the present: they regarded Jewish life in exile as inherently regressive and repressive, and believed in the need to promote some form of revival of Jewish national life as experienced in Antiquity. Although a harsh polemic on the route to achieve national revival split the Zionist movement for a while between the proponents of "cultural" and "political Zionism," it was the latter that became the dominant orientation of the Zionist Organization.[5] Focusing on the politics of rescue as the most pressing agenda, political Zionism advocated the resettling of Russian Jewry in Palestine as the beginning of rebuilding a secure home for all Jews in their ancient homeland. Thus, the first Zionist Congress proclaimed that "Zionism aims at the creation of a home for the Jewish people in Palestine, to be secured by public law."[6]

It was the particular bent of "practical Zionism," however, that became most influential among those who actually took the step of leaving Europe for Palestine at the beginning of this century. While Theodor Herzl's brand of political Zionism focused on the effort to secure political guarantees for the resettlement of Jews, the followers of practical Zionism insisted on immediate action, advocating the resettlement there even before such guarantees were obtained.[7] This position further accentuated the Zionist belief that Jews were to assume a more active role in changing the course of their own history. For the proponents of practical Zionism, the personal and the collective commitment to resettlement, even without waiting for external recognition or support, was a way of promoting such a desired change. This conviction, articulating the Zionist settlers' belief in their historical mission, also helped them endure the difficulties they encountered in the process of implementing their vision. Indeed, the belief that one could act in defiance of an unfavorable political situation in order to promote the national cause was deeply ingrained in the political consciousness of the emergent Hebrew nation in Palestine and represents a fundamental mode of thought in Israeli political culture.

The Zionist reading of Jewish history was an important facet of its political agenda. In fact, Zionist collective memory provided the ideological framework for understanding and legitimizing its vision of the future. The predominantly secular Zionist movement turned away from traditional Jewish memory in order to construct its own countermemory of the Jewish past. In its call for change and its critical attitude toward Jewish life, culture, and values in exile, the Zionist interpretation of history had a strong anti-traditionalist thrust. The majority of Orthodox Jews thus objected to Zionism as a challenge to traditional Jewish life and a negation of the belief in messianic redemption.[8] A religious Zionist minority who supported the Zionist advocacy of immediate action to promote the Jewish settlement of Palestine resolved the tension between the two frameworks by explaining the Jews' own initiative as a preparation for "the beginning of the blossoming of our redemption." Attempting to reconcile Zionist views with religious premises, their vision of the future focused on a Jewish nation governed by the laws of the Torah, a significantly different view from that of the secular majority.[9]

While the religious Zionists grappled with the vision of the future, secular Zionists were more concerned with reshaping the past.[10] This preoccupation with the past stemmed from the recognition that the development of a countermemory was in itself an effective tool for revitalizing Jewish national culture, to liberate it from the impact of centuries of life in exile. The Zionist discourse often resorted to oppositionist rhetoric toward traditional Jewish memory. This overt use, however, obscured the many links to tradition that Zionism retained, as we shall see. Even when the Zionist countermemory began to enjoy hegemony among the Jews of Palestine, thus transforming into collective memory, it continued to maintain an oppositionist pose to the larger and more established Jewish society in exile, in order to highlight the new Hebrew society's distinct identity.

The Zionist Periodization of Jewish History

Any commemorative system is based on certain guiding principles that are essentially ideological. For the Zionists the major yardstick to evaluate the past was the bond between the Jewish people and their ancient land. Influenced by European romantic nationalism on the one hand and drawing upon a long, distinctively Jewish tradition of longing to return to the ancient homeland on the other, Zionism assumed that an inherent bond between the Jewish people and their ancient land was a necessary condition for the development of Jewish nationhood. Indeed, the movement's name, Zionism, was based on the Hebrew name of the ancient homeland, Zion, articulating the centrality of this bond between the people and the land.[11] The 1903 "Uganda crisis" marked the failure of an alternative policy of substituting another territory for Palestine for the revival of Jewish national life. The vehement opposition to this idea within the Zionist movement served to affirm the Zionists' commitment to the Land of Israel as the only viable option for rebuilding the Hebrew nation.[12]

The Zionist periodization of Jewish history is thus based on the primacy of the people-land bond: the past is divided into two main periods, Antiquity and Exile. Antiquity begins with the tribal (prenational) history of Abraham and his descendants, leading to their migration to Egypt. Yet it is the Exodus from Egypt that marks the transition from a promise (to Abraham) to actual fulfillment. It also established the commemorative paradigm of national liberation in Jewish tradition, ritually affirmed every year in the celebration of three major holidays—Passover, Shavuot, and Sukkot.[13] The national past begins with the Israelites' conquest of ancient Canaan and extends over centuries of collective experience there. Antiquity ends with a series of revolts that fail—the Great Revolt against the Romans during the first century, followed by the failure of the Bar Kokhba revolt in the second century.

The period of Exile, in turn, covers the many centuries when Jews lived as a religious minority dispersed among other peoples. Exile thus embodies the loss of both physical bond with the ancient homeland and the Jews' collective experience as a unified nation. More problematic was the delineation of its ending, since Jewish life in exile actually continued at the time when the Zionist settlement in Palestine was in process, although it was expected to bring Exile to an end. The actual fulfillment of the Zionist ideology was thus motivated by the double vision of ending the state of exile and of beginning a new national era.

In itself this periodization of the Jewish past into Antiquity and Exile did not mark a revolutionary break with Jewish memory: Jewish tradition, too, differentiated Jewish life in exile from the ancient past in the Land of Israel. It, too, commemorated Zion and *galut* (the homeland and exile) as two distinct situations in the Jewish collective experience. But Jewish tradition also offered alternative periodizations of the past, such as classifying it by different generations of rabbinical scholars or the writings that they produced (namely, the Tana'anic period or the Mishna period).

For traditional Judaism, exile from Zion was a divine punishment, but it was also a condition that highlighted the Jews' spiritual mission as the chosen people. During centuries of life in exile the meaning of the concepts of Zion and *galut* continued to evolve and remained interconnected. No longer embedded only within a political-historical reality, they attained a spiritual, metaphysical meaning that made it easier to endure the state of exile: Zion was not only a physical homeland but also a metaphysical land that the Jews carried with them wherever they went.[14] Although Zionism pursued the traditional binary opposition of Zion and *galut*, it offered a primarily historicist approach to their interpretation. It thus forced Jewish memory to recreate itself by turning from a theological to a historical framework.

In its reconstruction of Jewish history, the Zionist commemorative narrative accentuated the perception of a "great divide" between Antiquity and Exile. The result of this process was twofold: it highlighted the contrast between these two major periods, but it also imposed a sense of uniformity within each period. By grouping eighteen centuries of Exile into one period, the Zionist commemorative narrative overlooked the considerable cultural, economic, social, and political differences in the development of various Jewish communities. Underlying this periodization is the assumption that the exilic condition is more central to Jewish communities' experience than any other dimension of their lives that would distinguish, for example, between the Babylonian Jewry during the fourth century and the Jews of Spain during the twelfth century, or the Jews of eastern Europe in the nineteenth century.

This periodization obviously requires a highly selective representation of many centuries of Jewish experience in a vast range of geographical territories and ignores historical developments that do not fit the principles underlying this mold. For example, it ignores the exile of the ten tribes of Israel from their land, which occurred within the period of Antiquity (722 B.C.), and the long stretches of time during that period when the Israelites lived under Babylonian, Persian, Greek, and Roman rule and their political freedom was severely curtailed. It also suppresses the memory of Jewish revolts against a foreign rule by those who remained in Judaea after the second century,[15] and incidents of Jewish self-defense during the Middle Ages, namely, within the Exile period.[16] The acceptance of the Zionist commemorative framework as given buries important social, economic, and cultural developments that do not relate directly to the political expressions of nationhood, and obscures the continuity within Jewish life between Antiquity and Exile.

Nonetheless, the emphasis on a great divide separating Antiquity from Exile articulates Zionism's ideological message that the political expression of nationhood stands above and beyond any other criterion of classifying Jewish history. Playing Antiquity and Exile against each other was necessary for constructing distinctive commemorative attitudes for each. It was also important for creating an equally dramatic contrast between Exile and the Zionist revival on the other end, marking the beginning of a new national period.

Exile: Suppressed Nationhood, Discredited Past

The Zionist binary model of Jewish history portrays Antiquity as a positive period, contrasted with a highly negative image of Exile. Since the main criterion for this classification is the bond between the Jewish people and their land, the period of Exile is essentially characterized by a lack. The dispersion to many localities resulting from the loss of direct contact with the land thus undermined the Jews' shared experience of nationhood. During centuries of exile, religion functioned as the adhesive bond for the dispersed Jewish communities. But this exilic way of life was a poor substitute for the earlier national phase, thus conveying a process of spiritual degeneration as well as political regression.

In its highly negative attitude toward the period of Exile and belief in the nation's inner vitality as a historical force, Zionism was influenced by European political and philosophical movements. But the negative view of Exile also continued a trend that began with the Jewish enlightenment, the Haskala, of portraying a highly negative picture of traditional communal life among observant Jews, with an emphasis on talmudic learning and use of the Yiddish language. Much of the Hebrew literature that was used by Hebrew schools in Europe and Palestine during the first decades of the twentieth century was written by Haskala writers and imbued with a critical portrayal that reinforced, in turn, the Zionist youth's negative attitude toward Exile.[17]

Zionism essentially emerged as a reaction against Exile and reflects an acute awareness of the need to find a solution to the problems of the Jewish people and exilic Judaism. In fact, even those who did not regard the return to the Land of Israel as the vital solution to the Jewish problem and who were reconciled to the idea of Jewish life outside the ancient homeland often shared a negative attitude toward Exile.[18]

Zionist collective memory thus constructs Exile as a long, dark period of suffering and persecution. Jewish life in exile constituted a recurrent history of oppression, punctuated by periodic pogroms and expulsions, of fragile existence imbued with fear and humiliation. For the Zionist settlers who left eastern Europe after pogroms, persecution was their final and decisive association with Jewish life in exile, both personally and collectively. They projected those memories back onto the period of Exile as a whole, enhancing the antiexilic attitude that had already marked Zionist memory.[19] The Socialist Zionist leader David Ben-Gurion stated that Exile consists of "'histories' of persecution and legal discrimination, the Inquisition, and pogroms; of self-sacrifice and martyrdom."[20] Another prominent Socialist Zionist, Ya'akov Zerubavel, similarly described Exile as consisting of "the Inquisition and the stake, the expulsion and the tortures, [and] the pogroms." He continued this statement by raising a rhetorical question: "Which other nation has such abundance of martyrs . . . in tragedies which have their source in the passivity of our faith?"[21] This view was later reiterated by a fictional character, Yudke (whose name means "the little Jew"), who protests vehemently against Jewish history in Exile: "You cannot imagine how I'm opposed to it, how I reject it, and how . . . how . . . I don't respect it! Now look! Just think . . . what is there in it? Just give me an answer: What is there in it? Oppression, defamation, persecution, martyrdom. And again oppression, defamation, persecution, martyrdom. And again, and again and again, without end."[22]

The highly negative perception of Exile often turned from *shelilat ha-galut* (the repudiation of the state of living in exile) to *shelilat ha-gola* (the condemnation of the people who live in exile), the product of its demeaning and regressive lifestyle. According to this view, life in exile turned the Jews into oppressed, submissive, weak, and fearful people who passively accept their fate, hoping to be saved either by God or by Gentiles' help. The Zionist image of the exilic Jew often seemed to incorporate antisemitic stereotypes to support this negative portrayal.[23] Exile, Ya'akov Zerubavel wrote, taught the Jew the need "to shrink and to bend one's back."[24] Yitzḥak Ben-Zvi, the Socialist Zionist leader who later became Israel's second president, expressed a similar view of the Jewish past: "The spirit of heroism and courage disappeared in the Jewish ghetto in which it had no place." Instead, he argued, the Jews adapted "a sharp mind, agility, submissiveness toward others, and patience, cowardice, and timidity in relation to neighbors and rulers." This Jewish behavior, continued Ben-Zvi, resulted in a tendency to rely on miracles, as Jews lacked either confidence or self-motivation to improve their situation.[25]

The period of Exile thus represents a "hole" between the two national periods, an acute lack of positive characteristics attributed to it. As a Zionist Revisionist youth articulated this idea: "I stand stirred by the heroism and greatness of the Maccabees, Bar Kokhba, and Elazar ben Yair, but all that happened thousands of years ago. We lack someone in the middle."[26] Exile displays the Jews' choice to prove their devotion to the Jewish faith through a martyr's death. Kiddush ha-Shem (i.e., death for the sanctification of God's name), the traditional Jewish concept of martyrdom, represents the Jews' failure to offer armed resistance to their persecutors and actively defend themselves. It was therefore criticized as an expression of passivity or perceived as an inferior form of "passive heroism" relative to the "active heroism" of armed resistance. As a result Exile turned into a dark and bloody period in Jewish history: "Much Jewish blood was poured during the entire period of Exile, all over the world. Not the blood of heroes, but the blood of 'sanctifiers.'"[27] The distinction between sanctifiers (i.e., martyrs) and heroes is thus significant. Heroes, the writer goes on to explain, can be found only when the nation lives in its own homeland. Therefore, those who die in the battle for their country are recognized as heroes, a status denied to sanctifiers who die for Kiddush ha-Shem in Exile.[28] Death for one's faith may have been the only form of heroism available to the displaced exilic Jew, but this was a mere substitute for the more honorable death for one's country. The same view was articulated by one of my informants, a man who grew up in Palestine during the prestate period:

> The Jews who live in Israel resemble much more the Jews of Masada, because they [the Masada people] had a state and had something to die for. While the Jews of Exile did not have a state and the only thing they could fight for was their lives. While here we have something else. Although according to traditional stories they [the Jews of Exile] fought for Kiddush ha-Shem and fought for the religion and for other things, these were substitutes. But the main reason they fought for substitutes was that they did not have the basic thing, and this is the state.

When the poet Bialik published his famous poem "be-Ir ha-Harega" (In the city of slaughter) in reaction to the Kishinev pogrom of 1903, it was largely perceived as a severe condemnation of the passivity of the Jews.

> Come, now, and I will bring thee to their lairs
> The privies, jakes and pigpens where the heirs
> Of Hasmoneans lay, with trembling knees,
> Concealed and cowering—the sons of the Maccabees!
> The seed of saints, the scions of the lions . . .
> Who crammed by scores in all the sanctuaries of their shame,
> So sanctified My name!
> It was the flight of mice they fled
> The scurrying of roaches was their flight;
> They died like dogs, and they were dead![29]

This highly negative portrayal of Exile was regarded as a crucial countermodel for the construction of a Hebrew national identity and was therefore raised as a central theme in the education of the New Hebrew youth.[30] "Anything that relates to Exile, or anything that has something of Exile's spirit in it, or anything that smells of Exile, should be out of the reach of this youth."[31] Exile was thus portrayed as "pollution" or "disease" that might undermine the development of the New Hebrew Man. During the first decades of the century, Hebrew literature became the central medium for transmitting the "repudiation of Exile." History textbooks, slower to respond to changing social views than literature was, began to emphasize the themes of pogroms and persecution in Exile from the 1930s on. Exilic Jews were thus portrayed as objects rather than subjects, victims rather than actors.[32]

The "repudiation of Exile" provoked criticism from those concerned about the youth's ignorance and dismissive attitude toward centuries of Jewish life and culture. Such critics warned that this attitude provides a highly biased view of Exile and undermines the youth's sense of historical continuity. "We have developed a contempt toward Exile that brought with it the neglect of the wonderful cultural and social values that developed in it," observed the historian Ben-Tsiyon Dinur in 1934.[33] Similar criticism of the highly negative and reductionist image of the Exile period was repeated by the philosopher Shmu'el Hugo Bergman in the early 1960s.

> The Jewish Israeli youth that has never seen Exile lacks the understanding of its greatness . . . To this youth, Exile seems a history of tears and humiliation, and they do not know the happiness and the light, the festivities and the exaltation that were part of Jewish life in exile. They erroneously believe that all the great classical achievements of our people have been accomplished in the Land of Israel, an error that was transmitted by their teachers.[34]

Yet if Zionist collective memory constructed a major gap between Exile on the one hand and the national periods of Antiquity and the modern National Revival on the other hand, it stopped short of its total rejection. As the historian Shmuel Almog notes, such an extreme position would have undermined the Zionist claim for historical continuity between Antiquity and the present, between the ancient Hebrews and contemporary Jews. Thus, even the most severe Zionist critics of Exile did not advocate a total rupture with it.[35] Indeed, when the small but vocal movement of the Young Hebrews (also known as the "Canaanites") advocated a full rupture between members of the new Hebrew nation and the Jews of Exile,[36] their views provoked a highly critical response. Their claim that the Hebrews of the Land of Israel and the Jews of Exile were two separate collective identities was thus largely rejected.

Having constructed a profound tension between Hebrew and Jewish identities, the secular Zionist collective memory showed a clear preference for presenting the former as a transformation of the latter. Although it wished to accentuate its break with Jewish tradition, it relied on this tradition as its legitimizing framework. As Yosef Gorni points out, the ambivalent attitude toward Exile was further complicated by the strong ideological, organizational, and economic ties between the new society in Palestine and the larger and more established Jewish community that remained in exile.[37] When Hebrew youth's critical approach to Exile and its Jews became more salient during the Holocaust, concerned educators urged introducing a more positive image of Jewish life in Europe and playing up examples of heroic behavior during Exile, to counterbalance that cultural trend.[38]

Jewish longing for Zion during centuries of life in exile as well as sporadic Jewish immigration to Palestine during those centuries supported the Zionist claim for the Land of Israel as its national home. The Zionist suppression of positive aspects of exilic life to promote the centrality of the people-land bond was reinforced by its denial of centuries of Palestinian life in that land. This double denial made it easier to reshape the period of Exile as a temporary regression between the two national periods, metaphorically suspending time and space in order to appropriate both into the Zionist commemorative narrative. Ironically, the recovery of the nation's roots in the ancient past implied playing down its roots in Exile as well as the renunciation of the Palestinians' roots in the same land.

In the formative years the repudiation of Exile provided a way of coming to terms with the enormous difficulties inherent in the task of tearing away from the old society and building a new nation. The darker the imagery associated with Exile, the greater was the promise that Zionism offered and the rationalization for the price it demanded. Yet even during the years following the foundation of the state, Israeli collective memory dwelled on the negative aspects of Jewish life in Exile and constructed a negative image of its Jewry. Although Israeli collective memory has been transformed and its negative construction of Exile has weakened, this representation has by no means disappeared, and the issue of the repudiation of Exile still occupies Israeli scholars and intellectuals.[39]

Locating the Nation: Antiquity and the National Revival

The Zionist collective memory constructs Antiquity as a period in which the ancient Hebrew nation flourished, enjoying an autonomous political, social, and cultural life. Antiquity is thus seen as the nation's golden age, the period to which the Zionists wished to return to recover their lost national roots: the national spirit, the Hebrew identity, the Hebrew language, their homeland, and the social, economic, and political structures of an independent nation. In Zionist memory the ancient Hebrews formed a proud nation, rooted in its land; they cultivated its soil and knew its nature;

they were ready to fight for their national freedom and, if necessary, to die for it. This romantic picture was clearly constructed as the counterimage of Exile and as an inspiration for the new modern era.[40]

Within Antiquity various biblical heroes appealed to the Zionist memory and imagination, among them Samson, Gideon, Saul, and David. But the secular national Hebrew culture displayed an even stronger fascination with the period of the Second Temple.[41] Judaea's wars of liberation against various imperial forces during that period—culminating in the Maccabees' revolt against the Syrians and the Jewish revolts against the Romans during the first and second centuries—gradually became the "hottest" events in the Zionist collective memory in Palestine. These revolts represented the ultimate commitment to national freedom, which the Zionists were so eager to revive: they provided examples of the ancient Hebrews' readiness, when oppressed, to stand up against a more powerful enemy and to sacrifice their lives for the nation. Such figures as Judah the Maccabee, Yoḥanan of Gush Ḥalav, Elazar ben Yair, and Bar Kokhba, who rose as leaders of those ancient revolts, provided the Zionist settlers and the Hebrew youth with historical models for their own struggle for national renewal, the importance of which they knew but whose outcome they could not predict.

These ancient heroes became vivid images for Hebrew youth: "Here I see the supreme heroes who served our people and who have become our symbols . . . I see them in my mind's eye: Judah the Maccabee standing in front of his army and making [his soldiers] take an oath of allegiance; Bar Giora, Elazar, the hero of Masada, Bar Kokhba."[42] The memory of the ancient revolts was also important as a proof that Judaea fell not out of indifference or lack of patriotic zeal, but in spite of intense and desperate fights for its autonomy. The Zionists would therefore continue the spirit of total commitment that the period symbolized. As the poet Ya'akov Cahan declared, "In blood and fire Judaea fell; in blood and fire Judaea will rise."[43]

In commemorating these wars of liberation, the tendency was to play up the national-political aspects of these conflicts and diminish their religious significance. This orientation also marked the teaching of history in the new Hebrew schools.[44] Although the subperiodization of Antiquity into the First Temple and Second Temple periods might appear to enhance the religious dimension, their common representation in modern Hebrew as the First or Second "House" eliminates the explicit reference to their sacred dimension and renders them closer in spirit to the English terms, the First or Second Commonwealth.[45]

The Zionist emphasis on the national-political significance of the past was clearly shaped by Zionist settlers' belief in their historical contribution to the modern era of nation building. No longer waiting for a divine sign or intervention on their behalf, they saw themselves as a group of ideologically committed individuals who left exile on their own initiative to return to the Land of Israel. This nonreligious approach was easily transformed into a more radically antireligious attitude, suggesting that "self-redemption" also expressed an act of defiance against God. "To arms, comrades! Seize sword and lance, spear and javelin—advance! Heaven's rage defy, and in storm reply. Since God denies us, his ark refuses us, we will ascend alone," wrote the Hebrew national poet Ḥayim Naḥman Bialik.[46] Although the explicit reference here is to that ancient generation who died in the desert on the way to the Promised Land, they can also be seen as representing the Jews of exile rebelling against God to free them from their imprisonment there.

Hebrew culture from the prestate period suggests that this shift from the religious to the national was pervasive. This was clearly manifested in the transformation of biblical or traditional allusions to God into a reference to the people of Israel.[47] Thus, the biblical verse praising God, "the guardian of Israel, neither slumbers nor sleeps" (Psalms 121 : 4) was applied to new Zionist "guards," the representatives of the ideology of Jewish self-defense. Changing the traditional memorial prayer (Yizkor) from "let God remember" to "let the people of Israel remember" is another expression of this orientation.[48] These transformations implied that the people's will would be the most important force for changing the course of history, an idea that was clearly articulated in a saying attributed to Herzl: "If you will, it is not a dream."[49] That this saying became an important slogan in the emergent national Hebrew culture indicates the centrality of the secular activist ethos that it reinforced.

Zionist collective memory not only defied Exile and its spirit; it also blamed it for a deliberate suppression of the national memory of the ancient struggles for liberation. The high commemorative density of these revolts was therefore seen as an important act of revolt against Jewish memory and its constraints. Consider the following quotation from a preface to the popular historical anthology on historical evidence of Jewish heroism, *Sefer ha-Gevura* (The book of heroism), written by Berl Katznelson, the prominent Socialist Zionist leader who was particularly active in the cultural and social spheres:

> With the loss of political freedom, Jewish historiography lost its freedom as well . . . The power of forgetfulness and omission in Jewish history is great . . . That which escaped from external censorship was caught by internal censorship. Did we get any of the Zealots' writings? Those expressions of Hebrew heroism that did not result in victory were doomed to oblivion . . .

> But with the rise of Zionism, a new light was shed on the defeated and neglected Jewish heroism. The forgotten people of Masada were saved from a foreign language; Rabbi Akiba now appears to us not only as the old man who sat in the Yeshiva [a religious academy of learning], but also as the prophet of the revolt; and Bar Koziba has been transformed back into Bar Kokhba in people's minds.[50]

The writer and Zionist activist who later founded the Zionist Revisionist movement, Ze'ev (Vladimir) Jabotinsky, made similar observations regarding the transformation of Jewish memory of the Hasmonean revolt. Jabotinsky accused "the sophistic mind of the ghetto" of distorting history by deliberately wiping out the memory of the Hasmoneans and turning the commemoration of the historical revolt to a celebration of a divine miracle of the flask of oil for the performance of religious worship at the Temple.[51] Indeed, Ḥanukka provides an excellent example of the transformation of traditional Jewish memory in the secular national Hebrew culture and the rising importance of its place in the curriculum of the Hebrew schools as a paradigm of a national struggle for freedom.[52]

The belief in Jewish collective amnesia as far as the national heroic aspects of the past were concerned led to a deliberate Zionist search for suppressed symbols of ancient heroism. Zionist collective memory thus turned to previously belittled leaders and groups involved in the ancient Jewish wars and rehabilitated them as part of Zionism's desired national revival. Thus, the terms *kana'im* (Zealots), *Sikarikim* (Sicarii), and Biryonim, which had been coined as derogatory names of extremist groups were now raised as positive references.[53] The discussion of Masada and the Bar Kokhba revolt in secular national Hebrew culture in chapters 4 and 5 will provide a closer examination of the drastic transformation of their commemoration along these lines.

The reawakening of a dormant "national memory" was thus seen as an expression of triumph over Exile and a means of obliterating its influence. The Zionist choice of an activist approach to the future was thus intimately linked to an activist view of the ancient past. The selective reconstruction of Antiquity was part of the historical mission of reviving the ancient national roots and spirit. Antiquity became both a source of legitimation and an object of admiration. Zionist collective memory emphasized the identification with heroes of the ancient past.

In fact, Zionist memory shaped the image of the young generation of New Hebrews as "grandsons" of the ancient heroes. This association acknowledged the existence of "fathers" (namely, the Jews of Exile) to allow for continuity within the Jewish past, but it enhanced the affinity between the ancient forefathers and the New Hebrews while marginalizing the exilic

Jews. A eulogy for Trumpeldor, the dead hero of Tel Ḥai, thus stated: "He fell dead, the hero of Israel! Like a figure of ancient magic this man was, *the great-grandson of the ancient heroes of Israel,* one of those who joined Bar Kokhba's host, one of those who followed the hero of Gush Ḥalav."[54] At times the need to emphasize symbolic continuity resulted in the projection of modern-day issues on Antiquity. This was the case in Ya'akov Zerubavel's statement that applied contemporary socialist concerns to the ancient Hebrews: "The Biryonim and the soldiers of Bar Kokhba were the last fighters for political freedom and *free labor* in the Land of Israel. Their grandchildren, the Hebrew workers, are the first fighters for free Jewish life, life of labor and creation in the Land of Israel."[55]

The use of the adjective *ivri* (Hebrew) to reinforce the tie with the ancient past and to dissociate from the concept *yehudi* (Jewish) had appeared prior to the emergence of Zionism as a political ideology.[56] But for the Zionists it was particularly appealing as a way of marking the symbolic discontinuity between the period of Exile and the modern National Revival. Zionism wished to present the "Jew" with an opportunity to transform into a "Hebrew" or, as Berdiczewski puts it, to be "the last Jews or the first members of a new nation."[57]

The pervasive use of the term "Hebrew" during the prestate period thus implied both symbolic continuity with the ancient national past and departure from Exile. The mere addition of this adjective was indicative of the national significance attributed to its referent. Thus, the Hebrew culture celebrated the emergence of "Hebrew youth," "Hebrew work," "Hebrew guards," "Hebrew labor union," "Hebrew literature," "Hebrew schools," "Hebrew language," and other such manifestations of its growing distance from traditional Jewish culture.

While the term "Hebrew" was also popular in Zionist circles outside of Palestine, the secular national Hebrew culture greatly enhanced the contrast between the "Hebrew" and the "Jew," along with its repudiation of Exile.[58] The highly negative image of the Jew of Exile was counterbalanced by the no less extreme positive image of the new native Hebrew, later known by the nickname *Tsabar* (Sabra).

> The Sabra became a mythological—and necessarily also archetypal—figure that forms a solid mold by which the Israeli-born would be shaped. The superior Sabra is characterized not only by what he possesses, but also by that which he does not have: he has no fear, weakness, or timidity; he has none of the exilic spirit [*galutiyut*]. He is the product of the Land of Israel, the outcome of generations' hopes, and he stands in contrast to the Jew of Exile. He is Hebrew

> and not Jew, and he is to put an end to the humiliation of his fathers. Anything that the Jew has lacked he has: strength, health, labor, return to nature, deep-rootedness, and a little of the peasant's slowness and heaviness.[59]

The New Hebrew was thus expected to be closer to his ancient forefathers than to his exilic parents. Accordingly, the uprooted Jew turns into a native who is deeply rooted in the homeland, settles in it, works its soil, and is fully prepared to defend it. Unlike the passive, submissive image of the exilic Jew, the New Hebrew is seen as active, self-reliant, and proud. The desire to compensate for what was seen as the excessive spirituality and verbosity of the exilic Jew resulted in the admiration of activism and physical strength.[60] The New Hebrew was thus portrayed as a man of action, not a man of words. His emergence would help recover the national pride and dignity that was lost during Exile.[61]

Within this context, it should not come as a surprise that the new Hebrew society in Palestine, which referred to itself as the Yishuv (Settlement), cultivated a special admiration for its youth, the new representatives of the Hebrew. For the Zionist settlers the young generation of Hebrews was the key to the future, the concrete evidence of the success of their vision and efforts to rebuild the nation. Youth worship, as the historian George Mosse points out, is characteristic of periods of dramatic political and social change.[62] Revolutionary movements mark their futurist orientation by symbols that revolve around young people or project youthfulness. In its portrayal of the New Hebrews as a radically transformed breed of Jews, Zionism reached closest to a revolutionary stance. However, even though the imagery of the New Hebrew often implied a dramatic contrast to its "Jewish" predecessor, Zionism rejected a total rupture between the two, as the response to the Canaanites showed. Zionism thus sought to induce a "fundamental" rather than a "radical" transformation,[63] using different periods of the past as both a countermodel and a source of legitimation.

More than realistic portrayals, the Zionist constructions of the exilic Jew and the New Hebrew suggest ideal types that provide another link between the Zionist view of the past and its vision of the future. Similarly, the construction of a new native Hebrew culture was more of an aspiration than a description of a reality. The cultural situation in Palestine was, indeed, much more complex. As the cultural critic Itamar Even-Zohar points out, many "exilic" and foreign elements were incorporated into the supposedly native Hebrew culture. The blend of new and old, Jewish and foreign, is particularly evident in such domains as dress, food, dance, and songs, which were the product of an attempt to construct indigenous cultural expressions.[64]

In spite of its constructed character as an ideal type, the "Hebrew" image was internalized by the Yishuv society and new Jewish immigrants were met with the social expectation that they would transform accordingly. The emergence of a literary archetype of the native youth in the literature of the late 1940s and the 1950s indicates the internalization of this image by Hebrew youth themselves. Ironically, one of the symbolic expressions of the parents' success in transmitting the ideal of a New Man is youth's self-portrayal in the literature as metaphorically "parentless." As the literary critic Gershon Shaked remarks, when Moshe Shamir chose to begin his 1951 novel, *Bemo Yadav* (By his own hands) with the statement that its young hero, Alik, was born of the sea, he was in fact articulating the social and literary expectations of that period.[65] Along with the admiration of the new Hebrew youth and culture, enormous pressures were exerted on new immigrants to relinquish their own languages and traditions and accept the values and norms of the Hebrew culture. Indeed, only during the last two decades has Israeli society begun to face the political and cultural manifestations of the deep psychological scars that these pressures produced.[66]

The Zionist vision of national revival centers around the image of the New Hebrew, but land and language were essential aspects of this revival. Here too, the construction of the past provided the guidelines to the future: national life degenerated in Exile as a result of the rupture from the ancestral land, Zion, and the use of a new hybrid language, Yiddish. The vision of the modern National Revival thus centered upon three main elements: the Hebrew man, the Land of Israel, and the Hebrew language.

National redemption was thus intimately linked to the idea of redeeming the land. The Zionist settlers believed that in the process of settling in and working the land they would find their own personal and collective redemption. As a most popular Hebrew song of the prestate period notes, "We have come to the homeland to build [it] and be rebuilt [in it]." The attachment to the land was further reinforced by the educational emphasis on the study of agriculture, nature, as well as local geography and history (known as a class on *moledet* [homeland]). *Yediat ha-aretz* (knowing the Land) did not simply mean the recital of facts in the classroom, but rather an intimate knowledge of the land that can only be achieved through a direct contact with it. As we shall see later, trekking on foot throughout the land was particularly considered as a major educational experience, essential for the development of the New Hebrews. During the prestate period, Hebrew schools and the highly popular youth movements assigned great significance to such trips.[67]

To erect a Hebrew settlement and work its land required a total commitment, devotion, and readiness for sacrifice.[68] Tel Ḥai emerged as a central myth of the settlement period because it was believed to demonstrate the significance of these values. Death for the country was itself a modern reenactment of the ancient spirit of heroism, indicating the beginning of a new national era.[69] The importance of working the land was particularly enhanced by the Socialist Zionists and received its most explicit expression in the teachings of A. D. Gordon. Gordon's writing, which focused on the link between the physical and spiritual dimensions of work, highlighted its sacred nature and gave rise to the concept *dat ha-avoda* (the religion of labor).[70] In the same vein, the poet Avraham Shlonsky portrayed the pioneers' work of building settlements and toiling on the land as sacred acts, using terms borrowed from the Jewish ritual domain:

> My land is wrapped in light as in a prayer shawl.
> The houses stand forth like frontlets;
> and the roads paved by hand, stream down like
> phylactery straps.
>
> Here the lovely city says the morning prayer to its Creator.
> And among the creators is your son Abraham,
> a road-building bard of Israel.[71]

Settling was a central pioneering activity that implied rerooting in the land. Founding a new settlement was defined as the ultimate realization (*hagshama*) of the pioneering ideology which Zionist youth movements transmitted to its members. Perhaps the most obvious expression of the prominence of this activity was the emergence of the concept of Yishuv, Settlement, as the collective reference to the new Hebrew society in Palestine. Rebuilding the nation thus became a sacred act, a work of creation; in Shlonsky's bold terms, the Zionist Settler replaced God as the creator.

The Hebrew language likewise emerged as a central component of National Revival. Zionist collective memory cast Hebrew as the language of the ancient Israelites who lived in the Land of Israel, which fell out of active daily use during Exile. Hebrew, accordingly, remained the Jewish sacred tongue of prayers and religious studies while other languages took its place as the languages of everyday life. As the Jews lost their unified territorial base in Zion, so they lost Hebrew as their unified national language. National Revival thus required a return to Hebrew as a means of reconnecting with the hidden national spirit.

For the European Zionists, the most notable example of the exilic substitute for Hebrew was Yiddish, the Jewish language spoken predominantly in eastern Europe. Compared to Hebrew, Yiddish was scorned as a language devoid of spiritual depth and artistic qualities. As Aḥad Ha-Am, the proponent of cultural Zionism, emphasized, only the Hebrew language could function as the tongue through which Jews could connect again with their national past and would be able to achieve a full literary and spiritual renaissance.[72]

Like other Zionist reconstructions of the Jewish past, this extremely dichotomized view ignored developments that did not fit its model. After all, Aramaic competed with Hebrew as the language spoken by Jews during the later part of Antiquity. Conversely, Hebrew did not remain constrained to the sacred domain during centuries of Exile but was also a language of poetry and writing, and served as the lingua franca for Jews who came from different countries.[73] Thus, the concept of the "revival of the Hebrew language" is not accurate, nor is the celebration of the "rebirth" of modern Hebrew in conjunction with Eliezer Ben-Yehuda's immigration to Palestine in 1881. That this event became a temporal marker of rebirth is an example of how collective memory reconstructs the past by selecting a symbolic "event" to represent a gradual process of transition. In spite of Ben-Yehuda's remarkable contribution to the development of modern Hebrew, efforts to expand the use of Hebrew as a spoken tongue actually predated his immigration to Palestine. Indeed, the decisive turn in the status of Hebrew in Palestine came later, during the second decade of this century.[74]

Like other aspects of the Zionist collective memory, the association of Hebrew with Antiquity and the negative attitude toward other Jewish languages associated with Exile predated the rise of Zionism. Yet Zionism presented a new insistence upon a full-scale "revival" of the ancient tongue with a more pronounced nationalist bent, and adjusted the perception of the past accordingly. The anecdote told by the archeologist Yigael Yadin of Ben-Gurion's reproach when he saw letters from the Bar Kokhba period that were written in Aramaic is quite revealing: "'Why did they write in Aramaic and not in Hebrew?' was [Ben-Gurion's] immediate angry reaction, as if the scribes had been members of his staff."[75]

The attitude toward the exilic languages and the commitment to turn Hebrew into an everyday language was not uniform, however, even among the Zionists. The emergence of Hebrew as the Yishuv's national language was a complex process that entailed a struggle on both ideological and practical grounds. The 1913 "Languages War" marked the success of the pro-Hebrew teachers and students, supported by the Socialist Zionist settlers of the Second Aliya, in abolishing the use of European languages in Jewish schools and establishing Hebrew as the main language of instruction.[76] For most Jewish immigrants, Hebrew was not a native tongue but a newly acquired spoken language. While its vocabulary was rich in some areas, it was severely limited in others. The use of the language thus required an ongoing effort to find (or construct) appropriate words, idioms, and concepts.

Yet the emergence of Hebrew as the primary and official language of the Yishuv was ultimately seen as a critical link to the ancient past, as constructed in Zionist collective memory. For this reason too, the eastern European settlers wished to adapt the Sephardi Hebrew pronunciation which, they believed, follows the ancient Hebrew accent. Thus, although Palestinian Hebrew actually formed a new system of pronunciation, drawing selectively on both the Sephardi and the Ashkenazi Hebrew,[77] it was seen as an adaptation of the Sephardi accent and therefore as closer to ancient Hebrew. That this was a new synthesis meant, however, that for both the eastern European Zionist settlers and the Middle Eastern Jews the new Palestinian Hebrew provided a further ritualized expression of change. This transformation thus symbolized the cultural transition from exilic to Palestinian Hebrew, from a primarily sacred and literary language to a secular language of everyday use and the official language of the revived Hebrew nation.[78]

Historical Continuity/Symbolic Discontinuities

The Zionist collective memory produces a master commemorative narrative that outlines three periods—Antiquity, Exile, and the modern National Revival. Within this semiotic framework, as it developed in the national Hebrew culture in Palestine, the meaning of each period is largely determined by its relations to the other periods. The following graphic display (figure 1) represents the Zionist vision of symbolic continuities and ruptures within Jewish history.

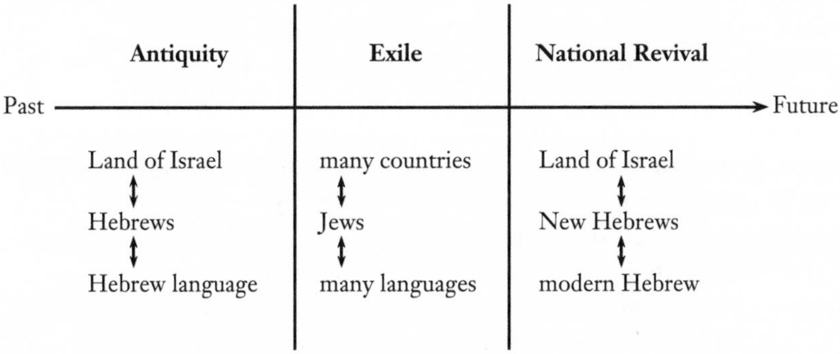

Figure 1

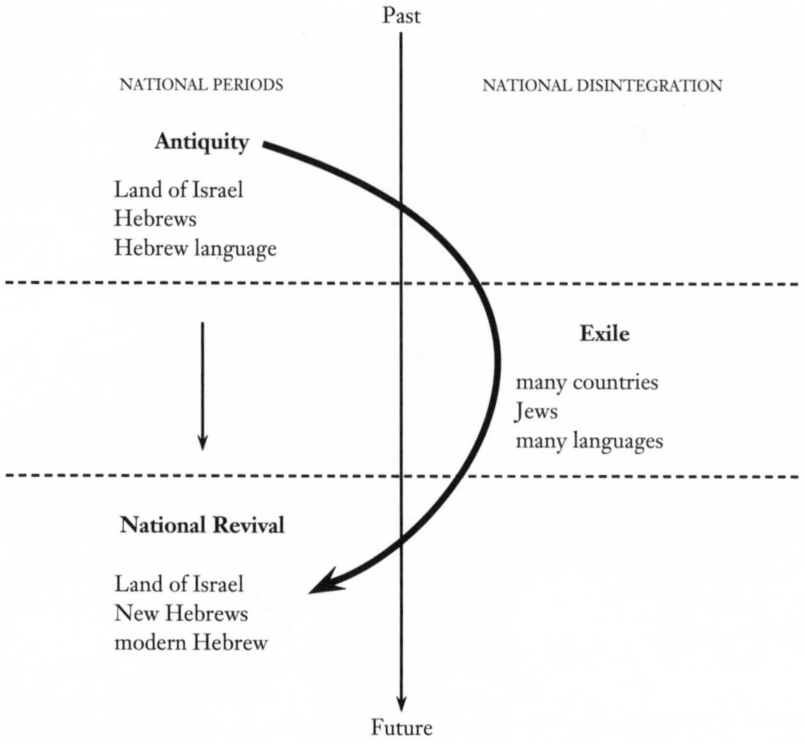

Figure 2

This semiotic system presents a basic conception of linear progression through historical time. But its segmentation into three periods also suggests some notion of historical recurrence that transcends this linearity. This does not imply a fully circular movement through time, but rather a spiral thrust forward to the future with a symbolic incorporation of certain features of the ancient past, as is demonstrated by figure 2.

Figure 2 thus displays how the national periods (Antiquity and the National Revival) became separated by a period of national disintegration. From a nationalist perspective, then, Exile is represented by blank space, a "historical detour" which denies continuity of national life. This gap, however, is not constructed by history, but rather by memory, imposing its ideological classification of the past.

To compensate for this disruption, the Zionist commemorative narrative constructs a *symbolic bridge* between Antiquity and the modern period, emphasizing their affinity and distancing both from Exile. The New Hebrews' renewed bond with land and nature as well as the revival of the Hebrew language help construct this bridge. This is clearly expressed in the Hebrew literature written for children. Nature is often described as supporting the Zionist efforts to bridge over Exile, thereby constructing the symbolic continuity that history denies. Thus, for example, the writer Ya'akov Ḥurgin informs his young readers that the ancient rebels' story had never left Zion to Exile and was, therefore, transmitted to him by the waves of the Sea of the Galilee.[79] The waves thus provide the symbolic bridge that makes it possible to "weave" the ancient past into the modern National Revival, skipping over the discredited exilic past. The result is an appearance of seamless continuity between Antiquity and the modern National Revival.

The alignment of the national periods on the one hand and Exile on the other plays up the positive images of the first and third periods against the highly negative image of the middle period. Even though Zionist memory acknowledges Exile as a very long period (often marked by the formulaic reference to "two thousand years"), it defines it by its lack, as if it were "empty" in substance. As a result, Hebrew education expanded greatly on Antiquity, with a special emphasis on the two centuries of national revolts against the Romans, and devoted relatively little time to the history of Exile.[80] Among his protests against Jewish history, Yudke, Ḥayim Hazaz's fictional hero, complains that Jewish history is boring because it consists of an endless recurrence of persecution and martyrdom.[81] Commemorative time created by the Zionist master commemorative narrative thus differs from historical time considerably, reflecting the different significance it attributes to each of the periods.

Historical Turning Points: Liminality and Transitions

The Zionist reconstruction of symbolic continuities and discontinuities in Jewish history was clearly designed to support the ideology of national revival. The dramatic contrast between the repudiation of Exile and the glorification of Antiquity accentuated the appeal of the future national era and highlighted the notion of a new beginning. The resettlement of Palestine represented a *national rebirth*. The Zionist settlers regarded themselves as engaging in the work of Creation, secularizing religious metaphors and drawing upon biblical images to highlight their own contribution to the formation of a new national era.[82]

While the early pioneering period symbolized the process of national rebirth, it was the 1920 battle of Tel Ḥai that provided the commemorative marker of a new beginning. Tel Ḥai was a sign that the expected historical transition was taking place. But a new beginning presupposes the end of the preceding period: The commemorative sequence strives to portray the transition as consisting of an end, a great divide, and a new beginning. The reality, however, is more complex and does not offer a clear-cut sequence. Jews lived in Palestine prior to the "first" Zionist immigration, and Jews continued to live in exile even after the beginning of the Zionist immigration and appeared to flourish more than their brethren in Palestine. To legitimize the delineation of a new beginning and reinforce their periodization, the Zionist settlers referred to the pre-Zionist Jewish population in Palestine as the "old Yishuv" (the "old settlement") and regarded it as a symbolic extension of Exile, thereby highlighting its distinction from the new Zionist Yishuv.[83]

The prestate period nonetheless continued to represent a highly ambiguous situation with regard to the end of Exile. Indeed, it was only with the Holocaust that the Zionist commemorative narrative was able to draw a clear boundary indicating the end of Exile. The fate of European Jewry sealed that period of misery and persecution and affirmed that the future belonged to the Zionist national revival in Palestine. It is not surprising, therefore, that the national Hebrew educational discourse emphasized this view of the Holocaust, implying a critique of the Holocaust victims for failing to understand that historical lesson in time and to join the Zionist effort.[84]

Thus, the master commemorative narrative allows for a liminal period in the transition between eras, beginning with the early pioneering period, culminating in the battle of Tel Ḥai. During this intermediate period of betwixt and between, historical forces shaped the emergent nation, but this process was still imbued with ambiguity as life in exile continued. The Holocaust, followed by the foundation of the State of Israel, provided a definitive boundary between the ending of Exile and National Revival. The representation of this symbolic order in the Israeli annual cycle of memorial days further affirms this commemorative sequence.[85] Within this semiotic system, then, the foundation of the state provides a symbolic compensation for the trauma of the Holocaust. This view, which the commemorative order suggests, is sometimes articulated explicitly in Hebrew textbooks that present the foundation of the state as a "happy end" for the Holocaust.[86]

Moreover, since Jewish life outside the State of Israel has continued to challenge this construct, a new term emerged following the foundation of the State of Israel to refer to Jewish communities abroad as "Dispersion" (*tefutsot*). This concept conveys that the State of Israel is the center of world Jewry and the Jews who live outside of Israel are defined in relation to it, namely, dispersed in its periphery. Furthermore, this new term reinforces a cognitive distinction between Exile as a past that preceded the foundation of the state and Jewish life in exile following 1948.[87]

Much like the liminal period marking the transition between Exile and

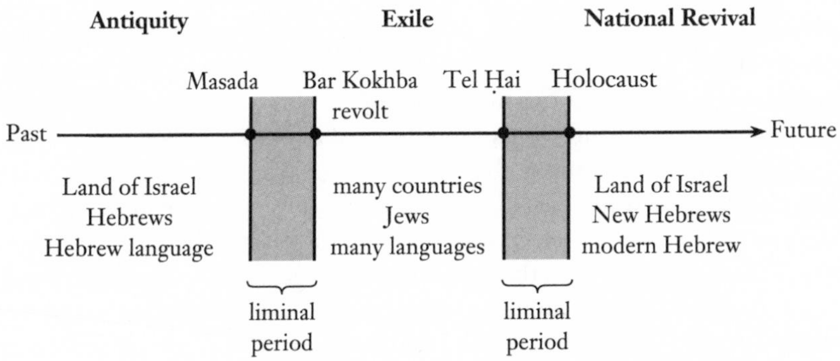

Figure 3

the Zionist National Revival, the Zionist master commemorative narrative constructs a similar liminal period that separates Antiquity from Exile. Although Masada was seen as a key turning point in Jewish history that indicates the conclusion of the Jewish revolt against the Romans in A.D. 73, this end did not actually represent a full transition from Antiquity to Exile. After all, Jews remained in Judaea under Roman rule while others continued to live in various diasporas throughout the Roman Empire. It was the outbreak of the Bar Kokhba revolt sixty years later that provided the Zionist commemorative narrative with an event to mark the conclusion of that transition: the Bar Kokhba revolt symbolized the final outburst of the ancient Jewish activist spirit, and its defeat ended the liminal period that had begun with the Great Revolt of the preceding century. Figure 3 represents the introduction of these turning points as temporal markers, signalling the entry to and exit from those liminal periods of transition. The three historical events that this book explores are thus located in the liminal periods of transition that the Zionist master commemorative narrative constructs. This commemorative location helps us understand why they emerged as major symbolic events in the national Hebrew culture and why they later became subjects of intense controversies over their meaning.

The designation of Masada and the Bar Kokhba revolt as major turning points that mark the transition from Antiquity to Exile and the emergence of Tel Ḥai as a symbolic marker of the onset of the Zionist National Revival were part of the Yishuv's attempt to shape its collective identity in relation to the past as well as the Jewish society outside of Palestine. While the division of the past into Antiquity and Exile continued the periodization constructed by traditional Jewish memory, the reinterpretation of Masada and Bar Kokhba as highly valued events marking the ending of Antiquity was a Zionist innovation. Jewish tradition emphasized the destruction of the Second Temple as the critical turning point ending this period, while it ignored Masada and was more ambiguous in its commemoration of the Bar Kokhba revolt. The reconstruction of these events as markers of major transitions in the nation's history was nonetheless essential for enhancing the ideological premises of the Zionist ideology.

The notion of a "national birth" is often linked to the themes of a national struggle and the sacrifice of life for its cause. The birth of the new Hebrew nation was no exception. It is not surprising, therefore, that the Zionist settlers focused on these themes with regard to their present reality and elaborated them in commemorating the ancient revolts. Here, the national struggles helped weave the end of Antiquity into the beginning of the modern National Revival to construct a symbolic continuity between the two periods and underscored their great divide in relation to Exile. This idea was so deeply ingrained in the secular national ideology that the first Hebrew organizations for self-defense in Palestine, Bar Giora and Ha-Shomer, chose the verse from Cahan's poem articulating this idea as their own motto: "In blood and fire Judaea fell; in blood and fire Judaea will rise."[88]

The Zionist collective memory emerged out of a deep concern for Jewish survival, both physical and spiritual, in exile. The issues of death and rebirth, sacrifice and survival, rupture and continuity were thus central to the Zionist views of the past and its vision of the future. The three turning points which this study explores likewise focus on national struggles and articulate the new Zionist outlook on those fundamental issues. That they became major heroic national myths of the emergent Hebrew nation in Palestine attests to the power of collective memory to artfully rework historical information in the construction of its commemorative narratives.

The basic premises of the Zionist collective memory described here relate mostly to the prestate period that shaped the foundations of the national Hebrew culture. Although the seeds of these ideas were formed in Europe, the emphasis of this book is on the development of the Zionist collective memory within the framework of the Yishuv and, after the foundation of the state, within Israeli culture. As the society has undergone considerable changes, its collective memory has also been transformed. And yet, even after the establishment of the state, Israeli society has confronted death and survival as part of its experience and these issues have remained central to its collective memory and political discourse. Israelis thus continuously engage in examining the relation between the past and the present and reconstructing symbolic continuities and discontinuities between them as they explore and reshape their identities as both Israelis and Jews.

THE BIRTH OF

Part Two

NATIONAL MYTHS

Three

THE BATTLE OF TEL ḤAI

In March 1920 news of eight Zionist settlers who died in the defense of a small settlement by the name of Tel Ḥai in Upper Galilee shook the Jewish society of Palestine. Although there had been other fatal incidents between Arabs and Jews in the preceding decade,[1] this confrontation was the first to be regarded as a full-fledged battle in which Zionist pioneers stood up to defend a new settlement. Tel Ḥai thus provided tangible and concrete evidence for the Zionists' readiness to sacrifice their lives for the national revival in their ancient homeland. With the death of eight settlers, Tel Ḥai seemed to have turned Cahan's prophetic verse, "In blood and fire Judaea fell; in blood and fire Judaea will rise," into reality.

Tel Ḥai was one of four Jewish settlements on the northern frontier of Upper Galilee, far from the center of Jewish population in Palestine. As a result of the prolonged negotiations between the French and British governments over their spheres of influence in the Middle East, the political fate of that region remained ambiguous following World War I. Only in November 1919, when the British withdrew their forces from the north into Lower Galilee, did control over that territory pass to French hands. The Zionist pioneers who had settled in Upper Galilee found themselves separated from the rest of the Yishuv, which was under the British mandate. The French, attempting to suppress a revolt against them in northern Syria, did not have enough forces to establish their control in southern Lebanon and Upper Galilee, where they were challenged by the local Muslim population. As the militancy of those rebels grew, the situation of the Jewish settlers became more precarious.

Although the hostilities were initially directed against the French forces and the local Christian population who supported them, the Jewish settlers, who had declared their neutrality in this conflict, were often robbed and harassed by "armed gangs" that controlled the region.[2] Shortages of food, supplies, and weapons and the difficulty of communicating with the rest of the Yishuv increased the settlers' vulnerability in the rapidly escalating tensions. Many Jewish settlers therefore decided to leave the northern frontier for the British-controlled south, and one of the four Jewish settlements, Ḥamra, was deserted. At the end of February 1920 the number of Jewish settlers in the remaining settlements (Tel Ḥai, Kfar Giladi, and Metula) declined to less than one hundred defenders, who felt committed to stay there despite the dangers facing them.[3]

On March 1, 1920, the eleventh of Adar in the Hebrew calendar, a large group of armed Arabs (estimates of their number vary from 150 to several hundreds) assembled near Tel Ḥai. Their representatives insisted on entering the yard and the building, which were enclosed by a wall, to see if the Jewish settlers had let in French soldiers. Although the Jewish settlers gave them permission to enter, lack of communication and misunderstandings led to the opening of fire inside the yard, and shooting continued for several hours, until the Arabs left. Five settlers died in that battle, and the group's commander, Yosef Trumpeldor, who was critically wounded, died a few hours later. Those who survived the attack decided to leave Tel Ḥai for nearby Kfar Giladi in the evening, carrying with them the dead and the wounded. Before they left Tel Ḥai, they burned down what they left behind. Two days later, upon hearing that large Arab forces were approaching Kfar Giladi, the rest of the Jewish settlers withdrew from the French-controlled region to the south, to the territory under the British mandate.[4]

Eight settlers died in the defense of Tel Ḥai: two were killed shortly before March 1 and six on that day. For the small Jewish society in Palestine (approximately 57,000 people)[5] this was a shocking figure. The death of Yosef Trumpeldor, a well-known military hero and Zionist activist, contributed to the traumatic impact of this event. Unlike most Zionist settlers, Trumpeldor had extensive military experience and had established his reputation as a hero prior to the battle of Tel Ḥai. During the Russian-Japanese war of 1904–5, he lost his left arm in combat and was later decorated for bravery. His unusual career as a Jewish officer and a hero of the czarist army thus brought him fame before his immigration to Palestine in 1911. During World War I Trumpeldor and Ze'ev Jabotinsky collaborated in the effort to form a special Jewish unit within the British army. When the British finally approved the establishment of a Zion Mule Corps, Trumpeldor served as its second in command under a British commander.

After World War I Trumpeldor diverted his energies to organizing Jewish emigration from Russia to Palestine and became the president of the Zionist organization the Ḥalutz in Russia. In fact, Trumpeldor joined the Tel Ḥai settlers only at the end of 1919, in response to a request to help them organize their defense in view of the growing instability there. He regarded his stay in Tel Ḥai as temporary and was planning to resume his mission of leading the Ḥalutz youth to Palestine.[6]

Trumpeldor, who was in charge of the defense of Tel Ḥai, was severely wounded early in the battle. According to eyewitness accounts, in spite of the great pain he must have suffered, he uttered no complaint during the battle but tried to encourage his comrades. When the settlers left Tel Ḥai in the evening, they carried him with them, and on the way to Kfar Giladi Trumpeldor died. A few minutes before he died, when the doctor asked him how he was feeling, he reportedly said, *ein davar, kedai lamut be'ad ha'aretz* (never mind, it is worth dying for the country).[7]

A New Commemorative Tradition

Several days passed until the news of the attack on Tel Ḥai, the settlers' resistance, the casualties, and the evacuation of the Upper Galilee reached the center of the Yishuv. The impact of the news was overwhelming. Reports, obituaries, stories about Trumpeldor, and articles discussing the significance of this event filled the newspapers. Parties planned for the celebration of the Jewish holiday of Purim were canceled or postponed, and the call for a meeting to commemorate the dead generated such a response that about fifteen hundred people could not enter the crowded hall.[8]

Trumpeldor's fame and heroic image added to the immediate impact of the news about the fall of Tel Ḥai. The story of his life as well as his death became an important part of the commemoration of this battle, and his last words constituted the peak of the commemorative narrative. The educational value of his final statement was instantly recognized as providing a succinct and powerful ideological message. With the omission of the qualifying beginning ("never mind") and some slight modification, it soon became a national slogan known as "Tov lamut be'ad artsenu" (it is good to die for our country). Teachers' custom of hanging posters of Trumpeldor's famous words around the eleventh of Adar highlighted the saying's centrality to the commemoration of Tel Ḥai and presented it as its legacy for future generations.

The Yishuv soon began to commemorate annually the defense of Tel Ḥai. Within a short time a new national memorial day made its way into the Hebrew calendar. The day was called Yom Tel Ḥai (Tel Ḥai Day), and was also designated by its Hebrew date, Yod Alef ba-Adar (the Eleventh of Adar). Every year on the eleventh of Adar, many local communities and public institutions held commemorative ceremonies for the fallen heroes of Tel Ḥai. These activities and the public speeches delivered on that day received wide coverage by the press. Public schools devoted special classes to the defense of Tel Ḥai and to Yosef Trumpeldor's heroic figure and held memorial ceremonies to honor the dead. Similarly, youth movements held educational programs and special activities for that day. The establishment of Tel Ḥai Day thus made room for an annual ritual that provided the occasion to shape and reinforce the memory of this event.

A few days following the Tel Ḥai battle, the writer Moshe Smilansky shared with the readers of the Hebrew daily *Ha-Aretz* his earlier concern about the lack of holy places for the education of Hebrew youth and announced with excitement: "And now a holy place has been created. Every year, on the eleventh of Adar, teachers and students from all over the free country will flock to the Upper Galilee, to Tel Ḥai and Kfar Giladi."[9] Within a few years, Smilansky's vision indeed materialized.

The first stage of this development occurred in 1924, when the bones of the six heroes who had died on March 1, 1920, were transferred from Kfar Giladi to the cemetery located between it and Tel Ḥai. The other two Tel Ḥai casualties as well as members of the small but prestigious Ha-Shomer defense organization were also buried in this cemetery.[10] A few years later the sculptor Avraham Melnikov constructed a large statue of a lion on the tomb of the Tel Ḥai heroes, inspired by ancient Babylonian statues. This monument, known as the Roaring Lion, was "the first modern monument in the country."[11] With this development a new sacred site emerged, and a new tradition of pilgrimage to it soon followed. The establishment of a separate date and a unique site for the commemoration of Tel Ḥai singled it out as a key turning point in the Yishuv's history. While the yearly commemoration provided a strong stimulus for the production of memoirs, poems, songs, stories, and plays written about Tel Ḥai, the new pilgrimage tradition added a central national ritual.

The rising importance of Tel Ḥai during those early years is also evident from the attempts of various groups of quite diverse political orientations to use the names Tel Ḥai and Trumpeldor as part of their symbolic identity. An experimental cooperative group of Ḥalutz members who immigrated to Palestine called themselves Gedud ha-Avoda al shem Yosef Trumpeldor (the Yosef Trumpeldor Work Legion), and a few years later they named their new communal settlement Tel Yosef after the dead hero.[12] Trumpeldor's name was also adopted by a Zionist group named the Yosef Trumpeldor Guard Association and by a commune of the Ḥalutz members in Poland, Kibbutz Tel Ḥai.[13] At the same time a group of students influenced by Ze'ev Jabotinsky formed a new, right-wing youth movement, Betar, whose name refers to the last stronghold of Bar Kokhba's revolt against the Romans in A.D. 135, but also is an acronym for Brit Yosef Trumpeldor (the

Yosef Trumpeldor Association). To achieve this desired double meaning, the Betarists changed the Hebrew spelling of Trumpeldor's name (from the Hebrew letter tet to tav) to fit the spelling of the ancient site. Betar also selected "Tel Ḥai" as a form of greeting and an official salute, and the Revisionists also named their financial agency Keren Tel Ḥai (the Tel Ḥai Fund).[14]

A Myth of New Beginnings

During the prestate period the historical battle of Tel Ḥai gave rise to a modern national myth, and Trumpeldor emerged as the first national hero of the young Hebrew society in Palestine. Tel Ḥai provided Israeli society with a myth of origin, a point in time that symbolized the rebirth of the nation and the beginning of a new era. The spontaneous response to Tel Ḥai revealed the Zionist pioneers' immediate recognition of the symbolic significance of this event as a major turning point in Jewish history.[15]

The construction of a myth of origins requires the twofold strategy of emphasizing a new beginning as well as discontinuity with an earlier past. "For something genuinely new to begin," Eliade notes, "the vestiges and the ruins of the old cycle must be completely destroyed."[16] The Zionist settlers therefore hailed Tel Ḥai for its symbolic rupture with Exile. Readiness to die for the country and the nation, so clearly expressed by Trumpeldor before his death, was in itself seen as a positive sign of breaking away from the exilic pattern of traditional martyrdom, namely, Kiddush ha-Shem. According to this view, the Jew of Exile always played the role of the victim. Hence, Trumpeldor's readiness to bear arms and fight was greatly praised as an innovative stance that marked the way of the future.[17] With pronounced admiration the poet David Shimoni welcomed Trumpeldor's patriotic message: "Your words, 'It is good to die for our country,' split our night like the rays of a proud sun."[18]

Neither the acts of Jewish self-defense nor the readiness to sacrifice oneself for the national cause was in fact new. As we saw earlier, these ideals originated in Europe, and Jewish organization for self-defense in its modern secular form predated the immigration to Palestine, most notably during the first decade of the century in Russia. Nonetheless, the Tel Ḥai battle provided a single, dramatic event to mark this transition within the context of the Zionist reconstruction of Jewish national life in Palestine. The recovery of the national spirit and its heroic manifestations were thus symbolically linked to the Zionist National Revival, and the establishment of this meaning helped accentuate the symbolic departure from Exile.

For the Yishuv, then, Trumpeldor became the symbol of the New Hebrew, the antithesis of the exilic Jew. His centrality to the commemoration of origins was not as an individual but as a collective representation, the model of the new type of man that the Zionist National Revival would produce. Tel Ḥai and its defenders were thus hailed as "the *first sign* of the future"[19] and as generating "a *new* voice and *new* words."[20] Trumpeldor and his comrades were congratulated for being "*the first* to know for what you lived and for what you died,"[21] and "the standard-bearers of our great ideal, those who went *in front of us* and showed us the way to Zion."[22] That the youth assimilated these ideas as central to the commemoration of Tel Ḥai is evident in the following piece written by a high school student in 1937:

> The Eleventh of Adar! Another date in the history of Hebrew heroism; yet perhaps this is a first date since it was then that Hebrew heroism reappeared after two thousand years . . . What is the essence of this date and its importance for us? If we examine Jewish self-defense during generations in Exile, it appears that we do not have a glorious past: a few incidents of self-defense by Russian Jews during pogroms, that's all. And until those incidents, Jews had extended their necks in front of the aggressors to be slaughtered. But on that day, the eleventh of Adar, a new chapter was opened in Jewish history.[23]

The educational message of Tel Ḥai was thus formulated on the premise that it provides a new paradigm of action for the new nation: "From this we can learn about the courage, the readiness, and the self-sacrifice of those people who wished to hold on to these isolated settlements. They knew well that the enemy outnumbered them ten times and that they had no hope of receiving real aid from the rear, which was also weak and lacking in resources. Nonetheless, they would not give up."[24]

Tel Ḥai assumed mythical dimensions as a symbolic event that stands for the new commitment to build Hebrew settlements in Palestine and to defend them at all cost. But it also signaled the heroic paradigm of the future struggle for national independence. The Tel Ḥai commemorative narrative thus stresses the theme of *a few against many* that encapsulates the Yishuv's as well as the later state's experience in the Israeli-Arab conflict.[25] The educational narrative in *Mikra'ot Yisrael*, the most widely used series of textbooks for the general public schools until the late 1970s, describes how "one day a mob of armed Arabs attacked Tel Ḥai. Trumpeldor and his brave comrades resisted them heroically, a few against many attackers." The story elaborates on this theme by describing how Trumpeldor fought against the enemy, "one hand against many hands."[26] This expression also emphasizes Trumpeldor's personal commitment to defense in spite of his own disability, an important theme in the literature that Tel Ḥai has inspired (see chapter 6).

The annual commemoration of Tel Ḥai thus provided a point in time in which the Yishuv society could celebrate its origins and highlight its symbolic departure from Exile. Yet the annual commemoration also marks the nation's indebtedness to those who sacrificed their lives to bring about this rebirth. Again a writer, Yosef Ḥayim Brener, articulated the moral burden of debt and guilt toward those who had spilled that blood: "And the question is asked: Do we, who live on, deserve such sacrifices? . . . Do we have the right to pronounce the name of 'Tel Ḥai'?"[27] The blood spilled in Tel Ḥai sanctified the renewed bond between the new nation and the ancient land.[28] Tel Ḥai thus became a modern variant of the myth of death and rebirth, representing a collective experience through the focus on the individuals who died in that battle.[29]

Tel Ḥai's special role as a symbolic beginning of the modern era of National Revival underlies the development of its commemoration. Tel Ḥai Day, the Eleventh of Adar, was also celebrated as the "Defense Day," providing an occasion to review Jewish heroism from a historical perspective.[30] Youth movements and military units still continue the pilgrimage tradition to Tel Ḥai, and special ceremonies are performed on the platform next to the Roaring Lion monument. The special prayer for Israeli soldiers who die in war, the military Yizkor prayer, follows the transformation of the traditional prayer implemented by Berl Katznelson's secularized Yizkor for the Tel Ḥai heroes.[31] Moreover, Tel Ḥai's status in secular national Hebrew culture is manifested in the unique place of the Eleventh of Adar in the Hebrew calendar: it is the only separate memorial day for those who fell for the country besides the national Memorial Day for Israeli soldiers. Whereas Israel's Memorial Day treats the fallen soldiers collectively and anonymously, the Tel Ḥai commemoration singles out one particular historical event and tends to center on Trumpeldor's heroic image. In fact, the preference for anonymous commemoration in Israeli culture culminates in what I call numerical commemoration, namely, the commemoration of heroic action through reference to the number of casualties involved.[32]

Tel Ḥai is also marked as a sacred site of modern Israeli society. With the graves of Ha-Shomer members and the Tel Ḥai defenders, the cemetery acquired a historical national significance early on, representing the pioneering ethos of heroism and self-defense. The large inscription of Ha-Shomer's motto ("In blood and fire Judaea fell; in blood and fire Judaea will rise") near its members' special lot, and the inscription of Trumpeldor's famous last words on the base of the Roaring Lion monument articulate the ideological framework of this memorial site.

With the later addition of a youth hostel to accommodate young pilgrims and other visitors, the establishment of a Ha-Shomer museum, and the transformation of the building and the yard of Tel Ḥai into a historical museum, the area surrounding Tel Ḥai has been expanded to offer a broader cultural reproduction of Israel's "beginning." The museum now displays old photographs of Tel Ḥai as well as historical artifacts and implements relating to the pioneering period. Tel Ḥai thus became a national site representing the period of *ḥalutsiyut* (pioneering), to which Israeli historiographic discourse also refers as *tekufat ha-meyasdim* (the period of the founders) or *ha-rishonim* (the first ones). The result is a large commemorative site that celebrates the nation's origins, an important institution for any modern nation.[33]

It is interesting to note that, unlike other important Israeli museums, the Tel Ḥai national site is not designed as an attraction for foreign tourists, including Jews from abroad. As a culturally reproduced beginning, it is primarily geared to Israelis themselves. The site is frequented by classes of schoolchildren, youth movement groups, army units, and families who visit its various components to explore and reexperience the essence of that period.[34] As such, a visit to Tel Ḥai is considered an educational lesson in the early history of Israeli society, an experience that has recently become increasingly popular in Israel.[35] The educational dimension has also been enhanced by the opening of Tel Ḥai Regional college at the site.

Within the historic cemetery the Roaring Lion stands apart and above other graves, representing Tel Ḥai as the focal point of beginning. The monument provides a visual representation of the Hebrew nation's primal experience of blood in its symbolic rebirth, its scream forever fixed in the lion's roar. But the lion also represents a universal symbol of power and domination that sets high hopes for the future, and as the emblem of ancient Judaea it is also associated with that glorified national past. The lion, like Trumpeldor himself, provides the missing link between Antiquity and the modern National Revival, compensating for the rupture of Exile. Indeed, the allusions to Trumpeldor as a modern reincarnation of the ancient heroes appeared in the first eulogies and obituaries: "Trumpeldor seemed like a soldier in Bar Kokhba's army who joined us from previous generations. Like this ancient soldier, he was whole, with no fear, full of bubbling energy, and quiet. Even his amputated arm reminded one of the legend about the Bar Kokhba heroes who proved their strong will and readiness to sacrifice themselves by cutting off their fingers."[36] As we shall see, this theme was greatly emphasized in the literature about Trumpeldor.

Tel Ḥai's importance as a national myth of beginning may be explained more by the timing of the historical battle than by its extraordinary character. The defense of Tel Ḥai happened early enough in the history of the Yishuv that it could serve to symbolize the departure from the Jewish society of Exile and the beginning of a new national era. During the following decades, as nationalist sentiments flared up in Palestine and the Arab-Jewish conflict escalated, the Tel Ḥai battle could no longer be seen as a unique historical incident. Nor was Trumpeldor the only one who uttered a highly ideological statement that might have become a national slogan.[37] At that point, however, Tel Ḥai was already established as a highly symbolic event and its paradigmatic character supported its status as a turning point in history.[38] Tel Ḥai emerged as a myth of origins to fulfill the classical role of a new national myth for a young nation in the process of defining its historical mission and forming its social and political foundations. Its historical battle thus opened the period of transition into nationhood that culminated with the establishment of the State of Israel. As the video presentation at the Tel Ḥai Museum asserts, "The circle that had been opened with Tel Ḥai closed with the War of Independence."

Four

THE BAR KOKHBA REVOLT

About sixty years after the defeat of the Jews' Great Revolt against the Romans and the destruction of the Second Temple, and a few decades following the failure of a revolt by Jewish communities in the Diaspora (A.D. 115–17), Judaea took to arms again, rebelling against the Roman Empire. This revolt, which broke out in A.D. 132 and lasted three years, is identified by its leader, Bar Kokhba. Having initially encountered success in liberating parts of the country from the Roman garrisons, the rebels established Bar Kokhba as *nasi* (president) of Judaea. Yet with the mobilization of additional troops to this area the Romans managed to suppress the Jewish revolt and ended this short-lived liberation.

In Zionist collective memory the Bar Kokhba revolt symbolizes the nation's last expression of patriotic ardor and the last struggle for freedom during Antiquity. As such it became an important symbolic event for the Jewish national movement. The fact that the revolt was commemorated did not constitute a dramatic change from Jewish tradition. Jewish memory continued to mark the fall of Betar, Bar Kokhba's last stronghold, as an important historical event. Yet the Zionist representation of the revolt differed considerably from that constructed in Jewish tradition and thus transformed the meaning of this event and the nature of its commemoration.

The written sources about the Bar Kokhba revolt are scant and provide only fragmentary information. They include works by Roman and early church historians, most notably Dio Cassius's account, some Samaritan sources, and several brief narratives in the rabbinical and talmudic literature that are more legendary than historical in character. Until the unearthing of archeological evidence from the Bar Kokhba period, including letters and coins bearing Bar Kokhba's name and complex subterranean constructions designed for hiding, little was known about the identity of the leader of the Jewish uprising, the popular following he had enjoyed, the organization and development of the revolt, and the extent of the destruction that Judaea suffered in its aftermath. Even with this additional evidence, information about the event is still limited.[1]

The available sources suggest that Jews took to arms in the year 132. Their revolt may have been triggered by their outrage at the emperor's plans to rebuild Jerusalem as a Roman city and erect a temple for Jupiter at the site of their own destroyed Second Temple. The Romans' prohibition of circumcision is likely to have been another reason for the outbreak.[2] It appears that initially the Jews succeeded in defeating the Roman army stationed in Judaea. The coins and letters from that period bear evidence that the rebels were successful in establishing their own government and administrative structure.[3]

Faced with the rebels' initial success, the Roman emperor Hadrian sent additional legions to Judaea and assigned his capable general Julius Severus as their commander. According to the Roman historian Dio Cassius, Severus's tactics were to progress slowly, besieging the rebels and destroying Jewish villages as his forces pushed ahead. Although these tactics prolonged the war, they eventually proved successful. Bar Kokhba and his men withdrew to a nearby mountain town, Betar. The Romans besieged this last Jewish stronghold and eventually overcame the rebels.

Both Jewish and non-Jewish sources describe the enormous scope of destruction and bloodshed during that war, although the numbers given are probably exaggerated. Dio Cassius writes that the Romans destroyed 985 settlements and "nearly the whole of Judaea was made desolate," 580,000 Jews fell in battle, and many others died in starvation and illness.[4] The Bar Kokhba revolt was crushed in 135. According to Jewish tradition, this happened on the ninth of the Hebrew month Av.[5]

Both Jewish and non-Jewish sources reveal that the revolt was also kindled by an upsurge of messianic hopes. In his history of the church Eusebius writes that the man who led the revolt was named Chochebas (star) and that he persuaded his people that he had come from heaven.[6] Rabbinical sources recount that Rabbi Akiba, the most prominent scholar of the period, attributed to Bar Kokhba the saying "A star shall step forth from Jacob." Alluding to the leader of the revolt as the "King Messiah,"[7] he articulated the belief that the revolt was not only a war of liberation from the Roman rule but also the first phase of the much anticipated messianic redemption.

Dual Image and Transformed Memory

Since the Bar Kokhba revolt is the only ancient war that is identified by a single leader,[8] his image plays an important role in the construction of the memory of this event. It is therefore interesting to note that the Jewish sources indicate a highly ambivalent attitude toward this leader, appearing to be far more negative than positive. This ambivalence is clearly expressed in the names attributed to the leader. While the name Bar Kokhba by which he is currently known was transmitted by non-Jewish sources, early and medieval Jewish sources called him Bar Koziba, which derives from the Hebrew word *kazav* (lie):

> Rabbi Yoḥanan said: Rabbi would expound "A star shall step forth from Jacob," thus do not read "star" [*kokhav*] but "liar" [*kozev*]. Rabbi Akiba, when he saw this Bar Koziba, would say: "This is the King Messiah." Rabbi Yoḥanan ben Torta said to him: "Akiba, grass will rise from your cheeks and the son of David will not yet have come."[9]

The two names thus articulate diametrically opposed perceptions of the revolt's leader. One is highly laudatory, relating to him as the Messiah; the other is extremely derogatory, accusing him of being a liar and betraying his people's trust and hopes. Prior to the discovery of the Bar Kokhba letters, the leader's actual name was an enigma; the letters revealed that his name is Shimon Bar Kosiba (or Koseba). On the basis of this recent information it appears that Bar Kokhba and Bar Koziba were both improvised forms that his followers and opponents, respectively, applied to him in order to convey their opposing views of his leadership.[10] That the glorifying name (Bar Kokhba) was preserved by non-Jews whereas Jewish sources until the sixteenth century referred to him exclusively as Bar Koziba is indeed striking.[11]

Only recently did the image of Bar Kokhba in the ancient and medieval Jewish sources become the focus of systematic inquiry. In his detailed study of the development of this image from Antiquity to the premodern period, Richard G. Marks demonstrates how the Jewish sources relate to Bar Kokhba as either a false messiah or a national hero, with only a few attempts to merge these two conflicting images.[12] Accordingly, the early rabbinical references recreate Bar Kokhba in the image of the biblical heroes who have extraordinary strength, courage, fighting ability, and charisma, but who also suffer from overconfidence and lack of sophistication, which lead them to disobedience to God. The rabbinical stories describe how Bar Kokhba "would catch the stones of the catapults on one of his knees and throw them back, killing many of [the Romans]," or would kill a man by the force of his kick. They imply that his enemy could not harm him and that he was eventually killed by a snake and not by a human. But Bar

Kokhba is also portrayed as a vain man who relied too much on his own power, challenging God not to interfere in the process of the war. "When he would go out to battle," the story goes, "he would say, 'Master of the world, neither help [us] nor shame [us].'" Bar Kokhba, according to those stories, was highly demanding of his men, testing their courage and commitment by requiring them to cut off one of their fingers, a demand that provoked the rabbis' rebuke. He was also described as a short-tempered, impulsive man who kicked and killed Rabbi Elazar of Modi'im upon hearing (unfounded) allegations that he betrayed the rebels. Betar's downfall is described as a punishment for this act of wrath, thus attributing the failure of the revolt to Bar Kokhba's character flaws and transgressions.[13]

These stories reveal admiration for Bar Kokhba's heroism but put an even stronger emphasis on his personal shortcomings. The tendency to dwell on the negative image may be more pronounced in the Babylonian than the Palestinian Talmud,[14] yet both sources indicate that he failed both as a person and a leader. Moreover, they ultimately show more appreciation of the rabbi than the leader of the revolt, suggesting that Rabbi Elazar of Modi'im, who was sitting in sackcloth and praying for God's help, contributed more to the revolt's potential success than Bar Kokhba.[15] These stories therefore imply that the way to redemption should follow the route of reliance on God, piety, and prayers.

A few medieval references to Bar Kokhba depart from this earlier, more negative approach, referring to the ancient leader as a king who had enjoyed glory and power for a relatively short time but who ultimately failed.[16] The great medieval Jewish scholar Maimonides wrote that Rabbi Akiba was *nose kelav* (armor-bearer) of Bar Koziba and that he "would say about him that he was the King Messiah and he and all the sages of his generation held the opinion that he was the King Messiah, until he was killed in his iniquities."[17] Bar Kokhba, according to Maimonides, was a promising hero who at the end turned out to be a false messiah.

As Marks points out, the twelfth-century scholars clearly focus on the messianic hope associated with the Bar Kokhba revolt. In describing Bar Kokhba's heroic image along with his emergence as a false messiah, they attempt to address issues pertaining to messianism that underlay their own polemics with the Karaites, Christians, and Muslims.[18] Similarly, the sixteenth-century references to Bar Kokhba deal with the man and his revolt in the context of the Jews' latest trauma of expulsion from Spain and Portugal. Whether they focus on his heroic stature and his revenge on his opponents or emphasize his role as a false messiah, they aim at encouraging exiled Jews by implying that redemption is possible and discouraging them from turning to false messiahs.[19]

With the emergence of Jewish interest in Antiquity during the nineteenth century, attention was first focused on the roles of spiritual leaders such as Rabbi Yoḥanan ben Zakkai and Rabbi Akiba. But as the national interest in the period of the Second Temple intensified, Bar Kokhba too became a central heroic figure, and his revolt was seen as an important manifestation of the ancient national soul and the readiness to fight for freedom.[20] Indeed, in the second half of the nineteenth century, when Masada was still considered a marginal episode in Jewish history, Bar Kokhba and the revolt began to attract attention as a subject of historical novels and plays.[21] This trend received great impetus from the rise of Zionism. Zionist writers and poets found Bar Kokhba a popular literary subject and referred to his revolt as a major turning point associated with the glorified national past.[22] The rising symbolic significance of Bar Kokhba was also evident in the use of his name for various groups and publications, such as the Bar Kokhba Association of Jewish students in Prague in 1893 and the *Bar Kokhba* magazine for young German Jews published in 1919–21; or use of the name of his last stronghold Betar for the Revisionist Zionist youth movement (founded in Riga in 1923), which became one of the important Zionist youth movements in eastern Europe and Palestine.[23]

The Zionist search for roots in the ancient national past clearly led to the enhancement of Bar Kokhba's positive image. The preference for the name Bar Kokhba over the traditional Jewish Bar Koziba symbolizes a departure from the predominant attitude of the earlier Jewish sources. Moreover, while the traditional Jewish turning point signaling the end of Antiquity and the beginning of Exile was the destruction of the Second Temple, the Bar Kokhba revolt provided Zionist memory with an alternative turning point, enhancing the national-political over the religious dimension of the periodization of the past. As the last war of liberation of Antiquity, it became a source of inspiration for the modern national movement.

Bar Kokhba was a "giant" figure who represented the greatness of the ancient national past. At a time of despair over the repeated victimization of the Jews, Ḥayim Naḥman Bialik wrote a poem calling on the Jews to begin a new era of armed struggle in their defense, using Bar Kokhba as an inspiration for his blunt and desperate call for revenge.[24] The Hebrew poet Sha'ul Tchernichovsky juxtaposed the image of Bar Kokhba the "giant" with that of a "crowd of contemptible midgets" who belittled him during centuries of life in "the filth of exile."[25] The Zionists' departure from the exilic tradition is thus articulated by their renewed admiration of "the son of the star" who has, in turn, inspired them by his light.

The invisible link between Bar Kokhba's men and the new Zionist pioneers was very much part of the attempt to construct historical continuity between Antiquity and the Zionist National Revival. When Herzl's associate, the famous Zionist leader Max Nordau, praises the Biluyim group of the First Aliya of the 1880s, he compares them to the legendary soldiers of Bar Kokhba, who had fought for national survival.[26] Rachel Yana'it, a prominent settler of the Second Aliya (later to become the wife of the second President of the State of Israel, Yitzḥak Ben-Zvi), describes her fifth-grade students' eagerness to hear about Bar Kokhba and their upcoming trip to Betar (around 1909). "I believe," she writes, "that we ought to raise Bar Kokhba's history in light of the reawakening of Galilee." In a revealing statement she then confesses: "I write about Bar Kokhba, but in fact I wish to write about anyone in our group. In my eyes, they carry the message of the beginning of a revolt . . . For me the connection between these histories is so clear that it does not require additional explanation."[27] This sense of identification is reconfirmed by Prime Minister David Ben-Gurion when the State of Israel was established. Ben-Gurion points out the symbolic continuity between the ancient Bar Kokhba followers and contemporary Israeli soldiers: "The chain that was broken in the days of Shimon Bar Kokhba and Akiba ben Yosef was reinforced in our days, and the Israeli army is again ready for the battle in its own land, to fight for the freedom of the nation and the homeland."[28]

The identification with Bar Kokhba and his men sometimes led to the projection of the present onto the past. As I mentioned in chapter 2, the Socialist Zionist leader Ya'akov Zerubavel attributes to the ancient heroes a concern not only with freedom but with the modern socialist agenda of "free labor." A student similarly employs an anachronistic term when he describes Bar Kokhba addressing his soldiers as *ḥaverim* (comrades), like members of the socialist youth movements and the kibbutzim of the student's time.[29] And a children's book tells of Bar Kokhba's "declaration of independence," a term conventionally applied to the foundation of the State of Israel in May 1948.[30]

Hebrew education in Palestine since the beginning of the century elevated the heroic image of Bar Kokhba and the importance of his revolt.[31] Hebrew literature and textbooks tend to draw more on the positive aspects of the traditional tales about the hero than on the negative ones.[32] Moreover, the construction of a new legendary lore about the ancient hero contributed to his heroic stature (see chapter 7). In this lore, Bar Kokhba's symbolic role as a model for the New Hebrews often took the literary form of an appearance in person in front of contemporary children, a common device in children's literature.[33]

The elevation of the ancient leader as a prominent historical and symbolic figure was an important feature of the Zionists' revival of what they regarded as the suppressed heroic national past. Yet some ambivalence underlies the representation of this transformation. Along with the desire to dramatize the departure from the traditional rabbinical attitude toward him, the Zionist commemoration of Bar Kokhba also implies that he had always been a folk hero. The most popular children's song about Bar Kokhba asserts that "the whole nation loved him."[34] Gershom Scholem, the famous student of Jewish mysticism, claims that "popular tradition did not subscribe to the rabbinic disparagement of Bar Kokhba's memory. He remained a kind of a hero-saint."[35] The archeologist Yigael Yadin makes a similar statement that Bar Kokhba's name was preserved by folk tradition but almost lost to authenticated history.[36] Elsewhere he remarks that the folk attachment to Bar Kokhba would withstand the pressure of historical inquiry, much as it resisted the rabbinical opposition to him.[37] In this statement Yadin asserts the primacy of collective memory over history in preserving a long, if at times suppressed, tradition of heroism around Bar Kokhba's folk image.

The Zionist elevation of Bar Kokhba and his revolt as a major turning point in Jewish history focuses on the act of initiating an armed struggle for national liberation. Zionist collective memory clearly preferred to dwell on the rebels' courage, determination, love of freedom, and readiness for self-sacrifice as a manifestation of the national spirit of Antiquity. Although the course and scope of the war are not clear, Hebrew educational texts state that Bar Kokhba freed Jerusalem, and highlight the initial successful phase of the revolt.[38] In this construction, the outcome of the war, the defeat, is clearly perceived as secondary to the symbolism of choosing to fight for national freedom and responding to oppression by taking up arms. In fact, in his address to the second Zionist Congress, Max Nordau went so far as to state that the Bar Kokhba war was superior to the Hasmoneans' victories.[39]

Various strategies are employed to diminish the significance of the defeat. One such strategy has been to demonstrate that the Romans also suffered heavy losses in the war. In reviewing the scant sources about the revolt, Yadin states:

> But perhaps the most important piece of information in Dio's description is recorded at its end and deserves verbatim quotation: "Many Romans, moreover, perished in this war. Therefore, Hadrian in writing to the Senate did not employ the opening phrase commonly affected by the Emperors: 'If you and your children are in

> health it is well; I and the legions are in health.'" Hadrian must have suffered heavy casualties indeed if he was forced to omit the customary formula.[40]

Another means of playing down the defeat is to show that the Romans' victory was short-lived from a historical perspective. In a polemic essay on the significance of the revolt Yisrael Eldad points out that Hadrian's statue is now standing in the garden of the Israel Museum in the capital of the State of Israel, after being unearthed by Bar Kokhba's descendants. In a triumphant tone he points out that now Israelis can "peek in the eyes of the 'victorious' Hadrian and pose the question, 'Where are you and where are we?'"[41]

The contrast between traditional Jewish memory, which highlights the outcome of the war and emphasizes Bar Kokhba's negative image, and the Zionist commemoration of his revolt is indeed striking. Rabbinical tales gloss over the rebels' initial success and provide harrowing descriptions of the massacre and destruction that the revolt brought upon Judaea: "And [the Romans] went on killing them, until horses waded through blood up to their nostrils. And the blood rolled rocks weighing forty 'seah' [an ancient measure], until the blood reached the sea forty miles away."[42] In the same vein, some later sixteenth-century sources dwell on the suffering, bloodshed, and persecution brought by the revolt. As Marks observes, this focus on Betar as one of the most horrifying examples of Jewish suffering inflicted by Gentiles was triggered by their recent memories of the expulsions from Spain and Portugal.[43]

The commemoration of the Bar Kokhba revolt during the annual festival of Lag ba-Omer reinforced the dramatic transformation of its traditional Jewish commemoration. Jewish tradition fixes the fall of Betar on the fast day of Tish'a be-Av (the ninth of Av) along with the destruction of the First and Second Temples. The commemoration thus focuses on the end of the revolt and its consequences and counts them among the most traumatic disasters of Jewish history and a major cause for collective mourning. Zionist collective memory, on the other hand, associates the Bar Kokhba revolt primarily with the celebration of the Lag ba-Omer holiday. This festive holiday shifts the commemoration from the outcome of the revolt to Bar Kokhba's victory over the Romans during the initial stages of the revolt. Since within the holiday framework itself there is no obligation to expand the commemorative narrative beyond that specific time, Lag ba-Omer serves to enhance the importance of the uprising and obscures the fact that the victory was short-lived. The revolt is transformed from a cause for collective mourning to a cause for collective celebration. For the majority of secular Israelis who do not observe the traditional fast of Tish'a be-Av, Lag ba-Omer becomes the exclusive commemorative setting for the revolt. As we shall see in chapter 7, this change has had far-reaching consequences for the memory of the Bar Kokhba revolt.

Archeological Findings and Symbolic Roots

The 1960s witnessed a new development in the rise of the Bar Kokhba revolt as a major national event from Antiquity. The impetus for this development came from archeological discoveries providing further evidence about the revolt that made Bar Kokhba and his men emerge as historical figures. Although letters from the Bar Kokhba period had been discovered in the early 1950s in Vadi Murabbat, these discoveries were not made by Israelis. In May 1960 Yigael Yadin, a professor of archeology at the Hebrew University and a former chief of staff of the Israel Defense Forces, turned an archeological discovery into a major national event.

In a meeting at the home of the president of Israel, Yitzḥak Ben-Zvi, in the company of the prime minister, cabinet ministers, members of the parliament, and other important guests, Yadin made public a "momentous secret," a discovery he had made in the Judaean desert only a few weeks earlier. In the opening of his book on Bar Kokhba, Yadin describes his dramatic buildup of this scene.

> A screen had been erected at Mr. Ben-Zvi's house, and when my turn came to report, I projected onto the screen through a film slide the colored photograph of part of a document and read out aloud the first line of writing upon it: "Shimon Bar Kosiba, President over Israel." And turning to our head of state, I said, "Your Excellency, I am honored to be able to tell you that we have discovered fifteen dispatches written or dictated by the last President of ancient Israel eighteen hundred years ago."
>
> For a moment the audience seemed to be struck dumb. Then the silence was shattered with spontaneous cries of astonishment and joy. That evening the national radio interrupted its scheduled program to broadcast news of the discovery. Next day the newspapers came out with banner headlines over the announcement.[44]

Yadin's skills in dramatizing the announcement about his finding clearly contributed to its impact. But the discovery of the Bar Kokhba letters turned into a national sensation because the ancient hero occupied a major symbolic place in the Israeli pantheon of ancient heroes. It is also important to note Yadin's rhetoric of continuity, linking the ancient past with contemporary Israel as he transmits a letter from "the last president of ancient Israel" to the current president of modern Israel. In this act he thus symbolically erases the rupture of eighteen hundred years of life in Exile.

Yadin's rhetorical skills are also evident in his writing about the expedition. The Hebrew title of his book *Ha-Ḥipusim Aḥar Bar Kokhba* (The Search for Bar Kokhba) reads like that of an adventure story, and the drama is accentuated by chapter titles such as "Behind the Legend," "The Curtain Rises," and "Rays of Hope." Similarly, Yadin invites the reader to join in the explorers' disappointments and hopes, their moments of extreme difficulties and excitement, adding to the dramatic unfolding of their discoveries.

Yadin's presentation had great appeal for the elite audience at the president's house and the Israeli public at large because it was nurtured by Israelis' long-standing interest in archeology. For Israelis, archeology is like a "national sport."[45] They volunteer to participate in archeological excavations, make pilgrimages to reconstructed archeological sites, and visit museums that display archeological findings, as if through these activities they ritually affirm their roots in the land. That the archeological excavation was considered a major national mission is evident also from the extent to which the military was involved in its planning and in carrying it out. According to Yadin's testimony, the idea of searching the caves for archeological remains was suggested to him by Israel's chief of staff in 1959. At the time Israeli politicians and archeologists were deeply concerned about the Bedouins' access to caves within Israel's territory where they found archeological remains, which they later sold outside the State of Israel. When the Israel Defense Forces were ordered to increase their patrol in that area, the chief of staff recommended a shift from a defensive strategy to "an all-out archeological offensive." "Why be on the defensive?" he argued, "the best defense is, after all, attack!" (32).

The military proved to be of vital help in the preparations for the excavation: the extremely difficult conditions of the terrain in which the archeologists were to work, the desert environment, and the proximity to the Jordanian border all required that involvement. The army's considerations dictated the duration of the excavation, and the minister of defense was to approve the archeologists' plan. The Israel Defense Forces also supplied helicopters for the exploration of the steep slopes of the canyons where the caves are located, prepared the sites for archeologists' overnight camps, and provided transportation, communication equipment, and security. Soldiers' involvement continued throughout the excavation, and in fact, some of them volunteered for dangerous assignments or provided useful technical assistance to the archeologists (42–46).[46]

The merging of the military and the archeological dimensions of this national project is manifested in Yadin's rhetoric. Not only was the archeological dig conceived in terms of an "attack" rather than "defense"; in describing the preparations for the excavation, Yadin resorts to paramilitary rhetoric, referring to the date for its beginning as "D-Day" (32–40). Moreover, he intersperses the narrative about the excavation with nationalist themes that emphasize the direct continuity between contemporary Israeli explorers and the ancient fighters for freedom. After describing the fellow who first discovered a fragment of a scroll, a red-haired, North African immigrant nicknamed Gingi (Ginger), Yadin adds: "I can still see his shining eyes as I write these lines. Alas, Gingi is no more; he was killed in the Six-Day War of 1967. He fought gallantly, and I am sure he visualized himself as a descendant of the Bar Kokhba warriors" (113–14).

Yadin himself, like another former chief of staff, Moshe Dayan, represents the integration of the military and the archeological. Both men belonged to the "Palmaḥ generation" educated by the prestate national Hebrew schools; both reached the highest rank as the Israeli Defense Forces' chief of staff and had an intense interest in archeology, Yadin as a professional archeologist, Dayan as an aggressive amateur. Both men also ended their careers as politicians. Indeed, Yadin's embodiment of the "Palmaḥ spirit" is visually represented in the photographs included in his book, displaying him wearing the Palmaḥ's famous wool hat (*kova gerev*) as he examines unearthed artifacts from the Bar Kokhba period.

The symbolic dimension of Yadin's career was later used by others as a way of enhancing the direct continuity between ancient and modern Israel.

> Bar Kokhba's army was the last national Jewish army, and Bar Kokhba was the last chief of staff of the historical armies of Israel. And he wrote letters, some of which survived hidden in a vessel, and the vessel was hidden in the Judaean desert and there they waited for 1830 years until they were discovered and deciphered. And by whom? By the one who in effect served . . . as the first chief of staff of the new army of Israel, Yigael Yadin . . . And is it not the act of God that the Bar Kokhba letters reached Yigael Yadin's hands as letters from one chief of staff to another?[47]

Yadin himself concludes his narrative with a personal statement imbued with a strong nationalist flavor.

> Archeologists are also human beings, and as human beings they are often emotionally attached to the history of their own people.
>
> Descending daily over the precipice, crossing the dangerous ledge to the caves, working all day long in the stench of the bats, confronting from time to time the tragic remains of those besieged and trapped—we found that our emotions were a mixture of tension and awe, astonishment and pride at being part of the reborn State of Israel after a Diaspora of eighteen hundred years. Here were we, living in tents erected by the Israel Defense Forces, walking every day through the ruins of a Roman camp which caused the death of our forefathers. Nothing remains here today of the Romans save a heap of stones on the face of the desert, but here the descendants of the besieged were returning to salvage their ancestors' precious belongings. (253)

Archeology thus becomes a national tool through which Israelis can recover their roots in the ancient past and the ancient homeland. The excavation itself symbolizes the historical continuity between Antiquity and National Revival, which the Zionist collective memory constructs and the archeologist's narrative reinforces. To participate in the archeological excavation—whether in person or symbolically, by reading Yadin's account—is to perform a patriotic act of bridging Exile to reestablish the connection with the national past and authenticate national memory.

Five

THE FALL OF MASADA

Masada is the site of an ancient fortress, a high plateau overlooking the Dead Sea and the Judaean desert. A dramatically elevated rock that is far from the center of the country, the site offers a sweeping view of its surroundings and an excellent place of refuge and seclusion. It is, therefore, not surprising that King Herod chose to use these natural qualities to build a palace that would serve as both a place of retreat and a defense post at the end of the first century B.C.[1] But Masada owes its present fame to a later event that took place at the end of the Jewish revolt against the Romans. Although the Roman emperor Titus celebrated his grand triumph over Judaea following the fall of Jerusalem in A.D. 70, three outposts continued to hold out against the Romans: Herodium, Macherus, and Masada. Having conquered the former two, the Romans turned to Masada, which had been the first site of attack on the Romans and the rebels' last place of refuge.[2]

The story of the fall of Masada was recorded by Josephus, a Jewish historian who was a contemporary of the people whose end he described. Since this is the only ancient narrative about the fall of Masada in 73, it is particularly significant for the examination of the collective memory of that event. Josephus reports that the Roman army besieged Masada and began an ambitious plan of construction to enable its machinery to destroy the fortress's walls. An estimated eight to ten thousand Romans, aided by thousands of Jewish slaves, engaged in this enormous undertaking.[3] When they finished this task, they discovered that the Jews had erected a second wall, better designed to stand the pressure of their machines. The Romans attempted to burn that wall down and, having set it on fire, prepared for the final attack the following day. At this point the unfolding events at Masada reached their dramatic peak.

When the leader of the Jewish rebels, Elazar ben Yair, realized that there was "no other way of escaping, or room for their further courage," he gathered his men to offer them what he considered the best possible alternative:

to slay their wives and children and then kill themselves so as to die as free people rather than be enslaved by the Romans.

> Since we long ago, my generous friends, resolved never to be servants to the Romans, nor to any other than to God himself, who alone is the true and just Lord of mankind, the time is now come that obliges us to make that resolution true in practice . . . We were the very first that revolted from them [the Romans] and we are the last that fight against them; and I cannot but esteem it as a favor that God hath granted us, that it is still in our power to die bravely, and in a state of freedom . . . (7.8.6)

Elazar continued his speech, arguing that it was God's will that the Romans succeed and that Jerusalem's fate had proven that true. When some of his followers objected to his idea of collective suicide, he persisted in a long speech about the immortality of the soul, the importance of life in the other world, the doomed fate of the Jewish people, and the grim prospects of slavery, torture, and death by the Romans (7.8.7).

This time, convinced by Elazar's arguments, the men hurried to carry out his plan.

> [H]usbands tenderly embraced their wives and took their children in their arms, and gave the longest parting kisses to them with tears in their eyes. Yet at the same time did they complete what they had resolved on, as if they had been executed by the hands of strangers, and they had nothing else for their comfort but the necessity they were in of doing this execution, to avoid that prospect they had of the miseries they were to suffer from their enemies [. . .] Miserable men indeed were they, whose distress forced them to slay their own wives and children with their own hands, as the lightest of those evils that were before them. (7.9.1)

After the men completed their terrible mission, they cast lots to select the ten who would slay the rest, until the last one set the palace on fire and fell on his sword. The next morning, when the Romans entered the fortress, they found the place engulfed by complete silence. According to Josephus, the sight of 960 bodies denied them the pleasure of victory, and they could not but wonder at the courage displayed by the dead. Although Elazar ben Yair and his followers wanted to ensure that no one would fall alive into the hands of the enemy, two women and five children who had managed to escape the collective death were later found by the Romans (7.9.2).

Josephus himself was hardly aloof from the events he reported. The commander of the Jewish army in Galilee, he had held a leading position in the Great Revolt against the Romans. According to his own testimony, when Vespasian succeeded in conquering some main posts in Galilee, Josephus chose to surrender to the Romans, thereby betraying his comrades who followed their agreed upon plan of collective suicide, similar to the one carried out later at Masada.[4] Whereupon Josephus joined the Roman court and devoted his life to historical writing, leaving behind a most important source on Jewish history in Antiquity, including a detailed account of the Jewish revolt from 66 to 73.

Although Masada is mentioned in two Roman sources, they do not relate the episode described by Josephus but rather mention the site itself.[5] The Talmud, which often relates historical events, makes no reference to the fall of Masada. As for Josephus's works, they were neglected by the Jews, who perceived their author as a renegade, and the original Aramaic version of his *Wars of the Jews* has not survived. In fact, its Greek translation was preserved because the church regarded his works an important source on the rise of Christianity. During many centuries, therefore, Jews were unfamiliar with Josephus's account of Masada's last days.[6]

Yet Josephus influenced Jewish historiography through another chronicle, *The Book of Jossipon*, which drew on his work. Written by an anonymous author around the tenth century, *The Book of Jossipon* became during the Middle Ages the most popular chronicle of Jewish history.[7] Jossipon's version of the fall of Masada differs from Josephus's version in one significant detail. Whereas Josephus reported that the men killed themselves after having slain their wives and children, Jossipon's version recounts that they went out to fight the Roman soldiers and encountered their death in that last battle.[8]

If the Jewish rebels at Masada entered later annals of Jewish Antiquity, it was largely through *The Book of Jossipon* and according to its version.[9] The story of the fall of Masada thus did not vanish from the records of Jewish history, yet it did not play a major role in Jewish collective memory. Even if Masada served as a historical model for medieval Jews, it represented to them an expression of extreme religious devotion leading to death for Kiddush ha-Shem.[10] In the absence of any explicit reference to Masada in this context, however, this possibility remains speculative.

The Rediscovery of Masada

The roots of Masada's contemporary symbolic significance lie in the emergence of a secular scholarly interest in Jewish history during the nineteenth century. No longer satisfied with traditional Jewish memory, the liturgical and philosophical works about the past, or popular chronicles such as *The Book of Jossipon*, Jewish scholars began searching for other historical sources and rediscovered Josephus. The first Hebrew translation of Josephus's works appeared in 1862.[11]

The new secular interest in the ancient Hebrew past prepared the ground for Masada's odyssey from the periphery of historical chronicles to the center of modern Jewish historical consciousness. The Zionist interest in the ancient national past encouraged the fascination with the Judaean wars of liberation. When a modern Hebrew translation of Josephus's *Wars of the Jews* was published in Palestine in 1923, the pioneers and the New Hebrew youth hailed it as a major text of historical and national significance. This reacquaintance with Josephus's account of Masada eventually led to its reconstruction as a major turning point in Jewish history, a locus of modern pilgrimage, a famous archeological site, and a contemporary political metaphor.

While the historian's task clearly calls for a careful examination of Josephus's story, Israeli popular culture does not question the validity of this account and the historicity of the event.[12] Moreover, selected paragraphs from Josephus's text are often reprinted in educational materials about Masada or read during visits to the site.[13] In analyzing Israeli collective memory of Masada I will therefore refer to Josephus's text as the historical narrative and focus on its relation to the Masada commemorative narrative.

In 1927 the publication of a poem entitled *Masada* by Yitzḥak Lamdan provided an important stimulus to the reintroduction of Masada to the Yishuv's collective memory. The contribution of this literary work to the rise of the Masada myth will be further explored in chapter 8. It is important to note here, though, that the popularity of the poem contributed greatly to the public's awareness of the historical event. Lamdan's *Masada* quickly became one of the "sacred texts" of the myth, second only to Josephus's historical narrative. The rising significance of Masada among Zionist circles can be attested by its adoption as a name of various Zionist organizations and publications from the 1920s on, both in Palestine and abroad.[14]

Three dramatic aspects of Masada contributed to its emergence as one of the most prominent national myths of Israeli society: a powerful story, a challenging site, and interesting archeological remains. The site too was discovered relatively late. Only in the middle of the nineteenth century did non-Jewish explorers identify and visit the Masada cliff. The first systematic archeological survey of the site was conducted in 1932 by a German archeologist who was more interested in the Roman camps than in the Jewish remains.[15] Masada began to attract Hebrew youth in the second decade of the twentieth century and gradually emerged as a site of pilgrimage. Not until the mid-1950s, however, did professional Israeli archeologists turn to Masada. Masada's appeal as a historical site of national value thus preceded Israeli archeological interest in it.

Reaching remote Masada was a complex and rather risky undertaking during the prestate period. In earlier trips visitors would arrive by boat through the Dead Sea.[16] But getting to Masada through the Judaean desert or along the Dead Sea shore was extremely dangerous. Field trips often lasted a week or longer under difficult physical conditions.[17] Trekking to Masada had an aura of adventure that became increasingly popular among Hebrew youth. The site's appeal thus contributed to the development of special rituals that underscored the growing importance of Masada as a national myth.

Youth trips to Masada led by Hebrew teachers took place as early as 1912 and continued through the 1920s and the early 1930s.[18] When casualties occurred, schools were forced to stop these trips. But during the early 1930s small groups of Hebrew youth began exploring the Dead Sea area, including Masada.[19] When these efforts were resumed in the 1940s, field trips to the Judaean desert and Masada became a popular tradition among youth movements and the newly formed Palmaḥ underground. Hebrew youth refused to let accidents disrupt their tradition. Field trips provided them an important opportunity to perform a patriotic ritual that linked them to the ancient spirit of Hebrew heroism and the love of freedom. The high degree of physical fitness, strong willpower, and daredevil mentality that a trip to Masada required clearly contributed to their growing fascination with the site.[20]

In 1934 the Jewish National Fund attempted to purchase Masada and the areas surrounding it, because of its historic significance for the emergent nation, but it did not succeed.[21] In fact, when the British government issued the white paper of 1936, outlining a plan for the future division of Palestine, Masada remained outside Jewish territory. Jews' historic claim on Masada and its surroundings was later brought up again in both national and international discussions on the issue.[22]

While Hebrew youth's tradition of field trips to Masada continued during the 1950s, that period also marked the beginning of professional archeological interest in its ruins. The involvement of professional archeologists and the Israeli government followed popular sentiment and the initiatives undertaken by archeological amateurs from the youth movements and the kibbutzim.[23] The first systematic surveys of Masada by professional archeologists from the Hebrew University took place in 1955–56. To facilitate the transportation of equipment and supplies and make

Masada more easily accessible, the Israel Defense Forces restored the ancient "snake path" that leads to the top of the cliff.[24] The construction of a new road that reaches the Dead Sea through the Judaean desert, the restored snake path, and the establishment of a youth hostel and a parking lot thus made Masada more easily accessible to the general public.[25]

Only in the mid-1960s did archeologists return to Masada for extensive excavation and reconstruction work. This expedition, which received much publicity and government support, marked the final stage in the transformation of Masada from a neglected cliff in the Judaean desert to a prominent archeological site and a major tourist attraction in Israel. Popular support and government backing joined forces here with professional expertise. The excavation was conducted on behalf of the Hebrew University, the Israel Exploration Society, and the Department of Antiquities of the Israeli government. The Israel Defense Forces took a major role in preparing the site, and the national water company (Mekorot) and the Naphta Oil company provided additional necessary aid. The project of excavating and restoring Masada was also supported by large donations and volunteers' work.[26]

Indeed, the response to the call for volunteers both in Israel and abroad was overwhelming. That Israelis, for whom archeology is of such national significance, would be eager to participate in this excavation is not so surprising, nor was it the first Israeli expedition to use local volunteers.[27] But the enthusiastic response of foreign volunteers, in spite of the rough conditions at Masada and the travel expenses involved, was unexpected and was taken as proof of the international appeal of Masada.[28]

From the early stages of preparation for this expedition, the archeological and national interests were closely intertwined. Professor Yigael Yadin, who headed this expedition, repeatedly emphasized the complementary nature of these two aspects. For him the excavation of Masada was not simply another archeological dig; it was the fulfillment of a national mission. In his earlier statements as well as in his book about the dig, Yadin's patriotic enthusiasm is evident and at times exceeds his professional restraint. Yadin admits that the decision to open the expedition to volunteers was partly economic, and then adds: "But the truth is that it would have never occurred to me to do this [call for volunteers] . . . if Masada hadn't been of such enormous significance. It is inconceivable that if we dig at Masada, people would not volunteer to take a part in this excavation, even for a short period only."[29] Similarly, Yadin justifies the unusual procedure of advancing with the excavation and the restoration simultaneously by the archeologists' obligation "to concern ourselves not only with our own immediate expedition but with the future—with the hundreds of thousands of visitors drawn by the drama of Masada, who would wish to see something of the physical remains of Masada's past" (88). Thus, while the archeologist's impulse is typically oriented toward the past, Yadin's awareness of the national value of this project led him to focus on the future.

Throughout his book Yadin expresses the awe stemming from the national historic significance of Masada and the excavators' identification with the ancient defenders: "Even the veterans and the more cynical among us stood frozen, gazing in awe at what had been uncovered; for as we gazed, we relived the final and the most tragic moments of the drama of Masada" (54). In the same spirit Yadin celebrates the continuity between Antiquity and the present, a theme evident also in the subtitle of the Hebrew edition of his book, *Ba-Yamim ha-Hem ba-Zeman ha-Ze* (In those days at this time), borrowing the phrase from the Ḥanukka prayer. The following passages demonstrate the importance he attributed to the national over the purely archeological:

> The site of the adjoining camps, Silva's and our own, was not without its symbolism, and it expressed far more pungently than scores of statements something of the miracle of Israel's renewed sovereignty. Here, cheek by jowl with the ruins of the camp belonging to the destroyers of Masada, a new camp had been established by the revivers of Masada. (21–22)

> [The Masada defenders] had left behind no grand palaces, no mosaics, no wall paintings, not even anything that could be called buildings, for they had simply added primitive partitions to the Herodian structures to fit them as dwellings . . . But to us, as Jews, these remains were more precious than all the sumptuousness of the Herodian period; and we had our greatest moments when we entered a Zealotian room and under a layer of ashes came upon the charred sandals of small children and some broken cosmetic vessels. We could sense the very atmosphere of their last tragic hour. (16)[30]

Indeed, thanks to Yadin's outstanding skills at organizing this large-scale expedition and giving it such publicity, the excavation and restoration of Masada became a national event in its own right. The preparation for the dig, the call for volunteers, their experiences, and new developments during the work on the site—all these became newsworthy topics that received ongoing coverage in the Israeli media.

Yadin's interpretation of the excavation as a patriotic engagement was not unlike other cases where archeology became a vehicle for legitimizing nationalist ideologies.[31] The archeological work at Masada thus grounded the nation's collective memory in excavated ruins and objects. A heroic venture to the past for the sake of the nation's future, it became a cause for national celebration. The archeologists and the volunteers who took part in it thus carried out a historical mission on behalf of the Israeli nation. While archeology was mobilized to substantiate the collective memory of Masada, it also became part of the commemorative narrative of Masada: texts about Masada tell the story of the famous dig and reproduce pictures of the excavation process, side by side with Josephus's narrative of the historical event and photos of the ancient objects.[32]

The excavation of Masada marks a turning point in its development as a national symbol. Masada emerged not only newly restored but also visibly enhanced in the public eye. The findings and the restoration of the site were seen as tangible proofs of Josephus's nineteen-hundred-year-old account. The archeological excavation thus reinforced the link between the appeal of the site and the importance of the historical event.[33] In the interviews I conducted in Israel in the late 1970s, some of my informants' accounts of their visits to Masada confirmed the importance of those relics as tangible evidence.

> I was very impressed. It is my nature to be very emotional, and I like archeological sites and history. At the moment that I see something like this, I begin to imagine what happened there. This is something ancient and it relates to me. And these are *my* people. It made everything real to me.

> [The visit] really impressed me and made me appreciate them [the ancient defenders] more. You come to a place and you see how and where they lived. The basket and the shoes, and the scrolls that were discovered at Masada impressed me. This makes one realize that indeed there were people who lived there, even though this happened two thousand years ago.

As a result of the enormous publicity about the expedition, Masada's history became better known to Israelis and non-Israelis. Visits to the archeological site became important as educational experiences not only for Israelis but also for foreign tourists. As early as 1966 Yadin suggested that "through visits to Masada we can teach [our brethren from the Diaspora] what we today call 'Zionism' better than thousands of pompous speeches."[34] Masada became one of the key attractions for non-Jewish tourists too and an official stop on state visits to Israel: it provides not only an interesting site but also an important lesson from Antiquity that could serve as valuable national propaganda for the State of Israel.

A Myth of Fighting to the Bitter End

> Masada is not just a historical site that researchers study; Masada is not simply an ancient fortress that one digs to find archeological remains through which one can learn about the past in order to support or refute theories.
>
> Masada is a symbol. Masada is a guideline. Masada is longing. Masada is a loud cry. Masada is a tower of light . . . Masada is a symbol of Jewish and human heroism in all its greatness. A generation of youth was raised by Masada. This is the generation that created the state, the generation of defense in its various manifestations. Masada has been the source of power and courage to liberate the country, to strike roots in it, and defend its whole territory.[35]

The pathos underlying this introduction to a book on Masada for young adults clearly stems from the author's wish to impress the readers with Masada's role as a major national myth. In less flowery language other Israelis have articulated similar views regarding Masada's potency as a symbolic event that provides modern Israeli society with a source of legitimation from the past and a model for the future. For Jewish settlers in Palestine and especially for the first generation of New Hebrews, Masada was not simply a geographical site nor a mere episode from Antiquity. For them it represented a highly symbolic event that captures the essence of the ancient Hebrew ethos and helped define their own mission of national revival.

Thus, the meaning of Masada was first and foremost shaped by the urge to forge a sense of historical continuity between the modern-day Zionist National Revival and Antiquity, when Jews lived in their own homeland, and to heighten their divergence from Exile. The Masada episode, marking the end of the Jewish revolt against the Romans, was seen as the essence of the national spirit that made the Jews stand up and fight for their freedom. In the period in which the Zionist settlers and the first generation of New Hebrews wished to define themselves as the direct descendants of the ancient Hebrews, they portrayed the Masada people as the authentic carriers of the spirit of active heroism, love of freedom, and national dignity, which, according to the Zionist collective memory, disappeared during centuries of Exile. Masada was therefore presented as a positive model of behavior and an important patriotic lesson. To fulfill this role, the Masada commemorative narrative required a highly selective representation of Josephus's historical record. By emphasizing certain aspects of his account and ignoring others, the commemorative narrative reshaped the story and transformed its meaning.

The new myth narrative highlights the defenders' courage in rebelling against the Romans in the first place and in sustaining their resistance long after the rest of Judaea had been defeated. It stresses their heroic spirit, devotion, and readiness to fight until the last drop of blood but does not dwell on the specifics of the final episode of death. In so doing, the myth narrative elaborates where Josephus is silent and silences some of his more elaborate descriptions: the ancient historian does not mention a direct confrontation between the besieged Masada people and the Roman soldiers, yet he does provide a long and detailed description of the collective suicide.

Israelis, however, accept as given that the Masada rebels actively fought against the Romans to undermine the siege construction around the fortress. One of the early explorers of Masada among Hebrew youth, Shmaryahu Gutman, articulated this view: "[E]ven though Josephus does not explicitly tell about the Zealots' war, it is clear to us that they did not sit with arms folded in their laps and wait for the Romans to advance with their siege work."[36] Most of a children's story entitled *The Glory of Masada* is devoted to description of the continuing fight against the Romans. The author highlights children's participation in the defense of the fortress and goes on to explain that this was "a sacred duty that transformed the weakest woman and the most tender child into disciplined soldiers who do not back away from any fear and danger." In contrast to the elaborate descriptions of this fight, he allows much less space to the collective suicide, thereby inverting Josephus's original structure and molding the meaning of the historical event to fit the symbolism of an active fight for freedom.[37]

The commemorative narrative plays up the defenders' *readiness to die* as an ultimate expression of their patriotic devotion and highlights it as the core of their exemplary behavior. But it plays down or ignores the particular mode of death that they chose. In this context the suicide becomes a marginal fact, a small detail within the larger picture of an "active struggle" for national liberation. Indeed, by shifting the focus from the mass suicide to the war that preceded it and by offering a generalized reference to death, the commemorative narrative attempts to avoid the more problematic aspect of the historical account, the suicide, which could threaten its activist interpretation.

This approach, clearly rooted in the Zionist collective memory of Antiquity, emerged in both scholarly and popular discourse. The historian and literary critic Yosef Klausner wrote as early as 1925 that the people of Masada who "fell in battle" were "the finest patriots Israel knew from the rise of the Maccabees to the defeat of Bar Kokhba."[38] Similarly, the geographer and educator Yosef Braslavsky wrote in 1942 that "in Masada, the fight until the very end was manifested in its most supreme and shocking meaning."[39] In my interviews informants repeatedly used phrases such as "fight until the bitter end," "until the last breath," or "until the last drop of blood" in discussing the fall of Masada and its symbolic meaning. This selective reference to the original account made it possible to commemorate the historical event as a symbol of uncompromising ideological commitment to national freedom that manifests itself in active resistance to the enemy.

This emphasis clearly made it possible for the Zionist settlers and the Hebrew youth to identify the Masada spirit with values promoted within secular national Hebrew culture. One of the students I interviewed said about Masada, "Thirty years ago they would have called this 'it is good to die for our country,'" thereby grouping Masada and Tel Ḥai in the same class of heroic historical events. Truly, within this commemorative context no major difference between these two prominent heroic myths emerged during the Yishuv period. Both provided positive models from the past, and both were used as patriotic lessons of loyalty to the national cause and readiness to die for it.[40]

The activist interpretation of Masada thus created an invisible bridge between this last heroic outburst that sealed the Jewish revolt in Antiquity and its reawakening by the Zionist settlers. This symbolic continuity was clearly important to underscore the distinction between both national periods and the discredited Exile period.[41] As one of my informants suggested, "Israelis are the continuation of Masada. Not in the sense of committing suicide, but in the sense of not giving up." Another informant articulated a similar reading: "The whole country is like Masada . . . We have to fight until the very end, not to yield and not to give up."

Masada and the Holocaust as Countermetaphors

During the Holocaust Masada's significance as a model of active resistance to persecution and a countermodel to the passivity of Exile further crystallized within secular national Hebrew culture. The glorification of the Masada people in contrast to the Holocaust victims began as early as 1942. At the time when information about the Nazis' systematic destruction of European Jews reached the Yishuv's leadership, the Yishuv was preoccupied by its own survival in the face of the German army's progress in northern Africa. The likelihood of a British withdrawal from Palestine and Arab support of the German forces left little hope for the Yishuv for a successful defense.[42] At this critical historical juncture the Zionist settlers and the younger generation often articulated their commitment to self-defense against all odds. Their commemoration of Masada therefore focused on this dimension of the historical event.

The anxiety over the fate of European Jewry and the impulse to dissociate from them and from what they represented thus pulled the Jewish society of Palestine in opposite directions. Side by side with expressions of concern over the fate of European Jews was a tendency to criticize the victims' behavior by emphasizing that the Zionist settlers would choose a different course of action. Moreover, the belief that the Zionist enterprise in Palestine was at the center of Jewish history inevitably marginalized Jewish life in the Diaspora and served to legitimize the focus on the Yishuv's politics and survival for its future role in absorbing Jewish refugees.[43]

In this context the Zionist settlers and the Hebrew youth turned to Masada as a historical model presenting a dignified alternative to the European Jews' response to the Nazi persecution. During the debate on the Yishuv's preparations for the German invasion, the prominent socialist leader Yitzḥak Gruenbaum presented the following argument: "If the Germans had encountered a Jewish armed resistance in Poland, it would not have made our situation there worse, for it is impossible for it to be worse than it is; but our honor would have been much greater in [the eyes of] the world." Gruenbaum continued by urging preparation for a last stand if the Nazis invaded Palestine. Even if the Jews of Palestine died in this war, he argued, they would at least leave behind another "Masada legend."[44]

The significance of the Masada defenders' example was thus explicitly juxtaposed with the "disgrace" displayed by the Jews' behavior in Europe. This open condemnation of the Holocaust victims is even more shocking if we consider that Gruenbaum himself had been a leading Jewish politician in Poland prior to his immigration to Palestine, was a member of the Jewish Agency Executive, the most important governing body of the Yishuv at that time, and served as chair of its committee for dealing with Polish Jews' affairs during the war years.[45]

Another socialist leader, Yitzḥak Tabenkin, did not explicitly refer to Masada in this political context. But his vehement objection to the proposal that women and children would be evacuated if the Germans invaded Palestine cannot but bring Masada's example of communal death to mind. Tabenkin dismissed the evacuation ideas not only on tactical grounds but also as a moral issue. "There is no justice in this demand to save the women and the children," he asserted and later referred to it as a "disgrace." Even if they all died while opposing the Germans, this was a better solution, for other Jews would follow their nation-building efforts in the future.[46]

In 1943 David Ben-Gurion made references to Tel Ḥai as a "second Masada" and contrasted it with Exile's tradition of passivity in the face of persecution. "And a new death we will guarantee to ourselves," Ben-Gurion declared, "not the death of powerlessness, helplessness, and worthless sacrifice; with weapons in our hands we will die."[47] In the context of the news filtering from Europe, his speech had a particularly biting edge, and its implied criticism of the European Jews could not have escaped his listeners.

If the Yishuv leaders who came from Europe vacillated between their deep anxiety about the fate of the Diaspora Jews and their ideological commitment to dissociate from what it represented,[48] Hebrew youth, who had no personal recollection of life in Europe, were even more critical of the victims' behavior. Brought up in the nationalist Hebrew education, which promoted a highly negative view of Jewish life of exile,[49] they were critical of the Jews for "going like sheep to the slaughter." Instead, they were determined to follow Masada's heroic route of fighting to the bitter end. Thus, the Palmaḥ underground's plan for a last stand in the north against the Germans in 1942 was named "the Masada plan."[50] In the same vein a youth rejected the national call for a three-day mourning period in solidarity with European Jewry, claiming that his youth group's gathering at Masada was a more appropriate symbolic measure: "We achieved our goal . . . in the field trip to Masada and the gathering there. This was our symbolic expression of our solidarity with the fate of Jews, the fate of the generation, with those, since Masada, who did not choose servitude."[51]

Clearly, the youth found it easier to bond symbolically with the ancient Jews' heroic stand at Masada than to identify with their contemporary brethren who were suffering in Europe. In contrast to the European Jews Masada represented a historical example of Jews who, faced with a similar horrible situation, understood that they had only one choice, to die a *dignified death*.[52] A poem by a member of that generation, writer and critic of children's literature Uriel Ofek, articulates the admiration of the Masada defenders' death.

> Under the swords they fell, the Masada heroes,
> For they had rejected eternal slavery.
> Their heroic act our hearts has filled
> Since the far days of our childhood.
>
> We stood still, the thunder roared,
> And we all knew so well:
> It is good to die and be ever free,
> Than become our enemy's slaves.[53]

In this commemorative context the meaning of Masada has slightly changed, although it remains firmly embedded within the activist framework. As before, the Masada commemorative narrative continues to emphasize the commitment to armed resistance and patriotic sacrifice, but it now acknowledges the theme of suicide. The suicide is defined as a heroic act and a patriotic choice that reveals the ancient Hebrews' national pride and moral integrity: when all was lost, the last rebels preferred to die free rather than suffer disgrace and humiliation, torture, or death at the Romans' hands. In this view the definition of their situation as that of "no choice" is not only accepted as unquestionable; it becomes an object of great pride and admiration. The rebels' courage to define the situation as such and act on that realization is seen as a symbolic departure from the behavior of the exilic Jews who, in Gruenbaum's words, "preferred the life of a 'beaten dog' over dignified death."[54] In this context suicide is not seen as an expression of despair but rather as *an act of defiance.*[55]

As we shall see in chapter 11, the definition of the Masada rebels' situation as having "no choice" other than suicide is clearly open to alternative interpretations. One can argue that the rebels could have yielded to the Romans like the people of Macherus before them and thus saved lives,[56] or that they could have decided to go on fighting until the last man, as the Jossipon version indeed has it. But the definition of "no choice" has become an integral part of the myth, and the glorification of the resolution to die free in that situation is often highlighted in commemoration of the historical event.[57] Moreover, since the theme of "no choice" as a rationale for activist stands is deeply ingrained in Israeli political culture, it is easily accepted as a satisfying explanation for past behavior.

At times the commemorative narrative incorporates the suicide metaphorically, ignoring its literal representation in the historical narrative. In these cases Masada represents a desperate ("suicidal") war in a situation that leaves no route of escape or hope for victory. For those who could only fear the fate they would suffer at the hands of their enemy, whether the Romans or the Nazis, death in a desperate war represented an act of defiance that combined a display of dignity with a desire for revenge. This was the symbolic meaning of Masada for Yitzḥak Sadeh, the Palmaḥ's commander, when he explained their Masada plan of 1942: "We knew only this: we would not yield, and we would fight until the very end. We would inflict many casualties on the enemy, as many as we could . . . We were a group of people . . . who decided to fight a desperate and heroic war . . . *to be a new edition of the people of Masada.*"[58]

While Masada clearly fulfilled the function of presenting an alternative Jewish model of behavior at a time of catastrophe, its use as a countermodel to the Holocaust was conditioned on blurring the distinction between literal and metaphoric references to suicide. This blurring was the only way Masada could be defined as a symbol of fighting until the very end. But Sadeh's Masada also discloses a desire to avenge an inevitable defeat and thus suppresses a significant part of Josephus's account of the suicide. The "new edition" of Masada differs greatly from the "original edition": Elazar ben Yair did not call his men to continue to fight the Romans until they all fell in the battle, and conversely, Yitzḥak Sadeh did not allude to the idea that members of the Palmaḥ should kill Jewish women and children and then commit suicide to avoid submission to the Nazis.

In fact, the activist interpretation of Masada during the Holocaust, represented by Sadeh's statement, resembles more closely the biblical account of Samson's death than Josephus's historical narrative. Samson's outcry—"Let me die with the Philistines"—delivers the message of readiness to kill oneself while inflicting death on the enemy, a message that the activist commemorative narrative attributes to Masada but which is missing in the single historical narrative about that event. This selective reference and interpretation of the original Masada edition explains what Marie Syrkin insightfully calls "the paradox of Masada": "Though the outcome of the struggle at Masada was the suicide of its last defenders, only the heroic resistance of which it was the scene has registered in the mind of Israel, not the grim 'un-Jewish' finale. However illogically, what happened at Masada permeates the imagination of Israel as the ultimate expression of active struggle, the reverse of an acceptance of death."[59]

It is important to note, however, that the activist interpretation of Masada and its elevation as the historical model of a dignified death in a hopeless situation was not unique to the Zionist settlers in Palestine. Indeed, this perception was rooted in the Zionist collective memory and was shared by its followers in Europe. Masada thus provided a historical model for those European Jewish youth who decided to organize resistance to the Nazis when the massive liquidation of the ghettos got underway. At the point when it became clear that life under the Nazi rule was likely to end in death, the youth were faced with the choice of either holding on to the small chance of survival or dying with weapons in their hands. For those who chose the latter, Masada served as a preferred paradigm of fighting a desperate war, motivated by pride and desire for revenge, and the Warsaw Ghetto revolt was also referred to as the "Masada of Warsaw."[60] Thus, in January 1942 the Socialist Zionist poet and activist Abba Kovner called the Vilna Zionist youth to organize self-defense, urging them "not to be led like sheep to the slaughter."[61] A similar call led to the organization of armed resistance in various ghettos, the most famous of which was the Warsaw Ghetto uprising, which broke out on Passover eve, April 19, 1943.

Ironically, the commemorative narrative praises the Masada defenders for dying with weapons in their hands, and this image, rather than Josephus's scene of mass suicide, provides the symbolic message of this text. The rhetorical use of activist expressions such as "they took their lives by their own hands" or "they preferred to die free" helps avoid the escapist dimension associated with suicide. Likewise, the tendency to quote Elazar ben Yair's strong statements favoring death over life in servitude, while glossing over Josephus's descriptions of the men's initial objections or their slaughtering of their wives and children and then themselves, similarly helps distance the image of that collective death.[62]

From the late 1940s to the 1960s, Israelis continued the prestate emphasis on the spirit of active heroism and displayed a strong trend of denial in relation to the Holocaust. The glorification of the Masada heroes' readiness to fight to the bitter end was intimately connected to the role of Masada as a counter-Holocaust model. The marginalization or suppression of the suicide within this activist commemoration thus went hand in hand with the suppression of the Holocaust in Israel during those years. Israeli writers avoided dealing with the subject. Israeli public schools devoted little attention to the discussion of the Holocaust.[63] Hebrew textbooks written during the 1950s and 1960s avoided direct condemnation of the victims' behavior, but their enthusiastic glorification of armed resistance contained clear expressions of their otherwise critical approach to the victims' behavior.[64] The Holocaust seemed to affirm what Zionist education had claimed, that the future belonged to the national revival in the Land of Israel; Jewish life in exile could lead only to death and destruction.

In the first decade following the foundation of the state, the reluctance to embrace the Holocaust as part of Israeli collective memory was clearly manifested in the commemorative domain. Only in 1953 did the Israeli parliament (the Knesset) pass a resolution establishing the Yad Va-Shem (Martyrs' and Heroes' Remembrance Authority) and a fixed day for the Holocaust commemoration, and six more years elapsed before it passed a law making observance of this memorial day mandatory and thereby an integral part of Israeli public life.[65]

While the establishment of a special day devoted to collective commemoration of the Holocaust indicates a recognition of the special significance of this event, the double focus of this commemoration articulates the Israeli ambivalence toward the Holocaust during those years. Official references to the commemoration of "the Holocaust and the ghetto uprising," "the Martyrs' and Heroes' Remembrance Day," or "the Holocaust and Heroism Remembrance Day" (*Yom ha-Sho'a veha-Gevura*, as it was eventually called), maintained a dual classification that marked armed resistance to the Nazis as "heroic" and lumped all other aspects of the Jewish experience under the label "Holocaust." Holocaust thus became the "nonheroic" category.

During those years Israeli collective memory showed a clear tendency to commemorate the "heroic" aspects of the Holocaust and suppress the "nonheroic" past. The establishment of the memorial day on the twenty-seventh of the Hebrew month of Nisan (i.e. close to the anniversary of the outbreak of the Warsaw Ghetto uprising) made the uprising the focal point of the commemoration. The reference to the partisans and the ghetto fighters as the "Zionist" or "Hebrew" youth (while referring to other Holocaust victims as "Jews") reinforced this attitude.[66] Israeli society thus embraced the ghetto uprisings and the partisans' fight as part of the Holocaust past with which it identified and which it eagerly glorified. The partisans and the ghetto rebels were symbolically separated from the Holocaust and Exile to serve as a symbolic bridge to modern Israel. Along with Masada and Tel Ḥai they became part of Israel's heroic past. Conversely, the rest of the Holocaust experience was relegated to Exile and associated with the "Other," the submissive exilic Jew.

During the first years of the state, the commemoration of Masada as a model of active heroism and a countermetaphor for the Holocaust continued. Yet as Israeli society began to undergo major changes from the late 1960s on, its attitude toward the Holocaust and Masada has been transformed, as we shall see in chapter 11.

During the formative years of Israeli society, the memory of the suicide at Masada was silenced in the activist discourse. Much of the interest in the site and the propagation of rituals around it stemmed from the premise that Masada would reinforce the youth's patriotism and the value of active heroism. These rituals were instrumental in the activist interpretation of Masada and its emphasis on the spirit of active heroism and fighting to the bitter end, affirming the marginality of the suicide to this commemorative narrative.

Part Three

Literature, Ritual, and the Invention of Tradition

HEBREW LITERATURE AND EDUCATION

During the formative years of Israeli society, concern with the social construction of a national Hebrew culture had a direct impact on the emergence of new literature and rituals relating to the national myths. Like other nations during their formative years, the Yishuv felt the need to create a new tradition that would help recover its historical roots and legitimize its nationalist aspirations. The new myths were an important element of the "invention" of a national tradition, but their successful integration into the collective memory of the New Hebrews depended on the formation of various literary and expressive forms that would reinforce their significance. The creation of stories, poems, plays, songs, and rituals imbued with the spirit of Zionist national ideology was thus essential to this process.

The task that the Yishuv faced was enormous. Even the revival of Hebrew as the national language seemed quite utopian at the turn of the century. Although the emergence of secular Hebrew literature was one of the greatest achievements of the Jewish enlightenment (the Haskala) in Europe, the literary language did not have the appropriate vocabulary for everyday use. The process of turning Hebrew into a native tongue was gradual and required tremendous commitment and effort from its speakers.[1]

The establishment of schools where Hebrew served as the language of instruction was a revolutionary and vital stage in this process. Indeed, schools took a leading role in introducing Hebrew as the national language and in developing a new Hebrew culture. But Hebrew education had to struggle for its place in the Yishuv. The first Hebrew kindergarten in Palestine was established in 1898 and the first Hebrew secondary school was officially founded in 1906.[2] In 1903 the number of primary Hebrew schools reached seventeen, and in that year fourteen Hebrew teachers formally established a professional association to encourage Hebrew education, regularize the Hebrew schools' curriculum, and issue textbooks.[3] By 1917 38 Hebrew schools were affiliated with the Zionist Organization (with 5,000 students), and in four years their number increased to 137 (with 12,830 students).[4]

While the early Yishuv period was still marked by the tension between the cosmopolitan and nationalistic orientations within the Jewish society of Palestine, the latter was soon to emerge as the dominant trend. The so-called Languages War of 1913 became a historiographic marker of the victory of the nationalist trend, championed by the Hebrew teachers and their students and supported by members of the Second Aliya. Their fight to abolish the use of European languages in Jewish schools and to establish Hebrew as the exclusive language of instruction was a major step toward the establishment of a Zionist hegemony in the Yishuv's educational institutions.[5]

The language question became a crucial factor in the construction of a new national culture. The victory of Hebrew as a language of instruction contributed to the widening of a great divide between the period of Exile and that of Zionist National Revival. This development also enhanced the role of the Hebrew language as a major instrument of change.[6] The emergence of a new Palestinian Hebrew, different from the Hebrew of both European and Middle Eastern Jews, further distanced the new generation from the world of Exile and its traditions.[7] Hebrew thus became a major vehicle in creating a new and more uniform national culture that propagated Zionist ideology and pioneering values.

During the first decades of the century, when Hebrew education in Palestine began to take shape, Hebrew schools suffered from a severe lack of appropriate teaching resources. The limited body of modern Hebrew literature available to Hebrew teachers had been written in Europe, and little fit the needs of children who grew up in a different reality and whose complete education was to be carried out in Hebrew. Faced with this vacuum, teachers felt immediate pressure to create new materials that would be age-appropriate and would contribute to the creation of a new national culture.[8] The first efforts at the turn of the century focused on adapting European textbooks to modern Hebrew. But as Hebrew education expanded, more textbooks were written to meet the particular needs of Hebrew students in Palestine.

Teachers regarded their work as the fulfillment of a national mission: the Hebrew youth was entrusted to them and so, to a large degree, was the future of the desired national revival. To achieve the transformation of immigrant Jews into a nation of New Hebrews, it was essential to provide the new generation with appropriate education. Teachers' investment in education not only would help shape the collective identity and values of those particular children, but also would form the social and cultural foundations of the future Hebrew nation. As educators, teachers became major actors in the construction of the nation. The broad conception of their role was clearly articulated in the custom of referring to the homeroom teacher as *meḥanekh* (educator), and not simply as *mo're* (teacher).

Socializing the young in nationalist ideology and pioneering values was the core of Hebrew education, and it superseded all other values and loyalties.[9] As one Hebrew teacher declared as early as 1895, "It is the teacher's obligation to teach nationalism, love of the motherland, love of the people and the language, even without the parents' agreement; and there is no need to ask their opinion about this issue."[10]

In fact, distancing the Hebrew youth from the world of their immigrant parents (or in the case of the old Yishuv, their observant parents) was necessary for securing their attachment to the new Zionist tradition. Hebrew education therefore stressed peer-group solidarity as an important aspect of the socialization process at school.[11] The centrality of Zionist youth movements to the Yishuv's youth culture contributed much to the strengthening of this trend.[12] The primacy of the collective needs over the individual's and the significance of each person's contribution to the nation-building efforts were major educational themes during that period, emphasized both at school and in the youth movement.[13] The Hebrew school curriculum reinforced the Zionist views of Jewish history, the values of pioneering, heroism, sacrifice, and love of the country. It also put major emphasis on the study of geography, nature, and agriculture as part of the return to the nation's roots in the land.[14] *Yedi'at ha-aretz* (knowing the land) thus became an important focus of Hebrew education and a means of fulfilling the goal of national redemption.

The desire to create a new "constructive" literature enhanced the national role of the Hebrew writers, many of whom also held teaching positions or were otherwise involved with the Hebrew educational system. The writers as well as the publishers considered the formation of national Hebrew literature an important aspect of nation building.[15] Their works contributed to the cultural life of the Yishuv as a whole, but were particularly significant for the development of Hebrew schools. Eliezer Smally points out that the motivation for writing new children's literature often arose in response to the children's needs. Smally recounts how, as a young teacher in Kfar Giladi in the 1920s, he assigned his class readings from the available Hebrew literature. One of his students protested loudly against those readings that dealt with the Jewish experience in Exile, exclaiming: "What? Stories about shopkeepers and *melamdim* [teachers of traditional Jewish schools]? I don't want!" And Smally continues: "I tried to explain to him that we had no other books for children, but he rejected my explanation and said: 'I have seen my father telling you stories every evening. Why don't you write down what he tells you?' I listened, and I thought: 'This child is right.'"[16]

Smally began to compose stories for his students. His works, with those of a few other writers, opened a new era in modern Hebrew children's literature. This new literature portrayed the Jewish settlers' new experiences in Palestine or focused on the world of their Palestinian-born children. It was inspired by the pioneering ethos, displayed children's love of nature and involvement in the national tasks of work, settlement, and defense, and was imbued with the spirit of heroism and readiness for sacrifice.

That Hebrew writers would have a major role in the construction of a new national tradition is hardly surprising. The prestige that Hebrew writers enjoyed within the Zionist movement in Europe around the turn of the century and their impact on the shaping of the Zionist discourse and internal debates were also manifested in the life of the Yishuv during the first decades of the twentieth century. The newly formed Hebrew schools provided writers with an eager and appreciative young audience. Given the limited body of new children's literature in modern Hebrew, those books were widely read and reread and became an important part of the new Hebrew culture. As such they contributed not only to the construction of a national culture, but also to its more uniform character vis-à-vis the diversity of Jewish exilic traditions. These literary works left their mark on later Israeli literature by writers who grew up during the prestate period.[17]

Whereas during the first two decades of the century Hebrew teachers enjoyed relatively high status and independence, Hebrew education became increasingly centralized and politicized during the 1930s and 1940s.[18] A similar process occurred within the literary scene, as Hebrew writers became affiliated with specific political parties and reflected on them the prestige of their work. Although Hebrew literature during the late Yishuv period was not political in the narrow sense—reflecting a political party's platform—it was nonetheless highly ideologized.[19] In the Yishuv, where eastern European Jews played a leading role, the perception of the writer as a major figure in the nation's political culture may also be a Russian legacy.[20] But similar phenomena may also be found in the history of other societies.[21]

The preoccupation with the here and now in the new Hebrew literature represents a major trend of writing in the prestate period. This trend was fueled by a strong conviction that those who participated in the nation-building efforts were shaping the course of Jewish history. The sense of historical mission thus provided both the motivation and the legitimation for the literary focus on the present. "Writers did not need imagination because reality seemed to them richer than any imagination," the literary critic Gershon Shaked comments. "Although the course of events may have appeared 'routine,' this routine was [nonetheless] 'wondrous.'"[22]

The very revival of Jewish life in Palestine was perceived as a wonder by those who actively participated in "making history" right then and there. Writers undertook to glorify and reinforce this "wondrous" dimension. Jewish history and experience were portrayed in their relation to the present; other subjects were often pushed aside and ignored. "Cosmopolitanism" and "universalism" became derogatory terms.[23] In its bias toward social realism and efforts to present "positive" heroes and "constructive" themes, this Hebrew literature sought to heighten historical awareness and reinforce social commitment to the formation of a new society in ways reminiscent of Soviet literature.[24]

The emphasis on the present national enterprise was reinforced by the retelling of major events in the ancient national past. "We need to reinforce our children's pride in their glorious past with the admiration for past heroic acts," stated the children's writer Ya'akov Ḥurgin in his preface to a book devoted to this subject.[25] The historical events of Masada, the Bar Kokhba revolt, and the defense of Tel Ḥai inspired nationalist Hebrew literature of the Yishuv period. The literature glorified the heroic spirit of the past and highlighted its analogy with the Zionist ethos. In some cases the literature simply alluded to these historical events and used them as poetic metaphors; in others it attempted to explore this past explicitly, laying out its own versions of history. Indeed, during the early Yishuv period, literature took a more active role than history textbooks in reintroducing ancient figures into the collective consciousness of the emerging Hebrew nation.[26] Children's Hebrew literature thus reinforced the basic premises of the Zionist master commemorative narrative, glossing over Exile to create a symbolic continuity between Antiquity and National Revival.

The new literary works articulated the admiration of the "wondrous" quality of the national past and its symbolic continuity with the present. Hebrew writers and educators turned history into "legends" that would inspire the Hebrew youth. After all, unlike historians, writers enjoy greater flexibility in transforming historical chronicles into meaningful stories and emphasize their symbolic and didactic messages. Their works could thus grip the audience by the power of imagination, the ability to dramatize the past and recreate its "authentic" spirit. The new literature was particularly useful for rendering the past more accessible and attractive to children than formal history lessons. Whereas history provided the legitimizing basis for the Zionist national revival, Hebrew literature contributed to the emergence of new forms of commemoration of the past.

Six

THE ARM, THE PLOW, AND THE GUN

Tel Ḥai: From "History" to "Legend"

In daily as well as scholarly discourse, "history" and "legend" suggest two very different cultural representations of the past. While "history" relates to the record of actual occurrences that took place in the past, "legend" implies a fictitious tale, the product of folk imagination. The early settlers who witnessed Tel Ḥai as part of their collective history nonetheless wished to glorify it as a legend. Their use of the term "legend" was not meant to challenge the historicity of the event. Rather, it indicated the desire to glorify it further by showing that Trumpeldor, the historical man, was a larger-than-life figure, a national symbol of extraordinary dimensions. The "legendizing" of history was thus designed to articulate and create an attitude of veneration for Trumpeldor and to establish Tel Ḥai as part of the Yishuv's national lore.

The outpouring of oral and written literature about Tel Ḥai reveals the frequent use of the Hebrew terms *agada* (legend) and *agadati* (legendary). "Days will come and songs will be sung about [the heroes of Tel Ḥai] and legends will be formed about them," pronounced the historian and literary critic Yosef Klausner a year after the historical event.[1] The important Hebrew socialist publication *Kuntres* carried the statement that Trumpeldor's "legendary, historical figure has already become a model and a flag to many."[2] Even biographical works about Trumpeldor did not shy away from alluding to the "legendary" dimensions of his life. Thus, early biographers stated that "this is the route of the real hero to appear at the right time, as if by miracle, in the place most in need" and that "he ended his legendary life with a legendary death."[3]

The oral and written literature about Tel Ḥai demonstrates a conscious attempt to "traditionalize" this past. Zionist reconstructions of Masada and Bar Kokhba could easily seem to be traditional narratives, since they relate events that took place in Antiquity. No such claim could be made about the recent defense of Tel Ḥai, yet Trumpeldor's life and character (like some other historical heroes[4]) lent themselves to the formation of a legend. Indeed, Trumpeldor was a natural choice for a counterimage to the Zionist stereotype of the traditional Jew. He was raised by assimilated parents outside the traditional Jewish community, had almost no Jewish education, and did not know Yiddish, the lingua franca of eastern European Jews at the time. While most Russian Jews tried to evade the military service, he joined the czarist army and excelled as a soldier. He received honorary military citations for his courage and was promoted to the rank of officer, an extraordinary promotion for a Jew.[5] With his amputated arm (due to a war injury), military mannerisms, and leadership qualities, Trumpeldor offered a "non-Jewish" image that was antitraditional at its core.[6] Moreover, the last words he was reported to have uttered before he died—"Never mind, it is good to die for our country"—provided a powerful ideological statement, imbued with the nationalist spirit of the new age.[7]

With this potential offered by Trumpeldor's biography, the Yishuv's educational agents undertook the mission of "turning the [Tel Ḥai] story into an enchanted legend that has its foundations in reality yet is wrapped with a glamorous halo."[8] Hence, a brochure of source material for nursery school teachers provides narratives about Trumpeldor and Tel Ḥai that would fulfill this goal. According to this brochure, teachers have "no obligation to tell anything . . . Each teacher can choose the appropriate stories for her and for her children and modify them according to her ability and work style."[9] Quite clearly, the blurring of the historical and the legendary was to be tailored to the desired ideological message in order to guarantee the impact of history on Hebrew children.

In analyzing the new literature about Tel Ḥai, we discern a variety of techniques used to imbue the narrative with the desired "legendary halo." The most explicit means to achieve that end was, quite simply, to include the word "legend" in the title. This is particularly striking in cases where the literary piece in question is not a prose narrative but a poem or a play.[10] It seems that by using this label, the authors did not attempt to present a generic classification of their work but rather to invoke the *appropriate attitude* of admiration toward their subject.

A common and effective legendizing device was to project on Trumpeldor an air of antiquity by creating a direct link between him and the ancient Jewish heroes: "He fell dead, the hero of Israel! Like a figure of ancient magic this man was, the great-grandson of the ancient heroes of Israel, one of those who joined Bar Kokhba's host, one of those who followed the hero of Gush Ḥalav."[11]

Trumpeldor's "antiquity" was widely featured in the Tel Ḥai lore. A popular song for Tel Ḥai Day describes the "legends of Galilee" and refers to Trumpeldor as an ancient hero.[12] A children's play for Tel Ḥai Day used a favorite literary technique of introducing a "medium" to create a link to the ancient past, in this case a shadowy image of a farmer of the Second Temple era. The author describes the image in accordance with the accepted modern stereotype of the ancient Hebrew Man—a person whose face is tanned, whose eyes radiate inner fire, holding a large shepherd's stick in his hand. The image tells the ancient tales of heroism and concludes with the story of Yosef Trumpeldor in Tel Ḥai.[13] That an ancient figure recounts the story of the later-day hero clearly reinforces the connection between him and his ancient predecessors. Paradoxically, the author seems to devise this unrealistic image to authenticate Trumpeldor's aura of antiquity.

The Rebirth of the Native Hebrew

The literary presentation of Trumpeldor as a modern reincarnation of the ancient heroes elevates him beyond the immediate historical situation and assures him a place of honor in the pantheon of Jewish heroes from the past. The "legendary" framework thus serves to legitimize the chronological incongruity of condensing two periods, historically separated by two thousand years, into a single heroic lore. This technique was correctly perceived as most effective for young children, for whom "there is not much difference between two thousand years ago—Judah the Maccabee and Bar Kokhba—and twenty-years ago—Yosef, the one-armed."[14] The success of this approach is evident in a piece written by a student in a school newsletter not long after the historical event: "Only fifteen years have passed since the wondrous defense of Tel Ḥai . . . Within a short period, though, we remember these heroes as if they lived thousands of years ago. So wonderful was this legend about the heroes, those spiritual heroes, [that] our hearts continue to tremble as we raise their names on our lips!"[15]

The resemblance to the ancient heroes was also geared to highlight Trumpeldor's contrast with the Diaspora Jews. Although Trumpeldor himself was a Russian Jew, his "legendary" image presented him as the forerunner of the New Hebrew and was based on the symbolic inversion of the stereotyped image of the Jew of Exile. As an obituary following his death remarked, Trumpeldor was "a hero—in the most simple, fundamental, positive meaning. Neither the hero of words, nor the hero of arguments, but a hero of action, a fighter for the liberation of our people."[16] The juxtaposition of a hero of words and arguments with the hero of action is clearly meant to suggest the fundamental opposition between the exilic Jew's ineffectual verbosity and lack of action with Trumpeldor's practical and heroic activism.

The attempt to recreate Trumpeldor in the image of the ancient heroes from Antiquity resulted in an interesting narrative from the popular *Mikra'ot Yisrael,* a textbook of the general public schools that was widely used until the late 1970s. This narrative illustrates the attempt to borrow traditional Jewish themes and styles yet adapt them to Zionist national ideology. The story of Yosef Trumpeldor begins:

> In Russia a child was born to a Jew, and his name was Yosef. He was courageous and brave. He always hastened to help the weak and defend them from the stronger and the more powerful.
>
> When Yosef grew up, he went out to his brethren and saw their misery in exile. He felt their sorrow and shared their pain. In his heart he thought about how he might raise his nation's honor and defend it against the enemy. For Yosef was a brother to all those who suffered and a friend to anyone in trouble.[17]

This first part of the textbook narrative borrows heavily from the biblical story of Moses, the mythical Jewish leader of Antiquity. Like Moses, Yosef went out to see his brethren's suffering in exile, and likewise he defended the weak against aggressors. By adopting specific expressions from the Bible (Exodus 2:11), the new text introduces an analogy between Moses and Yosef and implies that the modern-day hero is also a figure of mythical dimensions. Whereas Moses led his people from Egypt to the Land of Israel in Antiquity, Trumpeldor is portrayed as a symbolic leader of the Zionist settlement in Palestine in the modern period.

The Exodus from Egypt, which Moses led centuries ago, required the extension of the liminal period of wandering in the desert in order to produce a new generation of free-spirited Jews, qualified to establish a new nation in the promised land. In the twentieth century this process is obviously shortened and hence the human transformation that took place in the desert has to occur in Palestine itself. Trumpeldor's role was to serve as an educational model to assure the success of this change during the Yishuv period.

The adaptation of the biblical verses highlights the symbolic separation between Trumpeldor as a new breed of Jew and his contemporaries, the

"Jews of Exile." Although Trumpeldor himself was raised in exile, we are told that "he went out" to see his brethren there. The text implies that like Moses, who was brought up apart from his enslaved brethren, Trumpeldor did not share the exilic Jews' servile lot or mentality. Perhaps this is why the narrative begins with the rather awkward formulation that "a child was born to a Jew" rather than identifying him directly as "a Jewish child": for Trumpeldor was no longer the symbolic son of his biographical father, the Jew of Exile, but has been transformed into a New Hebrew, the descendant of the ancient Israelites.

The frequent reference to Trumpeldor by his first name also serves to associate him with the ancient past and enhance his Hebrew image. Although this technique may seem simply a way of making the hero's name more easily accessible to young children, it also eliminates his more problematic last name: "Trumpeldor" is not only a difficult name to pronounce, it is also a foreign name to a Hebrew speaker and associates the hero with Exile. Use of his first name thus makes Trumpeldor resemble the legendary figures of Antiquity, such as Abraham, Moses, and David, who have been known to generations by their first name. Similarly, the frequent addition of an epithet follows the ancient model of naming, rather than the modern use of a last name. Thus, the common epithets for Trumpeldor—"Yosef the hero," "Yosef the Galilean," or "Yosef the amputee"—resemble the popular references to ancient heroes (such as Judah the Maccabee and Yiftaḥ the Giladi) and rabbinical authorities (in this particular case, rabbi Yosef the Galilean).

Trumpeldor's resemblance to Moses and his difference from the Jews of Exile are also an important theme in a popular children's biography of the hero written by Uriel Ofek. In a chapter dealing with Trumpeldor's efforts to organize the Jewish prisoners of war in a Japanese camp during the 1905 Russian-Japanese war, the author describes how the hero, much like Moses (Exodus 2:13–14), encountered two fellow Jews who were bitterly attacking each other. Whereas the Jewish slaves in Egypt defied Moses' attempt to make peace between them, the modern Hebrew hero succeeded in mediating between the Jewish prisoners of war, who dared not challenge his authoritative behavior.[18]

Even more striking is Ofek's description of Trumpeldor's first dramatic encounter with traditional Jews, whom he had never met as a child or adolescent. To provide the image of exilic Jews, the men are stereotypically portrayed as elderly and religious, their talk punctuated by heavy sighs. The Jews tell Trumpeldor about an incident of persecution that ended with hundreds of casualties. Greatly agitated by this story, Trumpeldor responds to it with sharp criticism of Jewish passivity and helplessness in face of persecution. He, the hero proclaims, would always defend himself and others with weapons rather than behave like those Jews. Predictably, the men do not share his perspective.

> "But we live in exile," the elderly men replied and sighed again. "We are Jews and we depend on others' good will. Don't forget . . ." "Nonetheless," he argued against them, "we have to educate our children so that they know how to defend themselves. We have to send them to serve in the army so that they know how to use weapons, fight back, and protect their lives." He went toward the door, then turned back and added, "Thank you for the brief lesson you gave me in the history of my people."

Later Trumpeldor reflects on his brief encounter with traditional Jews and concludes: "And so, these are my own people. They live in exile and wait for the Messiah to come and redeem them. But the Messiah would not come by himself, as a result of prayers and talk. No. Words alone—no matter how beautiful and superior they are—will achieve nothing. Along with the talk there has to be some action."[19] Trumpeldor is thus portrayed as the spokesman of Zionist collective memory even while he lived in exile. His worldview and behavior explain how he became a Russian war hero and the forerunner of the New Hebrews.

To further distance the dead hero from the Jews of Exile, the settlers borrowed from non-Jewish eastern European folklore. One of the earliest and most popular songs for Tel Ḥai, "Ba-Galil be-Tel Ḥai" (In Galilee, in Tel Ḥai), which was composed immediately after the historical event, highlights Trumpeldor's role as a symbolic leader who calls others to follow him. It is no less significant that the Hebrew words were composed to the melody of a Ukrainian folk song that glorifies the death of a Cossack.[20] For his fellow pioneers Trumpeldor's new heroism is so non-Jewish in character that it evoked heroic images and lore that they had known from eastern Europe. Given the Cossacks' role in Jewish history, however, it is striking to see how Trumpeldor was associated with the Jews' archenemies, who had terrorized and murdered them ruthlessly. The association with the Cossacks implied in the adaptation of the Ukrainian song could not be missed by those who came to Palestine from that region.

The Tel Ḥai literature also enhances the hero's affinity for the land and nature. This emphasis contributes to his symbolic contrast with the Diaspora Jew, who lost touch with both land and nature, and brought Trumpeldor closer to the ancient Hebrews, who likewise worked that land. The literature therefore describes the hero's harmonious relations with nature, which was indicative of his "native" character as a New Hebrew. A poem for Tel Ḥai portrays nature's identification with Trumpeldor, describing how "[T]he whole Galilee carries his tune / Singing his last words: / 'It is good to live and good to die / For the homeland, for freedom.'"[21] Trumpeldor is also portrayed as a shepherd who protects the weak lambs and plays the flute to the flock while they cling to him.[22] More than the peasant, the shepherd represents the pastoral and evokes the romantic image of the ancient Hebrews as a nation of shepherds.[23] But the symbolism of the shepherd also enhances Trumpeldor's role as a leader and protector, a meaning reminiscent of more traditional Hebrew references to God as a shepherd.[24]

A particularly interesting example here is a children's story that describes how two lumps of soil were personally affected by Trumpeldor's enormous commitment to plowing the fields, holding the plow with his single arm. The two lumps, which had previously resisted the plow, now jump into its turning blade of their own free will so as to help the hero in his mission. When the blood of the dead hero later falls upon them, the two lumps produce radiant red poppies.[25]

It is quite likely that the theme of the poppy as part of the dead hero's commemoration was knowingly borrowed from John McCrae's poem "In Flanders Fields" (1915)—"In Flanders fields the poppies blow / Between the crosses, row on row." The poppy was established as part of the British commemoration of World War I, but it is also a highly erotic symbol.[26] In the Hebrew story mentioned above, the poppy symbolizes the union of the New Hebrew Man and Mother Earth: it is the product of the integration of Trumpeldor's blood into the soil. But it also functions as nature's monument for the dead hero. As much as the New Hebrew redeems the land of his ancient forefathers, the land also redeems him from his exilic constraints. This story not only suggests a regained intimacy with land and nature; it affirms Sha'ul Tchernichovsky's poetic idea that man becomes part of the landscape of his own country.[27]

Trumpeldor's highly glorified last words and his final act of sacrifice made him an object of great admiration. Indeed, earth itself follows the hero's example of devotion and self-sacrifice, and nature continues to deliver his ideological message. The story thus evokes a mythical structure that has a deep resonance in Jewish tradition, echoing the Agadic-Midrashic literature of the *akeda* (the binding of Isaac) and other Jewish tales of martyrdom.[28] But while the focus of the traditional tales is death as an expression of devotion to God, the new tale enhances the land as the current object of worship. Trumpeldor's blood thus sanctifies the land, and the red flowers represent this sacrificial act, which led to a renewed covenant between the New Hebrew, his ancient homeland, and nature.

The heroic spirit and the readiness for self-sacrifice are further emphasized by the theme of a "a few against many." As we saw earlier, this theme is central to Zionist collective memory. Tel Ḥai became the modern prototype of a defensive war in which the few managed to hold out against a superior enemy. Trumpeldor's disability further emphasized the defenders' disadvantage. The educational narrative in *Mikra'ot Yisrael* describes how "one day a mob of armed Arabs attacked Tel Ḥai. Trumpeldor and his brave comrades resisted them heroically, a few against many attackers." Not only does the term "mob" (or "robbers" in other narratives) allude to the Jewish defenders' moral superiority; the story emphasizes Trumpeldor's courage as he fought against the enemy, "*one hand against many hands.*"[29] By virtue of his disability, then, Trumpeldor surpassed all other Jewish heroes who fought the enemy "a few against many," for he literally resisted it single-handedly.

The Patriotic Legacy of Heroic Death

To a great extent the children's literature for Tel Ḥai Day can be characterized by its didactic tone, seeking to impress upon the younger generation the hero's patriotic message. A well-known poem emphatically states, "Yosef the Galilean / Left us his legacy / To work and to guard / The Land of Israel."[30] Similarly, a play for Tel Ḥai begins as three children get lost during a school trip to Galilee. An image appears in front of them at night, "dressed with gray clothes, a military shirt with its right sleeve hanging loose," which provides the clue for the image's identity. The image instructs the children as follows:

The image: If you wish to get rid of snakes and enemies . . .
The three: Then what?
The image: You must make the wilderness blossom . . .
The three: . . . what can we do, for we are still young?
The image: Don't say young. Everyone must do the best they can. The most important thing is willpower. I have only one single arm, and with it I plowed the mountains and I also expelled the enemy.
Yossi: Oh, oh, I know who you are!
The two others: You are the hero, Yosef the Galilean![31]

The literature also uses the monument of the Roaring Lion, which was erected on the tomb of the Tel Ḥai defenders, as a symbolic representation of the hero. The lion pursues the hero's role of guarding the nation, roaring when it perceives a threat to its security, or urging the Hebrew youth "to always be ready to defend the country."[32] As was mentioned earlier, the lion offers a visual image and a universal symbol of power and domination as well as a link to the past, when it was used as the emblem of ancient Judaea. The association of the modern hero with power and courage as well as with the glorified past thus reinforces his heroic image and the major themes of the Tel Ḥai myth.

The monument of the lion provides a more imaginative subject for writers of children's literature. Although the lion is made of stone, the literature often portrays it as having the ability to come alive again and to roar. Thus, one "legend" tells how the lion takes a child from Trumpeldor's grave to a cave where the child meets all the ancient heroes and the hero of Tel Ḥai. Although the story is framed as a dream, the lion serves as the symbolic link to Trumpeldor and the ancient heroes, collapsing them into a single group.[33] A different "legend" by the same author links Trumpeldor's lion with Bar Kokhba's.[34] In another literary work the lion comes to life every year on the Eleventh of Adar, and his roar can be heard for great distance.[35]

Perhaps the most distinctive feature of Trumpeldor that the literature was quick to exploit is his amputated arm. An amputation due to war injury was so unusual among the Zionist settlers that it became an integral part of Trumpeldor's heroic image. Thus, the epithets *ha-gidem* (the amputee) or *ha-gibor ha-gidem* (the amputee hero) became unique designations of Trumpeldor and were even used to name streets in his honor.

The mythical image of the Zionist pioneer in national Hebrew culture portrays him as holding a plow in one arm and a gun in the other.[36] The Tel Ḥai lore adjusts this image to Trumpeldor's condition to depict him as holding both the plow and the gun in his single arm. Indeed, Trumpeldor's sheer ability to perform such tasks made him an object of great admiration during his lifetime.[37] His single arm thus raised him above and beyond all other settlers and contributed to his legendary image. This admiration led to the creation of another epithet for Trumpeldor, *gibor ḥida* (the enigmatic hero). It is quite likely that this epithet was formed because it rhymes in Hebrew with the expression *zero'a yeḥida* (a single arm). Introduced by a popular poem for Tel Ḥai,[38] *gibor ḥida* became an accepted reference to Trumpeldor and was later used as the title of Ofek's biography of the hero.

The attempt to present Trumpeldor's role as a model for contemporary Israeli soldiers also appears in a children's story by Levin Kipnis, a well-known educator and writer of children's literature. The story, entitled "Ha-Yad ha-Ḥazaka" (The Strong Arm) focuses on Trumpeldor's arm that was amputated and left behind in exile. During the War of Independence, when Israeli soldiers found themselves in a critical situation, a mysterious object appeared and chased the enemy away. The astonished Israelis found out that this was Trumpeldor's amputated arm, which finally fulfilled its vow to come to the Land of Israel to continue to fight for its people.[39]

This rather gruesome story draws upon the fascination with Trumpeldor's amputated arm. It is interesting to note in this context that an early piece written by a student in a school newsletter reveals a similar interest in the fate of the arm that was left behind in exile.[40] Furthermore, following Trumpeldor's death, his artificial arm was preserved and put on display in a museum dedicated to his memory.[41] The story also highlights the intimate bond between Trumpeldor and contemporary Israeli soldiers, portraying the dead hero as greater than the Israelis who fought in 1948. Guidelines issued for seventh-grade teachers define the educational themes of this story quite broadly: (1) tales of heroism are remembered for ever; (2) Yosef Trumpeldor will be remembered forever; and (3) the Land of Israel will always be the most prominent concern of Jews.[42]

The strategy of "legendizing" Trumpeldor was designed to turn the hero and the historical battle of Tel Ḥai into a sacred cultural text of the new Hebrew nation. The educational message of Tel Ḥai has preserved the ethos of settlement and defense, the importance of fighting until the end, and the spirit of self-sacrifice. A major factor in the emergence of a new tradition revolving around Tel Ḥai is the establishment of a day of commemoration of the historic defense. The Eleventh of Adar, known also as Tel Ḥai Day, was designed to assure its place in Israeli collective memory and highlight the educational message of Tel Ḥai. The central commemorative ritual is performed at the grave of the fallen heroes and involves pilgrimage to Tel Ḥai by members of youth movements and military units that come from afar, as well as by school children and residents of the Galilee region. But Tel Ḥai's distant location in the north of the country prohibited its becoming the exclusive ritual for the commemoration of the historical defense. Local communities, schools, youth movements, and military units across the country therefore held their own commemorative rituals on the Eleventh of Adar.

The new literature about the Tel Ḥai heroes became an important educational resource for these commemorative rituals. School textbooks and special anthologies for Tel Ḥai Day drew upon these literary texts in order to turn "this tale of heroism into an educational treasure for the young."[43] The annual reading of poems and stories, collective singing and performance of plays on Trumpeldor and Tel Ḥai became part of a new tradition of commemoration on that day. The use of literature in these commemorative events thus contributed to the construction of a new national tradition.

Obviously, the annual commemorative rituals also left room for experimentation by individual teachers, particularly during the two decades following the event, before the commemoration of the Eleventh of Adar became routinized. The brochure for nursery school teachers mentioned above provides a variety of ideas for ritual performances for young children. One of the participating teachers suggests concluding the commemoration of Tel Ḥai with this ceremony:

> Accompanied by one of the melodies of Galilee, each child approaches [the teacher] and receives Yosef's photograph. The teacher explains in a few words how to preserve the picture, for it is precious to us, and [says,] "try to be like him." They then return to their seats. When the signal is given, everyone rises, holds up his photograph and repeats the vow as before. This concludes the ceremony.[44]

We have no evidence as to the prevalence of this kind of extreme hero worship, yet the symbolic meaning of the proposed ritual suggests the significance attached to the children's identification with Trumpeldor. Perhaps subconsciously, the proposed ritual follows the same principle underlying rituals of partaking of sacred food. The children's acceptance of Trumpeldor's photograph represents their embracing his legacy, much as members of a faith symbolically reaffirm their personal commitment to communal values and legacy through the consumption of a sacred substance. The conception of this ceremony highlights the sacred quality of the new national tradition. The vow articulates the educators' expectation that the children would personally see themselves as Trumpeldor's followers. Accordingly, each child would utter the following words:

> We shall go up and build,
> We shall defend and guard,
> Like Yosef, the hero.
> We will grow up a little
> And learn how to be heroes.
> We will go up to the Galilee
> And build Hebrew villages,
> Like Tel Ḥai. Hurrah![45]

The commemoration of Tel Ḥai Day during the prestate period was successful in recreating Trumpeldor as a hero of mythical stature. For children Trumpeldor was like one of the ancient heroes about whom they learned and whom they wished to imitate. A seventh grader wrote in his school newspaper in 1924, "Our hero, you should know that we will always remember you, like Judah the Maccabee and Bar Kokhba, with admiration and love."[46] Similar sentiments are also expressed in autobiographical or literary works relating to that period.[47]

The new literature and rituals thus support the myth's role as a paradigmatic text for a new age, creating a countertradition to the Jewish lore of Exile. The social construction of a new Hebrew national lore reveals a highly selective attitude toward Jewish tradition. Although much of the urge to create a new sacred text for a new age stemmed from a conscious reaction against the world of tradition, this overtly antitraditional attitude implied a heightened—even if negative—awareness of tradition. The very use of the traditional concept *agada* in reference to Trumpeldor and Tel Ḥai suggests unacknowledged ambivalence toward the old tradition. Indeed, in spite of its overt antitraditional thrust, the new narrative adopted some traditional patterns and techniques. The formation of a new legend about Trumpeldor follows a long Jewish tradition of creating legends about prominent historical figures. Like the traditional *agada*,[48] the Trumpeldor legend was largely developed for educational purposes and often follows literary strategies employed in traditional legends, such as condensing historical periods and linking heroes who were not historically connected in order to highlight the ideological message of the story.[49]

The differences between the traditional legends and this modern narrative are nonetheless significant. Whereas the former developed as a folk tradition, the modern text represents a conscious fabrication, supported to a large degree by Israeli educational institutions. While the traditional historical legends focus primarily on prominent *religious* figures and are imbued with theological significance, the Tel Ḥai literature was constructed within secular national Hebrew culture and deliberately sought to highlight an image of a *secular* hero.

Tel Ḥai was clearly a central myth of the prestate period that encapsulated much of the Yishuv's experience of settlement and defense, work and sacrifice, departure from Exile and movement toward National Revival. In that sense the desire to transform history into a sacred cultural text has been successful. The literature and rituals created around the annual commemoration of the historical defense have contributed to a new national tradition shared by several generations of Israelis. Following the foundation of the state, Tel Ḥai may have lost its prominent place in Israeli culture; yet, as we shall see in chapter 9, its symbolic relevance to the Israeli national tradition has not disappeared.

Seven

BAR KOKHBA, THE BONFIRE, AND THE LION

From Mourning to Celebration

The transformation of Bar Kokhba from a dubious leader of a failed revolt to a prominent heroic figure from Antiquity is an important feature of the Zionist reshaping of the past. While Jewish memory preserved both positive and negative images of the ancient leader, it was nonetheless the latter that had the strongest impact on Jewish tradition. Jewish memory recognized the significance of the revolt, but its focus was quite specific: it commemorated the revolt as a turning point that led to the destruction of Judaea and to the beginning of the period of Exile. Jewish tradition thus marks the fall of Betar, Bar Kokhba's last stronghold, on the annual fast day of Tish'a be-Av. Commemorating the greatest historical catastrophes in Jewish life, Tish'a be-Av focuses on the grim outcome of the Bar Kokhba uprising. That the same commemorative setting mourns the fall of Betar and the destruction of the First and Second Temples provides a measure of understanding of the traumatic impact of the end of this revolt.

It is therefore highly significant that this outcome, which is at the center of the traditional Jewish commemoration of Bar Kokhba, was marginalized within Zionist collective memory. National pride was a central Zionist theme, and the revolt was important because it symbolized the ancient Hebrews' proud and courageous stand that led them to defend their nation's freedom at all cost rather than yield to their oppressors. The Zionist commemorative narrative thus shifts its focus from the *outcome* of the revolt to the *act* of rebelling; it emphasizes the initial success that brought about the liberation of Judaea rather than the defeat that led to exile.

Such a major shift in collective memory clearly required a new commemorative event. The tragic character of Tish'a be-Av, so bluntly associated with the definition of the revolt as a national trauma, obviously hindered this desired transformation. It was therefore critical to the Zionist collective memory that the Bar Kokhba revolt become affiliated with another temporal marker that would make room for a new interpretation. The emergence of the festival of Lag ba-Omer as the primary commemorative event for the ancient revolt was thus a vital dimension in the reshaping of its memory.

Indeed, Lag ba-Omer offered an excellent occasion for the new commemoration of the Bar Kokhba revolt. A minor holiday of rather late origin, obscured by various traditions regarding its origin and significance, it was relatively open to yet another reconstruction of its meaning. The ambiguous nature of the holiday thus lent itself well to a modern nationalist reinterpretation: it provided both a traditional ritual and the flexibility of a loose meaning. Like other instances in the making of a new tradition, this combination legitimizes the new commemoration and makes it seem a generations-old tradition.[1] To appreciate the significance of this transformation of the commemorative locus of the Bar Kokhba revolt, it is important to understand the meaning of Lag ba-Omer in Jewish tradition.

Lag ba-Omer literally means the thirty-third day of a seven-week (fifty-day) period between the Jewish holidays of Passover and Shavuot. (This period, which is called Sefirat ha-Omer [counting of the sheaf] is often called simply Sefira [the counting].) The meaning of Lag ba-Omer is linked with that period. Although the biblical reference to this period associated it with the spring harvest,[2] the Sefira became a period of semimourning during the talmudic period, and various prohibitions against marriage, hair cutting, working during the evenings, and playing musical instruments marked its austerity.[3] Although the precise reason for the emergence of these mourning customs is not clear, the rabbinical account relates them to the death of 24,000 students of Rabbi Akiba who died in a plague during that time of the year, and explains the plague as a punishment for their maltreatment of each other.[4]

The designation of Lag ba-Omer as a unique date within the Sefira period is of even later origin. The first clear reference that singled it out is in a European Jewish source dating from the thirteenth century. Noting the festive character of that day, it suggests that the plague that had killed Rabbi Akiba's students stopped on that day.[5] Only in the sixteenth century did Lag ba-Omer become popular in Palestine, and its celebration was widely accepted only from the eighteenth century on,[6] recognizing the suspension of the Sefira mourning customs on that day.[7]

The reference to the halting of the plague that killed Rabbi Akiba's students became the standard explanation of the festival. In fact, Lag ba-Omer was also called "scholars' day," during which students did not study but were allowed to be outdoors and to participate in various sports, including play with bows and arrows.[8]

Yet the end of the plague was not the only reason given for Lag ba-Omer's emergence as a festive day. Some modern scholars argue that the story of the plague was fabricated in an effort to legitimize a folk ritual that had originated outside the Jewish religion but later became popular among the Jews.[9] Another early tradition attributes the Lag ba-Omer celebration to the beginning of the falling of manna in the desert following the biblical Exodus.[10]

A later mystical tradition that arose among the Kabbalists of Safed identified Lag ba-Omer as the date on which the great mystic Rabbi Shimon Bar Yoḥai (a student of Rabbi Akiba to whom tradition attributes the writing of the mystical book *Ha-Zohar*) died. In Palestine a new pilgrimage tradition to the rabbi's grave in Mount Meron emerged in the fourteenth century but became fixed only in the seventeenth century. Called Hilula de Rabbi Shimon Bar Yoḥai, this celebration marks the merging of the rabbi's departing soul with the heavenly world with great festivity, including lighting bonfires, singing, dancing, and burning clothes. The mystical account according to which Lag ba-Omer revolves around Rabbi Shimon Bar Yoḥai gradually spread to other Jewish communities that marked it by lighting candles in his honor and by visits to the other great rabbis' graves in those localities. The theme of fire and light was explained as symbolizing the light emanating from the rabbi upon his death, while the children's custom of playing with bows and arrows was accounted for by the legend that during his lifetime no rainbow ever appeared, as a sign of his greatness.[11]

Within this context of diverse traditions relating to Lag ba-Omer's origin, it is quite revealing that Zionist collective memory promotes a new commemorative locus, linking the holiday to the Bar Kokhba revolt through an allegorical interpretation of the rabbinical tradition relating to the plague. Given Rabbi Akiba's enthusiastic support of Bar Kokhba at the time, it suggests that the "plague" was used as a cryptic reference to the revolt when Judaea was still under Roman domination.[12] Although Zionism did not create this explanation,[13] it promoted it as the primary interpretation of Lag ba-Omer.

In his massive and influential compilation of sources about the origins of the holiday and its diverse customs, Yom Tov Levinsky confesses that "[w]e have no historical source that would withstand a critical historiographic examination for the celebration of Bar Kokhba on this particular date." But, he adds, "a folk tradition that has been transmitted from one person to another, from one generation to another, does not need a certificate of birth and a genealogical table."[14] The Zionist interpretation is thus sanctified as an ancient tradition. A recent brochure for Lag ba-Omer points out to students of the general public schools that

> [t]he Zionist movement . . . considered the holidays of a central national significance, and therefore added to them values that it regarded as important. Lag ba-Omer was among other holidays that the Zionist movement cherished since it was associated in the folk's mind with a revolt that had combined spiritual and physical heroism. Hence the Zionist movement turned it into a holiday [that promotes] national values: the struggle for freedom, the military heroism, and the hope for redemption.[15]

The emergence of Lag ba-Omer as the commemorative festival for the Bar Kokhba revolt is thus legitimized as the triumph of "folk memory" over an "official" rabbinical attempt to suppress it. During Exile, the memory of the revolt was encoded and preserved in the Lag ba-Omer ritual of children's play with bows and arrows. Although this custom is not central to the traditional holiday celebration, the Zionist collective memory uses it as an important foundation for its account of the holiday. This development led to changes in both the character of Lag ba-Omer and the memory of the revolt.

The explicit association of Lag ba-Omer with the Bar Kokhba revolt was greatly elaborated within secular national Hebrew culture. Songs, poems, stories, and plays for the celebration of Lag ba-Omer increasingly focused on Bar Kokhba and his revolt. While the rabbinical literature focused on Rabbi Akiba as the most prominent figure of that period and the principal historical figure associated with Lag ba-Omer, and the mystical tradition focused on Rabbi Shimon Bar Yoḥai, secular national Hebrew culture elevated Bar Kokhba as the main historical actor associated with that holiday.[16] Furthermore, secular textbooks assigned Rabbi Akiba, the most prominent rabbi of the period, a secondary role, recasting him as Bar Kokhba's follower and admirer.[17] Within this context Rabbi Akiba's memory was subordinated to the memory of the revolt. The mystical tradition relating to Rabbi Shimon Bar Yoḥai was usually presented as more esoteric, appearing only after the discussion of the Bar Kokhba revolt.[18]

The new Hebrew tradition revolving around the figure of Bar Kokhba thus marginalized the two rabbis that dominated the traditional accounts of the holiday while it promoted Bar Kokhba as the military commander of the revolt and its political leader. In 1927 this transformation of the meaning of the holiday in Palestine was noted in an article in the daily *Ha-Aretz:* "Lag ba-Omer is actually not the quiet holiday we would think, given its celebration in exile. Lag ba-Omer is not only a holiday in which the author of *Ha-Zohar* died; Lag ba-Omer is first and foremost the holiday of the revolt, the holiday of the uprising against the Romans."[19]

Zionist youth movements in Europe and in Palestine continued the tradition of Lag ba-Omer as a free day for students and enhanced its activist spirit by organizing sports, parades, races, and competitions.[20] For the emergent Hebrew society in Palestine, the new commemoration of Lag ba-Omer turned it into a highly symbolic day for military or paramilitary matters. Thus, the headquarters of the Labor-affiliated underground, the Hagana, passed the resolution to form the Palmaḥ youth underground as well as paramilitary training for schools (the Gadna) on Lag ba-Omer of 1941; and in 1948 Israel's provisional government approved the establishment of the Israel Defense Forces on Lag ba-Omer.[21]

It is important to note, however, that this transformation received great impetus within the new Hebrew culture and was not largely shared by Jews outside of Israel, except for members of Zionist youth movements. This was quite evident in my interviews, where parents who had been educated in Jewish schools abroad continued to refer to Bar Kokhba as Bar Koziba and referred to the rabbinical or mystic traditions for the Lag ba-Omer celebration. Parents who had a secular education abroad knew little or nothing about Bar Kokhba and his revolt, or had some vague notion about it from their Israeli-educated children. Similarly, all the Lag ba-Omer stories at the Israel Folktales Archive at Ḥaifa University, recorded from Jews who grew up abroad, refer to Rabbi Shimon Bar Yoḥai or to visits to other sages' graves, and none refers to Bar Kokhba.[22]

Like other changes that the Zionist collective memory introduced to traditional Jewish memory, the new significance attributed to the Bar Kokhba revolt was seen as a measure of success of the Zionist national revival. The reinterpretation of Lag ba-Omer shifted the focus of the holiday from major rabbinical figures to a national military hero, from "scholars" to "soldiers." This transformation provided an opportunity to articulate the important differences between these two representations. In a historical play on Bar Kokhba written by Avraham Goldfaden, the figure of Rabbi Elazar of Modi'im (whom Bar Kokhba is reported to have killed when he suspected him of treason) was contrasted to Bar Kokhba and the more militant Rabbi Akiba. Whereas the playwright portrays Elazar as calling his brethren to reconcile with the oppressive Roman rule, thus representing the passivity of rabbinical Judaism, Bar Kokhba calls his brethren to action, arguing that "our ancestors would have remained Pharoah's slaves in Egypt to this day if Moses had not taken them out of there with a strong arm."[23] Accordingly, Moses, not God, brought the redemption from Egypt; by analogy Bar Kokhba becomes the national leader who could lead his people to redemption.

The Lag ba-Omer Bonfires

In the Hebrew youth culture the most important ritual of Lag ba-Omer is kindling bonfires on the holiday eve. The bonfire has become the high point of the Lag ba-Omer celebration in secular national Hebrew culture. The association of bonfires with the holiday was not a new feature, but it highlighted the interplay between the traditional anchoring of the ritual and its new character and interpretation. As I mentioned earlier, kindling a large bonfire is one of the features of the Hilula de Rabbi Shimon Bar Yoḥai on Mount Meron since the High Middle Ages, and bonfires may have been lit in addition to candles in other places, too. Those bonfires, however, are associated with the kabbalistic tradition relating to Rabbi Shimon Bar Yoḥai. In contrast, the secular Israeli ritual of bonfires is explained by the ancient Hebrews' method of communicating news at the time of the revolt. "We all know," a children's book for the holidays states, "that we light these bonfires to commemorate the bonfires kindled by the Hebrew freedom-fighters who were camping on mountains and communicating with other rebel groups, informing them of the Roman legions' movements."[24] Readers for the (nonreligious) public schools point out a more specific message of victory: "One of Bar Kokhba's major victories occurred on Lag ba-Omer Eve, and Rabbi Akiba's students kindled bonfires on top of all the mountains around—and there was light in the whole country. To commemorate this victory, schoolchildren celebrate the Lag ba-Omer holiday, singing and dancing around the bonfire."[25]

In 1926 and 1927 the Hebrew daily *Ha-Aretz* reported on the spreading custom of kindling bonfires on Lag ba-Omer Eve.[26] That the newspaper found this custom newsworthy seems to indicate that bonfires began to be part of the Hebrew Lag ba-Omer tradition in Palestine in the mid-1920s. In examining the Hebrew children's literature for Lag ba-Omer, it is striking to see how many songs and stories revolve around the bonfires, reflecting and reinforcing their centrality to the youth's experience of the holiday.[27]

Wood is a relatively scarce resource in the Middle East, and in a culture that celebrates planting trees as a major patriotic act, the idea of chopping trees for fire is inconceivable. Gathering enough wood for a large bonfire that would go on for hours at night is therefore no small challenge for Israeli youth. In the days preceding Lag ba-Omer, children begin to look for scraps of wood and carefully hide or protect their findings because of the harsh competition over a limited supply. Humorous Lag ba-Omer lore describes the parents' need to protect their furniture from their children's overly zealous efforts to find materials for the bonfire.[28]

While younger children attend bonfires with their parents, older children celebrate with their friends from the neighborhood, the youth movement, or school. This form of partying around the bonfire, singing together, joking, frying potatoes, eating, and drinking is a youth ritual known as *kumzitz*. When performed by adults during trips or on special occasions such as Lag ba-Omer, the *kumzitz* is often imbued with some nostalgia for this youthful experience and attempts to recapture its spirit. On Lag ba-Omer Eve the *kumzitz* may go on for hours, and often until dawn.

The symbolic merging of the memory of the Bar Kokhba revolt with the youth movement spirit and experiences thus reinforces the symbolic continuity between the ancient fighters and Hebrew youth. The national dimension of the Lag ba-Omer bonfire was sometimes accentuated through the burning of an effigy of a leading enemy (Hitler during the 1940s, and either Hitler or Abdel Nasser during the 1950s and the 1960s). It is possible that the performance of this custom was borrowed from an earlier custom of burning an effigy of the Jews' archenemy Haman on Purim; or perhaps it developed from the burning of clothes in the Hilula celebration on Mount Meron.[29]

The burning of those symbolic figures of hostile leaders in the Lag ba-Omer bonfire demonstrates how collective memory often subverts historical time by collapsing different events into the same commemorative setting. It also indicates how the Zionist interpretation of Jewish holidays, further developed in secular national Hebrew culture, reinforced a sense that Jewish history is underlaid by repeated conflicts with enemies who wished to destroy the Jews.

The shifting of the temporal anchoring of the Bar Kokhba revolt from Tish'a be-Av to Lag ba-Omer made room for a radical change in its commemoration. Not only has the new commemorative locus been transformed from a grim fast day to a festive celebration, it has also shifted the focus from Bar Kokhba's ultimate defeat to a victorious moment during his struggle for liberation. The themes of courage, success, and revenge have become central to the commemoration of the Bar Kokhba revolt, thereby blurring the memory of the massacre, destruction, and exile it brought upon the Jews. Given the early and repeated exposure of the youth to the joyous Lag ba-Omer celebration, it is easy to understand its decisive impact on the memory of this event.

Bar Kokhba and the Lion

As in the case of the Tel Ḥai battle, the Bar Kokhba revolt gave rise to new literature that revolved around the image of its main hero. Yet Trumpeldor and Bar Kokhba represent two very different cases of historical heroes. While the former is a modern figure whose image was shaped through autobiographical memory as well as other substantial sources of information (recollections of people who knew him personally, his letters, and several biographies),[30] the memory of the ancient hero was primarily encoded in legendary narratives. Whereas the new Hebrew literature about Trumpeldor is characterized by the conscious effort to turn "history" into "legend," the new literature about Bar Kokhba continues a long tradition of creating legends about him. What is unique about this latter case is the radical transformation in tone of the new "legendary" reconstruction as compared to the older legends. While the rabbinical tradition tends to project a negative image of the leader of the failed revolt and to highlight his controversial character, the new Hebrew tradition portrays a heroic image of a courageous and resourceful man who succeeded in rallying the nation behind him in order to liberate it from oppressive Roman rule.

As we saw in chapter 4, Bar Kokhba and his revolt emerged as a favorite subject in European Jewish literature in the second half of the nineteenth century. Within this trend the most interesting literary phenomenon is the emergence of an utterly new and distinct corpus of legends relating to Bar Kokhba and his dramatic encounter with a lion. Although this purely legendary episode appears to be of relatively recent origin, it has nonetheless acquired an ancient appearance, by virtue of both its reference to Antiquity and the successful adaptation of familiar themes of folk literature. The following discussion focuses on this new legendary lore as an example of the role of literature in inventing a national tradition.

Several literary works describe the encounter between the ancient Hebrew hero and a lion. Despite considerable differences in genre, style, and literary quality, these works share a basic plot structure: When the lion and the hero meet, the beast initially threatens the man (or presents a potential threat to him), yet the hero manages to subordinate the fierce animal to his will and thus subverts the threat to his life. The lion ultimately helps the hero (either directly or indirectly) in his pursuit of freedom, hence becoming an instrument of support of the national cause.

The confrontation with the lion highlights Bar Kokhba's positive qualities: he either wins over the lion by his personal charisma and good heart, or overcomes it by his courage and physical strength. His success in this encounter eventually leads to a more significant development, namely, the beginning of his revolt. The story thus moves from a personal conflict (Bar Kokhba versus the lion) to a collective one (the ancient Hebrew versus the Roman Empire), and the success of the former leads the reader to expect (or assume) the success of the latter.

The best-known version of this fabricated encounter between Bar Kokhba and the lion in contemporary Israeli culture is a song written by Levin Kipnis. Indeed, Bar Kokhba's lion owes much of its fame to Kipnis's extraordinary productivity as well as his prominence as an editor of Hebrew educational literature from the early Yishuv period. Kipnis, who went to Palestine in 1913 as a young man exerted tremendous influence on the development of modern Hebrew literature for early childhood.[31] Concerned with the lack of appropriate songs for Hebrew nursery schools, he soon began to fill this gap. His song on Bar Kokhba and the lion is a testimony to his success: it is part of the standard repertoire for Lag ba-Omer, which Israeli children learn in nursery school, and has virtually acquired the status of a folk song.[32] The song presents a simplified, though dramatic, version of Bar Kokhba's encounter with the lion:[33]

There was a man in Israel,
His name was Bar Kokhba.
A tall, well-built, young man
With glowing, radiant eyes.

He was a hero.
He yearned for freedom.
The whole nation loved him.
He was a *hero*.

One day an incident occurred,
What a sad incident [it was]!
Bar Kokhba was taken captive
and was put in a cage.

How horrible was this cage
In which a lion raged.
As soon as it spotted Bar Kokhba,
The *lion* assaulted [him].

But you should know Bar Kokhba,
How courageous and daring he was.
He dashed and jumped on the lion
And raced [out] as fast as an eagle.

Over mountains and valleys he cruised,
Raising the banner of liberty.
The whole nation applauded him:
Bar Kokhba, *hurrah!*

The song provides the basic plot structure of Bar Kokhba's encounter with the lion. It introduces Bar Kokhba as a popular hero and sets the stage for the drama of his confrontation with the beast. The lion thus enters the scene in the role of the "villain" who challenges the hero. The situation changes, however, thanks to Bar Kokhba's courage and resourcefulness. A swift resolution of the conflict saves the hero and transforms his relations with the lion. At the end the man and the animal are portrayed as united under the banner of freedom, and the nation cheers them both. The melody of the song clearly emphasizes the most basic outline of the narrative, cheerfully rising and repeating the words (italicized in the text above)—"hero," "lion," "hurrah!"

The song provides little information about the specific historical context of the "sad incident." It does not tell who captured the hero and put him in the lion's den, nor why he is hailed as a lover of freedom. In fact, the lack of any allusion to the Romans or the revolt reinforces the legendary aura of this narrative, elevating Bar Kokhba beyond the constraints of time and place. Furthermore, on the basis of this song, one might legitimately conclude that the dramatic encounter with the lion is the single most important expression of Bar Kokhba's heroism and popular appeal.

In writing this song Kipnis was most likely inspired by a historical novel on the Bar Kokhba revolt, written by Israel Benjamin Levner and entitled *Bar Kokhba: A Historical Novel on the Destruction of Betar.*[34] Levner's work appears to be the first narrative in modern Hebrew literature to include the encounter between the hero and the lion. Levner constructs Bar Kokhba's captivity as a noble, voluntary act designed to save a female relative whom the Romans were keeping as a hostage. The author indicates that, even when the hero's followers planned to rescue him from prison, he refused to "run away like a thief" and shame the Jewish people.[35] When Bar Kokhba was thrown into the arena in Caesaria and was confronted with the starved lion, he prayed to God to help him and eventually overpowered the fierce beast with his bare fists.[36]

Levner's account of this dramatic confrontation in the Roman arena was later published as a children's short story for Lag ba-Omer.[37] In this short-story format, as in Kipnis's later song, the encounter ends with Bar Kokhba riding the lion to the rebels' camp, implying a connection to the revolt, yet leaving its precise nature vague. Levner's novel, however, offers a better insight into how the encounter with the lion was placed within the broader context of the revolt. Although the oppressive Roman rule had inflamed the Jews, the open revolt broke out only after Bar Kokhba's success in overcoming the lion in the Roman arena. Furthermore, the novel gives the lion a central place in promoting the Jewish national cause: it accompanies the hero throughout the war, and its ferocious roar backs up Bar Kokhba's call to arms. The lion's fatal injury is the direct cause of the hero's death: Bar Kokhba is hit by an arrow when he bends down to pet the dying animal.[38] The lion's death thus foreshadows the Jews' ultimate defeat.

Levner's novel serves as a bridge between the traditional Jewish and the new Hebrew construction of Bar Kokhba's revolt. The subtitle of the historical novel follows the traditional focus on the ending of the revolt and the destruction of Betar, but as the title itself reflects, the hero's glorified image looms large throughout the novel and is closer to the modern Israeli portrait of the ancient hero than to the traditional one. Kipnis further modified Levner's description of the encounter between Bar Kokhba and the lion in line with the predominant values in secular national Hebrew culture. His song version therefore ignores the religious theme of the hero's prayer to God and glosses over the revolt's ultimate defeat. By emphasizing the victory over the lion and the nation's love of freedom, Kipnis constructs the legend that articulates and reinforces the Zionist commemoration of the revolt, highlighting the very act of opening the revolt and diminishing the significance of its outcome.

Whereas his song version emphasizes Bar Kokhba's unusual physical strength as the source of his triumph over the lion, Kipnis also wrote another tale, offering a different version of the encounter with the lion. Like his song Kipnis's story enjoyed wide popularity and has been reprinted in textbooks for the primary grades and in special holiday anthologies.[39] In this story Kipnis provides the historical context that is missing from his song version and elaborates his account. The tale identifies the enemy clearly and moves the arena (previously described as in Caesaria) to Rome. This construction allows Bar Kokhba to confront the Roman emperor in person at the very heart of his empire, enhancing the symbolic significance of this encounter.

Kipnis also adds two important episodes prior to Bar Kokhba's public performance in Rome that alter the reading of his confrontation with the lion. According to this version, Bar Kokhba and the lion first meet in the Judaean mountains. The man and the animal befriend each other, and Bar Kokhba often rides the lion in the wilderness at night. One night Roman soldiers (who were searching for the Jewish hero) catch the lion, and when loyal Bar Kokhba looks for his lost friend, they capture him too and bring him to Rome.

The encounter with the lion in the Roman arena is described here as a result of the Jewish prisoner's direct and daring challenge of the Roman emperor. When the emperor orders Bar Kokhba to bow before him, the defiant hero breaks his chains and then reassures the scared emperor: "Don't be afraid! . . . the hero of Judaea would not hurt anyone, even his enemy, when he is unarmed."[40] He then challenges the emperor to a public duel. The emperor, however, prefers to have the hero fight a starved lion that turns out to be none other than Bar Kokhba's trusted friend. When the lion recognizes Bar Kokhba, it submissively crouches at his feet. The hero than leaps to its back, and the lion takes him out of the Roman arena, back to the rebels' camp.

This tale is fundamentally different from both Levner's earlier version and Kipnis's song version in that it emphasizes the harmonious relationship and intimate bond between the hero and the lion. The Judaean hero and the king of beasts meet each other as equal leaders who display mutual respect and trust.[41] The man does not use his strength to overcome the beast but rather wins its friendship and support prior to the encounter devised by the Romans. The underlying message of the story, then, is the natural alliance between the Judaean nation and nature, which Bar Kokhba and the lion represent, respectively. The Romans, whose devious plan is based on their "divide and rule" policy, fail to achieve their goal because they cannot possibly comprehend the special bond between the Hebrew nation and the forces of nature. This story too ends with Bar Kokhba riding the lion out of the Roman arena, rejoining his troops.

A more recent children's story by Shraga Gafni, published in 1976, incorporates the encounter between the hero and the lion in Rome into the narrative of Bar Kokhba's revolt. Gafni explains Bar Kokhba's imprisonment by the Romans as an act of retaliation for his public defiance of the Roman decree forbidding Jews to walk around the Temple's ruins.[42] Like Levner, he takes care to show that Bar Kokhba was not captured because he lacked courage or was careless but because Jewish national pride was more important to him than his personal freedom. Gafni introduces the theme of the lion early in the story, when the Romans announce that Bar Kokhba will serve as "a tasty meal" to a ferocious lion in Rome (22). The narrative includes harrowing descriptions of the cruelty that the hero suffers at the hands of the Romans on the way to Rome, and demonstrates that even these efforts did not succeed in weakening his defiant spirit.

The author attributes Bar Kokhba's triumph over the lion to his extraordinary physical strength. The hero, however, decides to spare the lion because it is not accountable for the Romans' vicious plan. In case the young readers suspect that Bar Kokhba might not be able to carry a fight to its end, the author hastens to assure them that "if, instead of the lion's neck, Bar Kokhba were holding Emperor Hadrian's neck, he would have pressed on and on and strangled him until he was completely dead" (53).

Although the lion leaves the narrative at this point, the confrontation contributes directly to Bar Kokhba's regained freedom: Hadrian, impressed with Bar Kokhba's performance (and oblivious to the hero's innermost desire for revenge, intimated to the readers), grants him freedom and makes him a Roman soldier. The Jewish hero uses this opportunity to return to Judaea and begin the revolt against Rome (50–54). While Gafni carefully builds up the dramatic tension culminating in the confrontation with the lion, his subsequent description of the revolt itself is significantly shorter and less dramatic. Since the book is entitled *Mered Bar Kokhva* (The Bar Kokhba Revolt), the reader is likely to remember the confrontation with the lion as the high point of Bar Kokhba's single-handed heroism and the climax of the historical event.

Other tales do not explain how the story of the lion is relevant to Bar Kokhba's experiences but rather assume this relevance as a cultural given.[43] These tales use the lion as a familiar symbolic representation of Bar Kokhba. The lion thus becomes a literary symbol that enhances the hero's mythical stature, indicating that the Hebrew man-nature bond has been continued and introducing mythical time into historical time. The following examples illustrate the use of the lion in these new Hebrew tales.

In yet another story by Levin Kipnis, Bar Kokhba's lion wanders about, searching for a hero to replace the dead Bar Kokhba. Having ceased its futile efforts, the lion "freezes" for centuries, until it learns about Trumpeldor and the new settlers of Tel Ḥai, and comes alive once again. When Trumpeldor dies during the defense of Tel Ḥai, the lion walks over to his grave and turns into a stone.[44] In another story Kipnis describes how a contemporary Israeli child sees Bar Kokhba riding his lion, urging Rabbi Akiba's students to join his revolt. The child persuades the hero to let him join the rebels' forces and contributes to the victory. The story ends with the child's waking up, reframing it as a dream that occurs, quite appropriately, on Lag ba-Omer Eve.[45]

Along similar lines the well-known children's writer Ya'akov Ḥurgin wrote a short story in which he describes how a group of the Jerusalem Hebrew boy scouts makes a trip to Betar on Lag ba-Omer Eve. The counselor tells the children about Bar Kokhba and his revolt and refers to Bar Kokhba's lion. At the end of his storytelling, the child protagonist inquires about the lion's fate, but this remains a mystery. The child's concern is later rewarded, however, when he encounters Bar Kokhba's armor bearer and the lion in a nearby cave at night. The armor bearer tells the Hebrew youth that both he and the beast "froze" in time and space after Bar Kokhba's death, but come back to life once a year on Lag ba-Omer. The ancient warrior also adds new information about the lion's historic role: after the Romans found Bar Kokhba's dead body, the lion guarded it and buried it in the Judaean mountains. When the Romans later caught the lion and put it in a cage, together with Bar Kokhba's armor bearer, hundreds of lions responded to its roar and devoured the Romans. "It was then that I understood," the ancient warrior explains, "that Bar Kokhba's lion was the king of the lions." The beast and the man remained locked in the cage, and the rocks formed a cave around them for their protection.[46]

Tamar Bornstein's story "The Escape of the Golden Arrow" uses an arrow as a bonding device that leads a contemporary modern Hebrew child to the ancient warrior on Lag ba-Omer. The child recognizes Bar Kokhba immediately because he is accompanied by a lion. The ancient hero reveals to the child that every year on Lag ba-Omer he reappears in order to tour the land, and offers him a ride on the lion. Before disappearing, Bar Kokhba tells the child that the arrow—once his—belongs to the heroes of Israel and asks him to keep it.[47]

Although the literary lore on Bar Kokhba's lion is of relatively recent origin, the encounter with the lion was quickly established as part of the story of Bar Kokhba's revolt in modern Israeli children's literature. The visual image of the ancient hero riding the lion became a common representation in the Lag ba-Omer materials (see example reproduced here). Tales that simply take the lion's association with Bar Kokhba for granted indicate the success of the invented tradition. The modern Hebrew legends about Bar Kokhba's lion thus serve as an excellent example of how a new tradition is constructed in support of a national ideology.

Since most of the traditional Jewish sources on Bar Kokhba are of legendary character, the new legends do not introduce a change in quality but rather transform the content of this legendary literature. As a result the lion story can be seamlessly woven into the Bar Kokhba lore without indicating the temporal gap between the old and the new legends. Ḥurgin's story "Bar Kokhba's Lion" illustrates this point. After describing the scouts' celebration, with singing and dancing around the bonfire, the author summarizes the guide's story about Bar Kokhba.

> Their guide got up and recounted for them Bar Kokhba's deeds: how he scared the great Roman emperor to death, how he swiftly rode the giant lion, looking like an angel of terror. And the guide told them about [Bar Kokhba's] heroic soldiers who uprooted cedars as they rode their mighty horses. But the Samaritan's treason brought their

> doom. One after another, the heroes of Israel fell. And as they were dying, they killed thousands of enemy soldiers. Their blood flowed in the valley as a powerful stream until it reached the faraway sea. But the cruel enemy was not satisfied with the heroes' death. They looked for Bar Kokhba. They were afraid of him. But they could not find him among the dead. Only in the evening were they able to find his giant body with a snake wrapped around its neck. All the enemy's troops could not harm him. A snake had bitten him and he died.[48]

The new tradition was thus incorporated into the story along with a selection of older traditions that seem to glorify the leader of the revolt. Israeli children can thus assume that the story of the lion is part of centuries-old tradition about the ancient revolt.

In light of the lion's persistence in the Lag ba-Omer materials, it is often the very first association that Israelis have when thinking about Bar Kokhba. Indeed, as my interviews indicated, this association may be far better established in Israelis' mind than the actual outcome of the historical revolt.

Invented Tradition: The Old and the New

The success of the new tradition about Bar Kokhba's lion in taking root in Israeli culture is, to a great measure, a function of its skillful adaptation of traditional tale structures and motifs, which lend it an aura of antiquity and credibility. At the same time the new lore adapted the traditional motifs to contemporary Zionist views to assure the desired ideological message. Ironically, this new literature used familiar folkloric forms to create a tradition that would reinforce an antitraditionalist ideology.

In its basic plot structure the new Bar Kokhba lore conforms to a familiar structure of heroic tales, in which the hero encounters and overcomes major obstacles on the way to fulfilling his major mission. In the new Hebrew tradition Bar Kokhba's imprisonment by the Romans and subsequent confrontation with the lion constitute obstacles that the hero needs to overcome before he can openly approach his main mission and challenge, namely, to start the revolt against the Romans.[49] This sequence is important, since the familiarity with the deep structure of heroic tales conditions us to expect that the victory over the lion foreshadows the successful resolution of the subsequent confrontation with the Romans.

The struggle with a lion, the symbol of mastery and might, is also a popular folk motif that is used cross culturally to glorify heroes (Gilgamesh and Hercules are two notable examples) and appears in traditional Jewish tales. In overpowering a lion with bare hands, Bar Kokhba follows the example of two famous biblical heroes, Samson and David.[50] Indeed, the literary descriptions of Bar Kokhba's impressive body and extraordinary physical strength appear to draw upon Samson's legendary image. Furthermore, in a few stories Bar Kokhba, like Samson, manages to break his chains.[51] And in Levner's tale Bar Kokhba's prayer to God before the confrontation with the lion echoes Samson's prayer to the Almighty to allow him a final show of strength in front of the enemy.[52]

Like other biblical heroes—Samson in his encounters with the Philistines and David's duel with Goliath—captive Bar Kokhba faces the Roman enemy alone. In all these cases, however, the significance of the heroes' success supersedes their individual fate: their victory has direct implications for the nation as a whole. In the case of Samson, as in Bar Kokhba's case, the tendency to elaborate on the heroes' earlier victories blurs the memory of their ultimate defeat.

If the heroic narrative tradition helped shape the new Bar Kokhba lore, the new tradition nevertheless departs from traditional Jewish tales in its distinctively secular tone. Although Levner's early version (which was written in exile) about Bar Kokhba's encounter the lion includes the hero's prayer to God, this theme dropped out of Hebrew tales written in the prestate period in Palestine. In light of the insistence of traditional Jewish heroic tales upon divine support of victories, this change is highly significant. The biblical stories of Samson and David attribute the heroes' ability to overcome the lion to God's help. Thus, "the spirit of the Lord came mightily" upon Samson as he killed the lion with his bare hands (Judges 14:6), whereas David tells King Saul that "the Lord who saved me from lion and bear also save me from the Philistine" (1 Samuel 17:37).[53] In contrast the new Hebrew texts attribute Bar Kokhba's success to his daring spirit, physical strength, resourcefulness, and strong bonding with nature (the lion), qualities that the new Hebrew culture associates with the ancient as well as the new Hebrews.

The secularization of tradition that this new lore reflects is typical of a broader cultural trend during the Yishuv period. It is interesting to note, however, that with the weakening of the secularist orientation of Israeli society during the 1970s and 1980s and the rise of a nationalist religious trend, Gafni's story (published in 1976) reintroduced Bar Kokhba's religious observance into the story. The hero, according to Gafni, risked his life when he refused to work on the Sabbath and preferred to starve rather than eat pork before the fight with the starved lion.[54]

As we have seen, the new tradition about Bar Kokhba's encounter with the lion emphasizes the cooperation between the human leader and the king of beasts. In the depiction of the lion as an agent of help, the modern

Hebrew tales draw upon other international tale motifs that are particularly popular in traditional Jewish tales: the lion does not harm a saint, the lion lies down at the saint's feet, the lion helps a saint out of trouble.[55] The new Hebrew tradition thus highlights Bar Kokhba's superior qualities as it describes how the lion crouches at his feet, licks him either in submission or gratitude, helps him out of captivity, and supports his fight for freedom.[56] In a typical departure from the traditional lore that describes how a lion helps highly observant Jews, the new Hebrew lore shifts to the leader of a national struggle for freedom. In the new tales, then, Bar Kokhba plays the role traditionally assigned to rabbis and other learned or righteous Jews.

A brief comparison of recent Bar Kokhba literature and traditional Jewish tales revolving around the lion motif illuminates the significance of this change. A popular traditional Jewish tale about a lion who provides protection and help focuses on a pious Jew who refuses to travel with a convoy on the Sabbath and is therefore left alone in the wilderness. A lion appears and guards him while he observes the Sabbath, and at the end of the holy day it gives the Jew a ride so that he can rejoin the convoy.[57]

Traditional tales, like the new Bar Kokhba lore, often highlight the lion's protective role during conflicts with foreign rulers. The lion defeats a vicious plan to use it as an agent of destruction, and its cooperation with the Jew ultimately changes the situation in favor of the Jewish community as a whole. This theme appears in the biblical description of Daniel in the lions' den (Daniel 6:16–21) and still thrives in oral traditions collected in modern Israel. The Israel Folktales Archive holds several examples of Jewish tales that use these motifs. For example, a Moroccan Jewish tale describes how a wicked king put two big lions in an urban Jewish quarter. When the hungry lions got out of their cage, a learned Jew ordered them to lie down, and they followed him to the king. The pious man made the king promise that he would never again cause trouble to the Jews.[58]

Much like Bar Kokhba's lion, these traditional lions are miraculously transformed from ferocious beasts to "pets" who lick pious men's feet and subordinate themselves to their will. The lion recognizes the superior power of a holy Jewish person, which the non-Jews fail to recognize. Yet while the traditional tales follow the "Purim paradigm" of assigning the Jews' deliverance to the foreign ruler's change of heart, the recent Bar Kokhba literature portrays the hero as a self-reliant man who saves himself in a critical moment.[59] That the ancient hero achieves this success by openly defying the Roman emperor clearly conforms to the Zionist emphasis on the ancient Hebrews' activism, resourcefulness, and self-reliance in sharp contrast to the Jews of Exile, who depended on others' help.

Another relatively recent tale about a hero's encounter with a lion supports these observations about the deliberate secularization of traditional

Jewish tales during the Yishuv period. The hero of this story is Michael Heilperin, a Jewish settler of the Second Aliya and an early advocate of Jewish self-defense. Responding to an Arab's challenge, Heilperin entered a lion's cage in a circus in Jaffa. The unarmed Zionist settler proceeded to sing the Jewish national anthem in the lion's cage before he safely got out.[60]

Like the Bar Kokhba lore this tale displays selective borrowing from Jewish tradition. A Jew's survival in the lion's den is a traditional Jewish theme. But this modern Hebrew tale introduces a deliberate inversion of the traditional tales. Whereas they describe Jews who are forced into the lions' den by their persecutors, Heilperin freely chooses to do this. And while the traditional Jew proves his religious devotion by praying to God at a moment of heightened personal risk, the modern Hebrew hero replaces the traditional martyr's prayer with the Zionist national anthem.[61]

In the peculiar ways in which historical memory and folk traditions intertwine, the story of Bar Kokhba's lion received an unexpected boost from later archeological findings. Long after the legend had become part of Israeli folk culture, an archeological dig in the Judaean desert uncovered letters signed by Bar-Kokhba, along with an engraved image of a man struggling with a lion, which was used as a seal. In his report about this excavation, Yigael Yadin remarks that this visual image was common in Greek and Roman seals representing Hercules's fight with the lion, and that Bar Kokhba's headquarters may have used this image to represent Judaea's struggle against Rome.[62] Two other Israeli scholars note the similarity between the seal image and the modern Bar Kokhba lore. Shmuel Avramsky remarks that "it is noteworthy that modern literature and art conceived this theme on an interpretive and intuitive basis";[63] and Yehuda Dvir vaguely states that "the late folk legend" about Bar Kokhba riding a lion may have had some actual foundation.[64]

Although one can only speculate about a link between the newly discovered ancient seal and the recent literary tales, it is possible that an old oral tradition about Bar Kokhba and the lion had escaped the written records for centuries but was preserved by folk memory and found its way into the more receptive nationalist orientation of modern Hebrew literature. Or one may argue that the universal appeal of this folk theme may have independently attracted both Bar Kokhba's followers in Antiquity and early modern Hebrew writers who wished to construct new legendary tales to support the emergent national Hebrew culture. By now, however, Bar Kokhba's lion is safely established in Israeli literary and folk traditions, representing the glorified image of the ancient hero who rebelled against Rome.

Eight

THE ROCK AND THE VOW

"Never Again Shall Masada Fall!"

As we have seen, the symbolic significance of the history and the site of Masada were intertwined in its rise as a national myth. Masada entered Israelis' collective memory as a highly charged symbolic event during the prestate period because it successfully combined what was considered a promising patriotic lesson from the nation's past with an appealing site. This change did not occur abruptly but evolved during the prestate and early state periods. In the early phase of this process, the publication of the poem *Masada*[1] by the Hebrew poet Yitzḥak Lamdan played a central role in reviving the memory of Masada among the Jewish settlers in Palestine.

In this long poem Lamdan expresses the experience of leaving the broken world of home and tradition in eastern Europe and the trials of returning to Masada. The poem begins with the description of other avenues chosen by Jewish youth who remain in Europe: a desire for revenge steeped in violent acts, a socialist activist stance for promoting a revolution, and fatalist acceptance of inevitable doom. As one by one these routes fail the youth, Masada emerges in the poem as the only viable option for the future.

The speaker describes the route to Masada as presenting almost insurmountable difficulties and demanding resolute determination. Those who set out on this difficult journey display a wide range of responses to these harsh conditions and challenges. The poem reveals their expressions of doubt, mental distress, and physical fatigue. Yet these descriptions are interspersed with bursts of ecstasy and exhilaration. Thus at a moment of great despair, the speaker says: "Everyone weeps, everyone . . . Listen, Masada weeps too . . . she knows she can give nothing, that she can deliver no more! She cannot deliver that consumed by the curse of generations; she cannot deliver that which Fate has commanded not to deliver!" (221)

But at night, charged with unforeseen fervor and ecstasy, the pilgrims cry out, "Ascend, chain of dance! Never again shall Masada fall!" (215). *Masada* is thus characterized by radical shifts in mood, swinging from utter despair, loneliness, and keen longing for the past to a feverish celebration of hopes for renewal. At the center of the work, however, lies the experience of the journey, not its destination. The poem depicts the trials of the process rather than unfolding its outcome.

Josephus's work, which was reissued in a modern Hebrew translation in 1923, was welcomed by the Zionist settlers, who considered it an important historical documentation of the nation's past.[2] Indeed, Josephus's historical narrative appears to have provided Lamdan not only with the story of Masada but also with the visual imagery of the site itself.[3] In the poem Lamdan does not dwell on the historical event that took place in Antiquity, and alludes to it only in passing.[4] Instead he uses Masada as a metaphor for Zion. The route to Masada thus represents the modern Zionist return to the Land of Israel and the struggle for a national revival. Masada provides Lamdan first and foremost with a dramatic visual image: a high mountain surrounded by a wall, hanging above the abyss. This image highlights the enormous difficulties of the process of return and dramatizes the perception of the Zionist immigration to Palestine as an upward struggle (i.e. Aliya).

If the text does not explicitly address the historical event, the memory of that past clearly serves as a subtext in the poem. Masada represents Zion because it symbolizes the broken link between the people and the land, which Exile introduced. Masada is important not for the historical details associated with it but for its historical location as a turning point. The return to Masada, therefore, does not imply the revival of the ancient Jews' struggle against the nation's enemies; it epitomizes a revolt against history itself.

> Against the hostile Fate of generations,
> an antagonistic breast
> is bared with a roar:
> Enough! You or I! Here will the
> battle decide the final judgement! (199)

Masada thus presents the last possibility for Jewish redemption, the only route still open to the Jews. This idea is clearly articulated in the poem. At a point near desperation, one of those who are climbing up begins to pray to God; referring to the "wasted hand of the people," he calls out to Him: "Oh God, look, it is stretched out, and on its palm is the last dream that it has drawn up from nights of wandering: 'MASADA'! / This dream and its interpretation have been entrusted in the hands of a few people on the wall" (229). This idea is reiterated toward the very end of the poem: "This is the frontier; from here onwards there are no more frontiers, and behind—to no single exit do all paths lead" (233). If indeed there is "a sign of 'no more exit'" (216), as the speaker asserts, then the selection of this route represents a no-choice situation. And yet choice is implied in the individual's will to go on in spite of the difficulties. The Zionist settlers' determination is the nation's only hope.

Published in 1927, *Masada* was greeted as one of the most important literary works of the early Yishuv period. With the exception of a few literary figures who were highly critical of this work, most of the literary critics, Zionist political leaders, Hebrew teachers, and the general public applauded *Masada* as a work of a great national importance.[5] In Zionist circles in Europe, too, *Masada* was met with great enthusiasm, and it soon became one of the major literary works of great ideological influence upon the Zionist youth.

As we saw earlier, the idea that the new Hebrew literature had an important national mission was quite prevalent. Indeed, Lamdan himself believed that Hebrew writers should contribute to the national cause, expressing their ideological commitment and public views through their writing.[6] Yet even within this context the great popularity that *Masada* enjoyed seemed remarkable, evident in its repeated publications, the great number of literary programs and articles devoted to it, and its place in the Hebrew school curriculum.[7] Furthermore, the poem also generated a famous national motto "shenit Masada lo tipol" ("Never again shall Masada fall!") and a folk song ("Ascend, chain of dance!"), which became highly popular. In fact, although the poem has lost its popularity since the late 1960s, the verse "Never again shall Masada fall!' outlives it as an independent expression of Israeli patriotic ethos.

Indeed, Lamdan's *Masada* presents an interesting case of the ways in which a literary work stimulates interest in the historical event and contributes to the shaping of its commemorative narrative.[8] Although this was not the first time that Masada was selected as a name (the Hebrew writer Ḥayim Yosef Brener, for example, called the association that published the literary magazine *Ha-Me'orer* "Masada" as early as 1906[9]), the poem was clearly instrumental in bringing the event into the public's historical consciousness. *Masada* thus played a major role in the revival of the memory of the historical event and its transformation from a marginal episode in Antiquity to a major national myth. As we shall see, the use of the verse "Never again shall Masada fall!" in youth rituals and national ceremonies and the frequent publication of excerpts from the poem in educational literature relating to Masada are indicative of the centrality of this literary work to the commemoration of the historical event.

Underlying the impact of the poem on the meaning of the myth is an intriguing process of selective representation and interpretation. This selectivity is evident not only in the relation of the poem to the historical narrative but also in the public's response to the poem itself. As I mentioned before, *Masada* is strikingly elusive as a commemorative text relating to the historical event: it assumes rather than provides information about it. Yet Lamdan's choice of Masada as a reference to Zion elevates the symbolic significance of this event as a pivotal turning point in Jewish history. The poem thus shapes the meaning of Masada as a key symbol in Zionist memory. The return to Masada will thus replace a historical rupture with a symbolic continuity. Lamdan's repeated use of the metaphors of rekindling the fire and adding a new link to the chain of history underscores the significance of the notions of continuity and survival to his work. His contemporaries welcomed the poem for this emphasis and for articulating the essence of the Zionist pioneering spirit and experience.

The poem provides a commentary on Masada's symbolic place in Zionist memory. In this respect it signals an obvious shift from a historical to a mythical representation.[10] Masada is elevated beyond its narrowly prescribed historical and geographical location to embody the Hebrew nation's life and soul. The merging of historical time into mythical time is further manifested in the conclusion of the poem, when the section entitled "Toward the Future" (representing linear temporality) is followed by the section "In the Beginning" (representing cyclical temporality). Rather than conclude with the future, the poem ends with a return to the beginning, highlighting its mythical framework. Lamdan's choice of the Hebrew form *Masada*, which evokes also the concept of "foundation" (*masad*),[11] and his use of the annual cycle of the reading of the Torah as a metaphor of renewal reinforce this cyclical notion of continuity: "And as did our fathers on finishing the book of the Law [the Torah] before starting it again, let us roar with a new and last roar of the beginning! / Be strong, be strong, and we shall be strengthened!" (234).

This conclusion of the poem conveys an optimistic note, suggesting renewal, vitality, and strength. The national Hebrew culture clearly focused on this and other parts of the poem imbued with an upbeat mood, an ideological fervor, and faith in the future. Yet the poem is by no means an optimistic work about the future of the Zionist enterprise, as those parts that are frequently quoted seem to suggest. *Masada* is pervaded by pessimism, sorrow, loss, and despair. Those who struggle on the way to Masada are seized by ecstasy and hope at night, but in the daylight they face the grim reality that leads to their "sober awakening" (215).[12] Even when Trumpeldor appears in the poem as the carrier of hope for a national redemption, the speaker observes that "in the camp, over the dying bonfires, stumbling heroes still bemoan their sorrow" (239). Furthermore, after that point the poem continues to a section entitled "Fall into the Abyss," depicting the ultimate despair that led one to suicide.

> Did you see? Today, in the midst of battle, someone cast himself from the top of the wall into the abyss . . . too weary to bear, exhausted. —Today? Tomorrow and the next day as well will many cast themselves from the wall. For no more as in ambush—but openly does despair stalk the camp, and many are its corpses amongst the corpses of battle. (230)

Thus, even though the poem does not address the theme of historical suicide, suicide does appear as a theme. In contrast to the activist interpretation of Masada, suicide is not presented here as a form of patriotic death nor is it seen as an act of defiance. Rather, the speaker regards the suicide as a negative expression of weakness, a form of escape in the middle of a struggle by the one who has given up the battle.

The suicide theme in *Masada* thus represents a different voice than the mythical representation of the historical event. It articulates feelings of fear, loss, and despair that appear to contradict the activist, heroic meaning of Masada as a national myth of commitment to fight to the bitter end. In light of this disparity, the poem's role in promoting the activist interpretation of Masada may be even more remarkable. Yet it is no mere incident that the popularity of the poem reached its peak in the 1940s,[13] during the same years that Masada became firmly established within secular national Hebrew culture as a counter-Holocaust metaphor.

These apparent tensions may be explained, as was suggested earlier,[14] by the multivocality of *Masada*. The poem had multiple messages that touched the readers simultaneously on different levels. The readers could focus on its messages of hope and renewal, which fit the prevailing political and educational discourse during the prestate and early-state periods. Within this framework they could hail the poem as an important literary work that would serve as a source of inspiration for Zionist settlers as well as future newcomers. Yet the poem could also appeal to Lamdan's contemporaries as an expression of the greater ambivalence about their situation, which their culture otherwise tried to suppress.

Indeed, historical evidence discloses the great psychological pressures that the early Zionist settlers experienced as they made the difficult transition to a radically new place and a different cultural environment. Despair and disillusionment forced many to emigrate and led to cases of suicide among the settlers.[15] These tensions were particularly acute in late 1920s, as the Yishuv faced a severe economic crisis and a threatening rise of Jewish emigration from Palestine.[16] In fact, Lamdan's diary attests to his own personal struggles, his own personal anguish at facing the gap between his ideological conviction of the value of manual work and the lack of personal fulfillment he experienced in pursuing this occupation.[17]

Thus, even though the ideological climate did not permit an open acknowledgment or awareness of these "negative" elements, the poem in effect became a collective representation of the psychological difficulties and ambivalent feelings that were part of the pioneering experience. While the Jewish society openly embraced the positive, optimistic portions of Lamdan's work as its explicit message, its enthusiastic response to the poem may have been reinforced by the settlers' identification with those other parts expressing the rarely acknowledged dilemmas of their own existence. The message of an ideological commitment to a national struggle for renewal was thus easily absorbed into their collective consciousness, at the same time that the unspoken experience of anxiety generated by a situation of no choice and the feelings of longing and loss about the world they left behind appealed to their collective unconscious.

Readers' familiarity with the historical event at Masada inevitably contributed to their subconscious response to this work. The historical event provided a concrete reference for their immediate fears of failure and death, and undermined the message of continuity and survival that the poem seemed to deliver. Thus, the poetic representation in *Masada* articulated and thereby reinforced the inherent duality of the Masada myth: both the historical event and the poem were interpreted as providing an unambiguous ideological paradigm for political action, yet both presented a more complex symbolic structure for the commemoration of the past than the society was ready to acknowledge.

A New Hebrew Pilgrimage

The importance of Masada as a symbolic event was clearly shaped by the selective reading of Josephus's historical narrative and Lamdan's poem. Yet the anchoring of this event in an exciting geographical location opened the opportunity to add alternative means of relating to the historical event, combining a patriotic lesson with an adventure. The emergence of new rituals relating to Masada was an important dimension in its rise as a national myth, enhancing its significance for the New Hebrew youth and reinforcing its activist interpretation.

It is difficult to appreciate the significance of Masada for modern Israeli society without dwelling on the emergence of new rituals associated with the site. The rituals are an important facet of the myth because they assume a certain interpretation of the historical event and reinforce it through their performance. Even when no explicit reference to the historical event is made in the ritual, the selection of Masada as the site assumes familiarity with the story of Masada and the ritual draws its symbolism from this association.

The rituals around Masada developed in various stages, each one adding or transforming the character of those which had already been established. During the first phase the ritual focused on the long and perilous trip to Masada and its surroundings. As these trips became more common, youth groups began to elaborate their rituals on top of Masada, and the stay on the site acquired greater significance. Following the archeological excavation, Masada became a tourist attraction as well as a national shrine. New ceremonies sprouted, expanding the earlier scope of ritual behavior and introducing new symbolic dimensions of the myth.

The first phase of rituals surrounding Masada marked the development of a youth pilgrimage to the site. It is not surprising, therefore, that this new tradition emerged in the critical years when the foundations of Hebrew youth culture were being shaped. Teachers in the newly formed Hebrew schools in Palestine were the first to recognize the potential of the site for the patriotic education of the New Hebrew youth.[18] During the prestate period field trips to Masada were not only highly demanding but also considered rather unsafe. Hebrew teachers' readiness to undertake the challenging trips obviously stemmed from their awareness of the symbolic significance of the historical event. The direct encounter with the site itself was likely to leave a far greater impression on the New Hebrew youth than any formal teaching setting.

But the Hebrew teachers' interest also derived from their broader conviction that field trips were an important educational tool. Knowing the land, its history and geography were the goals of special classes which, symbolically enough, were called *moledet* (homeland).[19] "Knowing the land" was more than the recital of facts in the classroom: it implied an intimate familiarity with the homeland, which can be achieved only through direct contact with it.

During the prestate period Hebrew schools and especially the highly popular youth movements assigned great importance to trips as an educational experience.[20] Field trips were considered a sacred activity through which Hebrew youth could reclaim their roots in the land. Trips reinforce the love of the Land of Israel, and the knowledge of its history, landscape, and nature. They also provide training for physical fitness and endurance and an opportunity for learning how to maintain group solidarity in difficult field conditions.

For many centuries Jews living in exile prayed for "Zion," yet their yearning remained enclosed within prayers and texts. Their knowledge of their homeland was thus ingrained in the knowledge of texts, and their bond to the land of their forefathers was ritually reaffirmed through the recital of prayers. In contrast Hebrew youth who grew up in Palestine had the advantage of being physically connected to the land. They did not need to resort to prayers to affirm this bond; they marked it by hiking across the sacred land, leaving their footprints on its soil. Going on field trips established a sense of ownership over the land and a new intimacy in their relations to it.[21]

Trips to Masada were particularly challenging because of the site's location in the Judaean desert. During the prestate period there were no established roads to Masada and no access by car. Travelers could see it from a distance from boats on the Dead Sea or reach it by trekking along the Dead Sea shores.[22] But trekking in this area was a life-risking operation, and after an earthquake in 1927 climbing up the cliff itself also became dangerous. That these trips were extremely demanding and required physical fitness, daring, and endurance only added to their ultimate impact as commemorative events. But when several fatal accidents occurred on school trips to Masada, schools were no longer permitted to pursue this track.[23] Field trips were then carried on by small groups of Hebrew youth exploring the Dead Sea area on their own. Yet during the early 1940s trips to the Judaean desert and Masada were resumed and became a popular youth tradition, embraced by the youth movements and the Palmaḥ underground.[24]

Throughout this period, field trips to Masada lasted for several days and were conducted under very difficult conditions. Accounts of the early field trips to the Dead Sea area and the Judaean desert are filled with descriptions of life-risking situations, problems of dehydration and fainting, the search for tracks, hostile encounters with Bedouins, fear of the British mandate police, the challenge of climbing steep rocks, and other such obstacles.[25] Indeed, these stories are part of a distinct Israeli genre of personal narratives about heroic youthful adventures into unfamiliar (or enemy) territory, in which the protagonists overcome successive obstacles by virtue of their daring spirit and resourcefulness; they face hardships and risk death, yet ultimately survive.

The most common and urgent problem was the scarcity of water. The stories typically focus on the experience of near-dehydration and the desperate search for water.

> We set out on our way . . . We didn't calculate accurately the water [supply], and we were left without any water. People started to dehydrate and were near fainting. I knew there was water in Ein Treibe, but we were still far from there. One of the women couldn't walk anymore. I ran forward and reached Ein Treibe and found water. I ran back immediately and took the group along. We all drank water, and the woman who had fainted got into the water with all her clothes on and absorbed the water through her entire body.[26]

Two of the three young men who set out for Masada in 1934, equipped with Josephus's description, later reminisced about their adventures on that trip. Shmaryahu Gutman, who later became a key figure in promoting Masada as an educational and archeological site, reveals the impact of this early encounter with Masada: "After that [field trip] . . . the thought of Masada did not leave me. As a person active in the youth movement, I realized it was possible to use Masada for educational purposes. At the same time, I started to think about the need to explore the site."[27] The friend who went along with him was clearly more impressed with the physical challenge posed by the cliff than with the historical lesson of Masada. In the same interview he recalls: "[Masada] didn't mean much to me . . . I knew it was something ancient, [that] Jews fought . . . I knew everything. But it didn't mean much to me. [*His voice rises with excitement as he continues.*] And then, of course, we had to climb down. How could we get down from there?" Typically, accounts of the early field trips are often concerned with similar logistic matters. Although Masada was selected as an important designation because of its national historic significance, the route to the site rather than the stay on the summit was the main source of appeal. Since during these early trips there were no "scripts" of behavior once the summit was reached, the stay on top of Masada could turn out to be quite anticlimactic.[28]

Whereas stories about the early field trips tend to emphasize the ultimate victory over difficulties, the trips did not always have a happy ending, and fatal accidents occasionally occurred on these expeditions.[29] When eight persons died in an accidental explosion of a hand grenade during a field trip to Masada in 1942, a commander of the Hagana underground published an article questioning the sacrifice of lives for such a purpose: "For what end did these youths die? Was it really death for Masada? Why were they added to our victims, victims without cause?" The youth responded to these open doubts dismissively, reaffirming the great importance of the pilgrimage to Masada.[30] This response echoed a familiar theme in the national literature on which these youth were raised: the glorification of patriotic death. A memorial brochure for those who died in that accident lauded the blood spilled during the field trips as sealing the covenant between the New Hebrews and Masada, "the heart" and "the soul" of their homeland. Thus, youth would continue to go up to Masada in the future, undeterred by the sacrifice of lives.[31]

It appears that for Hebrew youth the difficulties encountered on the way to Masada and the risks involved only served to enhance the appeal of the pilgrimage. To confront challenges, to persist in the effort despite obstacles, to overcome what appeared to be insurmountable hardships—all these were part of the prestate pioneering ethos they were taught to admire. Dangers highlighted the spirit of voluntarism and patriotism and the blood spilled on the way sanctified the pilgrimage and the bond with the land.[32]

The early field trips by small groups of youths were often made in defiance of elders' advice or authority. Gutman and his friends went on their trip in spite of warnings by Yitzḥak Ben-Zvi that such an excursion would be dangerous and "Don Quixotic."[33] Another group of fourteen youth movement members set out to trek around the Dead Sea, violating an explicit prohibition by their Hagana commander. As a result they had to evade not only the potentially hostile forces of the British, the Trans-Jordanian police, and the Bedouins, but their own authorities as well.[34]

Like the theme of endurance, the defiance of authority was deeply anchored in the prestate Hebrew culture. Daring, resourcefulness, and risk-taking were admired qualities in the underground activities against the British who stood for law and order. The education of the New Hebrews put greater emphasis on social solidarity than on obedience to authority. Socialization in these values was highly emphasized in schools and the youth movements. Field trips offered an important mechanism of reinforcing group solidarity, and teachers and youth movement counselors valued this aspect of the group experience.[35]

The emphasis on resourcefulness and risk taking in sharp contrast to obedience also presented another means of articulating the distinction between the New Hebrew and the Jew of Exile. This theme became even more pronounced in the 1940s, in response to the Holocaust. For the Hebrew youth who had difficulty in identifying with Jewish victims, defiance of law and order assumed an additional meaning: it was an affirmation that they were a new breed of Jews who chose to challenge authority rather than be victimized by it. It is by no means a coincidence that the youth pilgrimages to Masada crystallized during World War II, during the massive annihilation of Jewish life in Europe.

On a symbolic level the field trips to Masada through the Judaean desert can be seen as a reenactment of the historical passage in the desert after the Exodus from Egypt, the archetype of a rite of passage into nationhood. Reaching Masada on their own placed the Hebrew youth closer to the Bedouins, the long-established natives who represented the intimate bond between man and nature. But it also brought them closer to their own forefathers who walked through the desert and made it their home two thousand years earlier. The significance of the Masada trip as a rite of passage persisted even during the first postindependence years.

> A field trip to Masada, for example in 1951, was considered a real operation that lasted for five days and included trekking on foot for scores of kilometers, a chronic lack of water, no little fainting, and a breathtaking climb on ropes to the top of the Masada cliff. In general, the climb to Masada was a sort of "initiation ritual," some kind of a special status symbol for older members of the youth movement.[36]

The choice of Masada as the pilgrim's final destination highlighted the ideological significance of the historical event. The pilgrimage itself was a commemorative ritual that reenacted the spirit of active heroism and love of the country associated with historic Masada; the pilgrims' route became a symbolic reenactment of a struggle for survival. The young pilgrims' resolution to overcome hardships and their readiness to pay for it with their lives captured the essence of the activist commemoration of Masada. The youth's triumph over immediate obstacles thus became the triumph of the revived national spirit that had been suppressed by the long history of Exile.

More than any other trip, trekking to Masada through the Judaean desert became a rite of passage that activated an experience of primal belonging to an ancient history, land, and identity. Masada's location in the Judaean desert was thus critical to the symbolic meaning of the pilgrimage as a nativist ritual. The desert provides a most suitable space for experiencing liminality and communitas. In this distant and primal territory the youth could experience their profound transformation from children to independent adults, from Jews to Hebrews, from sons of immigrants to true natives. By trekking through the Judaean desert and up the cliff, Hebrew youth connected with the land on which their ancestors walked, and thus erased two thousand years that separated them from the ancient Jews who had died in Masada.

Climbing Up as a Patriotic Ritual

The pilgrimage to Masada reached its conclusion in the act of ascending to the summit where the ancient ruins were located. Climbing up with the help of ropes, hanging over the abyss, was both strenuous and dangerous. This dramatic ending of the field trip served as a last test of the pilgrims' courage, commitment, and persistence. Masada's topographical shape was clearly instrumental in enhancing the sacred character of the new pilgrimage tradition. The climb up the slopes to the ancient ruins conveyed a physical and spiritual upward journey that reached its climax when the pilgrims stood near the ancient relics, overlooking the Dead Sea and the Judaean desert. But this ritual climbing has a deeper meaning in the national Hebrew culture. The hikers refer to it as *aliya la-regel* (or *aliya ba-regel*) which is also the Hebrew term for the ancient pilgrimages to the Temple during the holidays of Passover, Shavuot, and Sukkot.[38]

The youth movement tradition of climbing up to Masada can be seen as a secular version of the ancient ritual that disappeared after the Romans destroyed the Temple. Like the ancient Israelites making regular pilgrimages to the holy Temple in Jerusalem, modern Hebrew youth made pilgrimages to their own sacred site at Masada.[39] The New Hebrews thus replaced the most important religious and spiritual center in Jewish Antiquity with the ruins of a fortress in the Judaean desert.

This substitution articulated a radical change in the new nation's commemoration of the past. Whereas Jewish tradition has preserved the memory of the destruction of the Second Temple in A.D. 70 as the most important marker of the transition from the period of Antiquity to Exile, the new Hebrew tradition assigned this symbolic role to the last stand at Masada in A.D. 73.[40] The fact that the fall of Masada could replace the destruction of the Temple as the marker of that critical historical juncture underscores the cultural shift from the traditional theological framework to a secular national one. From this new perspective Masada, not the Temple, represents to the New Hebrews the ancient national spirit that was lost with the transition to Exile. As we shall see, rituals developed during the post-1967 period would further show that Masada and the Western Wall (the only existing relic of the Second Temple) continue to present competing alternatives as sacred national sites of contemporary Israeli society.

The change of destination of the pilgrimage was further supported by the change of the pilgrimage's temporal locus from the three traditional major holidays mentioned above to Ḥanukka, traditionally a minor Jewish holiday. Selecting the eight-day Ḥanukka vacation for the modern Zionist pilgrimage obviously had a practical dimension—to allow sufficient time for the long trip to the desert. But the framework of a holiday associated with a national struggle for liberation reinforced the activist interpretation of the historical defense of Masada. The symbolic significance of the association of Masada with Ḥanukka is demonstrated in Yigael Yadin's subtitle for the Hebrew edition of his book on the Masada excavations and in the fact that both he and Shmaryahu Gutman, two Israelis who played major roles in the promotion of Masada, chose to sign their respective prefaces to publications on this subject on Ḥanukka Eve.[41]

For similar national historic reasons, Passover was also considered a symbolically appropriate time for trips to Masada. In 1963 a group of Israeli commando officers decided to hold the Seder (the ritual meal on Passover Eve) at Masada to celebrate "the feast of liberation on the spot which has come to symbolize the struggle for Israel's freedom."[42]

Clearly, the performance of pilgrimage and special ceremonies at Masada during these major national historic holidays reinforces Masada's association with the themes of national freedom and redemption, which the national Hebrew culture emphasizes in the celebration of these holidays. The pilgrimage introduces a mythical temporal framework that fuses into a single representation the Hasmoneans' revolt, the defense of Masada, and the modern Zionists' struggle for liberation. This mythical framework constructs Masada as another expression of the ancient national spirit that the Zionists revived, and shifts the commemorative focus to the act of resisting the nation's oppressors. Since Ḥanukka and the Zionist National Revival celebrate victories, this association was clearly instrumental in diminishing the significance of the grim ending of Masada.

On a deeper level the pilgrimage to Masada serves as a key cultural metaphor for the "ultimate" Zionist pilgrimage, immigration to Zion. Here again, language demonstrates the inner connections that shape the cultural understanding of symbolic acts. The Hebrew concept for immigration to Israel is *aliya* (ascension), implying that a Jew's "return to the holy land" is a spiritually upward journey.[43] The pilgrimage described as *aliya la-regel* (literally, ascension on foot) is, therefore, a ritual reenactment of *aliya* in its broadest sense.

The metaphor of a strenuous climb up a mountain often serves to represent the Zionist struggle of national revival. For example, it is used in a popular song from the prestate period calling for the participation in the

Zionist national revival: "Up to the top of the mountain, up to the top of the mountain, who could stop those redeemed from captivity?" And the chorus keeps urging, "Climb up, climb up, to the top of the mountain, climb up."[44] The climbing metaphor is also at the core of Lamdan's poem *Masada*.

In light of the multiple cultural meanings of the pilgrimage to Masada, it is not surprising that Hebrew youth refused to give up their sacred ritual for fear of injuries or deaths. Stopping this tradition—whether in response to parents' urging, leaders' advice, commanders' order, or British prohibitions—meant more than giving up an adventurous trip to the desert: it implied the betrayal of the very essence of the Zionist ethos. Death for the country was a central theme in the nationalist ideology of that period, articulated so well in Trumpeldor's famous last words, "It is good to die for our country." It was also seen as an inevitable aspect of the process of nation-building. In the above mentioned song, the speaker observes: "One fell to the abyss, a first victim but not the last." Yet this accident does not stop the speaker or the chorus from calling upon others to continue the effort of climbing up.

In this cultural context the resolution to go on, not to give up because of the blood spilled, assumes a positive patriotic meaning. The expression *lamut o likhbosh et ha-har* (to die or to conquer the mountain),[45] often said half-jokingly during strenuous acts of climbing, reflects the spirit that only death could excuse one from the patriotic obligation to reach the top. Sweating up the slopes of the Masada cliff and overcoming this challenge was a true test of strength and endurance, in the fulfillment of the more immediate task of reaching the summit as well as in the broader mission of contributing to the Zionist national revival in the Land of Israel.

Between Ruins and Texts

During the first decades of the century, getting to Masada was the high point of the pilgrimage. But as this new tradition began to consolidate during the 1940s, it was important to assure that the adventurous dimension of the route, as valuable as it was, would not overshadow the impact of the site and its historic significance. In fact, reaching the summit was often an anticlimatic moment, overshadowed by thirst, exhaustion, or concern with climbing back down the cliff. In order to keep the route a symbolic "prelude" to the "high point" of the pilgrimage, the pilgrims needed to develop a commemorative event that would be as memorable as the experience preceding it. It was therefore necessary to elaborate and expand the ritualistic aspects of the stay on top of Masada which have become part of the pilgrimage tradition.

To heighten the dramatic effect of the climb to Masada, leaders of youth groups often schedule it before dawn or late in the afternoon so as to reach the summit in time to watch sunrise or sundown. The changing hues of the Judaean desert and the distant Moab mountains and the remarkable blue of the Dead Sea offer a breathtaking view from the summit.

The pilgrimage to the top of Masada reconnect the ancient ruins with Josephus's text. While the ruins present mute evidence of life once lived in this desolate place, the text provides images and words to engrave meaning on those stones. Reading or retelling Josephus's narrative at the site is considered an important educational act that is likely to reshape the pilgrims' memory of the historical event. Elazar ben Yair's speech stirring his people to die free rather than be enslaved by the Romans is particularly forceful when read at the very site where, according to Josephus, the last rebels died. In the prestate era, the commemorative ritual usually included also a dramatic reading or performance of Lamdan's *Masada*.[46] The ritual reading transforms the listeners to symbolic actors who follow the steps of their ancient forefathers, sharing the weight and the uplift of a highly charged moment.

Although this ritual is highly secular, it clearly draws upon a long Jewish tradition of reciting texts at a sacred space, manifested in the weekly reading of the Torah in the synagogue. The new ritual of commemoration at Masada thus transforms *Wars of the Jews* and *Masada* from a historical narrative and a poem (respectively) into sacred texts of ritualized remembrance. Within this secular framework Josephus serves as the authoritative ancient text (reminiscent of the bible), while *Masada* provides a modern Zionist commentary to it.

This ceremonial reading is enhanced by its dramatic performance at night by firelight. In addition to campfires and torches, the youth often prepare fire inscriptions (made of canvas shaped into letters that burn in the dark) of Lamdan's famous verse "Never again shall Masada fall!" These fire inscriptions create a spectacular scene, literally highlighting the essence of Masada's national message.

The dramatic impact of the setting is sure to leave a lasting impression on the participating youths. The evocative power of fire for dramatic and stirring rituals has been recognized cross-culturally.[47] In Hebrew youth culture, bonfires, fire inscriptions, and torches are an important aspect of both formal ceremonies and informal pastime. On an isolated cliff, surrounded by the desert and engulfed by the quiet and darkness of the night, the sight of fire is certain to produce a strong visual and emotional effect.

Since youth movements often choose to organize field trips to Masada on Ḥanukka, "the holiday of lights," the use of torches, bonfires, and fire inscriptions reinforces the national-heroic symbolism of this connection.

During the Yishuv period, the rituals performed on top of Masada did not follow a tight script, but they provided the foundations for the commemorative behavior that continued to evolve in the coming years. The ceremonial readings of the Masada-related texts and the discussions of the significance of the historical event have become an integral part of the new commemorative tradition at Masada.

The pilgrimage to Masada gives ritual expression to the new collective memory of Masada as a sacred point in time and space. Through the act of pilgrimage, the New Hebrew youth articulate their bonding with the ancient fighters for freedom, ritually confirming their new native identity and ownership of the land, and contributing to the suppression of memory of two thousand years of Exile. The pilgrimage thus provides a minidrama that captures the essence of the youth's patriotic mission as defined within their transformed memory of the Jewish past.

The State's Sponsorship of Memory

The foundation of the State of Israel in 1948 signalled the beginning of a process by which the state has assumed control over the Masada site and the commemoration of the past. But more than a decade passed before the significance of this change became apparent. Indeed, the extensive excavation and restoration of Masada during the mid-1960s marked a new phase in Masada's career, in which the government and professional archaeologists followed the folk interest in the site.

Indeed, the archeological excavation of Masada demonstrates the state's increasing role as the custodian of national memory. Masada was not the only case in which the state symbolically assumed the role of the official representative of the Jewish people. This position has also been manifested in the Holocaust commemoration and in Israel's claim to act as the representative of the Nazi victims in relations with Germany.

This symbolic role received rather dramatic expression in an official 1969 ceremony in which twenty-seven skeletons, excavated at Masada and identified as the remains of its last defenders, were given a formal state burial. "In a full military ceremony, conducted at the top of the cliff of Masada," the news on Israeli national radio announced, "Israel paid last homage to the twenty-seven Zealots who died in the defense of the fortress two thousand years ago."[48] The chief chaplain of the Israel Defense Forces conducted the burial ceremony in the presence of government officials and other dignitaries. Israeli soldiers raised their weapons in salute to the remains of their ancient predecessors, who were brought to rest after a delay of two thousand years.

The state's decision to give the Masada defenders the honor of an official military funeral reflects the great significance it attributes to the historical event.[49] It also indicates that the ancient fighters for freedom are symbolically analogous to soldiers who die in the defense of modern Israel. Indeed, this anonymous ceremony was conducted in the spirit of the modern state-sponsored commemorations of the Unknown Soldier and demonstrates that the ancient dead have entered the same moral system of rights and obligations as its contemporary citizens.[50] In this sense the burial became a public display of the state's claim over memory along with the state's fulfillment of the moral-historical injunction to remember.[51]

Masada's greater visibility following its excavation and the introduction of a television network to Israel also brought into the limelight the state's cooptation of the youth tradition of pilgrimage to Masada. While various military units used Masada as a site to mark special occasions (often as the climatic end of difficult training), the Armored Corps established a new tradition of conducting its oath-taking ceremonies on top of Masada.[52] These dramatic ceremonies received regular coverage by the Israeli media, and books and brochures often include references to them.[53] Like the state funeral these military rituals emphasize the theme of continuity between the ancient and the present defenders of the nation. As one of these brochures explains,

> Today, other soldiers break the haunting silence atop Masada. Here, young recruits of one of Israel's crack armored units take their oath of allegiance to the modern State of Israel. The ceremony concludes with the solemn affirmation—Masada shall not fall again. The link between the 960 defenders of Masada and present-day Israel is inextricable, undeniable, unbroken. Through the historical account of Josephus, Jews drew strength and courage from Masada's tragic but heroic history for 1900 years in the hope that one day they could return to their native land.[54]

The picture above this text shows Israeli soldiers standing with their heads erect, peering into the depth of the night. Their faces are lit by a large torch, and a Hebrew fire inscription burns in the background, imprinting the verse "Never again shall Masada fall!" as a collective vow.

The army thus incorporated the youth movements' commemorative rituals into its official ceremonies. But the official and legal character of the oath-of-allegiance ceremonies transforms a tradition that was spontaneous and voluntary into a formal contract between the citizen-soldier and the state. By assuming the role of mediator, the state inevitably introduced a cognitive distance between contemporary Israelis and their ancient predecessors in an act that was originally conceived as a form of direct bonding between them.

The excavations of the mid-1960s changed the character of the commemoration of Masada. The remote cliff, which had given rise to a daring and adventurous folk tradition of pilgrimage, has now become easily accessible. New roads, bus tours, public transportation, a youth hostel, and hotels built along the Dead Sea offer a choice between a one-day trip to Masada or a longer stay in what has become a resort area. Masada's growing popularity as a tourist attraction and its official status as a national park have resulted in a growing bureaucratization and commercialization of the site. Entry, once gained by virtue of a patriotic commitment, strength of will, and physical endurance, is now purchased at the entrance to the site. The special rituals that used to follow a long trek through the desert now require special permits and coordination with the National Parks Authority.

Youth movements and schools attempt to pursue the Masada pilgrimage tradition by ascending on foot to the top of the cliff. So do other spirited and physically fit visitors to Masada. Yet even the climb up the slopes has paled in comparison to the adventurous experience of "the old days." Following its restoration, the ancient "snake path" up the slopes is now an easier, faster, safer route. This change is so dramatic that a recent guidebook to Masada warns tour guides to slow down the climb in order to make it last long enough to impress the climbers.[55]

The majority of Israeli and foreign tourists, however, reach the summit by means of a cable car. To protect the look of the summit and perhaps also preserve the symbolism of *aliya la-regel*, the cable car does not reach the very top but ends on a high point below it. While the cable car has made Masada accessible to those who could not have otherwise reached the archeological remains, rapid transportation to the top has clearly transformed the nature of the pilgrimage to Masada.

Most people I interviewed approved of the changes following the archeological excavations, claiming that visits to Masada make the historical event better known and more fully appreciated by both the Israeli public and outsiders.[56] Others, however, objected strongly to the cable car that substitutes an effortless ride for the strenuous climb which they considered a violation of the pilgrimage tradition.

Indeed, the cable car appears to symbolize more than anything else the transformation of Masada into a tourist site. Where Hebrew youth tradition expected the access to the summit to be gained by sweat if not blood, the ride offers visitors a fast, synthetic route to the top. Whereas the youth pilgrimage suggested an analogy to the ancient trekking to the Temple, the cable-car lift reminds one of the comfort associated with ski resorts. The more playful dimension of the experience is thus fundamentally at odds with the solemn character of a pilgrimage.[57] The opinion that the cable car represents a foreign element that is disruptive to the "authentic Hebrew spirit" of Masada has been expressed linguistically in at least two instances when Israelis referred to it by using foreign words within their Hebrew speech.[58]

Veteran Israelis, even those who do not object to this change, often talk nostalgically about the Masada of their youth and the deep and long-lasting memory of those early field trips. In fact, old timers' tendency to break into nostalgic adventure tales of their youth pilgrimages to Masada was so common that an instruction book to guides explicitly warns them against imposing those stories on tourists who may not share their memories or sentiments on the subject.[59]

The excavation changed the character of the visit to the site and expanded the range of rituals, both private and national, that are performed there. A visit to Masada is now a tour of the restored ancient ruins. The archeological interest, once secondary to the patriotic meaning, has thus become the core of the current Masada experience. At the same time the excavation and restoration of an ancient synagogue made it possible to add new rituals. As the secularist ethos of Israeli national culture declines, this dimension has assumed greater significance to Israelis and is a central attraction for Jewish tourists from abroad. The synagogue thus provides a religiously prescribed sacred space that legitimizes the performance of religious rituals at Masada. Today, as one reaches the partly reconstructed ruin identified as the synagogue, one often sees individual Jewish visitors reciting prayers wrapped in their prayer shawls, or groups gathered to collectively conduct religious ceremonies.

Before the excavation a private tradition of celebrating birthdays on top of Masada was considered an eccentric custom of a well-known general in the Israeli army; since then a new tradition developed of celebrating bar mitzvah ceremonies at the Masada synagogue. In 1967 the first collective bar mitzvah was reported as a novelty "that fired the imagination of the country."[60] Since then other schools followed the choice of Masada as a site for a collective celebration of this rite of passage in which children, parents, and teachers take a part. Masada and the Western Wall emerged during the post-1967 period as competing sites for collective rituals of this kind.[61] Indeed, this situation in itself provides evidence of fundamental changes within Israeli culture since the 1970s. The Western Wall, the remnant of the Second Temple and hence the most sacred religious site in Israel, has assumed a highly national significance, whereas Masada, which was associated with secular national tradition and developed later as an archeological site, has now become a religious site as well.

The new tradition of celebrating bar mitzvahs at Masada thus imbues a traditional rite of passage with a national historic significance. While the excavated synagogue makes Masada religiously appropriate for the performance of this ritual, the historical event associated with the site provides another symbolic message: the youths who celebrate their symbolic incorporation into the community of Jews as full-fledged members become a symbolic link in the historic chain that connects the ancient defenders of Masada with contemporary Israelis. Whereas the field trips during the prestate period stemmed from the secular national tradition, this new youth ritual places the religious tradition at the center of the Masada experience.

The Tourist Consumption of a Folk Tradition

Masada emerged from the excavations not only newly restored but also visibly elevated in the public eye. As a result of the enormous publicity won by the expedition, Masada's history has become better known to Israelis and non-Israelis. A visit to the site is now considered an important educational experience not only for Israelis but for tourists as well. Indeed, Yadin foresaw its potential when he suggested as early as 1966 that "through visits to Masada we can teach [Diaspora Jews] what we today call 'Zionism' better than thousands of pompous speeches."[62]

With its unique combination of exotic location, raw natural beauty, interesting archeological remains, and distinctive historical drama, Masada has emerged as one of Israel's prominent tourist sites, attracting a wide range of visitors. Furthermore, Israelis consider foreigners' encounter with Masada a valuable diplomatic lesson that explains Israel's uncompromising attitude toward issues concerning its security. Masada has therefore become an important stop on the itinerary of state visitors to Israel.[63]

Masada's emergence as a major tourist attraction has given rise to a flourishing tourist industry. Despite a decline in the earlier youth tradition, the tourist industry demonstrates a tendency to use this tradition for commercial purposes. Souvenir booths at Masada sell T-shirts with the emblematic image of the native Israeli, a young man wearing shorts, hiking shoes, and a typical Israeli summer hat (*kova tembel*), sweating on the way up the Masada cliff, with the inscription "I climbed Masada." While the image of the young man is an icon of Hebrew folk culture, its reproduction transforms both the symbolism of nativeness and the ritual climbing into a consumer commodity.

Souvenirs for tourists also carry other symbolic images of the folk commemorative tradition of Masada, such as the image of the cliff with Lamdan's poetic line "Never again shall Masada fall!" inscribed on it. Brochures on Masada often include, in addition to information about the archeological ruins, other evidence of Masada's symbolic place in Israeli culture: excerpts of Elazar's famous speech from Josephus, pictures of volunteers excavating Masada, and Israeli soldiers taking their oath of allegiance.

The Israeli tourist industry has also recruited for its own purposes one of the most sacred dimensions of the pilgrimage: the experience of reliving the past at the site itself. A full-page advertisement of Israeli national airline El Al demonstrates this trend. It features a picture of Masada inscribed with—"Masada: the mountain that will move you"—followed by a brief description of the physical setting and a reference to the ancient spirits of Elazar ben Yair and his "courageous band of Jewish patriots." The text concludes with the following statement: "In Israel, the past is always present. Every rock, every street, every city holds a secret centuries old. You only have to travel a few hours to go back thousands of years. You only have to move a few miles to be moved." While Hebrew pilgrims of the prestate and early state periods "earned" this mystical experience through a long and challenging *aliya la-regel* ritual in the desert, tourist-pilgrims can now expect to acquire the same privilege by taking an El Al flight.[64]

The tourist industry thus attempts to recapture the essence of Israeli youth and national traditions and turn them into a marketable commodity, thereby trivializing their original meaning.[65] It is not surprising, therefore, that this process threatens to devalue this tradition also for Israelis.[66] Whereas participants' loud cry during a ceremony, "Never again shall Masada fall!" once functioned as a collective vow that stirs patriotic sentiments, excessive use of this phrase as a publicity catchphrase, printed on ashtrays, shirts, and other souvenirs, inevitably trivalizes its meaning.

Along with the mechanical reproduction of the once scared images and themes, we witness a process whereby "authentic" rituals become staged performances for others' consumption. This transformation turns a ritual in which participants are fully engaged into a "spectacle" that allows passive involvement.[67] This process occurs when military ceremonies are broadcast on Israeli television, thereby becoming a show for Israelis who watch them on their television screens at home. Similarly, visitors who continue the *aliya la-regel* tradition, climbing up the "snake path" to the top of Masada, become a spectacle for those riding the cable car above them, who remain outside this ritual frame. This transformation of the sacred commemorative tradition into a show introduces an element of detachment and alienation that undermines its sanctity.

Indeed, as the state orchestrates ceremonial events at Masada, the line separating consumption for internal and external purposes often becomes blurred. For example, the state borrows for touristic purposes the youth movements' tradition of celebrating Ḥanukka at Masada. In 1971 the Ministry of Tourism organized the lighting of candles by Israeli schoolchildren on the eighth night of Ḥanukka for the benefit of three hundred guests. The following year the same ceremony featured not only the traditional Hebrew fire inscriptions but also an English translation for the tourists.[68]

In 1978 a light and sound show at Masada was among the special celebrations of the State of Israel's thirtieth anniversary. Produced in both Hebrew and English, it was designed for Israeli and non-Israeli tourists.[69] A decade later, Israel's celebration of its fortieth anniversary was marked by a special concert of the Israeli Symphony at Masada. Guests included the president, the prime minister, other Israeli dignitaries, and foreign celebrities such as Gregory Peck and Yves Montand. The high-priced tickets meant that most of the seats for this spectacle went to foreign tourists and well-to-do Israelis.

The use of an ancient site to mark a national anniversary was clearly deliberate. So was the choice of the music performed, Mahler's Resurrection Symphony. The symbolism of this choice was not unlike that which led the shah to celebrate Persia's twenty-five hundredth anniversary at Persepolis in 1971.[70] Although the Israeli celebration was hardly as elaborate as the Iranian, it nonetheless shared the aura of extravaganza. That this ceremonial concert drew cynical remarks from Israelis attests to the feeling of alienation at the incongruity between the imported foreign glitz and the indigenous Hebrew tradition associated with the place.[71]

Israelis' more recent tradition of celebrating bar mitzvahs at Masada is also exported to Jews living outside Israel. That this tradition would catch on is hardly surprising: the setting of an ancient synagogue in the Judaean desert has an obvious appeal as an alternative to the conventional synagogue setting in one's hometown. But the Masada bar mitzvah celebration is also used to stimulate tourism to Israel. This development, which draws upon the universal Jewish appeal of Masada as a commemorative site, erodes its distinctive Israeli patriotic character, typical of the early pilgrimage tradition.

Accommodating the site to foreign tourists similarly runs the risk of widening the gap between the average Israeli and Masada. This gap became apparent in Israel's celebration of its fortieth anniversary, when tourists who attended the concert on Masada became active participants in this commemorative event, and most Israelis watched it on their screens as mere spectators. Furthermore, a recent newspaper article warned that the high cost of the cable-car ride and the entry to the site makes a visit to Masada too expensive for many Israeli families.[72] The article's title, "Masada Fell Again," suggests that the excessive commercialization of Masada has brought about a symbolic inversion, defeating the tradition that elevated Masada and gave rise to this tourist industry.

To counteract the tourist consumption of Masada and the process of commercialization that the site has undergone, youth groups, schools, and military units attempt to preserve the tradition of climbing up the cliff on foot and performing special rituals. A recent guide to Masada explaining the importance of climbing it on foot reflects the efforts to fight off the impact of "the tourist's Masada" by preserving the activist spirit of the "old" pilgrimage tradition. The symbolic significance of the ritual climbing Masada, self-evident during the prestate and the early state periods, now needs to be spelled out for tourist guides.

> Why would one climb the Masada on foot? This may appear an unnecessary effort and a waste of time. Yet we often choose to "ascend on foot" with appropriate groups. Why?
>
> First, this is an act of sanctification. The value of Masada is enhanced for those who climb it on foot. You do not reach Masada "just like that" but only after you have proven yourself, prepared yourself, sanctified yourself, and you have become fit to step onto this awe-inspiring place.
>
> Second, this is the way they used to climb in the past. One of the secret charms and appeals of Masada was the possibility of forgetting the present and living in the past. Ascension by the cable car disrupts this illusion.
>
> Third, try to think what the visitor would remember in twenty years. Maybe a pretty mosaic, perhaps the color of the Dead Sea during sunset, the synagogue benches, or the sophistication of the bathhouse. Each has his own impressions. But maybe there will be quite a few who would remember how they "earned" the right to visit Masada by their sweat, as they ascended on foot.[73]

It may be tempting to conclude that excavations and tourism have ruined Masada's sacred character. Clearly, the influx of tourists to Masada has hurt the exclusive nature of the earlier rituals and transformed the commemorative tradition. Moreover, the cooptation of youth rituals by the state and its tourist industry threaten to desacrilize and destroy it. Yet two different processes seem to work against this decline. The first is the still popular youth trips to Masada. Their popularity may be reinforced by the still prevalent view of the desert as a free and challenging environment that appeals to the youth. For some older hikers too the tradition of climbing Masada is still important, even if quite different from their memories of their youth adventures. Unlike cases where a government's intervention destroys a folk tradition,[74] the ritual tradition of Masada has continued, if transformed. Second, the excavation of the ancient synagogue at Masada has redefined the space as sacred from a purely religious perspective and has stimulated a new tradition of individual and collective religious rituals at the site.

While attempts to preserve the early youth pilgrimage tradition may prove to be an uphill battle against the inevitable impact of bureaucratization and commercialization, the second process articulates a deep change in the conception of Masada's sanctity. The prestate and early-state tradition enhanced Masada as a unique native Hebrew symbol, the product of the particular type of secular Zionism of those years. The present appeal of the site to Jewish tourists and the unearthing of the synagogue highlight the universal Jewish significance of Masada and reinforce a traditional religious meaning. Furthermore, while the folk tradition made the pilgrimage to Masada into a secular, modern substitute for the ancient *aliya la-regel* to the Temple in Jerusalem, Masada and the Western Wall now present alternative locations for ceremonies that seek to combine religious and nationalist symbolism.

The development of Masada as a national shrine demonstrates that the binary opposition of sacred and profane is not sufficient to account for the transformation of its status and commemorative traditions. Rather, Masada as a sacred shrine has given rise to various interpretations, each of which promotes a somewhat different memory of the past and a different ritual tradition. Masada is thus the site of a secular folk pilgrimage that serves as a bridge between the ancient past and the present and suppresses the memory of Exile. At the same time it is an official sacred site for national ceremonies that alternate between the activist and tragic commemorations of the historical event that took place there. Yet it is also a religious site that proves the continuing vitality of religious tradition from Antiquity through Exile to the present. Finally, it is a tourist site that markets all these definitions of sanctity to a wide range of visitors, including Israeli, Jewish, and non-Jewish tourists.

CALENDARS AND SITES AS COMMEMORATIVE LOCI

The overlapping of the ideological, literary, educational, and political interests in the creation of a new tradition encoded the past with a new symbolic meaning and transformed the particular events into major historical turning points in the nation's memory. In the relatively small Jewish society of the prestate period with its highly charged ideological atmosphere, the literary contribution to the Zionist national revival was regarded as part of the ongoing attempt to construct a new national identity and culture. Writing, especially for children, became an activist expression of the Zionist pioneering spirit and an important instrument of change. The adaptation of literary verses such as "In blood and fire Judaea fell; in blood and fire Judaea shall rise" and "Never again shall Masada fall!" as popular national slogans demonstrates the contribution of Hebrew literature to the rhetoric of political activism during that period. At the same time, Hebrew schools and youth movements emerged as key agents in the socialization of the young and major contributors to the dissemination of a new national Hebrew literature and new youth rituals.

In spite of the obvious similarities in the literature inspired by the three events discussed here, it is important to note some significant differences. While the Bar Kokhba revolt has inspired the construction of a whole new body of literature for children, Masada has remained a marginal topic for children. As for Tel Ḥai, although it became a favorite topic for youth as well as adults, the children's lore did not develop a theme distinct from adult literature, like the new tradition of Bar Kokhba's lion.

One may argue that these differences relate to the nature of the historical events in question: the Masada episode, culminating in a mass suicide, does not lend itself to writing for children. Yet my analysis of the Masada myth suggests that its predominant interpretation during the prestate era highlights the resistance to the Romans and plays down the suicide at the end. Moreover, both the Bar Kokhba revolt and the defense of Tel Ḥai offer grim endings that could have posed a similar problem for juvenile readers: the former ended in horrifying bloodshed and destruction and the latter with a number of casualties, including the major hero, Trumpeldor. The events in themselves therefore do not seem to account for the differences in children's literature, which tends to be highly selective in its representation of the past.

The development of a richer body of children's literature about the Bar Kokhba revolt and the defense of Tel Ḥai may be more intimately linked to the nature of their commemoration. While in the early Yishuv period all these events seemed to offer a similar potential for educating the New Hebrew youth, their commemoration crystallized around different temporal and spatial sites. I propose that the specific choice of *a commemorative locus*—a particular point in the calendar or a certain geographical site—plays a major role in shaping the commemoration itself.[1]

The establishment of a memorial day for Tel Ḥai, the Eleventh of Adar, and the reshaping of the celebration of Lag ba-Omer around the Bar Kokhba revolt fixed specific dates in the Hebrew calendar that guarantee their annual commemoration. Those dates therefore serve as sanctified temporal loci for the commemoration of that specific past. Furthermore, the intersection of the Hebrew calendar with the school calendar becomes a most significant factor in shaping the nation's collective memory. When the commemoration of certain events falls within the school year, these events have a greater potential to emerge as distinct subjects of study and leave a greater impact on children. Thus, the timing of Tel Ḥai Day and Lag ba-Omer became an important element in promoting the modern Zionist commemoration of Tel Ḥai and the Bar Kokhba revolt and in turning them into important educational subjects. Conversely, the fact that the traditional commemoration of the fall of Betar occurs on Tish'a be-Av, which falls during the summer vacation, helped blur the memory of that defeat and its meaning within Jewish tradition.

In contrast to these two cases, the commemoration of the fall of Masada is not associated with any particular point in calendrical time. This lack implies that Masada does not enjoy a temporal locus that sanctifies its memory and renders it the primary focus of public attention.[2] Yet the memory of Masada is firmly attached to a spatial locus, and this site allows for greater flexibility in holding multiple commemorations throughout the calendrical year. Moreover, the site provides concrete images of the desert terrain, the mountain, and the various archeological ruins to support the memory of the historical event associated with it.

The establishment of temporal or spatial loci of commemoration appears to generate different kinds of commemorative events. For the specific dates within the calendar that are designated for specific commemorations, literature serves as the primary medium of representation. Commemoration thus revolves around the "performance of literature." On these occasions, children perform educational plays, read tales, recite poems, and sing songs about those particular past events. These performances are often conducted during large school assemblies or during ceremonies in the classroom.

The annual recurrence of these performances helps explain the enormous impact of literature on the emergence of a national tradition. Since children are introduced to these performances from a very early age and continue to be exposed to them year after year during the primary grades, these works essentially shape the meaning of these events and the attitude toward them. It is not surprising therefore that these performances may leave a strong imprint on people's memory. Indeed, some of these literary works, which have "nurtured" several generations of Israeli children, have become part of Israeli folklore and are intimately linked with the memory of these commemorations.

As we have seen, the new literature (especially that which was designed for the youth) often articulated the desire to recreate history as a legend to glorify that past. Following the universal pattern of creating legends about "great men" who shaped the course of history, the new legendary tales for children often focus on Bar Kokhba and Trumpeldor as the central heroes of those events. Although this process of singling them out as the main objects of worship supports the folk appeal of this new literature, it is clearly selective. In the case of Tel Ḥai, Trumpeldor is only one of a group of settlers who fought and died for the defense of the settlement. Along similar lines the emphasis on Bar Kokhba and his revolt during the celebration of Lag ba-Omer departs from the traditional emphases on Rabbi Akiba and Rabbi Shimon Bar Yoḥai as the main figures associated with that date.

In sharp contrast to the focus on individual figures in the cases mentioned above, the representation of Masada relates to a large and anonymous group of people, and its commemoration highlights a group action rather than a particular individual. Although Josephus identified the leader of Masada by name and he has entered the group of ancient heroes of that period who are mentioned by name, Elazar ben Yair has not become a prominent heroic figure of either Bar Kokhba's or Trumpeldor's stature. This may be the result of his primary association with that part of the historical narrative that focuses on the mass suicide rather than the act of defending Masada. We can only hypothesize what would have happened had Masada become associated with a specific calendrical locus that falls within the school year. I believe that such a commemorative locus would have created a greater incentive for Hebrew writers and teachers to form new legendary tales, plays, and songs about Masada and that those would have inevitably focused on the "legendary" leader of that group as a way of offering a more accessible and concrete image for children. Had Masada had a specific date of commemoration, it is quite likely that Elazar ben Yair would today enjoy higher status within the Israeli pantheon of ancient heroes.

There is, however, a fundamental difference in the perceived relationship between "history" and "legend" in the cases of Trumpeldor and Bar Kokhba. For the new Hebrew society, Trumpeldor was a historical figure whom quite a few people knew personally. The literary urge to create a legend out of history was an expression of the desire to glorify the historical event and recreate the historical man in the image of the legendary heroes of Antiquity. Bar Kokhba, on the other hand, was primarily a legendary figure whose history has been obscured by scant historical information and contradictory tales. In his case, history was mobilized in support of the legend. Here too the popular writing of the archeologist Yigael Yadin demonstrates this trend.

> As I remarked above, Bar Kokhba's war lacked a historian like Josephus Flavius, and therefore we have only scant and fragmented information about it. As a result, his memory was preserved in Jewish history more as a legendary figure than as a person of "flesh and blood." Centuries of persecutions and yearning gradually turned him into a national hero in Jewish tradition, a symbol of the Jews' ability to fight for their spiritual and political independence . . . It is therefore easy to understand the excitement that swept the country when it became known that the letters of this legendary hero have been uncovered.[3]

At the end of his children's story on Bar Kokhba's revolt, Shraga Gafni offers a revealing statement about its legendary character.

> Bar Kokhba, our hero, was so wondrous in his courage and wisdom, his great deeds for the freedom of the motherland, and his love for his nation that more legends have been told about him than any other hero. And now, we too have been telling about him in the language of a legend, for only legends can fit a hero like him. Any other form of a simple story would not convey the aura of his grandeur.[4]

Gafni reframes for the reader the nature of his "historical" account about Bar Kokhba and glorifies the legendary discourse as appropriate for a figure of the leader's stature. He goes on to argue that recent archeological findings show that "Bar Kokhba and his heroes were in reality better than anything that legends, even the most imaginary ones, can tell!"[5] That his book is part of a series entitled "Jewish History for Children" further highlights the author's casual approach to mixing history with legend. Indeed, literature for children often takes the liberty of blurring the line between fact and fiction, history and legend, in order to reinforce its educational message.

The Bar Kokhba revolt and the defense of Tel Ḥai thus demonstrate how the temporal anchoring of the commemoration of historical events encourages the emergence of a commemorative literature for that event and how this literature is primarily designed to provide us with a moral lesson.[6]

When a historical event is primarily linked to a spatial locus, commemoration shifts from literature to rituals revolving around the site. In this respect, whatever the Masada commemoration misses in terms of a calendrical representation it has gained by the emergence of a new ritual tradition anchored in the site itself. The emergence of a youth tradition of pilgrimage to Masada and the performance of a wide array of rituals on the site have served as major stimuli for the commemoration of the historical event associated with the site. Moreover, the climb up the cliff before sunrise or sunset, the tour of the ruins, the reading of Josephus's account of the historical event, and the performance of military ceremonies are all rituals that have helped shape the symbolic meaning of Masada in Israeli culture.

During the prestate and early-state periods the pilgrimage to Masada involved physical dangers that clearly enhanced the activist meaning of that ritual which, in turn, reinforced the activist heroic message of the historical event. While these dangerous conditions contributed to the appeal of the pilgrimage tradition for the youth, they also prohibited development of a site-oriented tradition for younger children, for whom such a challenge is not suitable. Unlike the defense of Tel Ḥai and the Bar Kokhba revolt, Masada did not develop an appropriate commemorative locus—either temporal or spatial—for the very young.

Theoretically speaking, both the Bar Kokhba revolt and the battle of Tel Ḥai have potential spatial loci in addition to their calendrical loci. Yet, while commemoration of the latter has also evolved around a specific site, the commemoration of the former has been primarily anchored in its calendrical locus. Thus, Betar, the site most distinctively associated with the Bar Kokhba revolt, has not inspired a major pilgrimage tradition. It is quite possible that Betar has been neglected because it calls attention to the rebels' retreat and ultimate defeat. Since the new commemorative tradition in Lag ba-Omer emphasizes an earlier and more successful stage of the revolt, it did not encourage focusing on Betar, the site of death and destruction. Furthermore, because the name Betar became strongly identified with the Revisionist youth movement by that name, its political opponents, who were more influential in shaping the social, political, and educational discourse during that period, had no incentive to enhance its visibility. Betar thus never developed as a major commemorative locus for the Bar Kokhba revolt.

The defense of Tel Ḥai, on the other hand, provides an example of multiple commemorations of a historical event with both temporal and spatial loci. The Eleventh of Adar, known also as Tel Ḥai Day, underscores the importance of its calendrical representation. The commemoration of the battle of Tel Ḥai also gave rise to a new annual tradition of pilgrimage to the tomb of the fallen heroes on that date. Youth movements, military units, and residents of nearby settlements continue this tradition today. The national memorial ceremony near the Roaring Lion monument at the Tel Ḥai cemetery became the central commemorative event on the Eleventh of Adar.

Yet Tel Ḥai's location in the far northern region of the country has inevitably limited participation in the pilgrimage ritual. Hence, during the prestate and the early-state periods, local communities and public schools throughout the country came to hold their own commemorative ceremonies on the Eleventh of Adar, drawing on its temporal locus only. These multiple commemorations of Tel Ḥai are therefore based on the performance of literature, while the tradition of pilgrimage to the site reflects greater emphasis on ritual orientation.

Whereas Masada and Bar Kokhba represent opposing models of commemorative events—the former based on a spatial commemorative locus with an elaborate ritual tradition and the latter based on a calendrical commemorative locus supported by a rich body of literature—Tel Ḥai represents a middle ground case that integrates some characteristics of both. Although a spatial locus allows for the pilgrimage to Tel Ḥai and the per-

Event	**Bar Kokhba's revolt**	**The defense of Tel Ḥai**	**The fall of Masada**
Temporal Locus	Lag ba-Omer	The Eleventh of Adar	
Spatial Locus		Tel Ḥai cemetery	The site of Masada
Commemoration	literature	literature and ritual	rituals

Figure 4

formance of its accompanying on any other day, their performance on the Eleventh of Adar clearly stands out as the most sanctified commemoration of the historic battle of Tel Ḥai. The combination of the temporal and the spatial loci thus contributes to the significance of this commemoration. At the same time, however, neither the ritual nor the literary orientations have been fully developed. Thus, Tel Ḥai has not generated the wide range of rituals performed at Masada, nor has it acquired the popular appeal of the new Lag ba-Omer tradition around Bar Kokhba.

The analysis of these commemorative patterns illuminates the role of literature and ritual in the development of the new Hebrew tradition during the formative years of Israeli society. By emulating traditional forms of commemoration as well as by adapting and secularizing various themes and forms of Jewish folk traditions, these new cultural constructs helped define the Hebrew nation and its relation to Jewish history and tradition. As years of established statehood have effected fundamental changes in Israeli cultural life, new interpretations of the historical events have emerged side by side with the earlier representations of this past. A more visible nationalist-religious trend within Israeli culture has created its own versions of the past, transforming the myths that the secular national ideology generated. The more accommodating attitude toward Jewish tradition is also articulated in the ritual domain, as the performance of bar mitzvahs in Masada and the growing significance of the Lag ba-Omer pilgrimage to Mount Meron and the tomb of Rabbi Shimon Bar Yoḥai, indicate. At the same time, a more critical attitude toward the representation of the past in Israeli national tradition is evident today. As a result, the cultural commemoration of all these historical events has been subject to critical reevaluation. These developments are the focus of part 4.

POLITICS OF

Part Four

COMMEMORATION

Nine

TEL ḤAI AND THE MEANING OF PIONEERING

The literature on national myths often emphasizes their function of reinforcing social solidarity among members of the society. Hence, the creation of myths is particularly important during the formative stage of a nation, when the need to foster social solidarity is acutely felt. In the early prestate period, when the Jewish society of Palestine was beginning to shape its identity as well as its social, political, and cultural foundations, the elevation of certain historical events to sacred national texts seems to have answered that need. From the 1920s to the 1940s new patterns of commemoration of those events crystallized, providing the emergent nation with symbolic texts that help it define its national historic mission.

Yet analysis of the rhetorical uses of three Israeli national myths challenges the functionalist view of myths as unifying cultural expressions that contribute to society's cohesiveness. A close examination of the interpretation of these sacred texts from a historical perspective discloses that national myths can also turn into a divisive cultural force. In pursuing this approach the present study is part of a growing body of literature exploring how cultural texts serve different groups and political agendas at one and the same time or at different points in history.[1] In fact, one can argue that, precisely because myths are so highly regarded as sacred texts, they are likely to be coopted by conflicting positions and thereby contribute to intensification, rather than easing, of internal social frictions.

In spite of some similarities in the controversies around the meaning of the three myths, each myth has generated discussion on distinct issues relating to the particular historical events and their interpretation. The politics of commemoration is thus shaped by the continuous negotiation between history and memory and the tensions between established commemorative practices and emergent political concerns. Whereas the three commemorative narratives have recently become subjects of public debate, Tel Ḥai is the only myth that has generated a diversified body of humorous texts. This humorous lore offers a different form of challenge to the myth text than do bluntly polemical narratives. Yet it too has modified the memory of the past, demonstrating its changing interpretation as a paradigm for the present.

The Plow versus the Gun

During the prestate and early-state periods, Tel Ḥai fulfilled the classic role of a new national myth of a young nation in the process of defining its historical mission. By providing a symbolic representation of collective death and rebirth, it dramatized the beginning of the new historical phase of National Revival. The blood of the dead heroes became a form of sanctification of this transition. The Jewish settlers' immediate response to the historical event indicated a general agreement on its political and educational significance as the embodiment of the new pioneering ethos. Even though the settlers initially put aside past and present disagreements in order to create a unified myth of Tel Ḥai, those differences were soon to enter the political discourse and transform the myth text.

From the end of the 1920s until the foundation of the State of Israel, Tel Ḥai continued to function as the most prominent national myth of the growing Yishuv. Yet during this period new political developments shattered the Yishuv's earlier agreement on the meaning of the myth and turned it into a subject of public controversy. During the 1930s and 1940s an intense conflict between the two major Zionist movements, the Socialists and the Revisionists, dominated the political life of the Yishuv. In the prevailing hostile atmosphere each party attempted to align the myth with its own political stance and accused the other of manipulating the past for its own political purposes. The heated dispute about the meaning of the Tel Ḥai myth thus provided another arena for the political struggle between the two movements.

The Socialists and the Revisionists advocated two different reactions to the deteriorating political situation in Palestine and abroad. The escalation of tensions between Arabs and Jews in Palestine, the British restrictions on Jewish immigration following the Arab revolt of 1936–39, the worsening situation of Jewish communities in Europe, and the outbreak of World War II intensified the internal debate on the Zionists' strategies of dealing with these issues. The Labor movement, from whose ranks rose the Yishuv's leadership, advocated self-defense with restraint vis-à-vis the Arabs and an official attitude of cooperation with the British mandate authorities, while covertly developing and training the Hagana underground.[2] The Revisionists called for a more activist stance of open opposition to the Arabs and the British authorities and a more aggressive policy of encouraging illegal Jewish immigration to Palestine in defiance of the British restrictions. The two underground groups that grew out of the Revisionist movement, Irgun Tseva'i Le'umi and Loḥamei Ḥerut Yisrael, advocated a more militant policy and were highly critical of the more passive stance of the Hagana, which they saw as a betrayal of the Zionist nationalist agenda.

In the growing political polarization within the Yishuv around these issues, each side interpreted Tel Ḥai in support of its own political and ideological stand. The ensuing controversy focused on both the historical event and the myth that it generated. The dispute raised conflicting ideological interpretations of Tel Ḥai and developed into a contest on the moral right to use it.

The discussion of the battle of Tel Ḥai revived a debate about the defensibility of Upper Galilee that had taken place prior to the eleventh of Adar in 1920. The Socialist Zionists vehemently condemned the use of "Tel Ḥai" and "Trumpeldor" by the Revisionist youth movement Betar (also called the Association of Yosef Trumpeldor). The Socialists reminded their opponents that in 1920 Ze'ev Jabotinsky had opposed the defense of the northern Jewish settlements and had called for their immediate evacuation.[3] They argued that the Revisionists had betrayed the defenders of Tel Ḥai at a time of need and therefore had no moral right to use the battle or the name of the fallen hero as their symbols. By coopting the sacred myth of Tel Ḥai and its central hero Trumpeldor, claimed the Socialists, the Revisionists were manipulating the past for their own political advantage.

> One should not blur and distort the historical truth; one cannot put a new face on the people of Tel Ḥai. One should not forget that the Tel Ḥai heroes fought and fell in a two-front war: not only the war against bandits who wished to destroy a place of peace and labor, but also a war against the indifference, helplessness, alienation, and fear at home, within the Yishuv and among its leaders. One should not forget their horrible isolation there and the response of those believers in "pure nationalism," those who had the ability and the influence [to help].[4]

Jabotinsky responded to the Socialists' accusation of his betrayal of Tel Ḥai by reiterating his earlier position on the issue of defending the northern settlements in 1920. In an article entitled "Between the Sixth and the Eleventh [of Adar]," Jabotinsky reconstructed the events that had led to the fall of Tel Ḥai and defended his earlier analysis of the settlements' situation.

Explaining why the decision to defend these settlements was unrealistic, he maintained that he had shown better judgment and more concern for the settlers in calling for their immediate retreat than those who had let them expect help which the Yishuv could not provide.

Jabotinsky now went further than he had in 1920, blaming the Socialists directly for the defenders' death and denying their moral right to the myth.

> When our "leftists" criticize the "Association of Trumpeldor" [Betar] or "Keren Tel Ḥai" [Betar's fiscal agency], they ask, "What right do you have to these names when your president suggested calling back Trumpeldor from Tel Ḥai?" He requested this, gentlemen, because he predicted that you would not send any aid in spite of all your heroic rhetoric. And knowing this, he thought that one should not abandon people to be slaughtered when one could not provide aid![5]

> There is a huge difference between the defenders of Tel Ḥai who were physically in that place and those who "defended" Tel Ḥai from a distance. The former had the right to be heroic and stay in the settlement, even when no aid was forthcoming. But those who served on the Provisional Committee, far from there, had no right to tell the Tel Ḥai people, "Be heroes and do not withdraw."[6]

The interest in this historical debate was far from academic. Underlying it was the desire of each movement to claim the moral right to the myth on the basis of the events that had led to the fall of Tel Ḥai in 1920, and to deny the other's right to do the same. The debate did not bring out any new information relating to the historical defense. In the 1930s and 1940s history was of interest to the rival parties only as long as it proved or disproved their moral claim to the myth. The intensity of the hostility that fired this debate was manifested, according to several of my informants, by the outbreak of skirmishes between Revisionist and Socialist youth on Tel Ḥai Day.

The resumption of the historical dispute over the defense of Upper Galilee a decade later is all the more interesting if we consider that, immediately following the fall of Tel Ḥai, the parties involved in that debate tacitly agreed to set aside their previous arguments about the plausibility of its defense. Eliyahu Golomb, who was a member of the commission sent to Tel Ḥai to explore the situation in March 1920, wrote: "After the event, there were no further arguments about the importance of the heroic stand of the Tel Ḥai defenders and of its value as a symbol and a model for the Yishuv and the entire Jewish world."[7]

The widening political gap between the Socialists and the Revisionists led to renewal of the old debate. In this controversy Jabotinsky's main line of argumentation was to separate the historical event from the myth in order to justify his opposition to the defense in 1920 and his later glorification of it. The Labor movement, on the other hand, denied the legitimacy of this distinction. For the Socialists, only those who had supported the defenders' determination to defend Tel Ḥai in 1920 earned the moral right to glorify that event and to use it as their political symbol.

The disagreement over the meaning of Tel Ḥai provided yet another front for the Revisionist-Socialist conflict. The rival interpretations of the myth did not simply highlight ideological differences; they also served as a useful means for mobilizing political support and attacking the other movement's policies by showing their inconsistency. By coopting the myth for their own political purposes, the two movements attempted to capitalize on Tel Ḥai's status as a major sacred text of the pioneering era. While Tel Ḥai's status as a national myth remained unquestioned, the controversy revolved around its meaning.

Each movement reconstructed the meaning of "pioneering" according to its political program, supported by its own version of Tel Ḥai. The Revisionists emphasized mostly the defenders' heroic, activist spirit, their strong sense of national mission, and their readiness for personal sacrifice. The Socialists did not neglect the heroic aspect yet preferred to emphasize the defenders' commitment to the ideology of settling and working the land. Since there was no disagreement about the heroic aspects of the myth, the dispute shifted to the theme of "settlement and work." While the Socialists emphasized this theme as central to the Tel Ḥai myth, the Revisionists denied its relevance for a heroic myth.

Today, the difference between these positions may seem quite insignificant. But at the time it represented the fundamental disagreement between these rival political movements. On more purely ideological grounds the Socialists' interpretation of Tel Ḥai integrated nationalism with socialism, whereas the Revisionist interpretation supported the principle of "monism," namely, exclusive adherence to nationalist Zionist ideology.[8] But the different versions of the myth also had a direct bearing on the immediate political scene. The Revisionists mobilized Tel Ḥai in support of their call for armed resistance, maintaining that it demonstrated the centrality of armed confrontation and readiness for sacrifice to the Zionist national revival. By shifting the focus from armed resistance to settling and working the land, the Labor movement argued that Tel Ḥai supported its advocacy of restraint in the use of arms against the Arabs and the British, thus proving the priority of the settlement mission.

In a polemical article on the eighth anniversary of Trumpeldor's death, Jabotinsky pointed out that Trumpeldor was remembered as a military hero and that this image would persist in the nation's memory. He openly acknowledged the relevance of this issue to the ongoing conflict between the Revisionist and Labor movements: "Among those who praise him [Trumpeldor], there are vocal opponents of anything related to the sword, the gun, and the pistol. But Trumpeldor's name is primarily associated with these weapons and others . . . In the collective memory of our people, Trumpeldor has essentially been remembered as a soldier."[9] Aba Aḥime'ir, the spokesman of a more radical faction of Revisionist youth, expressed a similar idea in a more confrontational style: "But what do they [the Socialists] have to do with Trumpeldor? Why don't they go on pilgrimage to the grave of [the Socialist ideologue] A. D. Gordon? Why do they too go on pilgrimage to the distant grave of Trumpeldor the militarist, Trumpeldor who volunteered for the Zion Mule Corps in Gallipoli?"[10]

The Revisionists focused on Trumpeldor's devotion to Jewish nationalism and military activism.[11] Their version of Tel Ḥai, they argued, represented the historical man more faithfully than the Socialists'. They also emphasized the historical cooperation between Trumpeldor and Jabotinsky during World War I, when the two men joined forces in lobbying for a Jewish legion within the British army, leading to the establishment of the Zion Mule Corps. This cooperation was thus presented as testimony of Trumpeldor's ideological affinity to the man who was later to become the head of the Revisionist movement.

To prove that Trumpeldor had been concerned primarily with nationalist and activist issues rather than with a socialist agenda, the Revisionist educational materials selected quotes imbued with this spirit from Trumpeldor's writings.[12] Jabotinsky interpreted Trumpeldor's famous words before he died as representing the hero's vision of pioneering, a total commitment to fulfilling the national needs without any other ideological considerations.[13] Since the Revisionist leader based his interpretation of Trumpeldor's words on a private conversation with the hero for which no other source is available, he could legitimately claim exclusive knowledge of Trumpeldor's views.[14] Furthermore, he could establish himself as a direct link between the dead hero and his own Revisionist followers, thereby presenting the latter as the authentic carriers of the Tel Ḥai legacy.

The Labor movement meanwhile advanced its interpretation of Tel Ḥai as a myth of settlement, work, and defense. To dramatize its distinction from the Revisionists', the Labor movement focused on Trumpeldor's ideological commitment to building Jewish settlements and working the land. This theme was not new: Trumpeldor had been portrayed in accordance with the conventional image of the Zionist pioneer who with one hand held the plow and with the other held his weapon.[15] In Trumpeldor's case, however, the image required some modification because his left arm had been amputated. The hero was therefore portrayed as holding both the plow and the gun in his one hand.

If the joined symbols of the plow and the gun served to glorify the ability of the average pioneer to carry out the highly demanding tasks of plowing and standing guard, Trumpeldor obviously rose above all other pioneers. Holding the two tools together, Trumpeldor symbolizes their inseparability, in defiance of the Revisionist position. The Socialists could thus clearly benefit from demonstrating the hero's personal commitment to the plow as a proof of his Socialist orientation.

The debate on the meaning of the myth during the 1930s and 1940s can be seen as a power struggle over the shaping of the Yishuv's collective memory from the vantage point of the ongoing political conflict between the two movements. In their interpretation of the Tel Ḥai narrative, the Revisionists and the Socialists used the gun and the plow as visual emblems of nationalism and socialism, respectively. Although the Labor movement had first presented both implements as equally important symbols of Socialist Zionism, it now attempted to introduce a hierarchical order into their representation: by asserting the plow's superiority over the gun, they wished to create a clear-cut contrast with the Revisionists' advocacy of weapons and armed struggle.

The Socialists therefore turned to the plow as the central icon of the Tel Ḥai myth. Their educational materials for the Eleventh of Adar highlighted Trumpeldor as a settler and a worker, a person who was holding his gun only to protect the plow with which he was tilling the fields. This theme was emphasized in a brochure for nursery school teachers for Tel Ḥai Day: "They were not the heroes of the sword and the spear, but the heroes of the shovel and the plow. [For them] the weapon did not exist but for supporting the builder's cubit. They knew how to die as heroes, because they knew how to live as heroes, the heroes of work and construction."[16]

The Socialists stressed time and again that the Tel Ḥai defenders who had been members of the Labor movement had been filled with "the love of the nation and the land, and believed in the principles of labor and social justice."[17] Trumpeldor himself, so the Socialists claimed, was committed to socialism and interested in the Labor movement's activities. The Socialists never doubted that the dead hero had been one of their own. To prove the point they, too, turned to his writings in search of appropriate quotations. Their educational materials for Tel Ḥai Day included a different sample of Trumpeldor's statements, which suited their purpose: "Not a sword but peace we carry to the Land of Israel. Only the most extraordinary circumstances will force us to transform our shovels to swords"; "Remember! To the Land of Israel you go not for heroic acts, nor to make sacrifices, but for work!"[18]

To support their respective interpretations of the myth, both rival movements drew upon the growing body of oral and written literature inspired by Tel Ḥai and often used for its commemorations. Since both the plow and the gun were important symbols in the literature of that period, each movement could selectively find literary support for its own position in this conflict.

A popular children's story, presented as a personal memoir, recounts how Yosef Trumpeldor led a small group of settlers to examine the damage that Arabs had inflicted on Ḥamra, a Jewish settlement near Tel Ḥai. The settlers found the place burned down and the fields deserted. As they approached the field, they saw a plow that had been left behind.

> It appeared a lifeless, cold, metal instrument, but it appealed to us as if it were a precious object. All of us surrounded the plow and stared at it. The plow was our symbol: they [the Arabs] have weapons and we have a plow. They left our plow here. They did not take it.
>
> "We will take the plow to Tel Ḥai!" exclaimed Trumpeldor after a prolonged silence. "We will go on plowing and sowing the land."

As they were about to leave for Tel Ḥai, the Arabs resumed the attack. Under the enemy's bullets, Trumpeldor carried the plow all the way back to Tel Ḥai. When they arrived there safely, one of his comrades asked him,

> "Did you risk your life for one plow, Yosef!?" . . .
>
> "This is not merely a plow," Yosef solemnly replied, "this is our flag, the flag of the awakening people of Israel. And one cannot abandon a flag at the hands of the enemy."[19]

A simple reading of the story suggests the importance of the plow as a major national symbol for Trumpeldor and his friends and demonstrates the Arabs' failure to understand the significance of this unassuming object. But when applied to the context of the Revisionist-Socialist conflict, the text gains a biting edge as it implies an analogy between the Revisionists and the Arabs: both believe in the power of weapons to win a war yet miss the ideological and moral strength that the plow bestows on its followers.[20] Trumpeldor's attachment to the plow also appears as the central theme of a popular song for Tel Ḥai Day (the original Hebrew rhymes).

In the Galilee Yosef plowed
And he was singing all along:
"My plow is with me, with me,
My plow is my work,
My joy and my flag . . .
My plow is with me, with me."

In Galilee Yosef fell
But his song did not die out:
"My plow is with me, with me.
It is good to die for my country,
My hand holding my plow.
My plow is with me, with me."[21]

Another poem describes the miracles performed by "the hero of Tel Ḥai" who made the wasteland bloom. In contrast to Jabotinsky's interpretation of Trumpeldor's expression "Never mind," this poem associates this phrase with the task of working the land: "Is the cliff burning? Is the thorn pricking? / Are there snakes in the desert? / 'Never mind!'"[22]

To counter the Socialists' use of the plow as the central emblem of the Zionist pioneer, the Revisionists turned to a story that focuses on the Tel Ḥai defenders' special attachment to the national flag. The story relates how the settlers made a flag out of a simple white sheet painted with blue. Throughout the battle with the Arabs this improvised flag, pierced by the enemy's bullets, continued to fly on high. Following the attack, the survivors of Tel Ḥai carried away the bodies of their dead comrades, wrapped in that flag. When the Jewish settlers later returned to Tel Ḥai, they brought back the flag. Stained with blood and riddled with holes, it served as the symbol of the battle of Tel Ḥai in future commemorations of the Eleventh of Adar.[23] Following this story the brochure reprints Jabotinsky's poem "The Flag" and presents an outline for a group discussion on the question, "Why would people be ready to be killed for the flag and not desert it?"

Both the plow and the flag stories, presented as accounts of a survivor of the battle of Tel Ḥai, were written by Eliezer Smally, who was a teacher in Kfar Giladi during the 1920s and published stories on the settlers' lives.[24] Their symbolic juxtaposition in the educational materials on the two movements, therefore, appears to have been imposed on the text rather than intended by the author. Furthermore, during the first few years following the historical event, the plow and the gun were not usually juxtaposed in the public discourse of Tel Ḥai. The themes of heroic last stand, activism, settlement, and working the land were all used interchangeably and across the political spectrum. In 1921, for example, the writer Yosef Ḥayim Brener, who published often in Socialist publications, stated that Trumpeldor was "first and foremost a military man," while Jabotinsky wrote two poems about the Tel Ḥai defenders that portray them plowing the fields.[25] At the time Jabotinsky had no qualms expressing his admiration for the Socialist settlers and the importance of plowing. Yet as the conflict between him and the Socialists intensified, he was less likely to use the plowing image in reference to Tel Ḥai.

By emphasizing their separate interpretations of the Tel Ḥai myth, the Revisionists and the Socialists accentuated their political differences. Projecting these differences onto the past, each movement attempted to prove itself the legitimate heir of the Tel Ḥai legacy. Trumpeldor's writings and career were so diverse that neither movement had any difficulty finding support for its position. Trumpeldor was a complex figure, and his personal correspondence encompassed a wide range of issues. He was inclined toward socialism and even tried to lay out systematic guidelines for future Jewish communal settlements.[26] As president of the Ḥalutz organization in Russia in 1919, Trumpeldor's main concern was to arrange for its members' emigration to Palestine. During his visit in Palestine in preparation for their arrival, he was deeply concerned that the severe economic problems might prohibit their successful integration into the Yishuv society. Thus, shortly before his death, Trumpeldor published an open letter in the Yishuv's main Socialist publications, urging the two Socialist parties to overcome their differences in order to improve the economic conditions in Palestine and help accommodate future Jewish immigrants.[27]

Yet Trumpeldor was also deeply concerned with issues relating to Jewish activism, which had brought him and Jabotinsky together. When Trumpeldor returned to Palestine in December 1919, Jabotinsky wrote an article in his praise and complained about the Yishuv's failure to give Trumpeldor a hero's welcome. And Jabotinsky was the person who gave the main eulogy in the public commemoration of the Tel Ḥai hero immediately after his death.[28]

Trumpeldor himself addressed the question of his ideological priorities in a letter to a friend. As early as 1911 he articulated his position clearly: "I have not found a conflict between Zionism and communism, and I do not believe that this will become an issue for me in the future."[29]

When the Revisionist-Socialist conflict subsided following the foundation of the State of Israel, there was no longer a need to separate the dimensions of work and defense in the Tel Ḥai myth. The symbols of the gun and the plow, previously interpreted as two polar representations of competing ideological systems, were once again restored to their earlier partnership. Indeed, it appears that the Zionist discourse emerged from that period of conflict strengthened, consolidating into an official discourse disseminated by the national educational system.[30] Public school textbooks thus continued to portray the plow and the gun as complementary symbols of Israeli pioneering ethos, reflecting Labor's political hegemony until the late 1970s.[31] The commemoration of Tel Ḥai emphasizes its meaning as a myth of heroism and national sacrifice, yet this interpretation is not necessarily associated with either Betar or the Revisionists.[32]

The intensity of the debate indicates the enormous political significance of the myth as a sacred text of the past that provides a model and legitimation for the present. It is not the historical event per se, but rather the encoding of its symbolic meaning, that provided fuel to this controversy. While the myth became an instrument of political struggle for hegemony and helped shape the political discourse during this conflict, the struggle also modified the political and educational meaning of the myth.

A Patriot's Legacy or a Victim's Curse?

Following the first decade of early statehood, Tel Ḥai began to lose its status as a prominent Israeli national myth. Although schools, youth movements, and the army continued to emphasize Tel Ḥai's educational value, and the historical event was annually commemorated in a national ceremony, the myth no longer seemed to occupy a central position in Israeli political discourse. The decline of the Tel Ḥai myth reflects the weakening of Israeli secular national ethos that had been generated by the eastern European Jewish settlers in the first decades of this century. As the new state struggled with major social, economic, and political problems, the gap between the earlier romantic anticipation of statehood and the reality of the 1950s led to skepticism and disappointment among those Israelis brought up in the Yishuv's Hebrew culture. The changing mood during this period of early statehood is captured by a group of young Israeli writers.

> Our present reality is not the enthusiastic atmosphere of the war years . . . Our reality now is gray, faded, and grim . . . The naïveté, this youthful belief that we would "conquer the world" with our own strength, has vanished. Skepticism, cynicism, and bewilderment have taken its place. We should therefore avoid pompous declarations and commitments that might lead to great disappointment.[33]

The national heroic lore lost much of its appeal after the first years of adjustment to statehood.[34] A new sense of disillusionment made young Israelis wary of the pervasive use of flowery ideological slogans in Israeli educational and political discourse. It was then that colloquial Hebrew transformed the term "Zionism" (*Tsiyonut*) to "Zionism in quotes" (*tsiyonut be-merkha'ot*), implying a form of preaching with pathos and pomp but without substance, a high-style discourse that serves to evade the real issues. From the late 1950s Israeli literature began to break away from its earlier engagement in the construction of a national heroic Hebrew culture, redefining its intellectual and aesthetic premises. A new cultural representation of the native Israeli appeared in literature, theater, and film, replacing the activist, self-assured, "constructive" hero of the 1940s and 1950s with a self-doubting, introspective, passive, and at times self-destructive character. This trend, which culminated in the 1970s and 1980s, deliberately attempted to demythologize the Israeli hero and to critically examine Israeli reality in the past and at present.[35]

It is hardly surprising, then, that the Tel Ḥai myth that had inspired much of the earlier nationalist-heroic lore became a primary target of this antiheroic trend in contemporary Israeli culture. For example, growing disillusionment with the heroic "legends" of the prestate period emerged as the subject of Aharon Megged's novel *Ha-Ḥai al ha-Met* (*Living on the Dead*) which was published in Israel in 1965. The protagonist, who is commissioned to write a biography of a fictitious pioneer-hero named Davidov, realizes that he cannot produce it as he uncovers the man behind the legend. The following monologue by a fellow writer reveals the new cynical attitude toward the heroic cult of the pioneering period:

> "Listen, who was Davidov actually? Just *an ordinary man* who knew how to work well, and from time to time killed a few Arabs. Anywhere in the world a man like that is born, lives, dies and is buried . . . Here they make a hero of him." And after a few steps in silence: "Not only of him. Every year on the Eleventh of Adar according to the Jewish calendar they wring tears from the schoolchildren and sing with great feeling: 'Once there was this wondrous hero, one arm alone he had.' *Who was this wondrous hero, after all?* An ex-officer called Trumpeldor, not a bad soldier, who defended his home against robbers. *So what?* There are any number of them like that all over the world, but nobody remembers their names. Here for almost forty years we've been standing at attention in his memory, singing the anthem, waving the flag, sending the kids home at eleven and letting the teachers lie down to rest . . . *What do we need heroes for in this country?*" (Emphasis added)[36]

Trumpeldor's famous last words, "It is good to die for our country," provided an easy and obvious target for this new skepticism toward the national heroic lore of the Yishuv period. Both the substance of Trumpeldor's saying and its function as an educational slogan generated new critical voices. As early as 1958 the writer S. Yizhar made one of his fictional characters of the 1948 generation express doubts about Trumpeldor's saying.

> If there is something great and beautiful and worthy and just, one ought to live for it and not to die for it. Or is that greatness measured by the scope of death and the readiness to die for it? What is wrong here? I have never thought about it. All of a sudden, it's all too big for me. Where am I wrong? And I want to cry out now that there is no compensation for the life of one young man who lived and died. That even a whole, large, and beautiful state could not give back what he has lost.[37]

Fifteen years after the publication of this novel and three wars after the War of Independence, a remarkably similar monologue of an Israeli soldier who fought in the Yom Kippur War was published.

> It is good to die for our country. Since my childhood I've known that this is either a supreme truth or a supreme lie, or both. For if Trumpeldor really loved this country, why did he think that it is good to die for it? And if he didn't love it, why didn't he say so? This [question] bothered me greatly when I was a kid. And my version, which has not had the privilege of being posted in any school, is—IT IS GOOD TO LIVE FOR OUR COUNTRY!!!—in giant, bright letters . . . I simply love to live for my country and hate to die for it or for anything in the world.[38]

Trumpeldor's saying, which used to evoke great admiration and awe, became subject to growing doubts about its authenticity and the legitimacy of its message. By the 1970s the discrediting of Trumpeldor's famous words was quickly spreading and became a subject for the media.[39] In the late 1970s about half of the adults and a quarter of the children I interviewed volunteered their opinion that it is historically unfounded, although I did not initiate a question focusing on those doubts.[40]

Skepticism about the authenticity of Trumpeldor's last words revolves around two issues. First, the argument goes, his knowledge of Hebrew was rather limited, and he could not have possibly uttered those Hebrew words that the commemorative narrative attributes to him. Second, it is inconceivable that any person would say that "it is good to die," much less so while he was actually dying. As one of my informants emphatically claimed: "It has been proven that he did not say, 'It is good to die for our country' . . . It is unnatural for a person to say such a thing, and Trumpeldor was not superhuman."

Thus, while the educational commemorative narrative continued to present Trumpeldor's heroic statement, a new popular version emerged, offering an alternative ending to the Tel Ḥai narrative. According to this version, when Trumpeldor realized that he was about to die, he uttered a rather juicy curse in Russian, most often identified as *iōb tvoyu mat* (fuck your mother). The new Russian version echoes the sounds of the first two Hebrew words of the glorified saying (*tov lamut*), but it radically transforms its message.

The contrast between the old and the new versions is dramatic. Substituting a Russian curse for a patriotic Hebrew statement suggests a complete inversion of the hero's legacy and public image. While the earlier text portrays Trumpeldor as glorifying death for the country, the new version claims that he in fact cursed his misfortune when he was about to die. Moreover, the revised text transforms Trumpeldor from the prototype of the New Hebrew Man into a Russian immigrant, from a prominent Zionist figure who provided the nation with a sacred slogan into a soldier who broke into profanities, and from a self-sacrificing hero into a reluctant victim.

This modified perception of Trumpeldor's saying is even more fascinating when we consider that the available historical sources suggest that Trumpeldor had in fact articulated the idea that it is good to die for the homeland before he passed away.[41] It is quite likely that the new version started as a joke, and it is often recounted half jokingly. The incongruity between the new and the old versions produces a deliberate comic effect: the new narrative is set to shock the listener with its irreverent ending. The assumption that the famous last words were fabricated is so widespread that it has become part of contemporary Israeli folklore, and it is often stated as a historical fact.

Jewish Settlements and the Politics of Withdrawal

The myth of Tel Ḥai became once again the subject of political controversy in the late 1970s and early 1980s when a new wave of newspaper articles, radio and television programs, and public debates brought Tel Ḥai back to the limelight. The renewed interest in the historical event and the myth that it generated is particularly interesting in view of the apparent decline in Tel Ḥai's status as a central Israeli myth.

The reawakening of an interest in Tel Ḥai was the result of the perceived analogy between its historical role as a frontier settlement and Israel's new "frontier settlements" in Sinai, the Golan Heights, the West Bank, and the Gaza Strip. The debate on the future of these territories and the government's policy regarding the establishment of new Jewish settlements in them has been a major factor in Israeli political life since 1967. This conflict escalated in the late 1970s, during the peace talks with Egypt. Israeli political factions on the far right were vehemently opposed to any territorial concessions in return for a peace treaty with Egypt, and hence regarded the Camp David Accord as compromising Israel's national interests. Many of the settlers in those territories objected to the evacuation of the Sinai settlements and participated in demonstrations organized by the Movement to Stop the Retreat; some others continued to resist the Israeli government's orders until they were evacuated from Sinai by force.

In this heated atmosphere the commemoration of Tel Ḥai reemerged as a political issue. The relevance of Tel Ḥai to the current political conflict provoked a public discussion on the meaning of the myth as well as a renewed interest in the 1920 debate on the evacuation of northern Galilee. Like their predecessors in the prestate controversy over Tel Ḥai, each side in the debate attempted to mobilize the myth in support of its own position. But the focus of the controversy shifted in response to the broader political issues underlying the conflict at hand. The debate revolved around the meaning of "holding on" to Jewish settlements, and the role of Tel Ḥai in shaping Israelis' defense strategy since then.

In 1978 Israel's national radio and television networks devoted a series of programs to Tel Ḥai. The key person behind these programs was Nakdimon Rogel, an Israeli journalist who had studied archival materials relating to the defense of Tel Ḥai and later published a book on this subject, entitled *Tel Ḥai: A Front without Rear.* Rogel's study focused on the historical developments in Upper Galilee at the end of 1919 and the beginning of 1920, challenging the interpretation of Tel Ḥai as a myth of no retreat that exemplified the successful defense of frontier settlements.

Although Rogel's examination of the historical event is likely to have been motivated by the relevance of the myth to the current political situation, his critique of Tel Ḥai rekindled the old political controversy between the Revisionists and the Socialists. Rogel supported the position Jabotinsky had taken in the original debate of 1920, agreeing that Tel Ḥai had no chance to survive the upheaval in Upper Galilee. Moreover, his analysis suggested that the Socialist leadership was at fault for advocating the defense of the Jewish settlements and failing to provide the necessary aid to assure its success. According to him, Tel Ḥai developed into a major national myth of a successful settlement and defense because Labor leaders were trying to redeem themselves by exaggerating the long-term contribution of the Tel Ḥai battle to Israel's future territorial gains.

It is little wonder, then, that the old Revisionists welcomed Rogel's much publicized position on the 1920 debate. Since Jabotinsky's historic opposition to the defense of Tel Ḥai, incongruent with the Revisionists' militant orientation later, was a highly sensitive point for them, they considered Rogel's statements a public rehabilitation of Jabotinsky's position in 1920.[42] Predictably, followers of the Labor movement criticized Rogel's interpretation of the 1920 debate on Tel Ḥai's defensibility. They emphasized again Trumpeldor's affinity to their movement and cleared the Socialist leadership from the charge of neglect by blaming it on the Yishuv's collective institutions.[43]

Despite the new information provided by Rogel's study about the historical event, the revival of the old debate on the plausibility of defending Upper Galilee differed more in style than in substance from the earlier revival of the 1930s and 1940s. The controversy of the late 1970s and early 1980s was more academic in nature and lacked the popular zeal that accompanied the earlier dispute. When the Revisionist-Socialist conflict developed, Tel Ḥai was still a recent past, and people who had been involved in the original discussion of 1920 were still alive and politically active. In the late 1970s and early 1980s the Revisionist-Socialist controversy belonged to a distant past, and the debate on the conflicting stances was marked by greater detachment.

Rogel's challenge of the meaning of Tel Ḥai as a national myth triggered a more emotional response. Rogel questioned the most sacred core of the myth, namely, the national significance of self-sacrifice for the defense of a Jewish settlement. His criticism was thus directed to two aspects of the commemorative narrative, (1) that Tel Ḥai represents a firm resolve never to abandon a Jewish settlement, and (2) that Tel Ḥai provides a successful historical model of holding on to territories through settlement and defense. Rogel emphasized that, although the settlers had made a firm commitment to stay on in Tel Ḥai and the leadership supported an antiwithdrawal policy, the settlers eventually retreated from northern Galilee after the attack of March 1, 1920. Moreover, he maintained, both the battle of Tel Ḥai and subsequent evacuation had no impact on the final agreement between the British and the French on the location of the northern border of Palestine.[44] Hence, despite what the myth suggests, neither the heroic defense nor the blood spilled on that land ultimately contributed to any long-term territorial gains.

Rogel's radical rereading of the historical battle of Tel Ḥai challenges the commemorative narrative that presents Tel Ḥai as a successful model of holding on to settlements at all cost. This interpretation of Tel Ḥai began to develop soon after the event and was accepted by different political elements in the Yishuv. Just a few days after the fall of Tel Ḥai, Jabotinsky publicly mourned the Tel Ḥai dead as "the men who knew no retreat"; and Yosef Klausner praised the settlers for their firm belief that no Jewish settlement in the Land of Israel should be abandoned.[45] Similarly, an editorial of the Socialist publication *Ha-Po'el ha-Tsa'ir* on March 12, 1920, stated that "we will not give up any portion of our land, we will not abandon any post." This idea was also articulated by Aharon Scher (one of the first casualties of Tel Ḥai): "One does not desert a place, nor give up that which has been built." Scher's words were published posthumously and, along with Trumpeldor's last words, served as an important theme in the Socialists' interpretation of the legacy of Tel Ḥai.[46]

That "no retreat" has been Tel Ḥai's legacy for future generations is reinforced by various types of educational materials. Young children learned this symbolic message of Tel Ḥai in a story in which Trumpeldor instructs his friends: "We will stand up together against the enemy. We shall guard the land that we have toiled on. We shall never desert the house that we built."[47] This message is also noted by *Encyclopaedia Judaica* in the discussion of Tel Ḥai's legacy: "It also established a new principle in the Yishuv's defense policy—"No Jewish settlement is to be abandoned for any security consideration whatsoever."[48]

Rogel attempted to challenge the validity of the Tel Ḥai commemorative narrative by highlighting its selective representation of the historical event. His historical analysis was thus designed to demythologize Tel Ḥai. The proponents of Tel Ḥai, on the other hand, focused on the historical impact of the myth. They reiterated the position that Tel Ḥai inspired the establishment of the Hagana underground in 1920 and the foundation of the *ḥoma u-migdal* (stockade and watchtower) settlements in the following decades.[49] Furthermore, the designation of the Eleventh of Adar as Defense Day during the prestate and early-state periods indicates Tel Ḥai's symbolic role in shaping Israeli conceptions of settlement and defense at the time. The historian Elḥanan Oren succinctly notes, "All the great acts in the area of settlement and settlement policy have been inspired by Tel Ḥai."[50]

It is important to note the general agreement about Tel Ḥai's function as the dominant myth of settlement and defense during the prestate period. The differences emerged only with regard to the evaluation of its effect. While advocates of the myth credited it with shaping a successful policy of settlement and defense, others pointed out the strategic and political shortcomings of the Tel Ḥai model that hindered its success. Tel Ḥai offered a static, and rather reactive, conception of defense that no longer fit the Yishuv's security needs in the face of escalating tensions in Palestine. As the historian Anita Shapira observes, although its ethos of "defensive heroism" continued to prevail in public discourse, after the late 1930s the Yishuv's defense policy in effect became more offensive in its orientation.[51] Rogel's criticism, however, focused mainly on the impact of Tel Ḥai in encouraging the loss of human lives in the defense of small and isolated settlements that had no chance of holding out against massive attacks.[52] Although Rogel did not spell out the implications of his criticism to contemporary Israeli politics, the implicit analogy is inescapable.

Indeed, although the debate about Tel Ḥai's influence on the policy of settlement and defense may appear to have been dominated by a past orientation, the ongoing political dispute on the future of the Jewish settlements in Sinai provided it with an acute sense of political relevance. The controversy over the Tel Ḥai myth may have been precipitated by an earlier attempt of the Gush Emunim (bloc of the faithful) movement to appropriate Tel Ḥai in support of its political agenda. Formulating its own brand of Israeli nationalism and Jewish fundamentalism, Gush Emunim had pursued an activist settlement policy since its formation in 1974 and forcefully advocated the permanent annexation of the West Bank and the Gaza Strip by Israel.

Criticizing the decline of the Yishuv's pioneering ethos in contemporary Israeli society, Gush Emunim claimed to be the current carrier of the Zionist ideals of settlement and defense. To support its role as a revitalizing movement, it turned to prominent national symbols of pioneering from the Yishuv period, such as Tel Ḥai, and incorporated them into its own political discourse. By using the highly respectable rhetoric of pioneering, the movement hoped to mobilize the largely secular Israeli society in support of its settlement policy and legitimize its oppositionist agenda.[53] In this vein, Gush Emunim issued a public call to join their settlement of the West Bank on the Eleventh of Adar, thereby reinforcing its claim of continuity with the Tel Ḥai legacy.[54]

There is a striking historical irony, however, in the attempt of an essentially religious movement to use the Tel Ḥai myth to promote its political agenda. Much of Trumpeldor's appeal in the prestate period stemmed from his image as a modern secularized Jew who offered a clear contrast to the stereotypical image of the Jew of Exile. Tel Ḥai emerged as a national myth within secular Israeli culture, and the Orthodox educational establishment reacted to it with reservation. My own experience of interviewing students of two religious public schools revealed that many did not know who Trumpeldor was or knew only little about him through the public media. (In the late 1970s, this stood in a marked contrast to the situation at the secular public schools where students were familiar with Trumpeldor's heroic image, even if some did not know or remember the historical details.)

Teachers in the religious public school explained to me that since the Eleventh of Adar falls three days prior to the Purim holiday, they are busy studying the Book of Esther and preparing for this traditional holiday and therefore have no time to devote to Tel Ḥai. It is interesting to compare this response with a prestate statement in a Zionist brochure of the 1930s that declares Tel Ḥai Day, the "symbol of Jewish renewal," much more important than Purim, which represents exilic Jewish mentality.[55] Gush Emunim, however, ignored the early antitraditional dimension of the Tel Ḥai myth in order to claim the legacy of the early Zionist pioneers. By so doing it wished to discredit those who oppose their settlement policy as violating the basic premises of Israel's national ideology.

In the late 1970s the peace negotiations with Egypt and the plans for the evacuation of the Jewish settlers from Sinai shifted the Tel Ḥai commemorative discourse from the symbolism of sacrificial death to a message of no retreat. Tel Ḥai became important again as a myth because it offered a channel to debate current positions on the future retreat from Sinai. Israeli newspapers dealt with the analogy between the current situation in Sinai and that of Upper Galilee in 1920; and Rogel's polemic position on the historical validity of Tel Ḥai as a myth of no retreat added fuel to this controversy.[56] Consider, for example, the following critique of Begin's government through the use of the Tel Ḥai myth:

> It so happened that sixty years after the events of Tel Ḥai, the situation on our southern border evokes arguments similar to those held in Trumpeldor's last days. A group of Betar members settled in Ne'ot Sinai, and Jabotinsky's heir, Menachem Begin, either sincerely or as an empty gesture, expressed his wish to make it his future home. This home, so to speak, he gave up in order to negotiate and sign a peace treaty with Egypt. His friends at Ne'ot Sinai woke up one morning and, suddenly, they found out that they were "a front without rear." If they decide to follow Trumpeldor's route and do not evacuate their own Tel Ḥai, they will have to rebel, no matter what, not only against the negative opinion of the one who considers himself Jabotinsky's heir, but also against his authority.[57]

The author resorts to the Tel Ḥai model in order to emphasize the enormous differences between the myth and Israel's current policy in Sinai. He further dramatizes this point in presenting a cynical version of the famous story about the deserted plow that Trumpeldor rescued.

> In order to sweeten the blow, the prime minister brought them [the settlers] a gift from his visit to Cairo—the washing machine that had

> been deserted during the first stage of the retreat [from Sinai] . . . and if Tel Ḥai has been the myth of settlement as territorial expansion and if the monument of the Roaring Lion has been the site of pilgrimage for generations of youth, the washing machine will become the monument of Menachem Begin's shrinking myth of peace. The difference is, indeed, tremendous.

Underlying the analogy between Tel Ḥai in 1920 and Sinai in the late 1970s were the following questions: Did the situation of the Jewish settlers in Sinai resemble that of their predecessors in Upper Galilee in 1920? Had the government betrayed the Tel Ḥai legacy by agreeing to abandon Jewish settlements in return for peace? Could the last stand at Tel Ḥai serve as a model for those contemporary Israeli settlers who oppose the evacuation of Sinai? Because the controversy of the late 1970s and early 1980s encompassed several issues—the 1920 debate on the defensibility of Upper Galilee, the historical validity of the Tel Ḥai commemorative narrative, and its relevance to the ongoing conflict on the future of the occupied territories—it sometimes diffused earlier political alignments around the interpretation of Tel Ḥai.

The political tensions between the various levels of this controversy were quite real: if one accepts the validity of the myth as well as its impact on earlier Israeli history, does this imply the support of contemporary policies of settling the occupied territories and an opposition to the retreat from Sinai? Or, put differently, if one agrees with Rogel's critique of Tel Ḥai and with his warning that it creates a dangerous model, does this necessarily lend support to the evacuation from Sinai?

Territorial maximalists can easily embrace the view that establishes a continuity between the Tel Ḥai myth and the present. Yet territorial minimalists who cherish Tel Ḥai's historic significance can find themselves in a more complicated position, supporting the symbolic and concrete value of holding on to Tel Ḥai in 1920, yet denying that this situation is applicable to Israel's current situation.

Once again, the commemoration of Tel Ḥai became an arena of conflict over present policies. As before, the controversy encompassed both the historical event and the myth that it generated. Whereas the earlier round took place when Tel Ḥai enjoyed a prominent status in national Hebrew culture, the later round erupted when the myth was in decline. In the 1930s and 1940s both sides supported Tel Ḥai's significance as a national myth but argued over its meaning; in the late 1970s and early 1980s the very process of mythologization became an important aspect of the debate. In both cases it was the relevance of the myth to the present that determined the discourse orientation and accounted for changes in the rhetorical uses of Tel Ḥai as a political metaphor.

Jokes and the Subversion of Myth

Along with the political and academic debate on the interpretation of the historical battle of Tel Ḥai, recent decades have witnessed the emergence of a large body of humorous narratives that defy the memory of Tel Ḥai and offer symbolic inversions of the myth. The new version of Trumpeldor's last words discussed above—the curse in Russian—is part of this trend. This new version and other humorous narratives explicitly call for the reconstruction of the Tel Ḥai commemorative narrative. Other humorous expressions do not openly challenge the myth, but the humor suggests a symbolic transgression of its sacred character.

This point is evident in the following exchange from an interview I conducted with an Israeli woman. When I suggested that we move on to Trumpeldor, she responded: "Hmmm . . . This reminds me of a joke. Can I tell a joke?" (She laughed and turned to her son whom I had already interviewed in school; while he nodded in agreement, I reassured her that she could go ahead). "It's an awfully nice joke about Trumpeldor." The joke that followed was of little relevance to the Tel Ḥai commemorative narrative. But her response demonstrates how humor can replace the glorifying lore as the first association with Trumpeldor.

It is difficult to point out when and how oral literary forms such as jokes are generated and to trace their circulation. I have collected the following jokes and humorous references from informants, acquaintances, friends, and written sources. It is quite possible that some of these humorous texts go back as far as the Palmaḥ generation. It is clear, however, that during the 1970s and 1980s these jokes gained greater circulation. From my own sample it appears that they circulate primarily among native Israelis who were educated in the secular public schools and were members of youth movements, and to whom the Tel Ḥai commemorative narrative had been presented as a sacred national text. The humorous narratives are therefore constructed in reaction to the myth and assume familiarity not only with the Tel Ḥai commemorative narrative but also with those "traditional" children's stories, poems, and songs associated with it.

Humor is clearly culturally bound, and what appears funny within a certain cultural context may seem senseless to outsiders. Moreover, humor is often generated by specific wording and rhythm in the original language, which is lost in translation. Non-Israeli readers may therefore find it difficult to perceive the humor in the following texts. In spite of these obvious shortcomings, I have included several jokes and other humorous narratives, for their value as symbolic inversions of the myth.

The first humorous text relating to Tel Ḥai that was generated by the 1948 generation is a *chizbat*, a distinctly Israeli humorous narrative produced by the Palmaḥ members. As the folklorist Elliott Oring suggests, the *chizbat* expresses the Palmaḥ members' need to explore their collective identity and attitude toward the exilic Jewish past. While the texts display the new values and experiences characteristic of this generation of Hebrew youth, the subtext often implies skepticism about the expected dissociation from Exile and the success of creating a new type of Jew.[58]

The following text, published in Oring's collection, focuses on the monument of the Roaring Lion and pokes fun at how it was created: "When they asked Melnikov to make the statue of the lion on the grave of Trumpeldor, they said that first of all he would have to see a real lion. They said to him, 'Find yourself a lion.' And in those days there wasn't one lion in the country."[59] The initial request for a real lion as a model seems quite appropriate for a hero of Trumpeldor's stature and in line with the glorifying myth text. But at this point the *chizbat* departs from the myth and begins its own sequence of symbolic inversions. We find out that, in spite of the prevalent rhetoric about the revival of ancient heroism, no real lion existed in the Land of Israel at that time. The sculptor is therefore obliged to go to Egypt, an Arab country, to look for a living model for the new Zionist monument marking a victory against the Arabs. Once there, Melnikov has to buy a ticket at the zoo and then bribe the authorities in order to sit and sketch caged lions. In this less-than-heroic setting Melnikov fails to fulfill his mission: the lions fall asleep, and when he attempts to wake them up, he awakens only the donkeys and then gets injured by an angry lion. As Melnikov flees from the zoo and receives first aid from an Egyptian pharmacist, he follows the latter's tip and goes to an Arab who has "a big cat, like a lion, who roared like a leopard." He buys the cat, starves it, and when the anguished cat roars, he makes his sketch of a roaring lion. The narrative concludes, "And anyone who doesn't believe it can go to Tel Ḥai and see if the lion there doesn't resemble a cat roaring like a leopard."

The *chizbat* presents the first Zionist monument in Israel as a ridiculous misrepresentation of a heroic symbol: the proud statue of the lion actually depicts an abused domestic animal. The glorification of Trumpeldor is largely undermined by its creator, an antihero who manages to fail at each step in his quest. Whereas heroes usually overcome fierce lions, the present narrative describes Melnikov as defeated by sleepy, caged lions and shows him using nonheroic methods of bribing, running away, turning to others for help, and starving an animal. Indeed, with all his mishaps Melnikov reminds one of the *schlemiel* (the Jewish antihero popular in Yiddish folklore and literature),[60] a rather unlikely exilic agent for the glorification of the New Hebrew of the Zionist National Revival.

The utter incongruity of the *chizbat* with the Tel Ḥai heroic lore is the source of its humor. This narrative clearly constitutes a countertext to the earlier literature of Tel Ḥai that raises the monument as an important feature of the myth and a favorite character in the new legends about Trumpeldor. Moreover, the more formal evaluation of Melnikov's monument in the *Encyclopaedia Judaica* (3:606) points out the resemblance of this first modern Israeli monument to ancient Middle Eastern sculpture. In contrast, the *chizbat* associates the same monument with exile and depicts the statue as a gross misrepresentation.

A relatively more recent *chizbat* by an Israeli humorist of the Palmaḥ generation pursues similar lines. "Trumpeldor on Gilbo'a" describes how a Palmaḥ commander, Moro, plans to leave an unforgettable mark on the settlements around Mount Gilbo'a during the 1948 War of Independence. He therefore plans to light a fire inscription of Trumpeldor's famous last words. His men, who do not share his enthusiasm for this project, agree to light only one word, a compromise that makes the inscription meaningless and the mission ridiculous. After carrying it out, they realize the mission was undermined by clouds surrounding Mount Gilbo'a and preventing the valley residents from seeing the inscription. The *chizbat* concludes: "They say that the pain that Moro's sunken face reflected was exactly like the pain reflected from Trumpeldor's face when he said 'It is good to die for our country,' but Trumpeldor at least had the opportunity to complete the whole slogan."[61]

Like Melnikov, Moro, who is from the very start identified as the *schlemiel* type, is an inappropriate agent to represent Trumpeldor's legacy. The *chizbat* informs us that he planned this "operation" while other Israeli soldiers were fighting on Israel's southern front. Thus, he was engaged in a rhetorical gesture while others were actually carrying out the burden of war and even at that he miserably failed.

In these narratives it is not Trumpeldor's heroism that is targeted but its glorification. These two *chizbats* offer a cultural critique of the gap between vision and reality that renders the glorification an empty gesture. This theme is also articulated in a cartoon published in Israeli papers in the late 1970s (and reproduced here), depicting a man peering inside the monument of the Roaring Lion only to find that it is hollow.[62] The cartoon shows the glorifying statue to be an illusory representation, a front without substance.

In the same vein other jokes target various primary and secondary symbols associated with the commemoration of Tel Ḥai. Such is the joke that the lion used to roar every time a virgin passed by, but in recent years it has had no opportunity to roar. This joke reverses the description of the earlier literature of the lion as a symbolic guard against the enemy. The substitution of guarding youth's sexual mores for a national security mission is in itself a violation of the sacred myth. Moreover, since the lion also exhibits an outdated position in relation to sexual norms, it can no longer roar and therefore does not deserve its title, the Roaring Lion. The joke suggests that the myth represents old, anachronistic values that have no place in contemporary Israeli culture.[63]

Another example of "youth folklore" about Trumpeldor is the composition of new, humorous lyrics to folk songs' melodies. I have heard the following song performed to several melodies in slightly different versions:

> Trumpeldor was a hero,
> The whole day long he was a hero.
> With one arm he held the plow,
> With the other he was a hero.[64]

This song is hardly as innocent as it may appear to someone ignorant of Israeli youth movement folklore, for it is a takeoff on an earlier joke on the image of the *ḥaluts*, the Zionist pioneer. Whereas the *ḥaluts* is usually described as holding a plow with one arm and a gun with the other, an earlier joke depicts him as holding the plow with one arm and hugging a woman with the other. This modified portrayal suggests that, although the lore about the first settlers creates the impression that their lives were totally consumed by the two national missions of work and defense, they were flesh-and-blood young men who were busier flirting with women than guarding at night. At this level the joke targets the excessive glorification of the pioneering generation, replacing the theme of national security by a humorous narrative of sexual activity.

The later improvised song, however, goes one step farther in undermining Trumpeldor's image. It implies that, unlike the other settlers, Trumpeldor could not hug a woman nor hold a gun because of his disability. That this reference to his amputation can be interpreted as an allusion to sexual incompetence is suggested not only by the phallic symbolism of a missing arm (amputation representing castration) but also in the double meaning of *arms* as limbs and weapons.[65] Whereas the joke appears to follow the tradition of singling out Trumpeldor by his amputation, it creates a dramatic inversion of its meaning, reducing the admired one-armed hero (whom the myth presents as superior to others) to a sexually inferior, crippled man.

The parody of Trumpeldor's glorified amputation is accentuated by the juxtaposition of the original lyrics of the melodies and the new words.[66] That the original songs used for this purpose include a heroic song about Bar Kokhba, a traditional celebratory hymn for Ḥanukka, and a merry children's song adds another macabre dimension to this seemingly innocent improvisation.

Even more explicit and crude is another takeoff on the traditional glorification of the one-armed hero. "With his one arm Trumpeldor held both the plow and the gun and with his leg he gave himself a hand job" (*uva-regel hu "asa ba-yad"*). The joke, which begins innocently enough with the familiar formula, goes on to portray Trumpeldor's alleged difficulties in the sexual domain: He was not sexually involved with a woman like the prototypical pioneer (whose second hand hugged a woman), but instead he masturbated. Yet the combination of his preoccupation with the national mission (holding both the gun and the plow in his one arm) and his disability made it impossible for him to masturbate "properly." The joke ridicules Trumpeldor for his commitment to work and defense as well as his heroic amputation and portrays a pathetic image that clearly subverts the sanctified myth text.

Other jokes about Trumpeldor's amputation reveal a similar transformation of his venerated heroic attribute into the butt of humor.

Q: Why didn't they play poker in Tel Ḥai?
A: Because they missed one hand.

Q: Why did Trumpeldor's plow have a white license plate?
A1: Because he was disabled.
A2: Because he was both disabled and a Russian immigrant.[67]

Trumpeldor is again identified first and foremost as a "disabled man" who suffers from a physical handicap. Whereas the Hebrew lore about the plow glorifies his heroic image, the second joke pokes fun at it as a disabled man's vehicle and transforms Trumpeldor from the model of the New Hebrew to a "new immigrant." Two other jokes poke fun at Trumpeldor's role as a model and the value of his sacrifice, two central themes of the Tel Ḥai myth.[68] A more recent cartoon (reproduced here) ridicules Trumpeldor's legacy of patriotic sacrifice by offering a special "economical model" of a one-sleeved T-shirt, inscribed with "It is good to die for our country."[69]

A visual joke, demonstrating that Trumpeldor could not gesture "follow me" to his soldiers (performed by the teller in a buffoonlike manner, mimicking the hero's disability to carry out this task), similarly undermines Trumpeldor's historical role as the model for the Israeli officer who steps out in front of his soldiers.[70] The joke implies that Trumpeldor could not perform the famous gesture "follow me," which is a source of great pride for the Israeli army, thus falling short of any contemporary Israeli commander. This joke stands in sharp contrast to Kipnis's earlier story "Ha-Yad ha-Ḥazaka" (The Strong Arm) that describes how Trumpeldor's amputated arm itself saved a group of Israeli soldiers (see chapter 6).

The most popular joke relating to the Tel Ḥai hero is the one-liner "I was Trumpeldor's right hand!" This joke obviously plays on the absurdity of the figurative meaning of this expression when applied to Trumpeldor. Curiously, this joke is based on the erroneous impression that his right arm was missing, instead of his left. I heard this joke time and again when I did the research for this study. The one time it really shocked me was when I went into a small Tel Aviv bookstore and inquired about new books on Tel Ḥai or Trumpeldor, and the owner asked me with a straight face if I had seen the new title that just came out, "I Was Trumpeldor's Right Hand!"

Other humorous references to the hero's amputation involve the use of "Trumpeldor" as an adjective denoting "one-armed." Such was the case, for example, in a rehabilitation ward of a hospital where patients referred to those who lost an arm as "Trumpeldors" and to those who lost a leg as "the crippled pilots."[71] Similarly, several informants told me that they named a pet or a toy with a broken limb "Trumpeldor." Thus, the hero who was raised as a *unique* figure in Israeli history is being reduced to a *generic* label. Whereas the adoption of Trumpeldor's name during the Yishuv period was a sign of collective veneration, its later use as an adjective is deliberately comic and irreverent.

A more explicit inversion of the myth text is created by a cartoon (reproduced here) that uses the popular educational narrative of Tel Ḥai.[72] In the tradition of talmudic commentaries, the original narrative appears side by side with its exegesis, provided by visual images. Yet these accompanying images deliberately subvert the meaning of the educational text. Trumpeldor the child is depicted as a Christ figure sitting on his mother's lap while Herzl, the prophet of modern Zionism, is standing by them. The cartoon emphasizes Trumpeldor's dissociation from "his brethren" in exile by depicting those around him (his mother, his father, and the angel) as traditional Jews, whereas Trumpeldor himself wears a soldier's uniform and is equipped with weapons. Subsequent drawings portray the hero in oversized dimensions and present a literal image of how he fights the enemy single handedly, "one hand against many." The cartoon pokes fun at other literary expressions used by the educational text and parodies Trumpeldor's amputation by projecting it on angels, the monument of the Roaring Lion, and the buildings of the city named after the Tel Ḥai defenders.

The humorous texts relating to Trumpeldor clearly have a close affinity with sick or cruel humor collected in other cultural settings.[73] Like the American jokes relating to Helen Keller, the Trumpeldor jokes transform a public figure admired for overcoming major disabilities into a grotesque invalid.[74] In Trumpeldor's case the focus on his amputation confirms Bakhtin's observation that grotesque humor tends to exaggerate one particular feature, often a protruding part of the body. The above jokes about the amputated arm suggest the underlying sexual connotations that Bakhtin discusses in his work.[75] The amputation becomes an allusion to symbolic castration, thereby diminishing Trumpeldor's identity as both a hero and a man. That the two are linked may be more obvious in Israeli culture where both Hebrew words (*gibor* [hero] and *gever* [man]) derive from the same linguistic root.

Humor, Wars, and Political Protest

Targeting Trumpeldor's amputated arm and patriotic statement obviously undermines the features that his contemporaries admired most as evidence of his heroism and readiness for self-sacrifice. For many Israelis the continuing Israeli-Arab conflict has been part of their lives, as is the call to risk their lives to defend the nation. Until 1967 the inevitability of this situation was little questioned. But the internal conflicts relating to the occupied territories and the Israeli response to Palestinian nationalism reflect growing doubts about this position. These doubts increased in the 1980s during the Lebanon War and the Intifada, which provoked the worst moral crisis that Israeli society had experienced, giving rise to public protests as well as some voices of criticism within the army itself.[76]

In this political context the Tel Ḥai commemorative narrative, representing the glorification of the call for patriotic sacrifice, emerged as a natural target for articulating deep-seated anxieties and fears and channeling feelings of ambivalence and resentment about this situation. It is not incidental, therefore, that the popularity of the macabre humor relating to Trumpeldor rose during the 1970s and 1980s. Indeed, it is part of a larger Israeli corpus of macabre jokes relating to wars, death, and injuries and has to be understood within this context.[77]

This kind of macabre humor is manifested in high school graduates' farewell greetings such as "We'll meet on the bulletin board" (or "on the memorial plaque" or "the monument"). These greetings refer to the Israeli custom of posting death announcements on public boards and schools' custom of inscribing the names of their fallen graduates on special memorial plaques. Whereas in normal circumstances high school graduates expect to meet in future school reunions, these graduates articulate the fear that, having to go into their military service soon after graduation, they might die in action before they have a chance to meet at a reunion.

Along the same line an Israeli joke suggests that Kiryat Sha'ul (Saul's City), a large cemetery near Tel Aviv where many war casualties have been buried, has been renamed Kiryat Ha-No'ar (the Youth's City). The joke points out a perceived incongruity in Israeli reality that makes the cemetery a major site for youth who die in action rather than a burial place for the elderly who die from natural causes. The theme appears also in a satirical piece entitled "One Hundred and One Ideas for Decorating the Teaching Space or the Classroom," which suggests hanging Trumpeldor's famous saying with breathtaking photographs of the Kiryat Sha'ul military cemetery.[78] The text thus brings Trumpeldor's famous glorification of patriotic death *ad absurdum*, demonstrating the logical yet highly unappealing destination awaiting students who would follow the hero's legacy. A popular song similarly pokes fun at the educational use of Trumpeldor's saying, citing it among the important lessons a child reports learning at the nursery school, leading him to express his hope that he too will be able to die for his country.[79]

That Trumpeldor's famous last words are part of official patriotic rhetoric that Isreali youth now find difficult to embrace is evident in a 1987 Israeli movie, *Late Summer Blues*.[80] The movie features a group of students during their senior year in high school. Shortly before their graduation party, they receive the news that Yossi, their first classmate to be drafted into the army, was killed. His friends prepare a morbid performance, accompanied by a mocking chant of "It is good to die for our country" in his memory. By applying Trumpeldor's famous last words to his contemporary namesake (Yossi is a popular Israeli nickname for Yosef), these youth parody the glorification of his heroic legacy. Typically, when the school principal finds out about this plan for their graduation party, she uses her last opportunity to exercise censorship and cancels this subversive performance. In spite of the movie's critical perspective toward the educational establishment, it also shows that, with all their ambivalence about the military service and critical view of the political situation, even the most radical of these youth ultimately conforms to Israeli norms and answers the call of duty.

In this situation humor offers an alternative to open political protest.

This function became clear during the Lebanon War, when Israeli soldiers developed a repertoire of morbid lyrics composed to well-known patriotic or folk songs.[81] Thus, a merry folk song expressing the wish to be buried in the first Jewish winery in Palestine where girls and red wine are abundant was modified as follows (note that the original Hebrew verses rhyme):

Original Lyrics	*Macabre Version*
When we'll die	When we'll die
They will bury us	They will scrape us
In the winery of	With a scraping knife
Rishon Le-Tsiyon.	Off the tanks' walls.
There are pretty gals there	There are pieces there
Who serve glasses	Of burnt flesh
Full of wine [which is]	In the colors of
Reddish red.	Red and black.

In December 1982 an Israeli television program on the Lebanon front included a scene portraying soldiers singing a new macabre version of a children's folk song (note that the original Hebrew verses rhyme):

Original Lyrics	*Macabre Version*
Come down to us, airplane,	Come down to us, airplane,
And take us to the sky.	And take us to Lebanon.
We'll soar up	We'll fight
To top of the trees	For Sharon
And will be	And we'll come back
Like birds.	In a coffin.

The soldiers' version substitutes Lebanon for the sky and asserts much more explicitly their protest that the war is not "for the country" but rather for Ariel (Arik) Sharon, the minister of defense who masterminded that war. Another song transforms an African-American song about slaves working in the cotton fields into a morbid battle march: "In a minefield / The Engineering Corps are marching / In a field of mines / Marching all day long. / Ho, ho, ho, my leg is blown up / Ho, ho, ho, my arm is blown up." The choice of this song reveals the soldiers' own alienation that made them identify with the slaves' situation of reluctant submission to authority, with no opportunity for open protest.[82]

Broadcasting soldiers singing these songs on Israeli national television infuriated the army who took immediate steps to prevent the future recurrence of such public displays. Yet the program succeeded in drawing public attention to the emergence of this macabre repertoire of war songs. As the folklorist Aliza Shenhar points out, the spontaneous performance of these improvised songs stands in sharp contrast to the Israeli tradition of broadcasting patriotic songs during wartime.[83] Whereas previous wars (most notably the Six-Day War) gave rise to a new repertoire of heroic songs, the Lebanon War generated an instant, antiheroic lore of macabre songs, presenting a harsh picture of war reality.

The response to war atrocities through humor is by no means a unique Israeli phenomenon. The development of macabre humor in Czechoslovakia during the Nazi occupation, in Jewish ghettos during the Holocaust, or in American popular culture during the Vietnam War provides other examples of the social and political significance of this humorous genre.[84] Consider, for example, the thematic resemblance of the Israeli joke "We'll meet on the bulletin board" with its Jewish predecessor during the Holocaust, "We'll meet in the same piece of soap."[85] The humor expresses fear of an untimely death in a situation over which one has no control and which one cannot avoid or challenge.

The most politically radical inversion of the Tel Ḥai myth I have seen is a satire written during the Intifada by the well-known Israeli writer and artist Amos Kenan. Subtitled "Trumpeldor of Kafr Ḥares," this short piece was published in the popular daily *Yediot Aḥronot:* "'It is good to die for our country,' said the girl who was murdered in Kafr Ḥares. Every day and every week Palestinian Trumpeldors fall for their country. Sometimes Trumpeldor is a boy, sometimes a girl. Sometimes a teenager, a young or middle-aged man, perhaps an old man."[86] Kenan suggests that using Trumpeldor as a symbol for a person who is ready for patriotic self-sacrifice is now more appropriate for the Palestinians than the Israelis. A "Jewish Trumpeldor" of today, he argues, is a settler who "with one arm kills a girl and with the other arm [kills] a donkey." By showing the disparity between the historic one-armed Trumpeldor and the present Jewish settlers of the West Bank, and by underscoring the continuity between him and the Palestinians, Kenan denies the political Right's legitimacy in using the Tel Ḥai myth, and casts the Jews into the aggressors' role.

This radical symbolic inversion that denies the Jews their traditional role as the victimized, persecuted group and portrays them as the aggressors can also be found in other satires by writers from the political Left. In this literature (most notably plays) the Palestinians are portrayed as the "victimized Jews" and the Israelis are cast as "Nazis." Designed to be shocking and profoundly unsettling, these inversions are meant to point out the subversion of Jewish values in current Israeli attitude toward the Palestinians.[87]

The analysis of the humorous Tel Ḥai texts in the context of similar expressions of Israeli morbid humor of the same period highlights their latent function as a form of political protest. That these texts are often characterized by their vulgarity only serves to emphasize their oppositionist character.[88] Israeli macabre humor articulates the horrors of war, the trauma of bloodshed and injuries, the terror of seeing friends burnt in tanks, blown up by mines, dead. The humorous framework, however, distances the pain, fear, and deep anxiety that accompany these experiences. Paradoxically, the humorous framework both reveals and suppresses ambivalence about the war and the legacy of patriotic sacrifice, thereby diffusing the impact of its own political message.[89]

Ten

THE BAR KOKHBA REVOLT AND THE MEANING OF DEFEAT

The dramatic transformation of the commemoration of the Bar Kokhba revolt from the traditional day of mourning of Tish'a be-Av to the festive celebration of Lag ba-Omer was integrated into national Hebrew culture during the prestate period and became part and parcel of Israeli national tradition after the foundation of the state in 1948. Whereas the Tel Ḥai myth became the subject of a heated dispute during the Revisionist-Socialist conflict, neither Masada nor the Bar Kokhba revolt emerged as a central polemical issue. Indeed, that Tel Ḥai entered the Yishuv's politics may suggest its greater significance as a recent historical event that had a more direct bearing on the present. In contrast, both the fall of Masada and the Bar Kokhba revolt belong to a more distant, almost mythical past that appeared to be beyond the politics of the present. The Jewish settlers thus acknowledged the significance of those two events as an inspiration for the Zionist national revival, but did not turn them into a contested arena in their ongoing political conflict.

In the cases of the fall of Masada and the Bar Kokhba revolt, archeology played a critical role in focusing public attention on these events. While the discovery of the Bar Kokhba letters in 1960 and the excavation of Masada in the mid-1960s enhanced their place in Israeli collective memory, these developments also provoked closer scrutiny of the commemoration of those events. Moreover, after the archeological discoveries the government's increased role in sponsoring these commemorations highlighted their relevance to contemporary Israeli politics. In light of these developments, the reconstruction of these events as major turning points in Jewish history, which had been taken for granted in national Hebrew culture, was reexamined and became a subject of public controversies.

Patriotic Dreams and Political Reality

In 1980 Yehoshafat Harkabi, a professor of international relations at the Hebrew University, published a critique of the Bar Kokhba revolt and its commemoration in modern Israeli culture. Harkabi, who first published his views in the daily newspaper *Ma'ariv*, elaborated on them in a short monograph in 1981, which he expanded to a full-length book in 1982.[1] The rapid escalation of a heated controversy on the subject was also evident in the proliferation of public debates, conferences, newspaper articles, and books of both popular and academic character.

Had Harkabi's challenge of the Bar Kokhba revolt been only historically and academically oriented, it would probably have received limited attention by scholars directly involved with the study of ancient Jewish history. Harkabi himself, as he readily acknowledged, was not an expert on Jewish Antiquity, and his critique was clearly directed to the commemorative, rather than the historical, narrative of the Bar Kokhba revolt. Harkabi, a former general in the Israel Defense Forces and a scholar whose areas of expertise are Israeli-Arab relations and strategic studies, was interested in applying lessons from the Bar Kokhba revolt to the current Israeli-Palestinian conflict. Since he had served as a head of military intelligence and later as an advisor to the government on issues pertaining to the Israeli-Arab conflict, his views attracted considerable public and scholarly attention.

Harkabi's main thesis is that the Bar Kokhba revolt was one of the three major disasters in Jewish history, along with the destruction of the First and Second Temples, and should therefore be commemorated as such. His analysis suggests that the revolt had no chance of success, because of the relative stability that Rome enjoyed in those years. Furthermore, Judaea's vital location within the empire would have made it highly unlikely that Rome would ignore the revolt.[2] Harkabi charges Bar Kokhba and his supporters with failing to comprehend the broader international scene in which they operated and hence the inevitability of their defeat. Because of their nationalist zeal and limited vision they aggravated the national situation considerably, and brought about massive destruction and exile.

Harkabi is even more vehement in his critique of the current commemoration of the Bar Kokhba revolt as a major heroic event in the nation's history. This commemorative narrative, argues Harkabi, ignores the horrible consequences brought by the revolt, second only to the Holocaust (27–30). That Bar Kokhba erred in his judgment of Judaea's chances of success in its revolt is understandable, but Israelis' admiration of this error is irrational and dangerous: "In admiring the Bar Kokhba revolt, we are forced into the straits of admiring our destruction, of cheering for a national suicide" (60). This view could develop, he argues, only from admiring "rebelliousness and heroism, detached from responsibility for their consequences."[3] Careful examination of the outcome of this revolt suggests that Jews have survived to date "not thanks to the Bar Kokhba revolt but in spite of it. We exist thanks to the Jews of Galilee and the Diaspora who did not take part in the revolt" (62).

At this point Harkabi applies the lessons from the historical revolt to the ongoing Israeli-Palestinian conflict. His call to return from memory to history thus claims to represent a more balanced view of the past for the sake of the future. The former general focuses on the fundamental distinction between tactical and strategic planning and points out that "a victory on the tactical level is not a final event from a strategic point of view" (60). When leaders can plan only at the tactical level and lack strategic understanding, they are bound to lead the nation to disaster, as happened in the case of Bar Kokhba's miscalculated revolt.

Within the context of Israel's post-1967 situation, this observation was essentially a warning. Harkabi criticizes what he identifies as a current trend in Israeli political culture that glorifies "unrealistic" activism as an expression of national pride and assertiveness, and warns against the blurring of vision and fantasy, messianism and "realpolitik" (69–82, 103–7): "In our day, prevalent in many circles in Israel is the faith that an act of *political audacity* that effects a *fait accompli* is a sure prescription for success. However, the alleged 'fait accompli' is liable later to be revealed as mere delusion or temporary gain."[4] In the Hebrew original, Harkabi uses a common Hebrew expression for "fait accompli," *litsor uvdot ba-shetaḥ* (literally, to create facts on the ground). The allusion to Israel's policy of building Jewish settlements in the occupied territories in order to guarantee their ultimate integration into its territory is clearly intentional. Harkabi rejects as highly unrealistic the underlying assumption that Israel can hold on to the occupied territories and warns against the long-term consequences of this policy. Furthermore, in the English edition of his second book, *The Bar Kokhba Syndrome*, published after Israel's 1982 invasion of Lebanon, he includes an epilogue discussing that war as a confirmation of his earlier analysis and warnings.[5]

Harkabi repeatedly (and unconvincingly) denies making a direct analogy between the Bar Kokhba revolt and Israel's present situation. Nonetheless, he readily admits that his motivation for discussing the past lay in its relevance to the present: "It appears to me that rational national behavior at the present is largely dependent upon a critical attitude toward the past"

(105). Harkabi thus uses the past as a means to deal with the present. For him the Bar Kokhba revolt served as a historical metaphor for contemporary Israeli politics and their future. His retelling of the historical event has a didactic purpose, to capture the attention of those who might otherwise refuse to listen to him had he begun by addressing the immediate conflict. In spite of his modern scholarly tools, Harkabi resorts to traditional methods used by the ancient Hebrew prophets: launching a political rebuke by telling a parable in order to disengage the audience from preformed stances in the immediate situation.[6]

Underlying Harkabi's approach is a fundamental belief in the power of the commemoration of the past to shape certain views and attitudes at present. Discussion of the prospects for the Bar Kokhba revolt was not an academic issue provoked by historical analysis of the records of the past. Rather, it stemmed from the recognition that a selective reading of the past might lead to an equally selective reading of Israel's present political situation. A similar recognition of the power of collective memory, he maintains, turned the rabbis against the Bar Kokhba revolt. Jewish tradition therefore collapsed the commemoration of this uprising with that of the destruction of the First and Second Temples to deliberately downplay its importance within this commemorative context.[7] Harkabi also provides personal testimony about the powerful effect of the selective commemoration of the revolt in national Hebrew culture, which had made him, like others, unquestionably accept the glorification of the Bar Kokhba revolt until quite recently.[8]

Like the Tel Ḥai controversy the debate that the Israeli professor triggered focused on both the historical event and its current commemoration in Israeli culture. Likewise, this dispute reached its most heated tones when it addressed the political implications of memory within current Israeli politics. Harkabi himself admits surprise at the vehement response that his initial newspaper articles unleashed, which greatly exceeded the public response to his earlier publications on Israeli-Arab relations.[9] This response made him pursue the debate further and continue to publish on the subject. Indeed, this response indicates that Harkabi's critique is perceived as a challenge to a sacred cultural text of Israeli society, touching a sensitive nerve in Israeli political culture.

The Bar Kokhba controversy remained in the news from May 1980 until after the outbreak of the Lebanon War two years later, furthering scholarly exchange on this subject in academic and more popular forums. In 1980, around the time when Harkabi's first articles appeared, a volume of articles on the history of the Bar Kokhba revolt was published in Hebrew.[10] During the debate the universities as well as other organizations (such as the Van

Leer Foundation and Siminar Shorashim) held public programs on this subject. A debate held by the Van Leer Foundation in January 1980 in Jerusalem reportedly attracted a crowd of several hundred Israelis. A follow-up debate in June 1980 brought the publication of Harkabi's first monograph on the subject, and a year later the Van Leer Foundation published a monograph of two rebuttals of Harkabi's views.[11] Following a two-day conference in spring 1982, cosponsored by Tel Aviv University, Ḥaifa University, and Yad Yitzḥak Ben-Zvi, another volume of articles was published, informing the Hebrew readers about recent research on the revolt.[12]

The continuing dispute over an event that took place eighteen centuries earlier demonstrates the importance that Israelis attribute to issues relating to collective memory and their relevance to Israeli political life at present. Indeed, the fact that such a debate was going on was in itself newsworthy for non-Israelis, who might have not expected an event from Antiquity to become a hot topical matter. "For Israelis, Bar Kokhba isn't ancient history," reported the *New York Times*, for it has turned into "something of an Israeli obsession."[13] "The crowd came because it is relevant," an Israeli journalist explained, referring to the overflow audience at the Van Leer debate. "History is contemporary business here. These are bread and butter issues."[14]

The duration and intensity of this debate on the commemoration of the Bar Kokhba revolt and the public interest in it show that the symbolic significance of the past for the present was not a purely academic affair.[15] Indeed, had Harkabi written either an academic article on the history of the ancient revolt or a plainly polemical article on the Israeli-Palestinian conflict, it would have not triggered such a debate. It is precisely because he challenged the accepted commemoration of the revolt on historical, political, and symbolic grounds that his views stirred such a stormy response. In his second book Harkabi points out the symbolic significance of this response: "I *do not* claim that it has become an obsessive myth—underlying all Israeli decision making or the formulation of policy. Still, its hold is of considerable tenacity, as I learned when I first published a booklet criticizing the rebellion, which was met by stiff opposition and which was considered by many a national sacrilege."[16]

Much of the criticism of Harkabi's views focused on the creation of a historical analogy between the Bar Kokhba revolt and Israel's post-1967 situation. Yisrael Eldad, a former leader of the radical-Right underground Leḥi and a well-known Revisionist ideologue and scholar, published his rebuttal of Harkabi's first monograph on the Bar Kokhba revolt, accusing him of shaping his ideas about the past by his immediate political agenda, namely, withdrawal from the occupied territories.[17] According to Harkabi's critics, the analogies he drew result in anachronistic analysis that fails to take into account the perspective of Bar Kokhba's contemporaries.[18] Harkabi claimed that neither Hadrian's plan to turn Jerusalem into a Roman city nor the prohibition of circumcision (which was not directed specifically against the Jews but against all the empire's subjects) could justify death for Kiddush ha-Shem. To further support his view, he pointed out that the Jews of Galilee and the Diaspora did not choose to rebel against the Romans in spite of these measures (43–44). Disputing this view, the historian David Roke'aḥ argued that Bar Kokhba's assessment of the situation, based on the Jews' knowledge at the time, had in fact been realistic. Furthermore, the rebels had no doubt in their minds that their fight and death were acts of Kiddush ha-Shem.[19] Harkabi's emphasis on the destruction following the Bar Kokhba revolt, Roke'aḥ added, did not acknowledge that the Jews of Palestine thrived at a later period and that the revolt did not threaten Jewish survival.[20]

Even some of those who agreed with Harkabi's assessment that the revolt had no chance of succeeding objected to the analogy he drew between the ancient revolt and the current political reality.[21] Criticism of the present on the basis of an analysis of the past is unfounded, the argument was raised, because the time and the circumstances are so dramatically different. Harkabi's method of applying lessons of the past to Israel's current situation, therefore, had no validity. In response Harkabi claimed that his lessons from Antiquity were only "at the universal level of principles and do not involve the making of comparisons and analogies."[22]

To support their opposing stances on the symbolic meaning of the Bar Kokhba commemorative narrative, both Harkabi and his critics drew on other historical events as well. In his rebuttal of Harkabi's views, Yisrael Eldad seemed to reintroduce the prestate Revisionist-Socialist controversy into the present discussion. Eldad thus set out not only to defend the Right's position in current Israeli politics but also to score points for the Revisionists' call to arms against the British during the 1930s and 1940s.[23]

Yet Eldad also wished to emphasize that Harkabi's position denied not only the more partisan Revisionist approach but a broader consensus within the early Zionist and later Israeli political culture. Harkabi's attack on the national commemoration of the Bar Kokhba revolt amounted in Eldad's and other critics' view to a betrayal of the Zionist ethos that Theodor Herzl articulated so clearly, "If you will, it is not a dream." They argued that Israelis' collective experience had disproved Harkabi's thesis: the Zionist movement's national aspirations did not seem realistic, yet they were, after all, fulfilled. The State of Israel owes its existence to the very ethos that raises ideological commitment beyond realistic calculations. That Israel has survived so far despite frequent wars against outnumbering forces demonstrates the ultimate superiority of this approach.[24]

The argument went further to claim that ideological commitment to national freedom has a greater symbolic and educational value than the outcome of a specific national war. One could not criticize a nation's struggle for freedom because it had failed.[25] As Yadin put it, "There are things that are measured not by lost territories but by lost values."[26] The significance of national myths, accordingly, goes beyond the specific outcome of the historical events they commemorate. Protecting them implies nurturing the nation's spirit. Harkabi's approach to the past was therefore condemned as a testimony of moral and ideological decline within contemporary Israeli society: "We do not address Harkabi here, but a fashionable trend that is part of a broader process of disintegration of values, supposedly in the name of pragmatism. The deheroization of our past is part of de-Zionization, part of a general decline."[27]

The subtext of this argument becomes clear within the context of the immediate political situation. For the Right debunking the Bar Kokhba myth was another sign of a broader process of ideological decay, evident in the government's readiness to return land for a peace agreement with Egypt. Israel's commitment to negotiate the West Bank and the Gaza Strip in return for peace, strongly advocated by the Left, was interpreted as another dimension of the weakening of its ideological integrity.[28] Even Yadin, who represented a more centrist position (although serving as the deputy prime minister in the Likud cabinet of Menachem Begin), regarded the logic of Harkabi's argument as threatening Jerusalem's status as a unified city under Israeli sovereignty: If Israelis were to pursue Harkabi's ideas, Yadin argued, they would have to give up Jerusalem because "there is nothing that provokes and unifies the world against us more than this issue." To underscore his disapproval of this approach, Yadin posed a rhetorical question: "Perhaps beyond some realism there are some ideals that hold together a people as a people?"[29]

The debate on the commemoration of the Bar Kokhba revolt thus turned into a controversy about the meaning of patriotism within the ongoing Israeli-Palestinian conflict. Whereas Harkabi's opponents criticized his stance as undermining the very foundations of Israel's history and national ideology, his supporters objected to this line of argument and defined their own position as patriotic: "It is not only permitted, it is a duty to shatter myths and slaughter 'sacred cows.' A national ideology based on false or only semitrue stories is built on shaky foundations."[30] Moreover, the danger in encouraging people to admire heroism regardless of its outcome is that they would judge their government by its gestures rather than the outcome of its policies.[31] "History," claims Harkabi, "is not an arena in which the party with the stronger faith in myth prevails."[32]

The debate on the Bar Kokhba revolt thus focused on both its history and memory. Yet it was clearly the latter that caused its emergence as a hot political issue. Within this context the history of the revolt assumed importance only as a way of supporting or disputing its current commemoration in Israeli culture. Memory was challenged in the name of history, and the past became a tool to criticize the present. Although both supporters and opponents blamed each other for working with historical analogies that would not pass a critical historical analysis, both sides based their views on the fundamental premise of a symbolic continuity between Antiquity and the present, choosing to emphasize those aspects best suited for their own stance within the ongoing Israeli-Palestinian conflict.

Archeology, Religion, and the War of the Bones

In late 1981 in the midst of the debate on the Bar Kokhba revolt, Israel's prime minister, Menachem Begin, agreed to provide a state funeral for the bones that were found with the Bar Kokhba letters two decades earlier. The initiative for this plan came from the chief Ashkenazi rabbi, Shlomo Goren, who had been the chief chaplain of the Israel Defense Forces at the time of the discovery.

The idea was not new. Shortly after their discovery in a cave, Goren recommended that the bones be reburied according to Jewish law near the site of their discovery and that a monument be erected there. David Ben-Gurion, then Israel's prime minister, nominally accepted those recommendations yet did not act on them.[33] In fall 1981 Goren reactivated his proposal and secured Begin's support.[34] From that point, and with the prime minister's full backing, plans for the state burial proceeded quickly.

Since the bones officially identified as the remains of the Bar Kokhba men had been discovered about twenty years earlier, Goren and Begin clearly had a political motive for the timing of their initiative. Indeed, the state burial seemed to offer an excellent opportunity to present an authoritative statement about the Bar Kokhba revolt as well as to carry multiple political messages of direct relevance to current issues in Israeli political life.

For Begin and other Likud leaders who came from the Revisionist old guard, Harkabi's critique of the Bar Kokhba revolt meant an attack on a key Revisionist symbol to which they had a special attachment.[35] Although the glorification of the Bar Kokhba revolt was not unique to the Revisionists, the revolt was clearly one of its most prominent symbols. What could better express the romanticized commemoration of the failed revolt than naming the youth movement after Betar, the site of Bar Kokhba's last stand? Challenging the political wisdom of the revolt not only tarnished the ancient rebel's heroic image but also the political wisdom of those who selected him as a model for the New Hebrews.

A state funeral thus provided a grand opportunity to respond to Harkabi's challenge and reaffirm the old Betarist view, presenting it as a national, rather than a partisan, position. This approach was typical of the Likud government's attempts to counteract earlier Labor hegemony by invoking national legitimacy through older Revisionist symbols and themes.[36] Since 1982 marked Israel's thirty-fifth anniversary and was officially labeled the "Year of Heroism," the timing of the bones' burial could further legitimize and accentuate the heroic symbolism associated with the revolt.[37]

The state funeral could also serve as a political booster for the Likud government, which had suffered from severe attacks by the radical Right on the Camp David Accord and on the withdrawal from Sinai. The funeral made it possible for the government to reassert its key position in the advocacy of national activism and readiness to fight "until the bitter end." The decision to bury the bones in the Judaean hills (near the site where they were found) would also display Begin's commitment to "Judaea and Sumeria," the ancient Hebrew names that the government had officially reinstated on the West Bank.[38]

For the chief Ashkenazi rabbi, the state funeral presented an opportunity to reinforce not only the Likud's policy with regard to the occupied territories but also the religious stance in an ongoing heated dispute over the excavation of Ir David (David's City). Rabbi Goren supported the ultra-Orthodox claim that the archeological excavation was desecrating an ancient Jewish cemetery, a charge that the archeologists vehemently rejected. The Ir David excavation brought out the tense and often highly adversarial relationship between the rabbinical authorities and the archeologists regarding their respective legal and moral claims over the past.[39]

While both the rabbis and the archeologists asserted their positions as guarding the nation's best interest in preserving the past, their sources of legitimation, grounded in tradition and science respectively, were radically different. For the archeologists the unearthing of evidence of the ancient Jewish past in Jerusalem was of primary historical and political significance; for the religious authorities it was necessary to leave the ground intact as a cemetery, to honor the dead whose presence there carries its own historical and national weight.

Adamant in his opposition to and disdain for archeologists, Rabbi Goren saw himself as fighting a sacred war. "I will not tolerate a science that is based on the violation of the Torah laws. I would fight any such science," he exclaimed in an interview. "The prayer for the dead, 'El Male Raḥamim,' ends with the phrase 'may he rest in peace.' The archeology is designed to contradict this prayer."[40] In the same interview he revealed the connection between the controversy on Ir David and his initiative to bury the remains of the Bar Kokhba men: "I do not believe one word of theirs. If the bones of the Bar Kokhba fighters remained scattered for twenty years without the possibility of burying them, if such a situation could have developed—how can I trust them?" In a private interview he admitted that the excavation had given him the opportunity to reopen the issue of the burial of the Bar Kokhba people's bones.[41]

The precise location of the burial site, which may seem a technical or marginal matter, emerged as another dimension in the political dispute. Goren declared that Jewish law requires that heroes be buried where they fall and that the Bar Kokhba bones should therefore be buried in the Cave of the Letters in Naḥal Ḥever (the Ḥever Creek) where they had been found.[42] This choice, nonetheless, would have served as a public demonstration of the primacy of religious law over archeological interests: by turning the cave into a "Jewish cemetery," the site would be ruled out of the archeologists' control. The chief Ashkenazi rabbi would have thus scored a symbolic victory over the archeologists and created a useful precedent for the dispute over Ir David.

Mistrusting the archeologists, Goren took it upon himself to personally enter that cave to prove its accessibility as a burial site as well as to search for additional bones that the archeologists might have left behind in 1960.[43] When his first attempt to reach the cave failed, he repeated his efforts, this time approaching the cave from the air, tied with ropes to a military helicopter. This daring and strenuous attempt by the sixty-four-year-old chief rabbi, who had had open-heart surgery the year before, received much publicity in the Israeli media. Whereas the book on the excavations written by Yadin, the former chief of staff of the Israeli Defense Forces, presented the archeologists and the volunteers as heroes undertaking a daring mission, Goren now threatened to replace them by creating his own heroic tale and by reminding the public of his earlier career as the chief chaplain of the Israeli Defense Forces. Consider the following newspaper report:

> An IDF helicopter lowered by rope ladder a helmeted Goren in harness down-to-near the cave entrances. But Goren had to do a fair bit of climbing. "It is very difficult, a juggling act with my legs," said

> Goren who last year underwent open-heart surgery in Cleveland. Goren said he had "felt no fear during the protracted descents and ascents over the 100-meter chasm of Naḥal Ḥever. Before setting out I had recited the traveler's prayer just to be on the safe side."[44]

Faced with the difficulty of reaching the cave, Rabbi Goren recommended burying the bones on the site of the Roman camp on Har Ḥever (Mount Ḥever) and building a commemorative obelisk on a higher spot so that it could be seen from a great distance. He sealed his plan by declaring that ground holy and the Bar Kokhba men "holy warriors,"[45] thereby taking them into his jurisdiction.

Not surprisingly, the archeologists perceived Goren's initiative as an aggressive attempt to invade their turf. Yadin protested against the chief rabbi's plan to enter the cave without an "excavation license," claiming that this was a violation of the Antiquities Laws of 1978.[46] Furthermore, Yadin had opposed burial in the cave itself because that would prohibit further archeological work there, and he later objected to burying the bones in the site of the Roman camp for a similar reason.[47] As for the obelisk monument, he opposed its separation from the burial site, quoting one of the most highly respected religious authorities, Maimonides, to the effect that one should not distance a marker from the grave, in order not to use up too much of the Land of Israel.[48] A site of burial was ultimately selected near the remains of the Roman camp.

This "War of the Bones" did not end with the settlement on the burial site. Once the site was decided, the focus of the dispute shifted to the bones and their "Jewish identity." Goren's crusade against the archeologists included a request that all bones related to the Bar Kokhba period be reburied in a state funeral. In December 1981 the Chief Rabbinical Council made this a formal demand, alluding also to bones that the archeologist Yoḥanan Aharoni had found in the Cave of Horrors in the 1950s. Although Yadin had expressed doubts about the Jewish identification of the Aharoni bones, he later refused to give his opinion about other bones added to the state burial.[49] He nonetheless reiterated his earlier position that the bones he himself had unearthed clearly belonged to Jews, claiming that they had been wrapped in prayer shawls and were found with other remains from the Bar Kokhba period. Yadin hypothesized that relatives and friends of the deceased must have collected their bones. However, the media reported that other archeologists had persisting doubts about this identification.[50]

The public dispute over the Jewish identity of bones that had been excavated more than two decades earlier became an important issue for the legitimacy of the state funeral, and its political implications depended on that identification. Goren thus dismissed all doubts about the identity of the bones as "nonsense" and referred to Yadin's and Aharoni's earlier publications as evidence. Curiously, in the course of this controversy, both sides resorted to each other's authority when it supported their position: Yadin quoted a religious source in opposition to Goren's plans, while Goren who had declared his contempt for archeology (which, he argued, "is based on hypotheses only"[51]) chose to quote the archeologists themselves to prove the bones' identification as Jewish.

When the bones were finally put to rest in a much-publicized public ceremony on May 11, 1982, the doubts cast on their Jewish identity were suppressed. Moreover, even though bones identified as belonging to adult males were a minority (the majority were those of women and children), they were referred to collectively as the bones of Bar Kokhba's warriors.[52] The Israeli army's involvement in preparing the site for this event and its pronounced representation in the official ceremony itself highlighted the military status of the buried.[53]

The list of those present also underscored the official character of that ceremony: the president of the state, the prime minister, the speaker of the parliament, cabinet members, senior parliament members, the two chief rabbis, generals, and other select dignitaries. Rank-and-file Israelis could watch the ceremony on their television screen.

Yadin and other archeologists refused to attend this ceremony, which they interpreted as a symbolic attack on them.[54] Their boycott expressed their view that the religious authorities manipulated this national ceremony in order to display their right to that past, represented by the excavated bones. The state burial of the bones identified as belonging to Bar Kokhba's men thus became an arena for testing competing religious and archeological claims over the control of the past and the moral and legal right to its commemoration and uses in contemporary Israeli society.

State Commemoration and Political Fictions

The state funeral was clearly designed to reinforce the established commemoration of the Bar Kokhba revolt, which Harkabi had tried to challenge. The State of Israel accepted the bones as the remains of the Bar Kokhba warriors and therefore provided them the same honors it bestows on its own soldiers. Begin's official eulogy at the ceremony, in which he addressed directly "our glorious fathers" whose remains were being buried, focused on their heroism and courage and avoided mentioning the outcome of that revolt.[55] As a commemorative event, then, the state funeral reaffirmed the symbolic continuity between the ancient and contemporary Jewish fighters for national freedom.

Furthermore, the decision to hold the state funeral on Lag ba-Omer reinforced the activist reconstruction of the historical event that emphasizes the rebels' courage and commitment and ignored the outcome of their revolt. As Myron Aronoff points out, this decision is particularly telling, since the committee that Goren headed in the early 1960s had recommended another date, the sixteenth of Av, as the appropriate date for the bones' burial according to Jewish tradition.[56] The burial on Lag ba-Omer, in line with the commemoration of the Bar Kokhba revolt in secular national Hebrew culture, indicates the priority of the activist agenda over the religious considerations in its planning.

In spite of their efforts, the Likud government and the chief rabbi were not successful in creating a national ceremony that would rise beyond partisan issues and become a unifying celebration of national magnitude. In fact, the ritual burial made the various frictions within Israeli society more visible. Whereas two years after the Six-Day War the state funeral at Masada enjoyed a wide consensus, the government could not recapture that spirit in a period in which Israeli society was embroiled in a bitter political controversy over the future of the occupied territories and the Jewish settlements there. The open hostility between rabbinical authorities and archeologists in 1981 fueled the conflict around the state burial and made both sides less inclined to compromise. The government thus failed to rally the parties involved behind its political agenda in the name of national solidarity, and the archeologists' ban on the ceremony highlighted the significance of this dispute.

Furthermore, the National Parks Authority, supported by other environmentalist groups, opposed the army's construction of a road to Naḥal Ḥever for the sake of the funeral, arguing that this would permanently damage the unusual natural beauty of that landscape. The primeval beauty of the site, they argued, should serve as a natural monument for those who fell during the Bar Kokhba revolt and would be of higher educational value than a man-made memorial. Like the archeologists, the environmentalists resorted to rhetoric that is no less central to Hebrew culture than the government's.[57]

Opposition politicians as well as the media criticized the enormous cost of the ceremony (estimated around $250,000[58]) and expressed a cynical attitude toward the government's performance of national ceremonies for the promotion of its political agenda. "The nation should be liberated from stories about bone burials, state funerals before the television cameras, emotion-charged speeches, and hovering helicopters," argued a member of the parliamentary Education Committee in a special session.[59] The journalist Amos Elon pointed out the cynical response to the ceremony: "There is a tendency to mock the rabbis who performed this week a state 'funeral' for archeological findings as well as the prime minister, who announced his 'vision of the air-lifted bones' of our glorious fathers. The latter could not respond, but among those present at the ceremony, some smiled and voiced cynical remarks."[60] Elon transforms the prophet Ezekiel's "vision of the dry bones" into a "vision of the air-lifted bones," thereby mocking the prime minister's modern version of the resurrection of the dead. He also refers to the ceremony as a "show," using the English word in his Hebrew text to articulate the foreign and alienating character of this contrived media happening.

While the successful model of a state burial at Masada may have encouraged Goren to renew his interest in a similar ritual for the bones of Bar Kokhba's followers, he seized upon the declining popularity of Masada to create an alternative site for the performance of national ceremonies. Thus, even though he had contributed to the earlier construction of the activist interpretation of Masada and its significance as a national site,[61] he now expressed reservations regarding its appropriateness as a site to enhance the value of his new plan: "It will be a site that IDF units will henceforth come to swear allegiance to the State. It is wrong that Israel should look to Masada as a symbol and example of its youth. Life, not suicide, should be the aim of our youth [. . .] We should live, not die, for Kiddush ha-Shem. This is what Bar Kokhba symbolizes.'"[62]

Goren's public recognition of the problematic ending of the Masada historical narrative was followed by his denial of a similar problem in the case of the Bar Kokhba revolt, in spite of the ongoing public controversy on that very issue. He thus attempted to replace one official activist commemoration with another, to promote one site of national ceremonies by withdrawing from the other. Yet in planning this symbolic ritual he and Menachem Begin, the two driving forces behind the state funeral, underestimated the extent to which the frictions within Israeli society would undermine the success of this ceremony. The ceremony that aimed to suppress the countermemory of the Bar Kokhba revolt by making a dramatic show of the nation's adherence to the activist commemorative narrative ultimately failed to achieve that end. Instead, the multiple voices opposing this ceremony highlighted the attempt to subject the memory of the past to current partisan agendas.

Eleven

MASADA AND THE MEANING OF DEATH

The Tragic Commemorative Narrative

As we saw earlier, the Holocaust played a major role in the consolidation of the activist commemorative narrative of Masada during the 1940s and 1950s. To a large extent, the emergence of new interpretations of Masada in recent decades continues to be a function of the relations between these two turning points within Israeli collective memory. The continuing interplay between the commemoration of Masada and the Holocaust thus becomes a key point in understanding the changing perception of Masada and its multiple meaning in contemporary Israeli culture.

The 1960s marked the start of a slow change in the Israeli attitude toward the Holocaust. A growing readiness to confront the Holocaust resulted from the much publicized Eichmann trial, exposing the Israeli public to testimonies that had not been heard before. Observance of Yom ha-Sho'a veha-Gevura (the Holocaust and Heroism Remembrance Day) also began to leave its mark on Israeli political culture. But it was the major trauma of the 1973 Yom Kippur War that made Israelis more aware of their own vulnerability and more open to empathy with Holocaust victims and survivors. The Lebanon War, the Intifada, and the tensions surrounding the future of the Palestinians, the West Bank, and the Gaza Strip continue to place matters of survival and death at the foreground of Israeli collective consciousness. Israeli society also went through other major social and political processes during those decades: the decline of Labor Zionism and the rise of the Likud government, the growing political and cultural impact of the more traditionally oriented Israelis of Middle Eastern descent, the greater role of religion in Israeli national culture, and Israelis' closer contact with Jewish communities abroad since 1967.

As a result of these developments, the commemoration of both the Holocaust and Masada has gone through a significant transformation. While the Holocaust has not lost its symbolic meaning as a collective trauma associated with the period of Exile, the perception of Holocaust victims has changed considerably. Israelis' shocking realization of their own vulnerability during 1973 weakened earlier condemnation of the victims for "going like sheep to the slaughter." A new sense of identification with Holocaust survivors has grown out of a new appreciation of *kiddush ha-ḥayim* (sanctification of life), embracing survival as a form of resistance to the Nazis and evidence of inner, if not physical, strength.[1]

As a result, the fundamental distinction between "heroes" and "victims" that underlay the earlier attitude to the Holocaust has considerably weakened. While modern Israeli society was earlier defined by its oppositional relations to Jews of Exile, the new Holocaust commemorative narrative implies that its victims have become a model of moral and spiritual strength that can inspire Israeli soldiers.[2] In spite of these changes, however, the ideal of heroism still appears to occupy a central position in the Holocaust commemorative discourse: even though Israelis reveal a readiness to redefine the meaning of heroism, they continue to examine the Holocaust experience through this modified concept.[3] Moreover, when former prime minister Menachem Begin proposed that the partisans and the ghetto fighters be commemorated on Israel's remembrance day for its fallen soldiers and the commemoration of the Holocaust victims be assigned to Tish'a be-Av, his suggestion was rejected. Israelis prefer to keep the two commemorations separate to highlight the unique character of each for cognitive as well as emotional purposes.

During the last two decades another commemorative narrative of Masada has emerged in Israeli culture, offering a competing reading of Josephus's historical narrative. Whereas the activist commemorative narrative emphasized the contrast between Masada and the Holocaust, the new narrative highlights the analogy between the two events. The new commemorative narrative thus underscores the importance of the suicide as the tragic climax of an extreme state of besiegement and persecution. In this framework, the situation, not the act of suicide, is strongly condemned. The new commemorative narrative continues to define suicide as an act of defiance in a situation that leaves no other dignified alternative, but it shifts the commemorative focus from armed resistance to the Romans to the situation of utter helplessness and despair, epitomized by the suicide. The narrative therefore elaborates the terrible oppression and victimization of the Jews that rendered death better than life and led them to choose suicide as the best possible alternative.

The "tragic version" thus reverses the commemorative trend established by the "activist version." Suicide is no longer suppressed under the glorification of "fight to the very end." Instead, it emerges as the focal point of the new version. Like Josephus's story the tragic commemorative narrative elaborates the descriptions of the mass suicide and highlights the desperation that led the defenders to choose death over life in servitude. The commemorative narrative thus redefines Masada, like the Holocaust, as a myth of death and destruction, a symbolic expression of an ending.

In contrast to the activist commemorative narrative that recreates Masada as a model to emulate, the tragic commemorative narrative emphasizes Masada's primary role as a historical metaphor for a major national trauma that should be avoided by all means. Lamdan's famous line, "Never again shall Masada fall!" now seems more consciously to evoke not just a strong resolution to guarantee the nation's survival, but also the fear that a "Masada situation" might recur. In this framework Lamdan's line is the symbolic equivalent of "Never again!" Both slogans function as national vows that convey Israelis' determination to avoid the recurrence of a deadly situation, alluding to Masada and the Holocaust respectively.

Indeed, the tragic commemorative narrative raises fears that Israel might face a similar catastrophe. In a society whose collective memory is punctuated by wars, Masada is no longer an obscure story from Antiquity but a vivid and powerful image that provides contemporary Israelis with a metaphor for their own situation: a small group of Jews living on an isolated cliff, surrounded by the desert and besieged by a powerful enemy, with no one to turn to for help. As the writer Avraham B. Yehoshua observes, "Masada is no longer the historic mountain near the Dead Sea but a mobile mountain that we carry on our back anywhere we go."[4]

For Israelis who feel surrounded by hostile Arab countries threatening their very survival, the image of besieged Masada is highly evocative. The trauma of the Yom Kippur War, more acutely felt after the period of collective euphoria and the sense of security that the victory of 1967 generated, clearly brought such fears to the surface. "The people of Israel do not want to reach the same situation of Masada," one of my informants stated, and another informant suggested, "The whole country is like Masada." His words were echoed by another informant's observation: "We sit here and do the very same thing. We are basically one large Masada."

In this commemorative context Israeli collective memory no longer defines Masada and the Holocaust as opposite historical metaphors. Rather, it groups them in the same class of collective traumas, as two major tragic events in Jewish history. Unlike the activist commemorative narrative, this reconstruction does not glorify Masada as a myth of revival that creates a bridge to Zionist National Revival. Rather, it redefines Masada as the very end of Antiquity and the beginning of Exile. The new commemorative narrative regards the collective suicide at Masada as the *first chapter* of "defeated heroism" in an extreme situation of persecution and helplessness that is typically associated with the period of Exile, culminating with the Holocaust.[5] The tragic commemorative narrative thus establishes a continuity between Masada, the Holocaust, and the State of Israel.

This fundamental change in Israeli memory, articulated in the shifting relations between the two historical events, reveals a greater readiness on the part of Israelis today to accept as their own the Jewish past—not only Antiquity but also the two thousand years of Exile. Underlying this renewed emphasis on historical continuity is the perception of a great threat to Jewish survival throughout Jewish history, which applies also to the State of Israel. Israeli collective memory has thus lost much of its oppositionist stance vis-à-vis traditional Judaism, now embracing a lesson deeply ingrained in Jewish memory: the experience of a persecuted group struggling to survive against all odds.[6] Within this commemorative framework Masada and the Holocaust become major historical metaphors for situations that generate fear and insecurity—feelings previously acknowledged only with reference to the Holocaust and Exile and suppressed in relation to either Antiquity or modern Israeli society.

The analysis of Masada and the Holocaust also underscores the multivocality of commemorative narratives. During the formative years of Israeli society, activist commemorations of Masada and the Holocaust (highlighting the ghetto uprisings and the partisans' resistance) enjoyed hegemony within the national Hebrew culture. The Masada suicide and the traumatic aspects of the Holocaust were largely suppressed. Although the 1970s and 1980s witnessed the emergence of competing commemorations of both events which dwell on their tragic elements, the earlier commemorative narratives have by no means disappeared.

In fact, the activist and the tragic commemorative narratives of Masada coexist in contemporary Israeli culture and are called upon in different situations. Masada thus continues to be a historical metaphor of active resistance and renewal in some instances and a historical metaphor of persecution, death, and suicide in others. A tourist guide told me that he was taught to emphasize for Israeli tourists the rebels' struggle and to focus on the shocking end in presentations for foreign tourists. The activist commemorative narrative is thus clearly perceived as still having a strong appeal to Israelis. Moreover, various military, national, and religious ceremonies that have been performed at Masada (such as the youth pilgrimage, the soldiers' oath-taking rituals, and the bar mitzvah rituals) have perpetuated the emphasis on heroism, patriotic sacrifice, and renewal promoted by the activist narrative. At the same time, a visit to Masada has become in many ways symbolically equivalent to a visit to Yad Va-Shem, the memorial site for the Holocaust. Tours of both sites are part of official state visits to Israel, designed to impress VIPs with vivid testimonies from the past that explain Israel's firm stand on issues concerning its security.

In spite of the perceived tension between the two commemorative narratives, both contribute to Israelis' commitment to be powerful and ready to sacrifice themselves for their nation to ensure that the Masada/Holocaust situation does not recur. In the words of my informants, "We'll always be strong so that the enemy won't cause us to be in the same situation as then" and "We would never have to be in a situation of either slavery or death."

Indeed, even when Israeli society clearly preferred to commemorate Masada as a myth of active heroism and renewal, familiarity with Josephus's historical record and his account of the collective suicide created a different, subversive subtext. While overt commemorations of Masada may have suppressed the suicide, it is quite possible that anxious responses to this repressed part worked against the explicit rhetoric of heroism, ideological resolution, and renewal, adding to Masada's evocative meaning as a historical metaphor.[7]

One could argue that, although Masada was used as countermetaphor to the Holocaust, it may have successfully served this role precisely because the two events share more than the national Hebrew culture was ready to acknowledge during the 1940s and 1950s. Cultural emphasis on differences between the two events provided comfort to unspoken fear and anxiety that they represent a historical pattern that might continue. Only when the need to emphasize the distinction between Jewish life in exile and modern Israeli society declined could the commemoration of Masada address the suicide more explicitly. At that point the analogy between the Holocaust and Masada shifted from the collective unconscious to collective memory.

The multivocality of the Masada commemorative narratives is also manifested in the emergence of countercommemorative narratives that provide alternative representations of the historical narrative. While the archeological excavations and the subsequent transformation of the site into a major tourist attraction brought Masada into the limelight, its enhanced visibility in Israel and abroad has made it subject to more critical scrutiny. Objections to the Masada commemorative narrative first came mostly from outside secular national Hebrew culture. During the last two decades, however, the cult of Masada has drawn criticism from Israelis as well.

Whereas both the activist and the tragic narratives essentially reinforce the Israeli collective memory of Masada as a major turning point in Jewish history, other versions defy this view. Some criticism has been directed at the construction of the historical narrative itself, but the main thrust of the criticism of Masada has been focused on the discrepancies between the historical and the commemorative narratives and has refuted the legitimacy of the latter from a wide range of perspectives. The following discussion of the debates on the interpretation of Masada therefore revolves around the specific arguments raised against its commemoration.

The Historical Debate: Between Facts and Fiction

In Israeli collective memory Josephus's account of the mass suicide at Masada is perceived as a reliable historical record that provides a vital document on a major chapter in the nation's past. But Josephus's precarious position in reporting the history of the Jewish revolt, due to his prominent role in it and his subsequent desertion of the Jewish cause, has long been a subject of critical evaluation of his writing. Clearly, Josephus was concerned with both the Roman and the Jewish readers' reactions to his writing, and this concern must be taken into account in evaluating his report.[8]

Yet Josephus's narrative about Masada is generally taken as the authoritative text about the event that occurred in A.D. 73. Although Josephus was critical of the Sicarii, the rebel group with which the Masada people had affiliated, so the argument goes, he could not help but display his admiration for them. Their boundless commitment to the national cause and their firm resolution to kill themselves rather than be enslaved to the Romans moved the ancient historian to faithfully record their heroic deed. Consider Yadin's comment on this issue.

> [N]o one could have matched his [Josephus's] gripping description of what took place on the summit of Masada on that fateful night in the Spring of 73 A.D. Whatever the reasons, whether pangs of conscience or some other cause we cannot know, the fact is that his account is so detailed and reads so faithfully, and his report of the words uttered by Elazar ben Yair is so compelling, that it seems evident that he had been genuinely overwhelmed by the record of heroism on the part of the people he had forsaken.[9]

Most questions about the validity of Josephus's account of the fall of Masada address Elazar ben Yair's speeches. Scholars seem to agree that Josephus drew on his own literary skills to construct these speeches in conformity with the historiographic norms of the period.[10] But this section is believed to be an exception within his otherwise reliable documentation of the historical event. Moreover, as we saw in chapter 5, the excavations are largely interpreted as authenticating Josephus's account.

The validity of Josephus's story was challenged, however, in the debates surrounding the elevation of Masada as a national myth. One of the early American Jewish critics of the Masada myth, Trude Weiss-Rosmarin, published a series of editorial articles on this subject in *The Jewish Spectator* from 1966 to 1969.[11] Extending the view that Josephus made room for literary fabrication beyond his account of Elazar ben Yair's speeches to include his story of the mass suicide, she argues that this explains why there is no other record of that event. Considering the Jewish prohibition against suicide and the Masada people's ideological commitment to the revolt, she argues, the idea that they would have killed themselves rather than continue to fight against the Romans is highly unlikely. Weiss-Rosmarin suggests that Josephus fabricated this story in order to clear from his conscience his betrayal of his comrades during an earlier stage of the revolt. Along similar lines historian Mary Smallwood argues that Josephus fabricated the suicide scene in order to cover up the Romans' barbaric behavior following the Masada people's real surrender.[12]

These speculations about Josephus's motives in constructing an imaginary end received attention but little support. Most scholars maintain that, writing his history at the time when people who had witnessed the death scene were still living, Josephus could not have invented the suicide. Although he did not record the sources of his information, it is most likely that he had access to the Roman archives with their testimony of the two women who survived the fall of Masada and that of the Roman soldiers who found the dead.[13]

Yadin's uncritical interpretation of Josephus's record was the subject of harsh criticism by the American Jewish historian Solomon Zeitlin, who triggered an intense and lengthy debate on this issue. Zeitlin's arguments were supported to varying degrees by other scholars, such as Morton Smith, Sidney Hoenig, and Yehuda Rosenthal. According to Zeitlin, Yadin misread the historical information that Josephus provides, ignoring the ancient historian's specific identification of the Masada men as Sicarii and referring to them as Zealots. Yet this misidentification was not naive. Zionist writers transformed the image of the Zealots, glorifying them as committed freedom fighters. As a result, the term Zealots has lost its negative connotations.[14] The Sicarii and the Zealots, Yadin's critics argue, are two distinct groups and their names cannot be used interchangeably. Moreover, these two factions pursued different courses of action during the Jewish revolt and were actually in conflict with each other.[15]

By referring to the Masada men as Zealots rather than as Sicarii, claim these critics, Yadin ignores Josephus's systematically negative descriptions of the latter's behavior. The Sicarii were members of an extremist sect who accepted only God's rule and defied any human authority. Their main opposition was directed not at the Romans but at those Jews who represented authority. After their leader had been murdered in Jerusalem, the Sicarii fled to Masada to find refuge there. From this point on, they did not take an active part in the war against the Romans and made no attempt to support the Zealots' struggle in Jerusalem. Instead, Josephus tells of how they terrorized and exploited the Jewish settlements around them.[16] In fact, even during the Roman siege of Masada, Josephus does not describe the Sicarii fighting the Romans; they maintained a policy of watchful waiting, and at the end they chose to take their own lives rather than fight or submit to the Romans.

These critics thus accuse Yadin of misrepresenting history in order to support the activist commemoration of Masada. Historically, claims Hoenig, we must distinguish between the Zealots, who acted as "defenders," and the Sicarii, those "anarchists and defeatists who contributed to the fall of the Jewish state."[17]

Zeitlin and Hoenig also assert that Yadin's material evidence of his portrayal of the Masada men as devout Jews is questionable. There is not enough evidence to substantiate his claim that certain structures had served as the *mikva* (ritual bath) and the synagogue, for laws concerning both developed later. The donation boxes unearthed at Masada could hardly be proof of the Masada inhabitants' religiosity, as Yadin asserted, for they can be part of the Sicarii's loot from neighboring Jewish settlements.[18]

While other scholars entered this debate "in defense of the defenders of Masada,"[19] Yadin deliberately refrained from defending his position. In a private communication, later published in the American Jewish journal *Ha-Do'ar*, he explains that he saw no point in arguing with Zeitlin on these and other issues.[20] A few months later, however, in an interview in the Israeli magazine *Ba-Maḥane*, published by the educational headquarters of the Israel Defense Forces, he said:

> Professor Zeitlin, as it is well known, argued against the early dating of the Dead Sea Scrolls and other findings at Masada that confirmed the early dating of the scrolls. And maybe, as a result of this, he has recently started to make statements that I, at least, consider a slander of the group of Zealot Jews who fought for freedom and who died for Kiddush ha-Shem because of their desire for freedom about two thousand years ago. Here I find it necessary to react strongly, and not necessarily as a scientist.[21]

Yadin's response reveals that he was ready to engage in a rebuttal of Zeitlin's critique *not as a scientist* but rather *as a patriot*, making this statement in an interview for a publication of the Israel Defense Forces. Whereas Yadin defended his view that those issues were not purely academic, his critics saw this very attitude as highly problematic. Indeed, Yadin's explicit nationalist bent was criticized not only by those mentioned above but also by other scholars, who point out that the goal he had set for the excavations "to see what evidence we could find to support the Josephus record"—shaped his interpretation of the archeological findings in accordance with the commemorative narrative.[22]

The Traditionalist Debate: Masada versus Yavne

Though Israeli collective memory constructed Masada as a key turning point in Jewish history that embodies the ancient national spirit, the "Masada spirit" became one of the main targets of the criticism of its status as a major symbolic text. Glorification of Masada, it has been argued, promotes an ethos that contradicts the authentic spirit of Jewish tradition. The much-celebrated message of the activist commemorative narrative, that death in freedom is preferred to life in submission, represents an extremist view that mainstream rabbinical Judaism has rejected. "In the scale of Jewish values, life occupies the highest rung. Unlike the Romans and the Greeks, the Jews did not glorify those who died by their own sword in the battlefield," argues Trude Weiss-Rosmarin.[23]

While Weiss-Rosmarin uses this argument to support her view that a mass suicide was highly improbable, other critics maintain that the Talmud's silence with regard to Masada clearly demonstrates that the sages disapproved of the collective suicide. The Sicarii's objection to any form of political submission as detracting from their total submission to God was not accepted by the majority of the more moderate Pharisee rabbis. The latter emphasized the importance of adherence to the principles of Judaism as the essence of Jewish life and accepted political submission when it was deemed inevitable.

> Respect for government and authority was always taught by the rabbis . . . Rome was regarded by many as an instrument of God. The priestly maxim was especially aimed to restrain strife and to preserve Israel from destruction.
>
> [. . .] The rabbis did not seek a political revolution. Their aim was to maintain the harmonization of law and life in the state by peace

Figure 1

Trumpeldor as an officer in the czarist army. Note his amputated left arm and the medals he received following the Russian–Japanese war of 1904. *Courtesy of the Lavon Archive of the Labor Movement.*

Figure 2

Trumpeldor's famous portrait as the commander of the Zion Mule Corps in the British army during World War I. *Courtesy of the Lavon Archive of the Labor Movement.*

Figure 3

The central building and part of the enclosed yard at Tel Ḥai as it looked after the battle. *Courtesy of the Lavon Archive of the Labor Movement.*

Figure 4

The monument of the Roaring Lion at Tel Ḥai. Trumpeldor's famous last words, "It is good to die for our country," and the names of those who died in the battle are inscribed on the monument. *Courtesy of the Lavon Archive of the Labor Movement.*

Figure 5

The Tel Ḥai monument in Upper Galilee is close to Israel's northern border, overlooking the Ḥula valley with the Golan Heights in the background. *Courtesy of the Government's Press Office, State of Israel.*

Figure 6

An official ceremony at Tel Ḥai near the monument of the Roaring Lion, with an honorary military guard and dignitaries, marking Tel Ḥai Day on the Eleventh of Adar, 1981. *Courtesy of Military and Defense Archives, Ministry of Defense, State of Israel.*

Figure 7

An aerial view of Masada. *Courtesy of the Government's Press Office, State of Israel.*

Figure 8

Youth raising a flag on top of Masada in 1943. *Courtesy of Military and Defense Archives, Ministry of Defense, State of Israel.*

Figure 9 (right)

Volunteers and soldiers excavating and restoring the archaeological ruins at Masada, 1963–65. *Courtesy of the Government's Press Office, State of Israel.*

Figure 10 (below)

Yigael Yadin leading David Ben-Gurion down the newly constructed stairs at Masada, 1963. *Courtesy of the Government's Press Office, State of Israel.*

Figure 11

The procession of the 1969 state burial for the remains of twenty-seven persons identified as the Masada defenders. The coffins, wrapped in the national flag, are carried by soldiers of the Israel Defense Forces to their burial site at Masada. *Courtesy of the Government's Press Office, State of Israel.*

Figure 12

An infantry unit of the Israel Defense Forces tracking on foot on the way to Masada in 1954. *Courtesy of the Government's Press Office, State of Israel.*

Figure 13

Israeli soldiers taking their oath of allegiance in a ceremony on top of Masada. The Hebrew inscription reads, "Never again shall Masada fall."
Courtesy of the Israel Defense Forces' Spokesman Office.

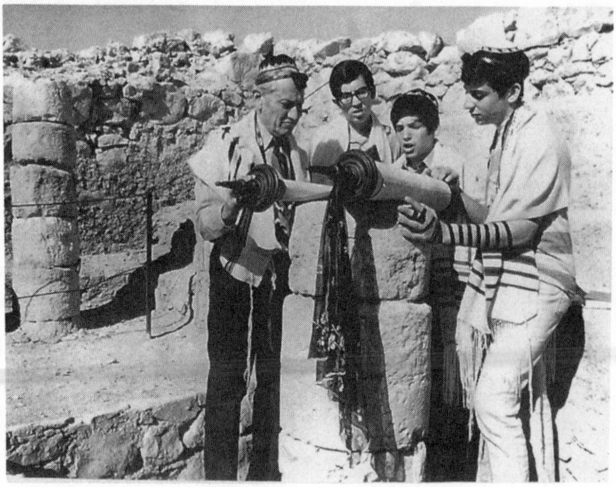

Figure 14

A bar mitzvah ceremony at the ancient synagogue of Masada.
Courtesy of the Lavon Archive of the Labor Movement.

Figure 15

A drawing from a children's book for Lag ba-Omer, depicting Bar Kokhba confronting the lion. Reprinted with permission from Levin Kipnis, *Mo'adei Yisrael: Lag ba-Omer* (Tel Aviv: Samuel Simson, 1974).

Figure 16

Soldiers carrying the coffins for the state burial of the bones identified as the Bar Kokhba warriors, which were transported by helicopter to the burial site in the Judaean desert. *Courtesy of the Government's Press Office, State of Isreal.*

Figure 17

Danny Kerman's cartoon of an Israeli peering inside the Roaring Lion monument and realizing it is hollow. Trumpeldor's words on the monument have been turned into a question: "Is it good to die for our country?" First published in *Devar ha-Shavua* (1979); reprinted with permission from Kerman, *That's It* (Tel Aviv: Zmora Bitan, Modan, 1981).

יוֹסֵף הַגִּבּוֹר׳

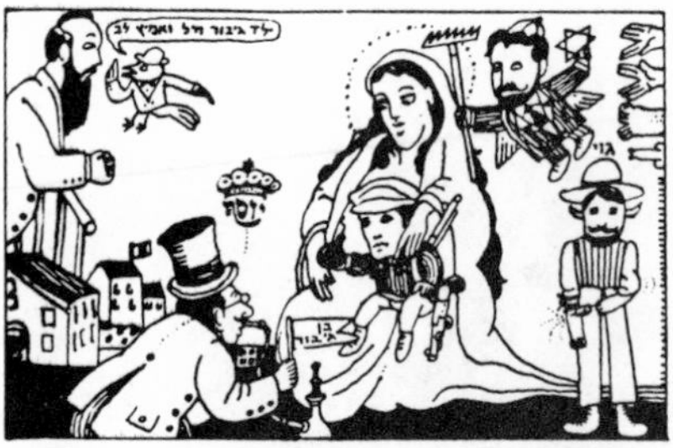

בְּאַחַת מֵאַרְצוֹת הַגּוֹלָה נוֹלַד לְאִישׁ יְהוּדִי יֶלֶד יִשְׁמוֹ יוֹסֵף. הוּא הָיָה יֶלֶד גִּבּוֹר־חַיִל וְאַמִּיץ־לֵב. תָּמִיד חָשׁ לְעֶזְרַת הַחַלָּשׁ לְהָגֵן עָלָיו מִפְּנֵי הֶחָזָק וְתַקִּיף מִמֶּנּוּ.

כַּאֲשֶׁר גָּדַל יוֹסֵף וַיֵּצֵא אֶל אֶחָיו רָאָה בְּסִבְלוֹתֵיהֶם בַּגּוֹלָה. הִרְגִּישׁ בְּצַעֲרָם וְכָאַב אֶת כְּאֵבָם. בְּלִבּוֹ חָשַׁב מַחֲשָׁבוֹת אֵיךְ לְהָרִים אֶת כְּבוֹד עַמּוֹ וּלְהָגֵן עָלָיו מִפְּנֵי צַר. כִּי הָיָה יוֹסֵף אָח לְכָל אֻמְלָל וְחָבֵר בַּצָּרָה לְכָל אָדָם.

בַּיָּמִים הָהֵם פָּרְצָה מִלְחָמָה בְּאֶרֶץ מוֹלַדְתּוֹ שֶׁל יוֹסֵף. הוּא הִשְׁתַּתֵּף בַּמִּלְחָמָה נֶגֶד אוֹיְבֵי רוּסְיָה, כִּי שָׁם נוֹלַד.

שְׁמוֹ יָצָא לִתְהִלָּה כְּחַיָּל אַמִּיץ וְגִבּוֹר. בַּמִּלְחָמָה זוֹ נִפְצַע יוֹסֵף הַגִּבּוֹר וְיָדוֹ נִקְטְעָה. מֵאָז נִקְרָא בְּשֵׁם הַגִּדֵּם.

כָּל יָמָיו נָשָׂא יוֹסֵף אֶת נַפְשׁוֹ לְאֶרֶץ־יִשְׂרָאֵל. הוּא חָלַם עַל גְּאֻלַּת עַמּוֹ, עַל חַיֵּי עֲבוֹדַת הָאֲדָמָה בְּאֶרֶץ־יִשְׂרָאֵל.

עָבְרוּ שָׁנִים וְיוֹסֵף טְרוּמְפֶּלְדּוֹר זָכָה לַעֲלוֹת אַרְצָה. הוּא עָבַד אֶת אַדְמָתָהּ, חָרַשׁ אֶת חֲרִישָׁהּ וְזָרַע אֶת זַרְעָהּ.

מְעַטִּים וּבוֹדְדִים הָיוּ אָז הַיִּשּׁוּבִים הָעִבְרִיִּים בַּגָּלִיל. יוֹסֵף טְרוּמְפֶּלְדּוֹר וַחֲבֵרָיו הִתְיַשְּׁבוּ בְּתֵל־חַי. עָבְדוּ בַּשָּׂדֶה וּבַכֶּרֶם, בַּגַּן וּבָרֶפֶת. בַּיּוֹם הָלְכוּ אַחֲרֵי הַמַּחֲרֵשָׁה וּבַלַּיְלָה שָׁמְרוּ עַל הַגָּלִיל מִפְּנֵי צַר וְאוֹיֵב.

וְכַאֲשֶׁר הַשּׁוֹדְדִים הָעַרְבִיִּים הִתְנַפְּלוּ עַל יוֹשְׁבֵי הַיְּהוּדִים בַּגָּלִיל, נִקְרָא יוֹסֵף הַגִּבּוֹר לְהָגֵן עַל אַדְמַת יִשְׂרָאֵל וְעַל כְּבוֹד עַמּוֹ.

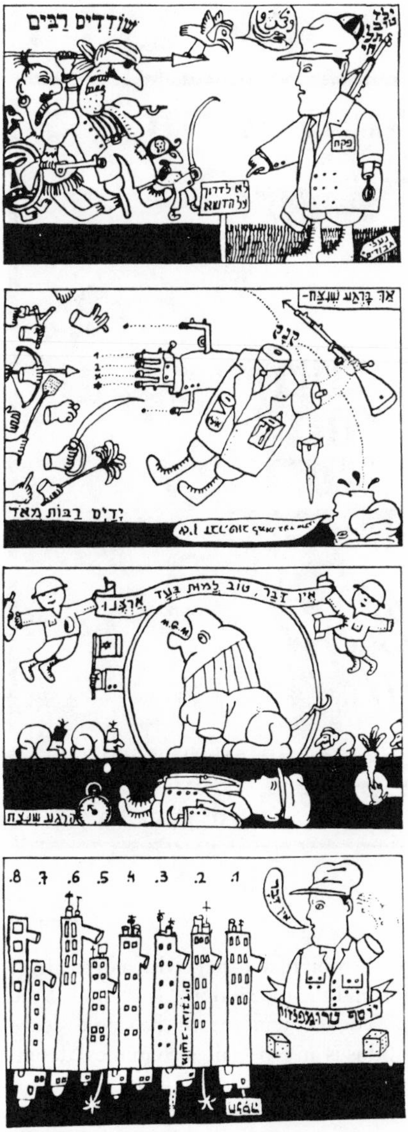

יוֹם אֶחָד הִתְנַפֵּל הָמָן עַרְבִי מְחָז עַל תַּל־חַי. טְרוּמְפֶּלְדוֹר חֲבֵרָיו הָאַמִּיצִים עָמְדוּ בִּגְבוּרָה, מְעַטִּים נֶגֶד פּוֹרְעִים רַבִּים. לָחֲמוּ בָּהֶם וְהָדְפוּ אוֹתָם.

וּבְיוֹם י״א בַּאֲדָר קָרְבוּ שׁוֹדְדִים רַבִּים אֶל חוֹמַת תֵּל־חַי. יָרוּ בְּרוֹבִים וּבְמִכְונוֹת־יְרִיָה וּכְשֶׁרָאוּ, שֶׁלֹּא יוּכְלוּ לִמְעַט תֵּל־חַי כִּי חֲזָקִים וְאַמִּיצִים הָיוּ, קָרְאוּ לָהֶם לְשָׁלוֹם וּבִקְשׁוּ לִפְתֹּחַ אֶת הַשַּׁעַר.

וְכַאֲשֶׁר הָעַרְבִים הָדְרוּ אֶל חֲצַר תֵּל־חַי, הִתְחִילוּ שׁוּב בִּירִיּוֹת וּבִקְשׁוּ לְהַחֲרִיב אֶת הַתֵּל וְלַהֲרֹג אֶת אֲנָשָׁיו.

טְרוּמְפֶּלְדוֹר פָּקַד עַל הַעֵת הַמָּקוֹם. יַחַד עִם חֲבֵרָיו נִלְחַם בְּעוֹ בַּשׁוֹדְדִים וְלֹא נָתַן לָהֶם לְגֶשֶׁת לַמֶּשֶׁק.

הַגִּבּוֹר נִלְחַם אֶחָד נֶגֶד פּוֹרְעִים רַבִּים. בְּיָד אַחַת נֶגֶד יָדַיִם רַבּוֹת מְאֹד. הוּא נִלְחַם בָּהֶם וְנִצַּח אוֹתָם, אַךְ בָּרֶגַע שֶׁנִּצַּח – נִפְצַע וְנָפַל.

בְּרֶגַע חַיָּיו הָאַחֲרוֹנִים דּוֹבְבוּ שְׂפָתָיו: „אֵין דָּבָר, טוֹב לָמוּת בְּעַד אַרְצֵנוּ".

בַּמָּקוֹם בּוֹ נָפְלוּ יוֹסֵף טְרוּמְפֶּלְדוֹר וַחֲבֵרָיו הוּקְמָה מַצֶּבֶת־זִכְרוֹן גְּדוֹלָה – אַרְיֵה שׁוֹאֵג.

וּמִדֵּי שָׁנָה בְּשָׁנָה עוֹלִים בְּיוֹם י״א בַּאֲדָר צְעִירֵי יִשְׂרָאֵל לְתֵל־חַי אֲשֶׁר בַּגָּלִיל וְנִשְׁבָּעִים עַל קִבְרוֹ שֶׁל טְרוּמְפֶּלְדוֹר לָלֶכֶת בְּדַרְכּוֹ – דֶּרֶךְ הָעֲבוֹדָה וְהַהֲגָנָה.

לְאַחַר הַנִּצָּחוֹן עַל הָעַרְבִים, נִכְבְּשָׁה חֶלְקָה הָעַרְבִית בִּידֵי צְבָא הַהֲגָנָה לְיִשְׂרָאֵל. בִּמְקוֹם הַכְּפָר, שֶׁמִּמֶּנּוּ יָצְאוּ רוֹצְחֵי יוֹסֵף טְרוּמְפֶּלְדוֹר וַחֲבֵרָיו, נוֹסַד מוֹשַׁב־עוֹבְדִים „קִרְיַת־שְׁמוֹנָה", עַל שֵׁם שְׁמוֹנַת גִּבּוֹרֵי תֵּל־חַי.

* הַטֶּקְסְט נִלְקַח מֵ„בְּאֶרֶץ יִשְׂרָאֵל", סֵפֶר לִימּוּד לִכִּתָּה ב׳
מֵאֵת אֲרִיאֵל / בַּלִּיד / פֶּרְסְקִי, כְּהוֹצָרֹת, 1974, עַ׳ 3־252.

Figure 18

Dudu Geva's macabre cartoon macabre cartoon parodying the public school's educational text on Yosef Trumpeldor (entitled "Yosef the hero"). Reprinted with permission from *Zoo Eretz Zoo?* (Jerusalem: Domino Press, 1975); cartoonist Dudu Geva.

Figure 19

Danny Kerman's cartoon of a T-shirt with a drawing of the Roaring Lion and the inscription, "It is good to die for our country." The text underneath the single-sleeve shirt explains that this is an especially economical design at a discount price but that it is also possible to get it "second hand." Reprinted with permission from *Davar Akher Legamre* (Tel Aviv: Am Oved, 1988).

> and by legal enactments, by interpretation of the law and a conformity to the traditional values in Judaism.[24]

To support their arguments against the glorification of Masada, the critics turned to another key historical event from the same period that, they believed, articulated better the spirit of Jewish tradition: the creation of a rabbinical center at Yavne, which provided spiritual leadership for the Jews in the aftermath of the destruction of the Second Temple in Jerusalem. Like Masada, the move to Yavne was a direct response to the Romans' success in suppressing the Jewish revolt. But while the Talmud refrained from even alluding to Masada, it contains several versions of Rabbi Yoḥanan ben Zakkai's initiative to found a new rabbinical academy in Yavne when he realized that Jerusalem was about to fall into the Romans' hands. Accordingly, the rabbi's students smuggled him in a coffin out of besieged Jerusalem in order to evade the Zealots, who guarded the city's exits so that no one would leave it. Reaching the Roman camp, he asked Vespasian to settle in Yavne (in some versions this was his reward for prophesying to the Roman that he would become the next emperor).[25] When Jerusalem fell to the Romans and the religious and political center of Judaea was destroyed, Yavne emerged as the new spiritual center to fill that void. Jewish tradition regards Yavne as a symbol of the vitality of Judaism in face of political oppression and credits Yoḥanan ben Zakkai with foresight that guaranteed this transition.

The critics of Masada's transformation into a major symbolic text point out its fundamental distinction from Yavne as a response to national catastrophe: whereas Masada represents the choice of death, Yavne represents survival. "We have survived as Jews and we have reconstructed Israel as the Jewish state not with the spirit of Masada but by the strength of Yavne," claims Weiss-Rosmarin.[26] This view was reiterated by the historian Binyamin Kedar in the Israeli newspaper *Ha-Aretz:*

> Indeed, Judaism's main road does not pass in Masada but in Yavne. Masada is a cul-de-sac, a dead end, a dramatic finale. He who tells the soldiers of the Armored Corps during the oath ceremony at Masada that "thanks to the heroism of the Masada defenders we stand here today" lives in error and misguides others. If Judaism has survived, if the Jewish people has survived, it is not by virtue of Masada but by virtue of Yavne; it is not thanks to Elazar ben Yair, but thanks to ben Zakkai.[27]

This contrast with Yavne challenges Masada on traditional grounds and defies the very act of raising it as a key turning point in Jewish history.

Whereas the activist commemorative narrative glorifies the resurrection of Masada as an important departure from traditional Jewish memory, this view essentially justifies the centuries-long collective amnesia regarding Masada by arguing for the incompatibility of the mass suicide with traditional Jewish values. Masada, these critics claim, is not the culmination of the ancient Jewish spirit that contemporary Jews should venerate and attempt to revive, but rather an unfortunate event that represents a fanatic response to political oppression that Jewish tradition could not, and should not, embrace.

The supporters of Masada refute this claim by belittling the significance of the lack of any reference to Masada in Jewish rabbinical sources. This avoidance does not reflect an agreement among the rabbis, for they were divided on the issue of the revolt. Some, like Rabbi Akiba who supported Bar Kokhba's revolt against Rome, were sympathetic to the idea of armed resistance; others, who did not believe that a revolt could be successful, sought a more peaceful accommodation to the Roman rule. The underlying issue, however, was not religious but political—a matter of realistic assessment of the prospects of such a war.[28]

Others acknowledge the tension between Masada and Yavne but present them as two different but valid traditional Jewish approaches. This approach was articulated earlier by Yosef Klausner: "Undoubtedly, Yavne saved the Jewish people from extinction. But maybe Masada saved it as well? Who knows if, in addition to the Torah, the memory of the heroism of Yoḥanan of Gush-Ḥalav, Shimon Bar-Giora, and Elazar ben Yair did not save the Jewish people from stagnation and extinction?"[29] A similar view is expressed in later publications that present both approaches as valid options. Beno Rotenberg refers to the Masada defenders' last act as a "heroic deed devoid of logic" and contrasts it with Yavne, which, he argues, represents "logic without heroism." Because Jewish history provides evidence of both approaches, he states, "there is no point in raising the question as to who was right in an argument that never took place between Yavne and Masada."[30]

Masada's compatibility with traditional Jewish values—a central issue in the religious and academic debates on its commemoration—does not necessarily articulate the average Israeli's concern. In the interviews I conducted in the late 1970s, no informant questioned the rabbis' attitude toward Masada or contrasted the spirit of Masada and that of Yavne. The few informants who objected to the suicide on religious grounds were not aware that this was a subject of an ongoing controversy in academic circles.

In fact, with the exception of Israeli intellectuals who followed and contributed to the debates on the commemoration of Masada and were well aware of the ambiguity that underlay the lack of reference to it in the talmudic-midrashic literature, the general public seems to take Masada's "traditional status" for granted. This assumption is quite obvious and is clearly reinforced by the commemorative narrative, which emphasizes the symbolic continuity between the Zionist National Revival and Antiquity. The lack of public awareness of the scholarly debate on the subject shows how the silencing of Masada in rabbinical sources has in turn been silenced in Israeli collective memory.

The Legal Debate: Suicide or Martyrdom?

The critical evaluation of the Masada commemorative narrative also turned to the issue of the communal death, examining it from a religious-legalistic perspective. At this level the controversy shifted from the traditional "spirit" of Masada to a more focused debate on the legal definition of the death at Masada. Since traditional Jewish sources make no mention of Masada, the legal interpretation of this case, based on inference from other cases specifically addressed by *halakha* (Jewish law), is open to discussion.

The legal debate returns to the historical narrative to examine the special circumstances of the participants' death and their motivation in executing a communal suicide. Josephus provides a detailed account of Elazar ben Yair's arguments to his people for ending their own lives and of how they carried that out. Once they were persuaded by their leader, the Masada men slew the women and children and then drew lots to determine the ten men who would slay the rest. The ten men later repeated the procedure to determine the one who would kill the nine others and then kill himself.

The historical narrative thus tells of people killing each other, with the single exception of the last person, who took his own life. Whereas causing someone else's death is usually labeled "murder," a voluntary death is usually classified as "suicide." Determining the voluntary basis of the Masada act is therefore crucial in assigning it to one of these two categories. It is extremely significant, however, that the issue of murder hardly appears in the legal debate. Rather, the controversy primarily focuses on the conflicting definitions of "martyrdom" and "suicide." We will return to the issue of murder later in this discussion, but at this point we should note the tacit assumption about the voluntary basis of the Masada people's death.

The legal controversy thus revolves around the question of whether the death at Masada can be interpreted as an act of Kiddush ha-Shem or defined as suicide. This issue is of primary significance, since Jewish law treats these two categories very differently, elevating the former as the most sublime manifestation of religious devotion while condemning the latter as a sin.

Jewish religion sets a high value on *piku'aḥ nefesh* (preservation of life) and objects to suicide as a violation of this principle. A person who commits suicide defies divine control over life and death and is guilty of destroying God's creation. Jewish law therefore denies persons who commit suicide certain posthumous honors and privileges that are customarily extended to all Jews, such as a public eulogy and the wearing of mourning garments for the deceased, and a grave in the communal Jewish lot. Furthermore, those who commit suicide are believed to be denied their place in the other world.[31] The legal position thus rules out the glorification of suicide as heroic unless it is defined as an act of Kiddush ha-Shem.

The laws concerning Jewish martyrdom crystallized in the second century in response to the Romans' religious persecution. The rise in cases of martyrdom during that period became so alarming that the rabbis felt obliged to provide clear guidelines as to when martyrdom is expected, in order to restrict it. Jewish law thus recognizes specific circumstances in which one is permitted—indeed, required—to choose death over life for one's faith. Accordingly, if a Jew is faced with a demand to perform one of the three most severe transgressions—idolatry, adultery or incest, and murder—one should risk one's life rather than comply with that demand. In the case of other transgressions, the principle of preservation of life supersedes the issue of religious violation. However, when one is forced to commit a minor transgression in front of at least ten Jews, one is called to die for Kiddush ha-Shem, since this becomes a matter of public display of religious devotion.[32]

If the Masada communal death can be legally defined as an act of Kiddush ha-Shem, this classification would justify its elevation as an important symbol; if not, that act should be condemned as suicide. Those who object to Masada focus on its incompatibility with the laws concerning Kiddush ha-Shem. First, they point out that Jews are expected to assert their devotion by being ready to be killed by others, not by killing themselves. To support this view the critics turn to the example of the famous Ten Martyrs whom the Romans killed and who had regarded their own readiness to endure terrible suffering from their persecutors as the ultimate expression of their devotion.[33] Second, argue the critics, the people of Masada were not faced with the three major transgressions that call for martyrdom, and therefore they were not permitted to kill themselves. Their act was inspired by Stoic ideas about life and death, which are in essence foreign to Jewish law concerning these matters.[34]

Those who maintain that the death at Masada was indeed an act of Kiddush ha-Shem attempt to refute these arguments with other legal points. They assert that the laws concerning Kiddush ha-Shem had been formed after the fall of Masada and therefore could not have served as guidelines for its people. Accusing them of choosing a solution that is incompatible with a later ruling is obviously anachronistic and highly unjust.[35] Moreover, even the later laws concerning Kiddush ha-Shem recognized the legitimacy of martyrdom in situations that involved a public demonstration of faith, and the Masada people's death can therefore be considered legitimate under those circumstances.[36]

Further arguments in support of Masada relate to other cases of death for Kiddush ha-Shem throughout the ages. For example, the legal precedent for the Masada people is the case of King Saul, who had fallen on his sword before the Philistines reached him. Based on later rabbinical justifications of his suicide, the supporters of Masada claim that, when Jews are faced with a situation in which they might be subjected to unbearable torture and pain, they are permitted to kill themselves.[37] Shlomo Goren, who served as the chief chaplain of the Israeli army, not only accepted the analogy between King Saul and Masada but went even further to apply it as a ruling for contemporary Israeli soldiers, stating that killing oneself in similar circumstances is a fulfillment of the requirement to die for Kiddush ha-Shem.[38]

The transformation of Kiddush ha-Shem during the Middle Ages provided further support for the legal definition of the death at Masada as martyrdom. The growing zeal that the medieval Jews displayed during the Crusades in dying for their faith was such a case in point. Jewish men's readiness to kill themselves and their families, and scenes of communal deaths quite similar to that of Masada, had been clearly considered acceptable acts of Kiddush ha-Shem, hence proving the legitimacy of Masada.[39] History demonstrates that Kiddush ha-Shem is a dynamic concept and has to be evaluated as such. This was manifested in the 1648–49 pogroms in Ukraine and again during the Holocaust, when victims who died because of their Jewishness were classified as martyrs regardless of the specific circumstances of their death.[40]

In the debate on the appropriate definition of the death at Masada as Kiddush ha-Shem or suicide, the assumption is that the death was the result of a collective decision and therefore could be considered "collective suicide." Within this context, *how* the "suicide" was carried out becomes a secondary, indeed a technical, issue. Although Josephus's narrative does not provide direct evidence that the communal death at Masada of 960 Jews was voluntary for all concerned, it is interesting to note that the issue of murder was hardly raised even by the critics of Masada. A rare exception is Bernard Heller's article "Masada and the Talmud," which accuses the Masada people of committing murder as well as suicide.[41] A later article that addresses the possibility of murder eventually dismisses it.[42]

Yet Josephus's historical narrative addresses only the men's response to ben Yair's plan of collective suicide and completely ignores the women's and children's perspective. Josephus does not tell us if the women and children agreed to be slain by their husbands and fathers or if their opinion, indeed, mattered at all. In his description the narrator clearly positions himself with the men, recounting how their leader persuaded them to carry out his plan, how each man embraced and kissed his beloved ones before he slew them, and how *the men extended their necks* to be slain by the others, thus expressing their voluntary agreement to this act.[43] We do not know, however, whether the women and children too extended their necks or whether they showed any reservations or resistance. The women's and children's ambiguous position was articulated by one of my informants who tried to adjust the intransitive verb "to commit suicide" to fit that scene: "The Masada men committed suicide the women and the children and then committed suicide themselves." In fact, the only place where women and children are transformed from objects to subjects occurs toward the end of the narrative, when two women and five children who had escaped the scene of death gave testimony to the Roman soldiers. This escape, revealing these women's opposition to the men's decision, made it possible for them to temporarily claim the center stage as witnesses, if not as dramatic actors.

Disregard of the women's and children's perspective, which might challenge the assumption of collective decision and hence of "voluntary death," is expressed not only by the ancient historian but also by most contemporary critics of Masada. Avoidance of this issue in the discourse about Masada may indicate that most critics have considered the charge of murder too extreme for those who acted out of religious zeal. The accusation of murder is much more severe than that of suicide: "Thou shalt not murder" is one of the Ten Commandments, and its violation is one of the three most severe transgressions by a Jew.

In this legal debate each side provides a number of arguments and supportive evidence from the legal literature to establish its definition of the Masada people's final act and its verdict about the legitimacy of the Masada commemorative narrative. This scholarly debate took place mostly in Jewish journals published outside of Israel (most notably, *Tradition*, *Or Ha-Mizraḥ*, *Ha-Do'ar*), although some Israeli academics and rabbinical scholars participated in it as well.

It is not surprising, therefore, that the legal debate has had little impact on the popular attitude toward Masada. In my own interviews most religious informants seemed to take it for granted that the death of the Masada people was an act of Kiddush ha-Shem. Only 6 out of 120 informants referred to the Jewish prohibition of suicide, and only 4 of them raised it to support their objection to the commemoration of Masada as a heroic act. While other informants often used terms that imply suicide ("they committed suicide," "they ended their lives by their own hands," etc.), they did not refer to the religious attitude toward suicide, nor did they provide any evidence that they were aware of the controversy around it. Only three of my informants objected to the final act at Masada on the grounds that it also involved murder. Two of them were Orthodox Jews, and one was a Holocaust survivor. While the religious definition of the final act would not be a major issue for secular Israelis to begin with, religious Israelis could find the excavations (especially the unearthed synagogue and ritual bath) and the official state funeral given to the remains of the Masada defenders a confirmation of the Masada people's religiosity that would eliminate any doubts about the appropriateness of their act on religious grounds.

The Activist Critique: Heroism or Escapism?

Criticism of the Masada commemorative narrative is also directed against the activist interpretation of Josephus's historical narrative. According to this argument the Masada men's behavior did not express a resolution to fight the enemy till "the last drop of blood" as the commemorative narrative implies, but a decision to *avoid confrontation* with the Romans when they entered the fortress. Rather than glorify the final act at Masada as heroic, one should see it for what it was—an escapist solution that brought death upon everyone in that community.

This line of criticism has been pursued at both the scholarly and popular levels. On the scholarly side the two staunch American opponents of the Masada commemorative narrative, the historians Solomon Zeitlin and Sidney Hoenig, voiced the most vehement opposition to the suicide on this ground. As Zeitlin stated: "[T]he Sicarii did not counterattack to protect Masada, they offered no resistance. They committed suicide and by this act they simply *delivered* Masada to the Romans."[44] Whereas the commemorative narrative emphasizes that the Masada men did not have any other dignified choice, Hoenig claims that Josephus's record of Macherus provides an example of how Jewish defenders fought against the Romans until they were forced to surrender, at which point the Romans gave them permission to leave safely.[45]

The Israeli historian Binyamin Kedar voiced a similar argument against elevating those who killed themselves to the level of a heroic symbol. Focusing on the gaps between the activist commemoration and the historical narrative, Kedar challenged the glorification of the suicide as a model of patriotic sacrifice for the Israeli youth: "[W]e ought to ask ourselves in the most critical way: Should we educate the youth by this myth? Is Masada indeed an example of 'sacrifice and voluntarism' as the commander of the Gadna [paramilitary youth education] recently said to several hundreds of seventeen-year-old boys and girls? Should we really present the collective suicide of the defenders of Masada as a model?"[46] Indeed, as we saw earlier, modern Hebrew culture has sought to promote the value of armed resistance to the enemy even in situations of fighting a few against many. This value is at the core of Israeli national ideology, supported by the commemoration of historical events from Antiquity and Israelis' own experience from the prestate and early state periods.

In fact, Jossipon's later modified version of Masada fits the activist conception of heroism in secular national Hebrew culture much better than Josephus's original version. According to Jossipon the Masada men killed the women and children and then went on to fight the Romans until they all fell in the battlefield.[47] One of the most curious developments regarding the collective memory of Masada may be that the activist commemorative narrative derives its legitimation from Josephus's historical account. Yet Masada's rise as a key turning point and a historical metaphor of fighting to the bitter end had been historically connected to the Jews' rediscovery of Josephus's historical works, and Jossipon's version has been largely ignored in the modern Hebrew commemoration of Masada.

Among the Israelis I interviewed the most common criticism of the Masada people was directed at their suicide on the grounds that it was an escape from confrontation. The following informants' statements are typical of this objection:

> They shouldn't have killed one another . . . They had to go on fighting against the Romans! What's the point of killing one another? In that way they could have done something so that [the Romans] would realize what heroism is.

> I would have wanted to fight against them and, at least, to kill one of them. But to die like that—killing one another—we don't gain anything by this!

> This isn't heroism. One should go on fighting till the end. A person who commits suicide has a weak character.

Although this was the most common objection to Masada among those I interviewed, it is important to note that they were only a small minority (16 out of 120 persons).[48] It is quite likely that today more Israelis would voice such criticism, disputing the value of suicide in the face of a greater cultural appreciation of *kiddush ha-ḥayim* (the sanctity of life). Like the other lines of criticism we have seen so far, this argument focuses on the commemorative, and not the historical, narrative. But unlike the previous arguments, this challenge was raised by ordinary Israelis who were not aware of a scholarly debate on the meaning of the myth.

The Political Debate: Realism or a "Complex"

Along with the arguments that point out various gaps between the historical and the commemorative Masada narratives, critics have raised a strong objection to the impact of the Masada commemorations on Israeli political culture. Accordingly, the reconstruction of Masada as a historical metaphor is detrimental to Israeli society's view of its own situation. Israelis' strong identification with the ancient Jews makes them look at the world as if they were still situated on top of besieged Masada, helpless and overpowered by their enemy. This defensive posture shapes not only Israel's perceptions but also its policymaking. Israelis therefore display an uncompromising attitude in negotiating with the Arab states and the Palestinians, an attitude that stems from what these critics call "the Masada complex."

The earliest use of the term "the Masada complex" I have found goes back to an editorial entitled "The Moral of Masada" in the London-based publication, the *Jewish Observer and the Middle East Review* (December 27, 1963). Yet the concept attracted more attention in 1971, when the American journalist Stewart Alsop reported in *Newsweek* that top State Department officials complained that Israel's prime minister, Golda Meir, suffered from a Masada complex that undermined efforts to reach a compromise with the Arabs.[49] Two years later, Alsop published another article, reporting Meir's direct response to his first piece on the subject.

> . . . She suddenly turned and fixed me with a basilisk eye. "And you, Mr. Alsop," she said, "you say that we have a Masada Complex."
>
> "It is true," she said. "We do have a Masada complex. We have a pogrom complex. We have a Hitler complex."
>
> Then she gave a small, moving oration about the spirit of Israel, a spirit that would prefer death rather than surrender to the dark terrors of the Jewish past."[50]

Alsop's articles called attention to the Masada complex and inspired further use of this concept in both Israeli and American political discourse. Government officials, journalists, and scholars reacted to the accusation that Israel suffers from a Masada complex. Alsop's second article provoked a letter from a top official in the Israeli Ministry of Foreign Affairs, arguing that "the Jewish imagination of disaster has, more than once, only too horrifyingly been confirmed by history."[51] A senior cabinet member, Pinḥas Sapir, declared in the Israeli parliament that "[w]e have a Warsaw Ghetto complex, a complex of the hatred of the Jewish people, just as we are filled with the Masada complex."[52] The official Israeli position was to acknowledge the centrality of Masada (as well as the Holocaust) to Israeli collective memory, yet to claim that the so-called complex is in fact a realistic outlook based on historical experience. This position further prompted discussion and criticism both inside and outside Israel, as journalists and scholars pointed out the selective commemoration of Masada and its influence on Israelis' perception of their present situation.[53]

Whereas critics of Israeli politics both inside and outside the country refer to the Masada complex, those who defend the Israeli government's position prefer to link it with a "Holocaust complex." By so doing, they group Masada and the Holocaust as interchangeable historical traumas, along the lines of the tragic commemorative narrative. The Holocaust, largely recognized as the major event that threatened Jewish survival in the modern era, thus becomes a source of legitimation for the commemoration of the ancient fall of Masada. Curiously, this move reverses the earlier trend that raised Masada as a model for contemporary events (e.g. Ben-Gurion's reference to Tel Ḥai as a "second Masada" and the reference to the Warsaw Ghetto revolt as "Masada of Warsaw"). Instead, Masada is described as an ancient Holocaust, thereby drawing on what is seen as a more powerful and immediate historical metaphor of persecution and death. While critics wish to highlight the difference between Masada and modern Israel, the proponents of the tragic commemorative narrative focus on the analogy between Masada, the Holocaust, and the State of Israel.

The critics' negative view of the symbolism of Masada and disapproval of its use as a historical metaphor for fear of blurring the past and the present is not new. A similar argument against the public's enthusiastic response to Lamdan's *Masada* as a representation of the modern Zionist National Revival was raised as early as 1927 by the literary critic Shlomo Tsemaḥ.[54] Almost twenty years later, Chaim Weizmann (then president of the World Zionist Organization) referred to Masada as a negative model when he voiced his opposition to Jewish terror against the British: "Masada for all its heroism was a disaster in our history. Zionism was to mark the end of our glorious deaths and the beginning of a new path whose watchword is life."[55] And even David Ben-Gurion, who had hailed Tel Ḥai as a second Masada on the Eleventh of Adar in 1943, later displayed a more critical attitude toward Masada.[56] Although reservations about the symbolism of Masada were pronounced earlier, this line of criticism has been voiced more often since the 1970s.

That the impact of Masada has become a focus of controversy during the last couple of decades is hardly surprising. Masada's increased fame following its archeological excavation has brought both the story and its commemoration to the limelight. The political use of Masada as a historical metaphor for contemporary Israel has also opened the door for counterinterpretations that caution against its impact on Israeli policies. Moreover, Israel's policies following its victory in the 1967 Six-Day War triggered blunt attacks on what was seen as its lack of willingness to compromise on the issue of trading territories for peace. The outbreak of the 1973 Yom Kippur War, the 1982 Lebanon War, and the Intifada were taken as evidence of the endless cycle of wars to which a Masada psychology can lead.

At the bottom of this line of criticism, then, is a perception that the elevation of Masada as a sacred symbolic text stems from, and reinforces, a pathological state. The introduction of psychological terms into the political discourse is furthered by social psychological studies that apply terms relating to individuals' pathologies to groups. An Israeli-born psychiatrist, Jay Gonen, diagnoses "Samson and Masada psychologies" in Israel, indicating a cultural disposition toward suicide and death.[57] Another Israeli social psychologist, Daniel Bar-Tal, studies the "Masada syndrome," which he defines as "a state in which members of a group hold a central belief that the rest of the world has negative behavioral intentions toward that group." His analysis of the consequences of the Masada syndrome focuses on how it turns into a self-fulfilling prophecy.[58]

The commemoration of Masada, according to these critics, gave rise to a Masada complex, which becomes part of Israeli political culture and shapes the leadership's views. "An Israeli leader who sees himself standing at the top of Masada might lose the ability to view reality as it is," warns Kedar.[59] The historian Bernard Lewis supports this caveat: "Care is needed not to carry it [Masada] beyond the stage of recovery into that of illusion. Dedication and courage are both noble and necessary—but they must not lead again to self-destruction in a dead-end of history."[60] The counterinterpretations of Masada thus present it as a model of a "dead-end" situation that would inevitably lead to self-extinction.

The criticism that the commemoration of Masada has generated a political neurosis appears to be limited to academics and political activists on the Left, and it is difficult to assess to what extent this reflects a popular concern.[61] The controversy over the Masada complex clearly has a more specific political reference, namely, the political debate over Israel's foreign policy and the Palestinian issue. Political parties and movements on the right advocate Israeli sovereignty over *Eretz Yisrael ha-shlema* (the entire Land of Israel of biblical dimensions) through the rapid settlement of the post-1967 territories. Despite important differences between them, the neo-Revisionists of the Likud and the radical nationalist-religious group of Gush Emunim share a fundamental belief that Israel is "a people dwelling alone" (Numbers 23:9) in a hostile Gentile world driven by antisemitism. This perception reinforces the political view that Israelis can rely only on their own power and resourcefulness, legitimizing the pursuit of unilateral policies that defy international pressures in the name of survival.

Within this worldview, where history, theology, and politics intertwine, Masada and the Holocaust become central political myths and historical metaphors. In its attempt to mobilize popular support for its settlement policy as a reenactment of the prestate pioneering spirit, Gush Emunim used the sanctified metaphor of *aliya* (climbing up) to the mountain, invoking Masada in support of its call to resist the withdrawal from Sinai.[62] Moreover, during the 1980s an extremist right-wing underground group selected for itself the name Sicarii (Ha-Sikarikim), borrowing Josephus's label of the Masada men and, like the ancient group, turning terrorist acts into an advocated policy. Such uses of Masada as well as the Left's accusations that its opponents suffer from a Masada complex indicate that within the immediate context of the Israeli-Palestinian conflict the debate on the Masada myth addresses the present as much as the past.

The debates on the religious, legal, and historical interpretations of Masada and on the emergence of a Masada complex developed as a result of the new visibility that both the story and the site have enjoyed since the excavation and changes in Israel's social and political reality. The multivocality of the Masada myth has generated the multivocality of its counternarratives. The activist commemorative narrative has given rise to a counternarrative that emphasizes an overzealous, uncompromising attitude to issues concerning Israel's security; the tragic commemorative narrative has generated a counternarrative that focuses on deep-seated fears of persecution and death. The dual meaning of "the Masada complex" thus echoes the coexistence of two commemorative narratives that enhance Masada's symbolic significance. While they focus on different aspects of the myth, both these Masada counternarratives underscore the formation of a vicious cycle: the Masada complex perpetuates the recurrence of military and political conflicts, which in turn reinforce the Masada complex.

In discussing these issues, critics point out that collective memory is not only a representation of the past but also a resource for shaping the future. The discussion thus focuses on the danger of using historical events as lenses through which one examines the present. Even though the critics may not be in full agreement about the meaning of Masada, they share a recognition of its powerful impact as a political myth.

In spite of these multiple voices of criticism, Masada has not lost its symbolic significance. Clearly, both the site and the myth have been transformed. In a more diversified and more politically polarized Israeli society, there is much less agreement on the interpretation of the past as well as its implications for the present. But Masada is still part of Israeli collective memory and still evokes strong responses. In this respect the criticism of Masada provides further evidence of its continuing, if transformed, symbolic significance for Israeli and Jewish political discourse.

CONCLUSION: HISTORY, MEMORY, AND INVENTED TRADITION

Nationalist movements typically attempt to create a master commemorative narrative that highlights their members' common past and legitimizes their aspiration for a shared destiny. Indeed, the establishment of such a narrative constitutes one of the most important mechanisms by which a nation constructs a collective identity for what Benedict Anderson calls an "imagined community." As we have seen throughout this study, this process of reconstructing the past entails a highly selective attitude toward the available historical knowledge. Although history serves as a source of legitimation, memory shapes the representation of the past. A dual process of "recovery" thus takes place at one and the same time: while some aspects of the past are uncovered or shift from the margins to the center of our historical consciousness, other aspects of the past are marginalized or fade into oblivion. Any remembrance thus entails its own forgetfulness, as the two are interwoven in the process of producing the commemorative narratives. This interplay and constant tension between these two forces contribute to their dynamic character and explain why memory has not vanished in the modern era in spite of the rise of history. They also account for the emergence of multiple representations of the past over time or by different groups.

The rhetoric of change and continuity is an important dimension of the construction of a national memory and tradition. Reformist and revolutionary movements tend to highlight their departure from the past and play down their continuity with what they regard as a discredited political and moral order. Conservative movements, in contrast, prefer to obscure changes and emphasize their continuity with the past. Such professed positions, articulated through the construction of the master commemorative narrative, often mask a more complex attitude toward the past and its traditions. By studying specific commemorations we can go beyond such ideological assertions to unveil the greater intricacy and ambivalence often implicated in the act of commemorating the past.

In the challenging formative years of Israeli society, the Zionist settlers' revolutionary rhetoric articulated most clearly their desire to depart from Jewish life in exile and its social, cultural, economic, and political manifestations. The Zionist collective memory elevated the period of Antiquity as the Hebrew nation's heroic past and enhanced its commemorative density. This was particularly evident with regard to the ancient Judaean wars of liberation of the first and second centuries. The revolts against the Roman domination of Judaea symbolized the continuing zest of the national spirit and the uncompromising drive to achieve national freedom that the Zionist settlers wished to revive in the modern period. The period of Exile was transformed into a negative reference point, and its main commemorative function reduced to creating a sharp contrast with the two national periods, the one experienced in Antiquity and the one beginning to take shape in Palestine. Despite these rhetorical stands the study of the new expressions of the Hebrew national tradition reveals their strong links to traditional Jewish culture. This continuity was, in fact, most instrumental to their rapid dissemination and ultimately contributed to their consolidation as a national tradition.

The desire to recover the Hebrew nation's ancient roots was a major motivating force in the construction of the Zionist master commemorative narrative. Yet in this process, Zionist collective memory suppressed other groups' memories that were in conflict with its own reconstruction of the past. Zionism, especially in its dominant socialist bent, struggled to discredit the memory of the non-Zionist religious Jews, arguing that it had led the Jews to a state of cultural stagnation, political inaction, and victimization that was characteristic of Exile. This oppositional stance vis-a-vis the religious view was clearly articulated in the Zionist discourse, thus expressing heightened awareness of the tension between the two.

In contrast to this awareness, Zionism suppressed the Arabs' memory of centuries of life in Palestine by ignoring its presence. Zionist memory portrayed the land as empty and desolate, yearning for the return of its ancient Hebrew inhabitants. The Zionist master collective memory was thus supported not only by the marginalization of Jewish experience in Exile, but also by shutting out others' experiences in the ancient land after the majority of Jews had left it. Conversely, that aspect of the past that the Zionist memory assigned to oblivion was central to the Palestinians' collective memory, providing the foundation for their collective identity and nationalist claims. The Israeli-Palestinian conflict grew out of this clash between their respective memories and their refusal, until quite recently, to acknowledge the problems inherent to their divergent reconstructions of the past.

Memory, Myth Plot Structures, and the Holiday Cycle

Analysis of the ways in which historical events give rise to national myths highlights the intersection of ideological, political, literary, and educational interests in the creation of a national tradition. Although detailed examination of specific commemorative narratives and rituals reveals that they provide a selective version of history, such gaps may not raise a controversy as long as the representation of the past conforms to and reinforces cognitive structures shaped by the master commemorative narrative. These structures, which govern the process of narrativization about the past, function as *myth plot structures*, molding the past into certain types of symbolic texts.[1] The conformity of a commemorative narrative to a myth plot structure contributes to its textual integrity[2] and makes it easier to ignore its selective representation of available historical data. The mythical structure thus reinforces the primacy of the ideological message over historical accuracy and enhances the symbolic significance of the event, beyond the historical constraints of a specific time and place.

The commemorative locus can further influence the degree of flexibility afforded in the process of adapting historical events to myth plot structures. By their very nature, holidays provide commemorative settings that allow greater freedom in the reconstruction of the past. The holiday cycle itself constitutes a traditional site of memory, anchored in a centuries-old tradition. Historical holidays offer rituals of remembrance that create "a shared network of practices around which clustered the common memories of the people as a whole."[3] Their celebration thus allows the society to replenish and reshape its memory of the past, while preserving an overall sense of continuity.

The holiday cycle can be seen as a semiotic system that offers a nonhistorical framework of representation of the past. The holiday cycle determines which aspects of the past become more central to collective memory and which are assigned to oblivion; which events are commemorated as highly significant and which are lumped together in a single commemoration,[4] or ignored. Holidays create commemorative narratives about specific events, detaching them from their broad historical context. This inevitable dissociation allows greater flexibility in delineating the narrative boundaries in order to accentuate a desired moral lesson, leaving out those developments that might detract from it. Moreover, since holidays are not arranged within the holiday cycle according to their dating, their nonchronological sequence within the cycle further contributes to the fragmentation and dehistorization of the past.

It is important to bear in mind these characteristics when we consider that the holiday cycle has a major role in shaping our basic views of the past. Children who are still considered too young for the formal study of history are introduced to the past through holiday commemorations. Learning about the holidays often occupies an important place in early childhood curriculum. The early introduction to the reconstruction of the past through holiday commemorations and their annual repetition therefore have a decisive impact on shaping our primary images of the past. Moreover, the holidays also stimulate the construction of an appealing commemorative literature designed to enhance the experience of their celebration. Since the context is commemorative and not strictly historical, and since much of this literature is directed to a young audience, this setting provides greater license for adding fictitious elements to the commemoration of the past. A further look at the specific cases that this study examines may help illuminate the interplay between the myth plot structures and the holiday cycle and its impact on the reconstruction of the memory of these events.

The Zionist collective memory did not invent new mythical structures. Rather, it promoted a closer association between existing Jewish myth plot structures and certain periods in Jewish history and reinterpreted their meaning. It thus linked Antiquity and the modern National Revival with the myth plot structure of a successful stand of the "few against many,"[5] and subsumed Exile under the plot structure of persecution leading to victimization and death. Furthermore, it shifted from the traditional, religious framework of attributing historical developments to divine help and punishment, to a secular national framework that emphasizes sociopolitical explanations.

The three cases explored in this study demonstrate how the conformity of new commemorative narratives to myth plot structures contributed to their acceptance as authoritative texts despite their selective representation of known historical sources. The position of these events within the "national periods" of either Antiquity (the fall of Masada and the Bar Kokhba revolt) or the Zionist National Revival (the Tel Ḥai battle) accounts for their activist interpretation as glorified expressions of armed resistance to the enemy. Within this context the available historical information that does not fit that commemorative pattern loses its relevance and fades into the background as negligible information. The conformity to the myth plot structures helps explain why the close resemblance between the historical narratives about the collective suicide at Masada and similar actions by Jews during the Crusades is ignored within the activist commemoration of Masada: the fall of Masada occurred in Antiquity and hence is associated with "active" heroism, while the Crusades are located in the period of Exile and hence become an expression of a "passive" response to persecution.

The transformation of the holiday cycle in the secular national Hebrew culture further facilitated the dissemination of these commemorative narratives. The founders of Israeli society showed a clear preference for transforming the meaning of traditional Jewish holidays to establishing a new holiday cycle. The addition of Tel Ḥai Day was, in fact, one of the few exceptions to this pattern during the prestate period. Preserving the structure of the traditional Jewish cycle, the Zionist Jews sought to counter what they considered to be an exilic overemphasis on the religious dimension of historical holidays, by reviving their national-political significance. Human rather than divine agents take the lead in the commemorative accounts of the holidays. In Ḥanukka, for example, the Maccabees' success in liberating their people from foreign oppressors has become the focal point of the celebration, rather than the divine miracle of the flask of oil and the renewal of services at the Temple. Passover brings forth the paradigm of liberation and national revival, led by Moses and Aaron. And in Purim, the celebration of a collective salvation underscores Mordechai's and Esther's resourcefulness in obstructing Haman's vicious plans.

In a similar revivalist trend the Hebrew commemorations also highlighted the natural and agricultural aspects of holidays, thereby enhancing the centrality of the Land of Israel and nature to Hebrew national culture.[6] Thus, purely religious holidays that have no historical reference lost much of their significance within that cultural context. For example, observance of the traditionally most sacred day, Yom Kippur, drastically declined among secular Jews during the prestate and the early-state periods, and the fast day of Tish'a be-Av was largely ignored.[7]

The overall tendency to dwell on the national-political aspects of specific historical holidays led to an ever stronger emphasis on national conflicts as the major theme around which the commemoration of the past revolves. Although the conflict theme also underlies many of the traditional Jewish holiday commemorations, the religious framework supersedes its political implications. The greater saliency of the political framework in the new Hebrew commemorations accentuated the pattern of besiegement, confrontation, and survival throughout Jewish history.

This basic *conflict formula* promoted by the holiday commemorations not only entails a gross simplification of complex developments but also suggests that Jewish collective experience is dominated by conflict situations.[8] That the holiday cycle represents historical events in a decontextualized, fragmented form and a nonchronological order serves only to enhance the centrality of this formula as a structuring scheme. The Passover Haggada reads, "For it was not only one who stood up against us to destroy us; in every generation they stand up against us to destroy us and the Holy One, blessed be He, saves us from their hand." A Hebrew children's poem for Purim articulates a similar idea, suggesting that Haman, the archetype of the Jew hater, appears every now and then to destroy the Jews, yet fails to achieve his goal.[9]

Revolving around this conflict formula, the holiday commemorations vary in their specific details. The enemy and the main heroic figures change according to the specific time and the place, yet the conflict situation persists. Thus, Ḥanukka commemorates the Maccabean revolt against the oppression of the Greeks (identified as Syrians in English texts), Purim revolves around the threat to the Jews of Persia, Passover marks the Jews' liberation from bondage in Egypt, and Israel's Independence Day commemorates the war against Arab forces. Fast days and memorial days further reinforce this emphasis on conflicts: Tish'a be-Av relates to the destruction of the First and Second Temples by the Babylonians and the Romans, respectively (as well as other, later historical traumas that were added on), and the Holocaust and Heroism Remembrance Day commemorates the Nazi atrocities. As a result of the prominence of the conflict formula as a myth structure, historical details pertaining to holidays seem interchangeable and can be easily confused. Such confusions are so pervasive that they have become part of Israeli folklore and are a popular subject of humorous lore.[10]

While each holiday commemoration embodies a myth plot structure, the nonhistorical sequence of holidays within the annual cycle constructs its own commemorative order that supports the Zionist master commemorative narrative. The temporal ordering of the holidays thus symbolizes a vast movement from bondage (Passover) and victimization (the Holocaust Remembrance) through a national struggle (the Memorial Day for Israeli soldiers) to national independence (Israel's Independence Day).[11] The representation of this macroprogression via the annual holiday cycle reinforces the commemorative structures shaped by the Zionist collective memory and accentuates the nationalist message of each individual holiday.

The holiday cycle promotes patterns of remembrance that are based on a rather simplified classification of commemorative events: festive celebrations commemorate conflicts in which Jews were victorious, while fast days and memorial days focus on conflicts that ended in death or defeat. Within this framework the Hebrew national tradition showed a clear preference for the former kind of commemorations: Ḥanukka, Passover, Lag ba-Omer, and Purim are favorite holidays around which a large repertoire of stories, songs, plays, and new rituals has been developed. Conversely, the secular national Hebrew culture largely ignored Tish'a be-Av and other, minor Jewish fast days.

These commemorative patterns help shed further light on the radical transformation in the collective memory of the Bar Kokhba revolt. Since festive celebrations usually mark a victorious resolution of a conflict situation, concluding the Lag ba-Omer commemorative narrative with Bar Kokhba's victory over the Romans seems only natural and appropriate. This logic was made explicit by a student whom I interviewed who could not remember how the revolt had ended; later, in the context of questions about Lag ba-Omer, she said: "It must have been a victory . . . For if there is a holiday, it means they won the war!" The "commemorative fit" between the narrative and its holiday setting thus helps obscure the actual outcome of the revolt in spite of available historical documentation.

When the constructed memory is shattered by the historical record, history can become a disturbing news. Both Rogel and Harkabi, who instigated public challenges of the Tel Ḥai and Bar Kokhba myths (respectively), reveal that they were motivated to reexamine these historical events when they realized that their childhood lore was based on a historical misrepresentation of which they had not been aware.[12] An Israeli woman recounted how her daughter came back from school visibly shaken, asking her mother if she knew that Bar Kokhba had actually lost the war.

Often, the ability to compartmentalize knowledge is so great that history and memory can coexist without apparent friction. This was evident in interviews where informants referred to the "defeat" and the "victory" of the Bar Kokhba revolt in different parts of the same interview. This duality indicates how history and memory can operate side by side within different commemorative frameworks as alternative knowledge about the past. Both the society at large and individuals may thus draw upon either history or memory, overlooking the tensions between their divergent representations of the same past.

The interchangeability of historical events within the conflict formula was also apparent in my interviews, where Lag ba-Omer and Ḥanukka were often mixed up. It is easy to see how these two holidays can be confused within the commemorative locus of the holiday cycle, even though Bar Kokhba's revolt was defeated within three years whereas the Maccabean revolt led to the creation of the Hasmonean kingdom.[13] Ultimately, it appears that offering armed resistance to the enemy is commemorated as a symbolic victory in itself, above and beyond the historical outcome of that act. The display of readiness to sacrifice one's life for the nation is thus glorified as a supreme patriotic value that diminishes the significance of the outcome.[14] In this respect there is no substantial difference between the actions taken by the Masada defenders, the Maccabees, or Bar Kokhba. The holiday cycle thus subverts history through its perpetuation of mythical representations of the past. By adjusting history into these mythical molds, the holiday cycle continues to shape the understanding of the past to a greater extent than we would like to acknowledge.

The Construction of Narrative Boundaries

As the earlier discussion of the politics of commemoration shows, one of the most interesting issues in the discursive reproduction of history is the delineation of narrative boundaries. Literary critics have noted the significance of the beginning and the ending for the construction of fictional narratives,[15] yet this issue is clearly more critical as far as historical and commemorative narratives are concerned. In the process of transforming history into a story, the decision of where to begin and end the story defines what constitutes the relevant event and determines its meaning.[16] Since the event is retrospectively identified, the act of imposing those points of beginning and ending upon an open-ended historical sequence is essentially interpretive.[17] As Hayden White suggests: "[N]arrative is not simply a recording of 'what happened' in the transition from one state of affairs to another but a progressive *redescription* of sets of events in such a way as to dismantle a structure encoded in one verbal mode in the beginning so as to justify a recording of it in another mode at the end. This is what the 'middle' of all narratives consist of."[18]

The construction of beginning and ending is clearly an important facet of ordering experience in a narrative form. Frank Kermode's brilliant analogy of the ticking of the clock reveals how the simple construction of boundaries confers a minimal fictive structure and meaning on an otherwise meaningless time flow. Whereas the tick-tock sequence indicates an intentional beginning and ending of a socially significant unit, the equally present tock-tick sequence is treated as meaningless and hence is ignored.[19] Similarly, the experience described between the points of beginning and ending in the narrative is assumed to represent the relevant part of that past, defining the information left out as nonimportant. The interdependence of the beginning and the ending shapes the construction of both in order to establish the desired message. "If one can say that the beginning of a narrative often dictates its end to some extent," Gerald

Prince states, "one can also say that the end conditions the beginning."[20] The construction of the beginning and ending of the narrative thus shapes the essence of the commemoration and highlights the literary dimension of memory.

Narratives that have a high textual integrity can clearly produce a more persuasive closure.[21] This point can easily be demonstrated by the contrast with modernist writers' techniques that are designed to undermine the textual integrity of their work. Their texts present a fragmented, alienated experience of reality that defies order and is resistant to closure and is designed to raise doubts in the reader's mind as to "what really happened."[22] In contrast, commemorative narratives tend to be tightly constructed and are meant to convince that their representation is reliable and complete, leaving no pertinent historical information out of the story. Their reliance on myth plot structures clearly reinforces their cultural acceptance as authoritative texts.

In all three cases I selected to study, the gaps between the historical and the commemorative narratives could justifiably raise questions regarding the construction of their endings. If the retreat from Tel Ḥai following the battle was recorded, how did it develop into a myth of successful defense and a historical model of never abandoning a Jewish settlement? If known ancient sources report on the destruction, death, and exile following the Bar Kokhba revolt, how did its commemoration successfully shift to a festive celebration of his war? And last but not least, if Josephus describes in detail the episode in which men killed women and children and then killed themselves, leaving close to a thousand persons dead, why did Masada become an inspiring myth for fighting until the last drop of blood? These questions are partly answered by the myth plot structure of the commemorative narratives of these particular periods. A closer look at the narratological strategies employed in the adaptation of historical information to myth plot structures further explains how this transformation is achieved.

In following the predominant myth plot structure of a successful struggle of the few against many associated with Antiquity and the Zionist National Revival, the commemorative narratives strive to produce a positive representation of these events. Two strategies are employed to achieve this end. The first is concluding at a high point during the struggle that suggests its success, leaving out further developments that might challenge this impression. The second is extending the conclusion of the story to a much later point in history that diminishes the significance of the outcome of that struggle. I refer to these narratological strategies as "curtailing" and "expanding" the end.

The commemorative narratives of the battle of Tel Ḥai and the Bar

Kokhba revolt best demonstrate the use of curtailing the end. Consider the following textbook narrative about the event that took place in Tel Ḥai on March 1 (the eleventh of Adar), 1920:

> And on the eleventh of Adar many robbers approached the wall surrounding Tel Ḥai. They fired guns and machine guns, and when they realized that they would not be able to overcome the defenders of Tel Ḥai because they were strong and brave, they asked for a truce and requested that they [the defenders] open the gate to them.
>
> When the Arabs penetrated the yard of Tel Ḥai, they reopened fire and wanted to destroy the settlement and kill its residents. Trumpeldor was in charge of the defense of the place. With his comrades he fought courageously and did not let them get to the house.
>
> Yosef told his friends: "We will stand up together against the enemy. The land that we plowed we will guard; the house that we built we will not abandon."
>
> For three days Yosef and his comrades defended Tel Ḥai—a few against many. He expelled the Arabs but was severely wounded in the battle.
>
> A few minutes before he died, his lips uttered: "Never mind, it is good to die for our country."[23]

A version written for younger children curtails the ending even further, leaving out the information about Trumpeldor's death: "Three days the robbers stood near the gate—many against few. Three days Trumpeldor and his comrades defended Tel Ḥai—few against many. And the young men won."[24] The narratives highlight the structure of a few against many. They use other techniques such as exaggerating the duration of the battle from one to three days to glorify the settlers' courage and persistence, and diminish the moral standing of the enemy by referring to the Arabs as "robbers" and by explaining their success in entering the yard by deception. The narrative does not mention the survivors' withdrawal from Tel Ḥai on that same day, thereby creating a closure with the defenders' victory and the Arabs' retreat. Tel Ḥai is thus constructed as a successful embodiment of the modern Zionist commitment to settlement and defense.

In the case of the Bar Kokhba revolt, a short version of the commemorative narrative is associated with Lag ba-Omer. The following example is likewise quoted from the public school textbook:

> Many years ago the Jews lived happily in the Land of Israel. The Romans came and conquered the country and burned down the Tem-

> ple. The Jews suffered terribly until they could not tolerate it anymore.
>
> The hero Shimon Bar Kokhba then came and called the entire nation to stand up and fight against the Romans. The heroes of Judaea heard him and gathered from all over the country. Bar Kokhba did not let all of them in but chose only the most courageous of them.
>
> In those days there was a very learned scholar, Rabbi Akiba was his name, who had twenty-four thousand students. Rabbi Akiba taught his students to love any fellow Jew as well as their country.
>
> When Rabbi Akiba heard about the Bar Kokhba revolt, he took all his students and came to support Bar Kokhba. Thousands of his students entered the army and fought against the Romans.
>
> Like lions the heroic Jews fought, led by Bar Kokhba. They defeated the Romans and expelled them from Jerusalem.
>
> One of Bar Kokhba's major victories occurred on the eve of Lag ba-Omer, and Rabbi Akiba's students kindled bonfires on top of all the mountains around—and there was light in the whole country.
>
> To commemorate this victory, schoolchildren celebrate the Lag ba-Omer holiday, singing and dancing around the bonfire.[25]

This narrative presents the Bar Kokhba revolt as highly successful. The story ends with the expulsion of the Romans from Judaea and the joyful celebration of the ancient rebels that contemporary Israelis continue today. The information that the Romans proceeded to crush the revolt, leading to the death of many Jews and the exile of others, is suppressed within this context as if it has no direct relevance to the memory of that revolt. In many respects the activist interpretation of Masada uses the same strategy. Although the collective suicide is not altogether suppressed, the broader, glorifying reference to the defenders' death while fighting against the Romans obscures the suicide. The direct fighting that is assumed to have taken place prior to the last scene of death thus becomes the high point that defines the meaning of the end, while the men's slaughter of the women and children and their own suicide fade into the background.

Even though the information about the withdrawal from Tel Ḥai, the defeat of the Bar Kokhba revolt, and the scene of collective death at Masada is part of known records, the commemorative narratives of these events were largely accepted during the prestate and early-state periods because they presented a convincing closure that was reinforced by the myth plot structures to which they conform. The strategic construction of boundaries thus manipulates historical time to establish the desired symbolic meaning of the commemorative narratives.

Although the battle and the retreat occurred within the framework of a single day, the narrative introduces a *thematic distance* between them and thus defines the withdrawal as essentially irrelevant to the story. Consequently, the narrative establishes the settlers' triumph in confronting the Arabs and avoids a possible challenge of this representation.[26] Trumpeldor's famous last words in the conclusion affirm the moral lesson of this ending, dispelling any doubt about the settlers' victory and its worthiness. Similarly, the Lag ba-Omer commemorative narrative introduces a thematic distance between the opening phase of the Bar Kokhba revolt and its ultimate defeat. This distance allows the glorification of Bar Kokhba's courage and patriotic commitment without diminishing it by the failure of his revolt. In both the case of Tel Ḥai and the Bar Kokhba revolt, the adaptation of history to story introduces a thematic distance between facts that are temporally close.[27] Historical time is thus transformed into commemorative time.

The other strategy used in commemorative narratives is to condense historical time in order to create a *thematic proximity* between events that are chronologically distant. The extended commemorative narratives diffuse the impact of the failure or death by a strategy of inclusion rather than exclusion. This strategy is used in educational narratives about Tel Ḥai that are designed for older children or adults. They include the information that the Jewish settlers evacuated the settlement and subsequently retreated from Upper Galilee. Yet these narratives also describe the settlers' return to Tel Ḥai seven months later and conclude with a coda stating that the battle of Tel Ḥai guaranteed the inclusion of Upper Galilee within Israel's territory in 1948. Within this framework the settlers' decision to burn down the place and withdraw to the nearby settlement of Kfar Giladi becomes a negligible fact. Consider the following example:

> After Trumpeldor's death the Arabs brought military reinforcements. The defenders saw no point in remaining in the place. They took with them their arms and withdrew to the south. But the battle and the sacrifices were not pointless. That part of the land for which they died was ultimately included within the territory of the [British] mandate and consequently within that of the [Jewish] "National Home." Today it belongs to the State of Israel.[28]

The text goes on to describe the precise scope and quality of the territory that Israel received thanks to "the battle and the heroism of the defenders of Tel Ḥai."

The portrayal of the later return to the settlement as an integral part of the narrative is also evident in a story told as a personal testimony by the last settler to evacuate Kfar Giladi after the fall of Tel Ḥai. Before he departs, the young man turns to the graves of his fallen comrades and vows: "'We will return'—I cried out in the direction of the graves—'we will return and rebuild everything anew! . . . ' And indeed we came back——"[29] Quite tellingly, this open-ended conclusion of the narrative defies the implications of closure, suggesting that the story does not end with desertion but with an open future following the settlers' return.

The two strategies of curtailing and expanding the end are combined in Tel Ḥai narratives that tell of Trumpeldor's fatal injury and ignore the subsequent retreat from the settlement, yet add a coda that expands the narrative time beyond March 1, 1920. Moreover, it diffuses the finality of death by introducing into the coda the themes of commemoration, revenge, and renewal:

> In the site where Yosef Trumpeldor and his comrades died a large monument was built—a roaring lion. Every year on the Eleventh of Adar, Israeli youth make a pilgrimage to Tel Ḥai in Galilee and vow on Trumpeldor's grave to continue his way, the way of work and defense.
>
> During the 1948 War of Independence, the Arab settlement of Ḥalsa was conquered by the Israel Defense Forces. In the place of this village from which the murderers of Yosef Trumpeldor and his comrades came, a large Jewish settlement was built [and was named] Kiryat Shmona [the City of the Eight], after the eight heroes of Tel Ḥai.[30]

Along similar lines Zionist collective memory reconstructed Masada and the Bar Kokhba revolt as sources of inspiration for the renewed Hebrew nation. The death encountered in both events becomes a connecting tissue to the Zionist national "rebirth." The symbolic bridge between Antiquity and the modern National Revival (illustrated in figure 2) transforms death into a temporary regression redeemed by return and renewal. The Zionist commemoration of these events suggests that the modern resettlement of Palestine has symbolically liberated the Masada defenders and the Bar Kokhba rebels from the historical constraints of their immediate situation.

The challenge of the finality of death through the introduction of the concept of renewal is made explicit in a children's story entitled *Tehilat Metsada* (The Glory of Masada). The author first presents the notion of "end" as problematic and then attempts to resolve this ambiguity:

> This was the end of Masada, the fortress of supreme heroism. But this was not the end of the revolt. There is an end that is in essence a

> beginning. Such was the glorified end of Masada. Because at the very moment that the last Jew fell on his sword at Masada and the fierce battle reached its end, the Jewish people began to live again. How could it be?[31]

The author then explains that Josephus's account of the end of the Masada people "spread all over the country and beyond, and revived the rest of the Jewish nation, even though others believed that this nation was doomed forever."

The same idea was articulated by Yigael Yadin in a speech to new recruits of the Armored Corps during a ceremony at Masada.

> We will not exaggerate by saying that, thanks to the heroism of the Masada fighters, like other links in our nation's chain of heroism, we stand here today, the soldiers of a young-ancient people, surrounded by the ruins of the camps of those who destroyed us. We stand here, no longer helpless in the face of our enemy's strength, no longer fighting a desperate war, but solid and confident, knowing that now our fate is in our hands . . . We, the descendants of these heroes, stand here today and rebuild the ruins of our people.[32]

Like other national myths the commemorative narratives of the fall of Masada, the Bar Kokhba revolt, and the battle of Tel Ḥai reframe death as leading to rebirth: the loss of individual life contributes to the survival of the collectivity.[33] Patriotic death thus becomes a form of sacrifice that is rewarded within the larger context of the nation's history. If the religious sacrifice mediates between man and divinity, as Hubert and Mauss suggest,[34] the death of those who die "on the altar of the homeland" mediates between the citizen and the nation. As a source of inspiration to future generations, it thus generates a sense of continuity.

Narrative time thus takes liberties in shrinking the temporal distance of seven months (from the battle of Tel Ḥai until the return to it), three decades (from that battle until Kiryat Shmona was built), or eighteen to nineteen centuries (from the fall of Masada and the defeat of the Bar Kokhba revolt to the Zionist settlement of Palestine) by constructing a direct commemorative sequence between these events. This strategy offers a more ideologically appropriate conclusion to events associated with the national periods, thereby avoiding tensions between the commemoration of specific events and the Zionist master commemorative narrative.

Yet the concept of renewal is not always successful in transforming death into survival. This becomes apparent in the following examples from my interviews. One person said, "Thanks to [Masada], many Jews may have *continued to survive*, who did like them . . . and *died heroically;*" and another informant asserted: "It is heroic that they could live there about three years . . . that they weren't discouraged for so long. If you want to teach your children to love the country, you have to do it through past generations. And this is an example of people who did everything *to remain* in the country" (emphasis added). The incoherence of these statements stems from the informants' reference to both death and survival in line with the accepted mythical meaning. A student answered my question as to how the revolt ended, saying that it was defeated. Later, in the context of discussing the Lag ba-Omer celebration, the same student struggled, not quite successfully, to integrate the two reconstructions of the ending: "One calls it 'victory' but . . . this is a kind of victory which they [the rebels] did not manage to hold on to for long. They succeeded, they, like, had a victory with defeat . . . One celebrates it as a victory, but one doesn't look at how it continued!"

The tensions underlying such statements disclose a cultural ambivalence regarding the finality of death and defeat that the commemorative narratives attempt to suppress. Beneath the explicit message of survival and renewal, the knowledge that the historical records relate to death, suicide, retreat, and exile—even if this information is belittled or left out of the commemorative narratives—contributes to their dramatic intensity. As part 4 of this study shows, these tensions were later brought into the limelight by the emergence of countercommemorative narratives.[35] The strategies of curtailing and expanding the end, which were earlier accepted as given, have recently become the subject of political controversies, shaking the foundation of the myth plot structures that underlie the activist commemoration of these events.

In light of the particular significance of the end, it is not surprising that the delineation of the narrative boundaries often emerges as a major point of contestation as far as commemorative narratives are concerned. In the three cases I have explored here, political controversies emerged around the issue of endings, as various individuals and groups challenged the "lessons" of the past promoted by the activist commemorative narratives formed in the prestate and early-state periods. In no case did such a controversy follow the discovery of hitherto unknown historical facts that called for reinterpretation. In fact, the critics drew attention to information that was previously known yet was marginalized within the commemoration of that past. Their insistence on relocating the narrative endings at a different point in history challenged the memory of the "event" as it was previously shaped in the commemorative narratives.

Turning Points and Multiple Meanings

By insisting upon new endings, the critics of the three myths called for the reinterpretation of the historical events and the reevaluation of their symbolic significance. Their challenge was, in fact, broader than the specific construction of these endings: it essentially targeted the myth plot structure that governed their creation. By moving from the specific details to the myth structure, the critics also contested the mythical status of those events and its impact on the perception of the present. In spite of the academic discourse that dominated some of these debates, their focus and orientation were no doubt determined by current political issues. Thus, concern about the politics of the present, as much as the memory of the past fueled the controversies over the construction of the ending. The debates addressed sensitive issues with which Israeli society continues to struggle: death and renewal, exile and return, territorial gain and loss, defeat and victory, and above all, the meaning of survival.

Like parables the commemorative narratives offer the possibility of distancing critical issues relating to the present, into the past. But the controversies also stem from an awareness that the collective memory of the past contributes to the shaping of the perception of the present. Indeed, the practice of creating analogies between the past and the present is quite prevalent in contemporary Israeli culture (as manifested in political satires, plays, television discussions, and lectures), even though the validity of such analogies is often questioned.

I suggested earlier that turning points are particularly interesting for the study of collective memory because their liminal position within the master commemorative narrative allows greater ambiguity in their interpretation than the culture itself is ready to acknowledge. More than other events, turning points reveal that the meaning of events is, to a large extent, constructed by their commemorative context.

The construction of the memory of the three events discussed here was functional in reinforcing the Zionist master commemorative narrative. The fall of Masada and the Bar Kokhba revolt could highlight the departure from Exile because they still occurred in Antiquity, when the Jews lived in their own homeland. The elevation of these events as heroic myths therefore dramatized the historical rupture between Antiquity and Exile, demonstrating the change that took place when the ancient Israelites were exiled from their land. The battle of Tel Ḥai emerged as a secular national myth of new origins because it occurred early enough in the Zionist era to dramatize the desired break from Exile. Its location as a turning point thus helped highlight the historical rupture between Exile and National Revival.

The recent debates on the meaning of the myths reflect the weakening of the Zionist master commemorative narrative and the deeper cleavages within contemporary Israeli society. During the formative years of Israeli society, Zionism could produce a master commemorative narrative that provided a shared political framework for the Yishuv and that marginalized the non-Zionist views of the past. But Israeli collective memory can no longer be taken as a given. We now witness a weakened collective memory that confronts other memories and is forced to face their interpretations of the past. Various groups within Israeli society, such as Middle Eastern Jews, Orthodox and ultra-Orthodox Jews, and Israeli Arabs, challenge the authority of the secular national commemorative narratives constructed by the European settlers during the first decades of this century, and demand greater representation of their divergent views of the past.

The growing political assertiveness of groups whose voice was largely marginalized during earlier decades has gradually weakened the image of the New Hebrew, fashioned by the secular eastern European Jews at the beginning of the century. In a society in which ethnicity has become a major political factor, a Russian Jewish hero can no longer serve as a self-evident collective representation of "the Israeli." The humorous lore articulates this discrepancy by pointing out Trumpeldor's identity as an eastern European Jewish immigrant who resembles more the Jews of Exile than contemporary Israelis. In fact, his earlier glorification as the prototypical New Hebrew can now be seen as a function of the hegemony of eastern European Jews in the Yishuv; the continued efforts to preserve his mythical image can be regarded as evidence of their desire to perpetuate it. An Israeli man of Middle Eastern descent told me in an interview, "Honey, if Trumpeldor were a Yemenite, no street would have been named after him!"

As we have seen, the interpretation of the three events as national myths was to a great extent shaped by the Zionist construction of a binary opposition between the national periods and Exile. The debates over their commemoration, however, reflect significant changes in Israelis' growing interest in Jewish history and tradition during Exile. Although the periodization of the Zionist master commemorative narrative, emphasizing the bond between the nation and the land, still structures the perception of the past, the earlier emphasis on a sharp contrast between Exile and the national periods has clearly weakened.

The more positive attitude toward Exile is now evident in a desire to understand better both the richness of Jewish life and the traumas of persecution during that period. This is evident in the proliferation of autobiographical works, novels, and films relating to Jewish life in Europe and the Middle East prior to the immigration to Israel, and the revival of religious customs and communal festivals that originated in Exile. The recent fad of trips to a family's birthplace abroad or places of special significance to exilic Jewish history and culture reveals a desire to recover both individual and collective roots in Exile that had previously been a cause of embarrassment, shame, or indifference. Sephardic Jews' strong identification with the "golden age" in Spain prior to the 1492 expulsion not only indicates a reversal of *shelilat ha-galut* (repudiation of Exile); it also provides them with a distinct past that challenges the exclusive role of Antiquity as a national golden age. Israelis' increased interest in the commemoration of the Holocaust and attempt to understand its impact on their collective experience manifest a sharp contrast to the earlier emphasis on mental distance between them and the Holocaust victims.

This weakening of the binary opposition between the national periods and Exile is clearly evident in the emergence of counternarratives relating to the specific events discussed here. While the earlier activist interpretations of these events emphasized the contrast with Exile, the liminal location of these turning points made it possible also to present patterns of historical continuity with it. In the three cases, the counternarratives challenged earlier readings of the past by adapting the grim plot structure that highlights the association with Exile.

Turning points can thus provide the commemorative flexibility that allows for multiple, even contradictory, meanings. Masada can be interpreted as representing the ancient spirit of resistance to the enemy, emphasizing its sharp contrast to the exilic pattern of martyrdom, but also the traditional pattern of martyrdom in face of persecution (Kiddush ha-Shem), associated primarily with Exile. In the same vein, counternarratives of Tel Ḥai and the Bar Kokhba revolt dismiss the activist myth plot structure, glorifying the stand of a few against many, and emphasize an indefensible situation in which an effort to raise armed resistance leads to a futile sacrifice and greater destruction. Such portrayals come dangerously close to the grim descriptions of the vulnerability of Jewish life in Exile. Thus, whereas Zionist collective memory favored emphasizing deep historical ruptures between the national periods and Exile, the countermemories illuminate patterns of continuity within Jewish history, typical of all three periods.

The Frailty of Invented Tradition

The emergence of countermemories and the greater visibility that they enjoy in contemporary Israeli culture have become so pronounced during the last two decades that Israeli discourse has labeled this phenomenon *niputs mitosim* (shattering of myths). While some Israelis regard this process of "demythologization" as a necessary response to the excessive glorification of the national periods by earlier generations, others consider the shattering of myths a subversive act that undermines the sacred foundations of Israeli society. It is not surprising, therefore, that the publication of new critical works about historical events or figures often provokes controversies similar to those described in this book.

The emergence of counternarratives that defy the earlier drive to create a modern Hebrew national tradition raises further thoughts on the nature of invented tradition. While any tradition is socially constructed, the concept of invented tradition suggests a more conscious attempt to produce new cultural forms that seem as if they are of older origin. The formation of such cultural forms is designed to support social and political changes with the legitimacy of "tradition." But invented tradition can be successful only as long as it passes as tradition, with little or no concern about its relatively new origins. An awareness of its deliberate construction inevitably undermines its acceptance as tradition.

The strength of the national Hebrew culture of the prestate period lay in its successful production of new commemorative narratives and rituals that were easily accepted as traditional. In this case, the success did not stem from a totalitarian regime's forceful imposition of new cultural forms to propagate its ideology. Rather, it was the product of ideologically motivated, collaborative efforts by educators, writers, politicians, ordinary settlers, and Hebrew youth. The emergence of a national tradition was seen as a sign of the vitality of the Zionist National Revival and evidence of its future success. Even when controversy developed around the Tel Ḥai myth during the Yishuv period, the disagreement did not focus on the legitimacy of its constructed nature but on its interpretation. In the last two decades the debates on the commemoration of the three events have also addressed the very process of their "mythologization."

The popular discourse on Tel Ḥai is particularly interesting because it reveals the vulnerability of national traditions to public suspicions about their intentional fabrication. Whereas the founding generation hailed the process of turning history into a legend (*agada*) as a major contribution to the emergence of a secular national Hebrew tradition, the process of "legendizing" ultimately undermined the credibility of this tradition. Trumpeldor's public image began to suffer from a "loss of character," being now perceived as a two dimensional, cardboard figure lacking human qualities.[36] Trumpeldor therefore became a two-dimensional, cardboard character. Given this transformation, the discovery of the human figure behind the legendary image was used as a publicity pitch for Shulamit Laskov's 1972 biography which praised the portrayal of the hero as a flesh-and-blood man.[37] Laskov's biography received an award for military history upon its publication. In its public statement the selecting committee pointed out the merit of this historical work as a contribution to the ailing legend:

> Shulamit Laskov's book, which was written fifty-two years after his death, evokes a forgotten hero. It provides his life with a realistic quality, a quality by which one can educate no less than by the halo of a legend . . . Shulamit Laskov's biography does not abuse the Trumpeldor legend. It illuminates it, explains it, and it becomes better clarified and understood and more humane.[38]

Yet Laskov's biography, although it was well received, was not enough to dispel the public questioning of the historical validity of the Tel Ḥai commemorative narrative. Israelis' awareness of Trumpeldor's glorification by his contemporaries has contributed to growing skepticism about the authenticity of his last words, "It is good to die for our country," which became an educational motto and a national slogan during the prestate and early-state periods. As we saw in chapter 9, a new humorous version of Trumpeldor's words has replaced this lofty statement with a crude curse in Russian that Trumpeldor had supposedly uttered before he died. Even though historical evidence seems to support the earlier version, the view that it was fabricated later is quite pervasive. An Israeli-born teacher whom I interviewed expressed her objection to what she considered the excessive constructedness of the Tel Ḥai commemorative narrative: "It is typical of the Jews that if they finally have a hero, his own heroism is not sufficient; they have to 'decorate' it further . . . Wasn't it enough that his arm was amputated and that he organized the people around him so well when he was wounded . . . They didn't need to add 'It is good to die for our country.' And now, as it turns out, this isn't true." The popular view thus considers the curse as "history" and discredits the earlier commemorative narrative as a "legend," in spite of the historical evidence to the contrary.

The changing meaning of the term *agada* is important because it indicates a new conception of the relationship between "history" and "legend" and discloses the problems facing a new tradition. During the prestate and early-state periods the term indicated an attitude of veneration toward the dead hero and the recognition of the importance of this narrative as a cornerstone of a new national tradition. Several decades later, when the same Hebrew term is applied again to the Tel Ḥai commemorative narrative, it alters its meaning, now discrediting that same narrative as fictitious and false. Whereas the historical and the legendary aspects of the new tradition were earlier praised as complementary, the "legendary" now appears to diminish the value of the "historical."

These changes reveal a growing Israeli concern about the blending of history and memory in the process of constructing a national tradition. Although the explicit discourse revolves around the authenticity of Trumpeldor's saying, the relatively little impact of historical research on the public's view of his last words indicates that the crux of the matter lies not in the historical validity of the Tel Ḥai commemorative narrative but in its credibility.[39] The scholarly support of Trumpeldor's last words cannot dispel pervasive doubts about its authenticity. Although the version of Trumpeldor's curse probably began as a joke, it has taken root in Israeli popular culture because it is currently considered a more believable representation of historical reality than his reported statement. Such developments demonstrate how "history" and "legend" are culturally constructed and subject to change, articulating the credibility of their representations of the past at a certain point in time.

It is quite possible that the increased role of the state as a custodian of national memory has actually contributed to the decline of the national Hebrew tradition constructed during the pre-state period. The bureaucratization (and, at times, commercialization) that this process entails has undermined the more spontaneous appeal of earlier rituals. Furthermore, the government's visibility in this domain has made the public more aware of the constructed character of these commemorative traditions and has drawn attention to their political implications. The growing divisions within Israeli society and the government's initiatives in the domain of public ritual enhance the awareness of partisan cooptation of national memory. The marked difference between the public's response to the two state funerals for the excavated bones identified as the "Masada defenders" and the "Bar Kokhba warriors" indicates the growing skepticism and cynicism in relation to state-sponsored commemorative activities.

The case of Tel Ḥai demonstrates also the impact of the interaction of collective and autobiographical memory as far as invented tradition is concerned. When the first controversy about Tel Ḥai broke out, leading figures who had been active players in the historical event took part in that debate. Since they had a personal as well as a collective stake in the construction of its memory, the autobiographical dimension clearly added fervor to the political dispute. During the second Tel Ḥai debate the personal dimension was still evident, but to a much lesser degree. The second generation, who remembered the rise of the myth rather than the historical event itself, took the lead in that public argument. From this perspective, the current Israeli attitude toward Trumpeldor reflects the ambiguity that underlies his liminal position as far as memory is concerned: his image evokes both a feeling of cultural intimacy (he is the representative of the founders' generation) and social distance (he is two generations removed from middle-aged Israelis). The proliferation of humorous lore about him is one of the expressions of this tension, which is missing in the cases of Bar Kokhba and the Masada men: their images, constructed through the collective recovery of memory, are clearly a part of the mythical past for contemporary Israelis.

From Collective Memory to Multiple Memories

The study of the commemoration of the battle of Tel Ḥai, the Bar Kokhba revolt, and the fall of Masada demonstrates the dynamic character of collective memory and its continuous dialogue with history. It reveals how collective memory, which can help construct the nation's identity during its formative years, can turn into a contested arena that highlights social and political divisions.

Israeli culture today encompasses a greater diversity of commemorative narratives that offer different interpretations of the past. These multiple texts may at times coexist without apparent tension; at other times they become subjects of intense debate. The growing diversity within the society and the increased pressures from within and without have challenged the hegemony of the commemorations that crystallized during the prestate and early-state periods and gave rise to multiple commemorative texts. Indeed, it should not come as a surprise that a society divided over the conflict with the Palestinians and neighboring Arab states and strained by the mass immigration of Ethiopian and Russian Jews, the religious-secular conflict, and ethnic tensions, would generate more than one version of its past.

The analysis of the politics of commemoration relating to the three events indicates that the development of symbolic texts is neither linear nor uniform. The intensification of an internal political dispute over Tel Ḥai in the late 1970s and early 1980s was, in fact, instrumental to injecting new blood into the myth after a period of relative decline. The power of the myth to confront present issues through the discussion of the past evoked a new political interest in it. The myth resurfaced as an active political narrative and provided a framework for registering protest and frustration through its humorous inversions.

Similarly, rituals of commemoration relating to these events have been transformed, but not necessarily in a uniform fashion or direction. The relative decline of the Tel Ḥai myth has recently caused Israeli prime ministers to limit or cancel their attendance at the annual memorial ceremony at Tel Ḥai. Recent ceremonies seem to indicate that this commemoration may gradually assume a more local character, as its national component declines.

The commemorative rituals at Masada now offer a new emphasis on the national-religious significance of the site, manifested in the bar mitzvah rituals as well as in pilgrims' use of the excavated synagogue for prayer. This added religious dimension, coupled with the now famous archeological excavations, has moved Masada beyond the youth culture and its more local Israeli fame. Masada has become a place of pilgrimage for Jews outside and inside Israel and an internationally known tourist attraction; at the same time, it has lost some of its earlier appeal for Israelis.

Lag ba-Omer bonfires continue to enjoy wide popularity, especially among families with young children and the youth. Yet the older tradition of pilgrimage to Mount Meron, revolving around the figure of Rabbi Shimon Bar Yoḥai, once owned by observant Jews, is attracting a growing number of participants and receives wider publicity in Israeli media. This religious celebration has therefore come to be a viable alternative to the secular national emphasis on Bar Kokhba and his revolt. It also serves to illustrate the growing cultural visibility of Orthodox and ultra-Orthodox Israelis who reject (some or all) premises of secular national Hebrew culture, and immigrants of the postindependence era who subscribe to its premises only partially.

Although countermemories now challenge the primacy of the Zionist collective memory as developed within the Yishuv and the early-state periods, the earlier commemorative narratives have by no means lost their significance within Israeli culture. Side by side with the emergence of counternarratives, the society continues to transmit the older commemorative narratives and reinforce them by the performance of its "traditional" Hebrew literature and rituals. Although the Tel Ḥai commemorative narrative has clearly lost the prominence it enjoyed earlier, it is still embraced by many Israelis as part of an important legacy of the pioneering period. Similarly, for most secular Israelis the Bar Kokhba revolt is still associated primarily with the merry celebration of Lag ba-Omer more than with the fast of Tish'a be-Av, and Bar Kokhba has remained a heroic figure of the ancient past. Despite the relative decline of these myths, youth movements, school classes, army units, and private families take trips to Tel Ḥai and Masada in recognition of their historical and educational value.

The multiplicity of texts about the past is not only evident among various groups within the society, but also in individuals' engagement in different, even conflicting, commemorations of the past in different situations. This phenomenon can be observed in shifts from the activist to the tragic commemoration of Masada, the dual meaning of "legend" in reference to the Tel Ḥai commemorative narrative, and the changing allusions to Bar Kokhba's "victory" and "defeat." In different contexts people draw upon the cultural resources at their disposal, often without noticing the tensions between their various references to the same event.

The emergence of humorous lore relating to the past is a particularly interesting form of countermemory. These texts debunk the myth, but the playful, nonserious framework helps blur the ideological import of their challenge. Although my analysis of jokes highlighted their subversive nature, Israelis who tell Trumpeldor jokes do not see this activity as unpatriotic. One of my best sources for these jokes was an elementary school teacher who, in his capacity as an educator, also engages in the formal transmission of the myth texts. Others were a war widow and an air force career officer. These individuals clearly saw no tension between their patriotism and the jokes they were telling me about Trumpeldor.

The emergence of conflicting interpretations of the past reflects the vitality of memory in contemporary Israeli culture. The multiplicity of texts and the debates on the past indicate that contemporary Israeli culture has become more pluralistic and that Israelis display a greater readiness to examine critically the essence of their collective identity and multiple roots. Israeli public discourse continues to deal with issues of the past because of the awareness of its impact on the shaping of the present. The emergence of competing versions of the past and the moral claims regarding its use are central issues that continue to occupy contemporary Israelis as they negotiate the meaning of the present within the framework of their understanding of the past.

NOTES

Introduction

1. Interviews with the children were conducted in two general (secular) and two religious public schools in the Tel Aviv district; interviews with the parents were conducted at their homes.

Chapter 1: The Dynamics of Collective Remembering

1. Carl L. Becker, "What Are Historical Facts?" in Phil L. Snyder, ed., *Detachment and the Writing of History: Essays and Letters of Carl L. Becker* (Ithaca: Cornell University Press, 1958), 61.

2. Maurice Halbwachs, *La Mémoire collective* (1950), trans. F. J. and V. Y. Ditter, *The Collective Memory* (New York: Harper & Row, 1980), esp. 50–87. See also his *Les cadres sociaux de la mémoire* (1925), English translation and introduction by Lewis A. Coser, *Maurice Halbwachs: On Collective Memory* (Chicago: University of Chicago Press, 1992), 37–189.

3. Halbwachs, *Collective Memory*, 86.

4. Whereas autobiographical memory relates to events that the individual experiences firsthand, collective memory also encompasses events of a past that were not directly experienced by an individual but are transmitted by others. However, Halbwachs points out that the two forms of memory interact, as the practice of dating personal experiences through societal markers (such as wars) indicates; *Collective Memory*, 44–49.

5. See, for example, Barry Schwartz, "The Social Context of Commemoration: A Study in Collective Memory," *Social Forces* 61 (1982): 374–402; Pierre Nora (sous la direction de), *Les Lieux de mémoire*, vol. 1, *La République* (Paris: Gallimard, 1984); David Lowenthal, *The Past Is a Foreign Country* (Cambridge: Cambridge University Press, 1985); Barry Schwartz, Yael Zerubavel, and Bernice Barnett, "The Recovery of Masada: A Study in Collective Memory," *Sociological Quarterly* 27, no. 2 (1986):

147–64; Patrick H. Hutton, "Collective Memory and Collective Mentalities: The Halbwachs-Ariès Connection," *Historical Reflections/Réflexions Historiques* 15, no. 2 (1988): 311–22; Paul Connerton, *How Societies Remember* (Cambridge: Cambridge University Press, 1989); Michael Kammen, *Mystic Chords of Memory* (New York: Knopf, 1991); John R. Gillis, ed., *Commemorations: The Politics of National Identity* (Princeton: Princeton University Press, 1994).

6. Halbwachs, *Collective Memory*, esp. 78–87.

7. Ibid., 78–83. Yosef Hayim Yerushalmi's observation about the decline of Jewish memory with the rise of a modern, secular interest in Jewish history in the nineteenth century reinforces the same view; *Zakhor: Jewish History and Jewish Memory* (Seattle: University of Washington Press, 1982).

8. Pierre Nora, "Between Memory and History: Les Lieux de Mémoire," *Representations* 26 (1989): 8.

9. Ibid., 12.

10. Patrick H. Hutton, *History as an Art of Memory* (Hanover, N.H.: University Press of New England, 1993), 73–90.

11. See R. G. Collingwood, *The Idea of History* (Oxford: Clarendon, 1946), 236–49; Becker, "What Are Historical Facts?" E. H. Carr, *What Is History?* (New York: Penguin Books, 1971); Hayden White, *The Content of the Form: Narrative Discourse and Historical Representation* (Baltimore: Johns Hopkins University Press, 1987).

12. Amos Funkenstein, *Tadmit ve-Toda'a Historit ba-Yahadut uvi-Sevivata ha-Tarbutit* (Perceptions of Jewish history from Antiquity to the present) (Tel Aviv: Am Oved, 1991), 28.

13. Schwartz, "Social Context of Commemoration," 393. See also Schwartz, Zerubavel, and Barnett, "Recovery of Masada," 149–51, 158–61; Michael Schudson, "The Present in the Past versus the Past in the Present," *Communication* 11 (1989): 105–13; and Lewis A. Coser, introduction to *Maurice Halbwachs*. Hutton, who discusses the tension between Halbwachs's theoretical position on this issue and his study of the topography of the Holy Land, concludes that he was a "historian of memory despite himself"; *History as an Art of Memory*, 80–84.

14. See also Natalie Zemon Davis and Randolph Starn, introduction to a special issue on collective memory and countermemory, *Representations* 26 (Spring 1989): 5.

15. Geoffrey H. Hartman points out that the public's oversaturation with docudramas and other media productions of memory creates a paradoxical situation where these productions overpower our sense of reality and of history. Hartman refers to this process as "derealization"; "Public Memory and Modern Experience," *Yale Journal of Criticism* 6 (1993): 240.

16. Halbwachs, *Collective Memory*, 82. See also Nora's statement that the *lieux de mémoire* survive by virtue of their capacity for change; "Between Memory and History," 19.

17. See Émile Durkheim's discussion of commemorative rituals in *The Elementary Forms of the Religious Life*, (1915); English translation by Joseph Ward Swain (New York: Free Press, 1965), 414–33.

18. Toni Morrison, *Beloved* (New York: Knopf, 1987).

19. See also Yael Zerubavel, "The Holiday Cycle and the Commemoration of the Past: Folklore, History, and Education," in *Proceedings of the Ninth World Congress of Jewish Studies* (Jerusalem: World Union of Jewish Studies, 1986), 4:111–18.

20. White, *Content of the Form*, 42. See also Louis O. Mink, "Narrative Form as a Cognitive Instrument," in Robert H. Canary and Henry Kozicki, eds., *The Writing of History: Literary Form and Historical Understanding* (Madison: University of Wisconsin Press, 1978), 143; Lowenthal, *Past Is a Foreign Country*, 219–24.

21. See White's distinction between "the discourse of the real" and "the discourse of the imaginable" in *Content of the Form*, 20; see also his earlier discussion in *Tropics of Discourse: Essays in Cultural Criticism* (Baltimore: Johns Hopkins University Press, 1978), 51–80, 81–100; and Mink, "Narrative Form as a Cognitive Instrument," 144–45.

22. Jean François Lyotard's contention about the death of the metanarrative as a source of legitimation of the postmodernist society holds a great literary appeal; *The Post-modernist Condition: A Report on Knowledge*, English translation by Geoff Bennington and Brian Massunmi (Minneapolis: University of Minnesota Press, 1984). Yet I believe that a basic human need to construct meaning through the creation of stories continues to reassert itself on both an individual and a collective level. Thus, even in experiences of trauma that break down memory, individuals may generate new narratives that work to disguise ruptures of forgetfulness. Even the technologically advanced society may need a master narrative, although it is quite likely to reshape it to fit its changing needs.

23. In discussing the nature of nationalism, Hans Kohn states that "nationalism is a state of mind, permeating the majority of a people and claiming to permeate all its members"; *The Idea of Nationalism* (New York: Macmillan, 1944), 16. Benedict Anderson and Homi Bhabha further elaborate on the constructed nature of the nation as an "imagined political community"; Benedict Anderson, *Imagined Communities: Reflections on the Origin and Spread of Nationalism* (London: Verso, 1983), esp. 14–16, 31; Homi K. Bhabha, "DissemiNation: Time, Narrative, and the Margins of the Modern Nation," in Homi K. Bhabha, ed., *Nation and Narration* (London: Routledge, 1990), 290–322.

24. In contrast to the prevailing association of modernity with temporal linearity, Eviatar Zerubavel demonstrates how a cyclical conception of time still governs much of modern everyday life; *Hidden Rhythms: Schedules and Calendars in Social Life* (Chicago: University of Chicago Press, 1981); and *The Seven Day Circle: The History and Meaning of the Week* (New York: Free Press, 1985).

25. See Richard Terdiman, "Deconstructing Memory: On Representing the Past and Theorizing Culture in France since the Revolution," *Diacritics* 15 (Winter 1985): 28–32. Homi K. Bhabha, "DissemiNation," 297, discusses the tension between what he calls the "pedagogical" and the "performative" aspects of narrating the nation. While the pedagogical represents "the continuist, accumulative temporality," the performative presents a "repetitious, recursive strategy" of writing the nation.

26. For a discussion of the cultural significance of origins, see Mircea Eliade,

26. For a discussion of the cultural significance of origins, see Mircea Eliade, *Myth and Reality* (New York: Harper & Row, 1963), 21–53. See also W. Lloyd Warner, *The Living and the Dead: A Study in the Symbolic Life of Americans*, Yankee City series, vol. 5 (New Haven: Yale University Press, 1959), 156–225; Schwartz, "Social Context of Commemoration," 374–402.

27. As Eviatar Zerubavel suggests, the social construction of "great divides" introduces "mental gaps" to a reality that would otherwise be perceived as continuous. For a further discussion of these concepts, see *The Fine Line: Making Distinctions in Everyday Life* (New York: Free Press, 1991), 21–32. The relevance of this issue to new (or renewed) national claims is evident in Europe following the breakdown of communist regimes.

28. William A. Wilson, *Folklore and Nationalism in Modern Finland* (Bloomington: Indiana University Press, 1976); Michael Herzfeld, *Ours Once More: Folklore, Ideology, and the Making of Modern Greece* (New York: Pella, 1986); Richard Handler, *Nationalism and the Politics of Culture in Quebec* (Madison: University of Wisconsin Press, 1988); Carol Silverman, "Reconstructing Folklore: Media and Cultural Policy in Eastern Europe," *Communication* 11 (1989): 141–60.

29. Bernard Lewis provides examples from the Middle East and Africa for efforts to reshape a national past; *History: Remembered, Recovered, Invented* (Princeton: Princeton University Press, 1975).

30. Nora, "Between Memory and History," 16–17.

31. Claude Lévi-Strauss observes the creation of "hot" and "cold" chronologies as a result of the pressure of history; *La Pensée sauvage* (1962), English translation, *The Savage Mind* (Chicago: University of Chicago Press, 1970), 259–60. See also Warner, *The Living and the Dead*, 129–35; Schwartz, "Social Context of Commemoration," 375–77.

32. Sigmund Freud discusses the phenomenon of collective amnesia in *Moses and Monotheism* (1939; New York: Vintage Books, 1967). Like memory, amnesia is not a fixed state but a fluctuating process. Thus, a group may be able to recover from collective amnesia and reclaim a repressed past; see Bernard Lewis's discussion of recovering the past in *History*. On the dialectics of remembering and forgetting, see the special issue entitled "La Mémoire et l'oublie," *Communications* 49 (1989).

33. In introducing the concept "commemorative time," I expand Gerald Genette's concept of "narrative time." See his *Narrative Discourse: An Essay in Method* (Ithaca: Cornell University Press, 1980), 33–35.

34. Edward Shils observes that "great moments" are those events that are believed to have shaped later developments and hence infuse the past with sacredness; *Center and Periphery: Essays in Macrosociology* (Chicago: University of Chicago Press, 1975), 198. For an example of how a historical process is obscured by the selection of one particular event as the focal point of its ritualized commemoration, see Eviatar Zerubavel, *Terra Cognita: The Mental Discovery of America* (New Brunswick: Rutgers University Press, 1992).

35. Henry Tudor, *Political Myth* (New York: Praeger, 1972), 137–40.

36. Arnold Van Gennep, *The Rites of Passage* (1908; Chicago: University of Chicago Press, 1960), 11.

37. Victor W. Turner, *The Ritual Process: Structure and Anti-Structure* (Harmondsworth, Middlesex: Penguin Books, 1974), 81.

38. See, for example, Edmund Leach, *Political Systems of Highland Burma* (Boston: Beacon Press, 1954); Bruce Kapferer's analysis of how competing views of the past fueled bloodshed in contemporary Sri Lanka, in *Legends of People, Myths of State: Violence, Intolerance, and Political Culture in Sri Lanka and Australia* (Washington, DC: Smithsonian Institution Press, 1988); Peter Van Der Veer, "Ayodhya and Somnath: Eternal Shrines, Contested Histories," *Social Research* 59, no. 1 (1992): 85–109.

39. See Michel Foucault, *Language, Counter-memory, Practice: Selected Essays and Interviews*, trans. and ed. Donald F. Bouchard (Ithaca: Cornell University Press, 1977). See also George Lipsitz's discussion of the use of this term, in *Time Passages: Collective Memory and American Popular Culture* (Minneapolis: University of Minnesota Press, 1989), 213.

40. See Silverman, "Reconstructing Folklore," 141–60.

41. Leonard Thompson, *The Political Mythology of Apartheid* (New Haven: Yale University Press, 1985).

Chapter 2: The Zionist Reconstruction of the Past

1. Theodor Herzl's vision of a Jewish state was first published in German, *Der Judenstaat: Versuch einer modernen Lösung der Judenfrage* (The Jewish state: An attempt at a modern solution of the Jewish question). Although Leo Pinsker published his *Autoemancipation* in German in 1882, outlining similar ideas, Herzl's leadership as the founder and head of the World Zionist Organization made his views more widely known. According to David Vital, seventeen editions of Herzl's work were published between 1896 and 1904, and it was translated into Hebrew, English, Yiddish, French, Romanian, and Bulgarian; *The Origins of Zionism* (Oxford: Oxford University Press, 1975), 259–66.

2. Ben Halpern, *The Idea of the Jewish State* (Cambridge: Harvard University Press, 1961), 55–94; Vital, *Origins of Zionism*, 201–45.

3. The First Aliya was initiated by the followers of the Ḥibat Tsiyon (love of Zion) movement, a forerunner of the Zionist movement. Various groups affiliated with this movement were active in Russia and Romania, two countries that had increased their oppressive policies toward Jews; see Vital, *Origins of Zionism*, 49–186; Arthur Hertzberg, ed., *The Zionist Idea: A Historical Analysis and Reader* (New York: Meridian Books, 1960), 40–45.

4. The poet Ḥayim Naḥman Bialik was sent to Kishinev to collect testimonies from the pogrom survivors. For excerpts see Yisrael Heilperin, ed., *Sefer ha-Gevura: Antologia Historit Sifrutit* (The book of heroism: A historical literary anthology) (Tel Aviv: Am Oved, 1941), 3:4–27. See also Bialik's powerful poem "Be-Ir ha-Harega" (In the city of slaughter), which was written under the impact of this pogrom, re-

printed in *Shirim* (Poems) (Tel Aviv: Dvir, 1966), 350–60; English translation by A. M. Klein, in Alan Mintz, *Ḥurban: Responses to Catastrophe in Hebrew Literature* (New York: Columbia University Press, 1984), 132–41; and Ya'akov Cahan's "Shir ha-Biryonim" (The song of the Zealots), in *Kitvei Ya'akov Cahan* (Collected works) (1903; Tel Aviv: Hotsa'at Va'ad ha-Yovel, 1948), 2:13–17.

5. On the emergence of political Zionism, see Vital, *Origins of Zionism*, 233–370. On the brand of so-called Spiritual or Cultural Zionism, advocated by Aḥad Ha-Am (aka Asher Tsvi Ginsberg) in opposition to Theodor Herzl's Political Zionism, see Hertzberg, *Zionist Idea*, 249–77; Halpern, *Idea of the Jewish State*, 20–27; Shmuel Almog, *Zionism and History: The Rise of a New Jewish Consciousness* (New York: St. Martin's, 1987), 84–176.

6. Vital, *Origins of Zionism*, 368 (Vital's translation).

7. Halpern, *Idea of the Jewish State*, 25–31; Almog, *Zionism and History*, 252–53. Later, Chaim Weizmann's concept of "synthetic Zionism" was designed to suggest the Zionist movement's double goal of pursuing resettlement and diplomatic efforts for approval of a national home for the Jews in Palestine.

8. Ehud Luz, *Makbilim Nifgashim: Dat u-Le'umiut ba-Tenu'a ha-Tsiyonit be-Mizraḥ Eiropa be-Reshita, 1882–1904* (Religion and nationalism in the early Zionist movement) (Tel Aviv: Am Oved, 1985), 233–34, 269–98. On the development of Orthodox anti-Zionist stance in Palestine, see Menaḥem Friedman, *Ḥevra va-Dat: Ha-Ortodoxia ha-Lo Tsiyonit be-Eretz Yisrael, 1918–1936* (Society and religion: The non-Zionist orthodoxy in Palestine) (Jerusalem: Yad Yitzḥak Ben-Zvi, 1978).

9. On nationalist-religious thought see Hertzberg, *Zionist Idea*, 397–465; Halpern, *Idea of the Jewish State*, 81–94; Arnold M. Eisen, *Galut: Modern Jewish Reflection on Homelessness and Homecoming* (Bloomington: Indiana University Press, 1986), 105–14. On the early development of the religious Zionist movement, see Luz, *Makbilim Nifgashim*, 299–335.

10. Dan Horowitz and Moshe Lissak, *Mi-Yishuv li-Medina* (The origins of Israeli polity) (Tel Aviv: Am Oved, 1977), 182–83.

11. *Zion* refers to both Jerusalem and the Land of Israel. The use of the German term *Zionismus* (Zionism) as a political concept is attributed to a Jewish writer and activist by the name of Nathan Birnbaum (1864–1937). See Vital, *Origins of Zionism*, 222.

12. Almog, *Zionism and History*, 238–304.

13. Yerushalmi, *Zakhor*, 42–45; for a discussion of the Exodus as a paradigm of liberation that emphasizes its function as a historical turning point, see Michael Walzer, *Exodus and Revolution* (New York: Basic Books, 1985).

14. For the development of the concept of *galut* in Jewish thought, see Yitzḥak F. Baer, *Galut* (New York: Schocken, 1947), and Eisen, *Galut.* See also Eliezer Schweid, *Mi-Yahadut le-Tsiyonut, mi-Tsiyonut le-Yahadut* (Between Judaism and Zionism) (Jerusalem: Ha-Sifriya ha-Tsiyonit, 1983), 155–60.

15. Yosef Braslavi [Braslavsky], "Milḥama ve-Hitgonenut shel Yehudei Eretz Yisrael ad Mas'ei ha-Tselav" (War and defense of Palestinian Jews until the Crusades), *Maḥanayim* 41 (Ḥanukka issue, 1960): 57–68.

16. See, for example, Robert Chazan, *European Jews and the First Crusade* (Berkeley: University of California Press, 1987).

17. Halpern, *Idea of the Jewish State*, 70–71; Almog, *Zionism and History*, 26–29, 108–17; Schweid, *Mi-Yahadut le-Tsiyonut*, 155; Rachel Elboim-Dror, *Ha-Ḥinukh ha-Ivri be-Eretz Yisrael, 1854–1914* (Hebrew education in Palestine) (Jerusalem: Yad Yitzḥak Ben-Zvi, 1986), 1:361; Ruth Firer, *Sokhnim shel ha-Ḥinukh ha-Tsiyoni* (The agents of Zionist education) (Ḥaifa: Ḥaifa University Press; Tel Aviv: Sifriyat ha-Po'alim, 1985), 19.

18. Aḥad Ha-Am, the proponent of Cultural Zionism, similarly held a critical view of exilic Judaism yet insisted that Jewish national revival should begin with a spiritual-cultural renaissance. The territorialist orientation within the Zionist movement, on the other hand, saw the solution for the acute situation of European Jews in their resettlement in a territory of their own, and not necessarily in Zion. See also Eisen's discussion of Aḥad Ha-Am in *Galut*, 69–80, and Almog on both issues in *Zionism and History*, 129–41, 238–304.

19. Yosef Gorni, "Yaḥasa shel Mifleget Po'alei Tsiyon be-Eretz Yisrael la-Gola bi-Tekufat ha-Aliya ha-Sheniya" (The attitude of "Poalei Zion" of Palestine to Exile during the Second Aliya), in *Ha-Tsiyonut* 2:74–89; Firer, *Sokhnim shel ha-Ḥinukh ha-Tsiyoni*, 93–94; Jonathan Frankel, "The 'Yizkor' Book of 1911: A Note on National Myths in the Second Aliya," in *Religion, Ideology, and Nationalism in Europe and America: Essays Presented in Honor of Yehoshua Arieli* (Jerusalem: Historical Society of Israel and the Zalman Shazar Center for Jewish History, 1986), 368; David Biale, *Power and Powerlessness in Jewish History* (New York: Schocken, 1986), 137. See also Schweid, *Mi-Yahadut le-Tsiyonut*, 172.

20. David Ben-Gurion, "Di Ge'ula" (The redemption), *Der Yidisher Kampfer*, November 16, 1917, quoted in Gorni, "Yaḥasa shel Mifleget Po'alei Tsiyon," 77.

21. Ya'akov Zerubavel, "'Yizkor': Shivrei Ra'ayonot" (In memory: Fragmented ideas), *Ha-Aḥdut*, nos. 11–12 (1912): 30–31, quoted in Frankel, "'Yizkor' Book of 1911," 375 (Frankel's translation).

22. Ḥayim Hazaz, "Ha-Derasha" (The sermon), in *Avanim Rot'ḥot* (1942; Tel Aviv: Am Oved, 1970), 219–37; English translation by Ben Halpern, in Robert Alter, ed., *Modern Hebrew Literature* (New York: Behrman House, 1975), 274–75.

23. Eisen, *Galut*, 98; Firer, *Sokhnim shel ha-Ḥinukh ha-Tsiyoni*, 95. On the impact of this approach on the stereotypes of Israeli schoolchildren in the early 1970s, see Simon N. Herman, *Jewish Identity: A Social Psychological Perspective* (Beverly Hills: Sage Publications, 1977), 183. See also Amnon Rubinstein, *Liheyot Am Ḥofshi* (To be a free people) (Tel Aviv: Schocken, 1977), 134.

24. Ya'akov Zerubavel, "Savlanut" (Patience), *Ha-Aḥdut* no. 35 (1911), quoted by Gorni, "Yaḥasa shel Mifleget Po'alei Tsiyon," 76.

25. Y. Avner [Yitzḥak Ben-Zvi], "Ha-Yehudim veha-Pe'ula ha-Medinit" (The Jews and political action), *Ha-Aḥdut*, nos. 11–12 (1913), quoted in Gorni, "Yaḥasa shel Mifleget Po'alei Tsiyon," 76.

26. Quoted by Ya'akov Shavit, *Ha-Mitologiot shel ha-Yamin* (The mythologies of the Zionist Right) (Kfar Saba: Bet Berl, 1986), 48, n. 16.

27. M. Derr, "Min Metsada ve-Ad Ata" (From Masada to the present), *Metsada* (Masada), 25. Ya'akov Zerubavel suggested that "martyrs are remembered in the hours of helplessness; heroes are taken for an example in times of courage and action"; quoted in Frankel, "'Yizkor' Book of 1911," 375.

28. This less favorable view of martyrs' death was also supported by an argument that martyrdom involves a personal benefit, namely, gratification from belief in a divine reward after death. Conversely, death for the country constitutes a pure act of self-sacrifice for the collectivity, devoid of any benefit for oneself. See A. Z. Rabinovitch, "Hirhurim" (Reflections), *Kuntres* 72 (March 15, 1921).

29. Bialik, "Be-Ir ha-Harega," (English translation by A. M. Klein), in Mintz, *Ḥurban*, 132–41. In his discussion, Mintz points out Bialik's deliberate subversion of the traditional martyrological ideal in this poem.

30. As early as 1912, Ḥayim Tchernovitch (Rav Tsa'ir) observed that the negative attitude toward Exile became a cornerstone of Hebrew education; "Rishmei Eretz Yisrael: Matsav ha-Ḥinukh" (Impressions from the land of Israel: The state of education), *Ha-Olam*, June 10–July 2, 1912, 3–4, quoted in Frankel, "'Yizkor' Book of 1911," 376, n. 58.

31. Michael Ish-Shalom, "Anu Ḥotrim le-Atid" (We strive for the future), *Metsada* (Masada) (Jerusalem: Hitagdut ha-Setudentim ha-Revisionistim, 1934): 13.

32. On the negative representation of Exile and its passivity in Hebrew textbooks, see Firer, *Sokhnim shel ha-Ḥinukh ha-Tsiyoni*, 65–69, 94–95. Even during the 1960s, a textbook often used in the general public schools reinforced this outlook by entitling the chapter on Exile "Gola va-Sevel" (Exile and suffering). See A. Buchner, Y. Levinton, and L. Kipnis, eds., *Sefer ha-Kita Zayin* (Reader for the seventh grade) (Tel Aviv: Dvir, 1965), 362–64.

33. Quoted in Firer, *Sokhnim shel ha-Ḥinukh ha-Tsiyoni*, 95–96. See also Gorni, "Yaḥasa shel Mifleget Po'alei Tsiyon," 82.

34. Sh. Hugo Bergman, "Ha-No'ar ha-Yisraeli ve-Yahadut ha-Tefutsot" (Israeli youth and the Jews of the Dispersion), *Maḥanayim* 66 (1962): 22–23. For a critical approach to the emphasis on the passivity of the Jews of Exile, see also Funkenstein, *Tadmit ve-Toda'a historit*, 232–42; Biale, *Power and Powerlessness in Jewish History*.

35. Almog, *Zionism and History*, 45–51, 308.

36. The Young Hebrews, as the group members referred to themselves, were labeled "Canaanites" by the poet Avraham Shlonsky, a name by which they became widely known. The group, which crystallized during the 1940s around the poet Yonatan Ratosh and remained active until the early 1950s, included young writers and artists. For a study of the Canaanite ideology and its origins in radical secular Zionism, see Ya'akov Shavit, *Me-Ivri ad Kena'ani* (From Hebrew to Canaanite) (Jerusalem: Domino Press, 1984).

37. Gorni, "Yaḥasa shel Mifleget Po'alei Tsiyon," 74, 80–85.

38. Firer, *Sokhnim shel ha-Ḥinukh ha-Tsiyoni*, 44, 140–44. See the anthologies on heroism, which attempt to emphasize Jewish heroic behavior during Exile: Heilperin, *Sefer ha-Gevura* (1941), including Berl Katznelson's preface to it; Zrubavel

[Gilad], ed., *Moreshet Gevura* (The heroic heritage) (Tel Aviv: Ma'arkhot, 1947), including Zalman Rubashov's preface; *Masekhet Gevura le-Yom ha-Hagana, Yod Alef ba-Adar* (The story of heroism for the Defense Day, the Eleventh of Adar) (Israel Defense Forces, 1949); Avraham Levinson, "Gevurat Yisrael" (Jewish heroism), in *Magen va-Shelaḥ: Sheloshim Shana la-Haganat Tel Ḥai* (The shield and the weapon: Thirtieth anniversary of the defense of Tel Ḥai) (Tel Aviv: Histadrut, 1950), 79–89.

39. See, for example, Funkenstein, *Tadmit ve-Toda'a Historit;* Avraham B. Yehoshua, *Bi-Zekhut ha-Normaliyut* (Between right and right) (Tel Aviv: Schocken, 1980), and Schweid's essays on *shelilat ha-gola* (The repudiation of Exile) in *Mi-Yahadut le-Tsiyonut*, 139–208, including his discussion of Mordekhai Bar-On's and Avraham B. Yehoshua's polemic positions on this issue.

40. There were obviously variations in the delineation of this period in line with other ideological differences between the Zionist parties. On the differences between Po'alei Tsiyon and Ha-Po'el ha-Tsa'ir within Socialist Zionism, see Yosef Gorni, "Ha-Yesod ha-Romanti ba-Idi'ologia shel ha-Aliya ha-Sheniya" (The romantic element in the ideology of the Second Aliya), *Assufot* 10 (1966): 55–75; see Charles Liebman and Eliezer Don-Yeḥiya on the differences between Socialist and Revisionist Zionism, *Civil Religion in Israel* (Berkeley: University of California Press, 1983), 25–80.

41. Elboim-Dror, *Ha-Ḥinukh ha-Ivri be-Eretz Yisrael*, 1:383–87, 2:351; Gorni, "Ha-Yesod ha-Romanti," 59–61; Anita Shapira, *Halikha al Kav ha-Ofek* (Visions in conflict) (Tel Aviv: Am Oved, 1988), 27–28; Ya'akov Shavit, *Me-Ivri ad Kena'ani*, 31.

42. Zrubavel [Gilad], ed., *Sefer ha-Palmaḥ* (The Palmaḥ book) (Tel Aviv: Ha-Kibbutz ha-Me'uḥad, 1963), 1:283.

43. Ya'akov Cahan, "Shir ha-Biryonim." The Hebrew verse reads *Be-dam va-esh yehuda nafla, be-dam va-esh yehuda takum.*

44. Shmu'el Klausner, "Ha-Ivri he-Ḥadash" (The New Hebrew man), *Zemanim*, nos. 323, 325, 329, 330 (September–October), 1954.

45. In this historiographic context, the Hebrew term for the Temple *bet ha-mikdash* (the house of sanctuary) is shortened to the First or Second House (*ha-bayit ha-rishon* or *ha-bayit ha-sheni*).

46. Ḥayim Naḥman Bialik, "Metei Midbar" (The dead of the desert) (1902), reprinted in *Shirim*, 340–49, English translation by Ruth Nevo, in *Selected Poems: Bialik* (A Bilingual Edition) (Tel Aviv: Dvir, 1981), 114–15. Shortly thereafter, still under the impact of the Kishinev pogrom, Bialik wrote another poem in which he expresses doubts about God's presence; "Al ha-Sheḥita" (On the slaughter), 1903, reprinted in *Shirim*, 152–53.

47. This transformation occurs in a popular Ḥanukka song that substitutes praise for the "glories of Israel" for the "glories of God" and indicates that "in our days, the people of Israel will rise, unite, and be redeemed," conditioning redemption on the people rather than on God; see Liebman and Don-Yeḥiya, *Civil Religion in Israel*, 38; Schweid, *Mi-Yahadut le-Tsiyonut*, 176.

48. Frankel, "'Yizkor' Book of 1911," 377.

49. The literal translation of the Hebrew saying is "If you will, it is not a legend" (*Im tirtsu ein zo agada*). Posters carrying this saying often adorn classrooms in the public schools to transmit its message to the younger generation.

50. Berl Katznelson, Introduction to Heilperin, ed., *Sefer ha-Gevura,* 1:9–10.

51. Ze'ev Jabotinsky, "Kaddish" (Prayer for the dead) (1928), reprinted in *Ketavim: Zikhronot Ben Dori* (Collected works: Memoirs of my generation) (Tel Aviv: Ari Jabotinsky, 1947), 103–9. See Gedalyahu Alon's historical challenge of this perception of traditional memory with regard to the Hasmoneans, in *Meḥkarim be-Toldot Yisrael bi-Yemei Bayit Sheni uvi-Tekufat ha-Mishna veha-Talmud* (Studies in Jewish history of the Second Temple, the Mishnaic, and the Talmudic periods) (Tel Aviv: Ha-Kibbutz ha-Me'uḥad, 1967), 15–25. The folklorist Dov Noy challenges the broader notion that Exile highlighted spiritual heroism and suppressed physical heroism, by pointing out how folk literature continued to focus on physical heroism during that period; "Gevurat Yisrael ba-Maḥteret" (The underground Jewish heroism), *Maḥanayim* 52 (1961): 122–28.

52. The emphasis on the national heroic aspects rather than the religious aspects of Ḥanukka began in Zionist circles in Europe. See Almog, *Zionism and History,* 52; Halpern, *Idea of the Jewish State,* 83. These Ḥanukka celebrations were criticized by Rabbi Elijah Akiva Rabinovitch as early as 1899; see Almog, *Zionism and History,* 172–73. On their evolution in the Jewish society in Palestine, see Liebman and Don-Yeḥiya, *Civil Religion,* 51–53.

53. Ya'akov Cahan's "Shir ha-Biryonim" or Uri Tsvi Greenberg's "Song of the Sikarikim" are such two literary examples. Radical Zionist groups selected for themselves the names of those ancient extremists in different periods. See, for example, Brit Ha-Biryonim in Palestine during the 1930s, and Ha-Sikarikim underground in Israel today.

54. *Ha-Aretz,* March 5, 1920, 1 (emphasis added).

55. Ya'akov Zerubavel, "'Yizkor,'" quoted in Gorni, "Ha-Yesod ha-Romanti," 59 (emphasis added).

56. See Ya'akov Shavit, *Me-Ivri ad Kena'ani,* 30–33; Itamar Even-Zohar, "The Emergence of Native Hebrew Culture in Palestine: 1882–1948," *Studies in Zionism* 4 (1981): 167–84.

57. Mikha Yosef Berdiczewski, *Ba-Derekh* (Lipsia: Shtibl, 1922), pt. 2, 20. Berdiczewski contributed greatly to the popularity of the concept of the New Hebrew among the followers of Zionism; Luz, *Makbilim Nifgashim,* 224–27.

58. In Palestine the contrast between Jew and Hebrew was promoted by members of the Second Aliya as well as Hebrew teachers and their students. See Frankel, "'Yizkor' Book of 1911," 361; Elboim-Dror, *Ha-Ḥinukh ha-Ivri be-Eretz Yisrael,* 1: 359–60.

59. Rubinstein, *Liheyot Am Ḥofshi,* 102.

60. Max Nordau's concept of "muscular Jewry" articulates the idea that the exilic Jew's rehabilitation was both physical and spiritual. See also Almog, *Zionism and History,* 108–18; Elboim-Dror, *Ha-Ḥinukh ha-Ivri be-Eretz Yisrael,* 2:352–55.

61. Almog, *Zionism and History,* 23–38, 305.

62. George L. Mosse, *Fallen Soldiers: Reshaping the Memory of the World Wars* (New York: Oxford University Press, 1990), 54–69. Mosse refers to Germany before World War I, but the same observation applies to the Hitler Youth in Nazi Germany or the communist youth in Russia after the Bolshevik Revolution.

63. For Edward Shils's distinction between fundamental and radical change, see *Center and Periphery*, 216.

64. Even-Zohar, "The Emergence of Native Hebrew Culture in Palestine," 167–84.

65. Gershon Shaked, *Ha-Siporet ha-Ivrit, 1880–1980* (Hebrew narrative fiction) (Tel Aviv: Ha-Kibbutz ha-Me'uḥad and Keter, 1988), 3 : 185–89, 235–41. See also Rubinstein, *Liheyot Am Ḥofshi*, 104. The portrayal of a "positive hero" in this Hebrew literature also drew upon the Russian literary tradition transmitted by their eastern European parents and teachers; see Katerina Clark, *The Soviet Novel: History as Ritual* (Chicago: University of Chicago Press, 1985), 46.

66. These traumatic effects are most powerfully expressed by Middle Eastern Jews who immigrated after the foundation of the State of Israel. But pressures were also exerted on eastern and central European immigrants since the 1930s, including those who survived the Holocaust in Europe. The outpouring of literary and autobiographical writing on the transition from their native lands to the Jewish society in Palestine (or later, Israeli society) since the 1970s is not only indicative of the importance of this phenomenon, but also of the greater readiness of Israeli society today to acknowledge the problems of this transition.

67. Elboim-Dror, *Ha-Ḥinukh ha-Ivri be-Eretz Yisrael*, 1 : 387–88, 2 : 346; Mordekhai Na'or, ed., *Tenu'ot ha-No'ar 1920–1960* (Youth movements 1920–1960) (Jerusalem: Yad Yitzḥak Ben-Zvi, 1989), 246–56. Uri Ben-Eliezer, "Tsva'iyut, Status, ve-Politika: Dor Yelidei ha-Aretz veha-Hanhaga ba-Asor she-Kadam la-Hakamat ha-Medina" (Militarism, status, and politics: The generation of Israeli-born and the Yishuv's leadership) (Ph.D. diss., Tel Aviv University, 1988), 255–56; Zali Gurevich and Gideon Aran, "Al ha-Makom" (About the place), *Alpayim* 4 (1991): 27–34.

68. Gorni, "Ha-Yesod ha-Romanti"; Liebman and Don-Yeḥiya, *Civil Religion in Israel*, 30–40. This theme is most central to modern Hebrew literature during the Yishuv period, but continues also in postindependence Israeli literature. For a study of its articulation in Hebrew drama, see Gideon Ofrat, *Adama, Adam, Dam: Mitos he-Ḥalutz u-Fulḥan ha-Adama be-Maḥazot ha-Hityashvut* (Land, man, blood: The myth of the pioneer and the ritual of earth in Eretz Israel settlement drama) (Tel Aviv: Gome, 1980).

69. Gorni, "Ha-Yesod ha-Romanti," 63, 66; Frankel, "'Yizkor' Book of 1911"; Shapira, *Halikha al Kav ha-Ofek*, 26–38.

70. Avraham Shapira, *Aharon David Gordon u-Mekorotav ba-Ḥasidut uva-Kabala* (A. D. Gordon and his roots in Hasidism and Kabbala) (Tel Aviv: Am Oved, forthcoming).

71. Avraham Shlonsky, "Amal" (Labor) (1927), in T. Carmi, ed. and trans., *The Penguin Book of Hebrew Verse* (Harmondsworth: Penguin, 1981), 534. See Ḥanan Ḥever's analysis of labor poetry in "Shivḥei Amal u-Fulmus Politi" (The praise of

labor and a political controversy), in Pinḥas Ginosar, ed., *Ha-Sifrut ha-Ivrit u-Tenu'at ha-Avoda* (Hebrew literature and the Labor movement) (Be'er Sheba: Ben-Gurion University Press, 1989), 116–57.

72. Aḥad Ha-Am, "Teḥiyat ha-Ru'aḥ" (Spiritual revival), in *Kol Kitvei Aḥad Ha-Am* (Aḥad Ha-Am's collected works) (Tel Aviv: Dvir, 1956), 173–86.

73. Ze'ev Chomsky, *Ha-Lashon ha-Ivrit be-Darkhei Hitpat'ḥuta* (The Hebrew language and its development) (Jerusalem: Re'uven Mass, 1967), 235–53. On the development of Hebrew language and literature in Europe as challenging some of these Zionist hypotheses, see Lewis Gilnert, ed., *Hebrew in Ashkenaz: A Language in Exile* (New York: Oxford University Press, 1993); Dan Miron, *Im lo Tiheye Yerushalayim: Ha-Sifrut ha-Ivrit be-Heksher Tarbuti-Politi* (If there is no Jerusalem: Essays on Hebrew writing in a cultural-political context) (Tel Aviv: Ha-Kibbutz ha-Me'uḥad, 1987), 103–14; Robert Alter, *The Invention of Hebrew Prose: Modern Fiction and the Language of Realism* (Seattle: University of Washington Press, 1988).

74. Chomsky, *Ha-Lashon ha-Ivrit*, 254–74; Ya'akov Felman, "Terumato shel Eliezer Ben-Yehuda li-Teḥiyata shel ha-Lashon ha-Ivrit" (Eliezer Ben-Yehuda's contribution to the revival of the Hebrew language), *Katedra* 2 (1976): 83–95; Shlomo Morag, "Ha-Ivrit ha-Ḥadasha be-Hitgabshuta: Lashon be-Aspaklaria shel Ḥevra" (The shaping of modern Hebrew: Language in a social mirror), *Katedra* 55 (1990): 70–92; Benjamin Harshav, *Language in Time of Revolution* (Berkeley: University of California Press, 1993), 133–52.

75. Yigael Yadin, *Ha-Ḥipusim aḥar Bar-Kokhva* (In search of Bar Kokhba); English edition, *Bar Kokhba: The Rediscovery of the Legendary Hero of the Second Jewish Revolt against Rome* (Jerusalem: Weidenfeld & Nicholson, 1971).

76. Elboim-Dror, *Ha-Ḥinukh ha-Ivri be-Eretz Yisrael*, 1:309–56.

77. Even-Zohar, "Emergence of Native Hebrew Culture," 167–84; Harshav, *Language in Time of Revolution*, 153–66.

78. For a fuller exploration of the development of modern Hebrew in its social, literary, and political contexts, see Harshav, *Language in Time of Revolution*.

79. Ya'akov Ḥurgin's historical novel, *Ha-Kana'im ha-Tse'irim* (The young Zealots), published in 1935, was a highly popular work among the Hebrew youth. See Uriel Ofek *Sifrut ha-Yeladim ha-Ivrit, 1900–1948* (Hebrew children's literature) (Tel Aviv: Dvir, 1988), 2:478–80. For further examples of the role of nature in children's literature, see chapters 6 and 7.

80. The emphasis on the ancient heroes was by no means limited to formal history classes. In fact, since history books take longer to respond to changing cultural trends (see Firer, *Sokhnim shel ha-Ḥinukh ha-Tsiyoni*, 43), poetry, stories, novels, and plays were more instrumental to the elevation of these heroes and their wars of liberation in Hebrew culture. See Elboim-Dror, *Ha-Ḥinukh ha-Ivri be-Eretz Yisrael*, 1:383–87, 2:351; Firer, *Sokhnim shel ha-Ḥinukh ha-Tsiyoni*, 65–68, 122.

81. Hazaz, "Ha Derasha."

82. See Shlonsky's poem "Amal," above, for the explicit reference to the pioneers as creators. Similarly, Eliezer Smally's famous novel on the early Zionist

settlers was entitled *Anshei Bereshit* (The people of Genesis) (Tel Aviv: Shtibel, 1933), alluding to the biblical myth of Creation. *Anshei Bereshit* enjoyed immediate acclaim and was one of the most widely read books by Hebrew youth of the prestate period. See Ofek, *Sifrut ha-Yeladim ha-Ivrit,* 2:465–66; Shaked, *Ha-Siporet ha-Ivrit,* 1:294, n. 17.

83. On the political dimension of the classification of "old" and "new" Yishuv in a historical and sociological perspective, see Yehoshua Kni'el, *Hemshekh u-Temura: ha-Yishuv ha-Yashan veha-Yishuv he-Ḥadash bi-Tekufat ha-Aliya ha-Rishona veha-Sheniya* (Continuity and change: The old and new Yishuv during the First and Second Aliyas) (Jerusalem: Yad Yitzḥak Ben-Zvi, 1982); and Ḥana Herzog, "Ha-Musagim 'Yishuv Yashan' ve-'Yishuv Ḥadash' be-He'ara Sotsiologit" (The concepts of "old Yishuv" and "new Yishuv" from a sociological perspective), *Katedra* 32 (July 1984): 99–108. On Hebrew textbooks' critical representation of the old Yishuv, see Firer, *Sokhnim shel ha-Ḥinukh ha-Tsiyoni,* 140–42.

84. Firer, *Sokhnim shel ha-Ḥinukh ha-Tsiyoni,* 96–102; Liebman and Don-Yeḥiya, *Civil Religion in Israel,* 100–104. For a more extensive discussion of the commemoration of the Holocaust during the prestate and early state periods, see chapter 5.

85. See Liebman and Don-Yeḥiya, *Civil Religion in Israel,* 100–104, 113–20; James E. Young, "When a Day Remembers: A Performative History of Yom Hashoah." *History and Memory* 2, no. 3 (1990): 54–75.

86. Firer, *Sokhnim shel ha-Ḥinukh ha-Tsiyoni,* 101.

87. On the use of the concept of *tefutsot* (dispersion) in Hebrew textbooks, see ibid., 97–98.

88. Heilperin, *Sefer ha-Gevura,* 3:242.

Chapter 3: The Battle of Tel Ḥai

1. Heilperin, *Sefer ha-Gevura,* 3:276–97; Frankel, "'Yizkor' Book of 1911," 355–84.

2. The earlier oral and written testimony about Tel Ḥai relates to "gangs of bandits," "Bedouins," or "Arabs" interchangeably. In later texts, however, the common reference is to "Arabs." The change, noted also by Liebman and Don-Yeḥiya (*Civil Religion in Israel,* 46–47), may be the result of the later establishment of the "Arabs" as the archenemy of Israeli society.

3. Since most settlers decided to leave and some volunteers arrived to support those who remained in the settlements, the number of Jewish settlers in the northern region fluctuated. According to Nakdimon Rogel, at the end of February there were 45 people in Metula, 35 in Tel Ḥai, and 25 in Kfar Giladi; *Tel Ḥai: Ḥazit Lelo Oref* (Tel Ḥai: A front without rear) (Tel Aviv: Yariv-Hadar, 1979), 136.

4. For a more extensive discussion of the developments in Tel Ḥai, see Rogel, *Tel Ḥai,* 171–91, and Shulamit Laskov, *Trumpeldor: Sipur Ḥayav* (Yosef Trumpeldor: A biography) (Ḥaifa: Shikmona, 1972), 237–47.

5. *Encyclopaedia Judaica* (Jerusalem: Keter, 1972), 9:474.

6. For further biographical information about Trumpeldor, see Laskov's most recent biography, *Trumpeldor*, and earlier works such as Pesaḥ Lipovetsky [Ben-Amram], *Yosef Trumpeldor: Ishiyuto, Ḥayav, Pe'ulotav* (Yosef Trumpeldor: His personality, life, activities) (Kovna: Semel, 1924); Menaḥem Poznansky, ed., *Me-Ḥayei Yosef Trumpeldor* (On Yosef Trumpeldor's life) (Tel Aviv: Am Oved, 1953); N. Ben-Ari and E. Kena'ani, eds., *Yosef Trumpeldor: Po'alo u-Tekufato/Yosef Trumpeldor: His Life and His Times* (Hebrew and English) (Tel Aviv: Mif'alei Tarbut ve-Ḥinukh, 1970).

7. This was the version reported by Dr. Gary, who accompanied him on the way to Kfar Giladi. Some other witnesses provided slightly different versions of Trumpeldor's last words conveying the same idea. See Laskov, *Trumpeldor*, 243, 248; Rogel, *Tel Ḥai*, 190, 195. For further discussion of Trumpeldor's saying, see chapters 6 and 9.

8. See the daily newspapers *Ha-Aretz* and *Do'ar ha-Yom* from March 5, 1920 on; *Ha-Po'el ha-Tsa'ir*, March 12 and 20, 1920; *Kuntres*, no. 29 (March 1920). See also Laskov, *Trumpeldor*, 252.

9. Moshe Smilansky, "Makom Kadosh" (A holy place), *Ha-Aretz*, March 14, 1920, 1.

10. On the reburial of the defenders' bones in Tel Ḥai, see *Kuntres*, no. 166 (Adar 2, 1924): 20–21.

11. *Encyclopaedia Judaica* 3:606; Elik Mishori, "Leida me-Ḥadash shel Omanut Ivrit" (The rebirth of a Hebrew art), in Nurit Gertz, ed., *Nekudot Tatspit: Tarbut ve-Ḥevra be-Yisrael* (Perspectives on culture and society in Israel) (Tel Aviv: Ha-Universita ha-Petuḥa, 1988), 183–84.

12. Yehuda Slutsky, *Mavo le-Toldot Tenu'at ha-Avoda ha-Yisra'elit* (Introduction to the history of the Labor movement in Israel) (Tel Aviv: Am Oved, 1973), 282.

13. C. Ben-Yeruḥam, ed., *Sefer Betar: Korot u-Mekorot* (The book of Betar: History and sources) (Jerusalem: Betar, 1969), 1:76; Ya'akov Zielberscheid and Arie Pialkov, eds., *Tel Ḥai: Kibbutz Hakhshara be-Folin* (Kibbutz Tel Ḥai in Poland) (Tel Aviv: Ha-Kibbutz ha-Me'uḥad, 1979), 7.

14. Ben-Yeruḥam, *Sefer Betar*, 1:39–45; Ya'akov Shavit, *Me-Rov li-Medina: Ha-Tenu'a ha-Revisionistit, ha-Tokhnit ha-Hityashvutit, veha-Ra'ayon ha-Ḥevrati, 1925–1935* (Revisionism in Zionism: The Revisionist movement, the plan for colonizatory regime and social ideas) (Tel Aviv: Hadar, 1983), 98–106, 272.

15. The immediate recognition of the symbolic significance of Tel Ḥai was manifested in the first obituaries for Trumpeldor and his comrades. See, for example, *Ha-Aretz*, March 5, 8, 9, 12, 1920; *Do'ar ha-Yom*, March 5, 8, 1920; *Ha-Po'el ha-Tsa'ir*, March 12, 20, 1920.

16. Eliade, *Myth and Reality*, 51. For other examples of this attitude, see Eviatar Zerubavel, "Easter and Passover: On Calendars and Group Identity," *American Sociological Review* 47 (1982): 284–89; and *Hidden Rhythms*, 82–95.

17. See, for example, Ḥadash, "Mi-Saviv: Al Mot Loḥem" (From around: The death of a warrior), *Ha-Po'el ha-Tsa'ir*, March 12, 1920, 26; Yosef Klausner, "Hem Naflu Ḥalalim" (They are dead), *Ha-Aretz*, March 9, 1920, 2; Jabotinsky, "Kaddish," 105; Ḥayim Harari, ed., *Mo'adim le-Simḥa* (Festivals and holidays) (Tel Aviv:

Omanut, 1941), 282; David Ben-Gurion, "Tsav Tel Ḥai" (The Tel Ḥai legacy), *Kuntres* 1, no. 381 (1943): 3.

18. David Shimoni, "Le-Trumpeldor" (To Trumpeldor) (1929), reprinted in *Shirim* (Poems) (Tel Aviv: Masada, 1954), 2:226–27.

19. A. L., "Le-Zekher Aḥai she-Naflu ba-Galil" (In memory of my brothers who fell in Galilee), *Ha-Po'el ha-Tsa'ir*, March 26, 1920, 17 (emphasis added).

20. Ḥadash, "Mi-Saviv," 26 (emphasis added).

21. Yosef Klausner, "Hem Naflu Ḥalalim," 2 (emphasis added).

22. Max Nordau, "Ha-Kapitan Trumpeldor: Divrei Hesped" (Captain Trumpeldor: An obituary) (1920), reprinted in *Yosef Trumpeldor: Ḥai Shanim le-Moto* (Yosef Trumpeldor: Eighteenth anniversary of his death) (Tel Aviv: Keren Tel Ḥai, 1938), 50 (emphasis added).

23. P. Aviv, "Le-Yom Tel Ḥai" (For the Tel Ḥai Day), *Ha-Lapid* (Monthly of the ninth grade of the High School for Commerce in Tel Aviv), no. 2 (February 1937): 1–2, Aviezer Yellin Archives for Jewish Education in Israel and the Diaspora, Tel Aviv University, file 3.149/7. I would like to thank Nili Arie for bringing this text to my attention.

24. *Ha-Hagana* (The defense), 4th ed. (Israel Defense Forces, Education Headquarters, 1975), 36.

25. For the centrality of this theme in Israeli culture, see Nurit Gertz, "The Few against the Many," *Jerusalem Quarterly* 30 (1984): 94–104; Yael Zerubavel, "Holiday Cycle."

26. Z. Ariel, M. Blich, and N. Persky, eds., *Mikra'ot Yisrael le-Khita Bet* (Israel's reader: Textbook for the second grade) (Jerusalem: Masada, 1974).

27. Yosef Hayim Brener, "Tel Ḥai," *Ha-Adama* 1 (March 1920), reprinted in G. Rivlin, ed., *Moreshet Tel Ḥai* (Tel Ḥai's legacy) (Tel Aviv: Ma'arakhot, 1947), 131–33.

28. See also Liebman and Don-Yeḥiya, *Civil Religion in Israel*, 44.

29. On the roles of modern national myths of death and rebirth, see Robert N. Bellah, "Civil Religion in America," *Daedalus* (Winter 1967): 1–21, reprinted in *Beyond Belief* (New York: Harper & Row, 1970), 176–79.

30. *Masekhet Gevura le-Yom ha-Hagana; Magen va-Shelaḥ: Sheloshim Shana la-Haganat Tel Ḥai* (The shield and the weapon: Thirtieth anniversary of the defense of Tel Ḥai) (Tel Aviv: Histadrut, 1950), 79–89; *Zekhor Yemei Tel Ḥai* (Remember the days of Tel Ḥai) (Tel Aviv: Teachers Council for the Jewish National Fund, 1960), 23.

31. Berl Katznelson's "Yizkor" (memorial prayer) for the Tel Ḥai heroes was published in *Kuntres*, no. 29 (March 11, 1920), 1. On the military Yizkor prayer, see Liebman and Don-Yeḥiya, *Civil Religion in Israel*, 119–20.

32. Consider, for example, the naming of Israeli settlements Netiv ha-Lamed Hey (the thirty-five route) or Ma'ale Ha-Ḥamisha (the hill of the five) in commemoration of specific heroic events. On anonymous commemorations, see also Liebman and Don-Yeḥiya, *Civil Religion in Israel*, 98.

33. On national celebrations of origins, see also Warner, *The Living and the Dead;* Schwartz, "Social Context of Commemoration," 377–78.

34. According to the director of the Tel Ḥai historical museum, the number of visitors is estimated at 81,000 per year. I am grateful to Tamar Katriel for this information.

35. See also Tamar Katriel, "Remaking a Place: Cultural Productions in an Israeli Pioneering Museum," *History and Memory* 5 (Fall/Winter 1993): 104–35.

36. *Ha-Aretz*, March 21, 1921, 2. See also *Do'ar ha-Yom*, March 8, 1920; Nordau, "Ha-Kapitan Trumpeldor"; Snir, "Trumpeldor," *Kuntres*, no. 208 (March 6, 1925): 6.

37. Similar statements were made by other Hebrew youth in the Yishuv period. See, for example, Yosef Nedava, *Sefer Olei ha-Gardom* (The book of the executed) (Tel Aviv: Shelaḥ, 1952), 265. That patriotic statements by youth affiliated with the Revisionist movement were not accepted as national slogans clearly reflects Labor's hegemony during those years.

38. Anita Shapira suggests that Tel Ḥai's rise as a national myth is linked to the centrality of "defense" as the guiding principle of the settlers' policy in the Arab-Jewish conflict during those early decades. This defensive conception was later replaced by a more offensive ethos; *Halikha al Kav ha-Ofek*, 42–44.

Chapter 4: The Bar Kokhba Revolt

1. References to the Bar Kokhba revolt are made in Dio Cassius, *Roman History*, trans. Earnest Cary (London: Heinemann, [1925], 1955), 69.12–14, pp. 447–51; Spartianus, *De Vita Hadriani*, quoted in Shmu'el Yeivin, *Milḥemet Bar Kokhva* (The Bar Kokhba war) (Jerusalem: Mosad Bialik, 1957), 59–61; and Eusebius, *Ecclesiastical History*, trans. Kirsopp Lako (London: Heinemann, [1926], 1975), 4.6, pp. 311–13. For a review of the study of these and other sources, see Benjamin Isaac and Aharon Oppenheimer, "The Revolt of Bar Kokhba: Ideology and Modern Scholarship," *Journal of Jewish Studies* 36, no. 1 (1985): 33–60.

2. These two reasons are given, respectively, by two Roman historians, Dio Cassius and Spartianus. See also Yadin, *Bar Kokhba*, 19–23; Aharon Oppenheimer, ed., *Mered Bar-Kokhva* (The Bar Kokhba revolt) (Jerusalem: Merkaz Zalman Shazar, 1980), 11; Isaac and Oppenheimer, "The Revolt of Bar Kokhba," 45–48.

3. Yadin, *Bar Kokhba*, 15, 24–27; Isaac and Oppenheimer, "The Revolt of Bar Kokhba," 53–57.

4. Dio Cassius, *Roman History*, 69:12–14; see also Yeivin, *Milḥemet Bar Kokhva*, 115–21; Shmu'el Avramsky, *Bar Kokhva Nesi Yisrael* (Bar Kokhba, the leader of Israel) (Tel Aviv: Masada, 1961), 120.

5. Babylonian Talmud, *Ta'anit* 29:1, 30:2.

6. Eusebius, *Ecclesiastical History*, 4:6.

7. Palestinian Talmud, *Ta'anit* 4:8; Midrash *Ekha Rabba* (Lamentation Rabba) 2:5.

8. Isaac and Oppenheimer, "The Revolt of Bar Kokhba," 57.

9. *Ekha Rabba* 2:5; a slightly different version of this paragraph appears in the Palestinian Talmud, *Ta'anit* 4:8.

10. Yeivin, *Milḥemet Bar Kokhva*, 61–62; Avramsky, *Bar Kokhva Nesi Yisrael*, 53–54; Yadin, *Bar Kokhba*, 18, 28–29, 124. Richard G. Marks argues that later generations may have believed Bar Koziba to be his real name and therefore its use does not necessarily reflect a negative view of the leader; *The Image of Bar Kokhba in Traditional Jewish Literature: False Messiah and National Hero* (University Park, PA: Pennsylvania State Press, 1993), 15. Nonetheless, the name clearly evokes negative associations.

11. According to Marks, the first association of the name Bar Koziba (used in the Jewish literature) with the names Barchochebas or Chochebas (used by non-Jewish sources) was made in the sixteenth century by the Jewish historians Azarya dei Rossi (*Me'or Einayim* [Light to the eyes], 1573) and David Ganz (*Tsemaḥ David* [The sprout of David], 1592). See Marks, *The Image of Bar Kokhba*, 162–64, 174.

12. Marks's research, first made available as a doctoral dissertation (University of California at Los Angeles, 1980) has made a most important contribution to the study of the traditional Jewish perception of Bar Kokhba.

13. *Ta'anit* 4:8; *Ekha Rabba* 2:5. See also Marks, *The Image of Bar Kokhba*, 13–57.

14. See Yehoshua Efron, "Milḥemet Bar Kokhva le-Or ha-Masoret ha-Talmudit ha-Eretz Yisra'elit ke-Neged ha-Bavlit" (Bar Kokhba in the light of the Palestinian and Babylonian Talmudic traditions), in Aharon Oppenheimer and Uriel Rappoport, eds., *Mered Bar-Kokhva: Meḥkarim Ḥadashim* (The Bar Kokhba revolt: A new approach) (Jerusalem: Yad Yizḥak Ben-Zvi, 1984), 63–64.

15. Rabbi Elazar's importance for the rebels' cause is clearly articulated in a story about a Samaritan's advice to Hadrian to kill the rabbi in order to guarantee the Romans' success: "So long as that old cock wallows in ashes, you will not conquer it [Betar]"; *Ekha Rabba* 2:5.

16. The exception here is Avraham Ibn Daud's reference to a three-generation dynasty of Bar Kokhba in *Sefer ha-Kabala* (The book of tradition), ed. Gerson Cohen (Philadelphia: Jewish Publication Society, 1967), 3:28–36.

17. Maimonides (Moses ben Maimon), *Mishne Torah: Hilkhot Melakhim* [Maimonides' Code: Laws concerning kings] 11.3, quoted in Marks, *The Image of Bar Kokhba*, 81–82.

18. For a detailed analysis of the twelfth-century references to Bar Kokhba by Rashi (Rabbi Solomon ben Isaac), Ibn Daud, and Maimonides, see Marks, *The Image of Bar Kokhba*, 57–134.

19. Ibid., 135–83.

20. Lewis, *History*, 29–30.

21. Jewish historical novels written first in European languages and only later in Hebrew became a popular genre in the second half of the nineteenth century. The rise of interest in Rabbi Akiba and Bar Kokhba therefore extends beyond works written in Hebrew. Among historical novels and plays on that period are the novel *Rabbi Akiva* by Meir (Marcus) Lehmann which was translated into Hebrew in Kra-

kow, 1896; Judah Leo Landau's *Bar Kokhva: Shir Ḥezyon Tuga ba-Ḥamesh Ma'arakhot* (Bar Kokhba: A play in five scenes) was published in Lvov in 1884, and Kalman Shulman's *Harisot Betar* (The Ruins of Betar) published in Vilna in 1900.

22. For examples of poems relating to Bar Kokhba, see Bialik, "Ein Zot Ki Rabat Tsrartunu: Mi-Shirei Bar Kokhva" (You have oppressed us unbearably: From Bar Kokhba's poems), 1898; reprinted in *Shirim*, 96; Shaul Tchernichovsky's poems "le-Nokhaḥ ha-Yam" (Facing the Sea), 1910–1920, reprinted in his *Shirim* (Poems) (Jerusalem: Schocken, 1959), 119–224; "Betara" (To Betar), 1903; reprinted in *Shirim*, 273–74; and a play "Bar Kokhba" in *Kitvei Tchernichovsky* (Tchernichovsky: Collected works) (Tel Aviv: Hotsa'at Va'ad ha-Yovel, 1932); Ya'akov Cahan, "Bar Kokhva" (1933), reprinted in *Kitvei Ya'akov Cahan*, 3:127–28; Shmu'el Halkin, *Bar Kokhba: Dramatisher Poeme* (Bar Kokhba: A dramatic poem) (Moscow: Emes, 1939) in Yiddish. For examples of prose, see Israel Benjamin Levner's work on Bar Kokhba, first published in *Ha-Ḥayim veha-Teva*, 1905; reprinted posthumously as *Bar Kokhva: Sipur Histori mi-Yemei Harisot Betar* (Bar Kokhba: A historical novel on the destruction of Betar) (Warsaw: Barkai, 1923); Avraham Goldfaden's musical play in Yiddish, *Bar Kokhba: Der Zuhn Fun dem Shtern: A Musikalishe Melodrama in Raymen* (Bar Kokhba, the son of star: An enlightened melodrama in rhymes) (New York: Hebrew Publishing Co., 1908); David Pinsky, *Meshiḥim: Dramen* (Messiahs: Dramas) (1928), translated into Hebrew *Meshiḥim: Dramot* (Tel Aviv: Am Oved, 1952). Bar Kokhba has continued to be the focus of literary works.

23. On the Bar Kokhba Association, see *Encyclopaedia Judaica* 4:228; on the magazine *Bar Kokhba*, see Leo Baeck Institute, *Library and Archives News*, no. 22 (June 1985); on the Betar youth organization, see Ben-Yeruḥam, *Sefer Betar*, I: 39–45.

24. Bialik, "Ein Zot Ki Rabat Tsrartunu." Note that this poem was written on Lag ba-Omer.

25. Tchernichovsky, "le-Nokhaḥ ha-Yam."

26. Shapira, *Halikha al Kav ha-Ofek*, 28.

27. Rachel Yana'it Ben-Zvi, *Anu Olim* (We climb up) (Tel Aviv: Am Oved, 1962), 103.

28. David Ben-Gurion, in a speech in a ceremony of pledging allegiance, June 27, 1948, reprinted in *Medinat Yisrael ha-Meḥudeshet* (The renewed state of Israel) (Tel Aviv: Am Oved, 1969), 1:207–8.

29. Quoted in Yonathan Shapiro, *Ilit Lelo Mamshikhim* (An elite without successors) (Tel Aviv: Sifriyat ha-Po'alim, 1984), 110.

30. Tamar Bornstein-Lazar, *Lag ba-Omer* (Revivim, n.d.), 62.

31. Elboim-Dror, *Ha-Ḥinukh ha-Ivri be-Eretz Yisrael*, 2:351–55; see also Shapiro, *Ilit Lelo Mamshikhim*, 110.

32. See, for example, Lag ba-Omer stories by the prominent children's writer and educator, Levin Kipnis, reprinted in *Mo'adei Yisrael: Lag ba-Omer* (Israel's holidays: Lag ba-Omer) (Tel Aviv: Samuel Simson, 1974); Z. Ariel, M. Blich, and N. Persky, eds. *Mikra'ot Yisrael le-Khita Ḥet* (Israel's reader: Textbook for the eighth grade) (Jerusalem: Masada, 1966), 510–18; Bornstein-Lazar, *Lag ba-Omer*;

Shi'urim be-Historia le-Veit ha-Sefer ha-Mamlakhti (Lessons in history for the public schools) (Jerusalem: Ministry of Education, Center for Curriculum Development, 1987), 2:115.

33. See, for example, Levin Kipnis, "Yigal Asher Yigal" (Yigal who redeems) in *Mo'adei Yisrael*, 17–28; Tamar Bornstein, "Menusato shel Ḥets ha-Zahav" (The escape of the golden arrow), in *Sipurai ha-Ahuvim* (My beloved tales) (Tel Aviv: Zelkovitz, 1960), 7–13. For a similar use of this device in works relating to Trumpeldor, see chapter 6.

34. The lyrics of the song "Bar-Kokhva veha-Arye" (Bar Kokhba and the lion) were written by Levin Kipnis. For further discussion of this song, see the section relating to Bar Kokhba and the lion in chapter 7.

35. Gershom Scholem, *Sabbatai Sevi* (Princton: Princeton University Press, 1973), 285, quoted in Marks, *The Image of Bar Kokhba*, 10.

36. Yadin, *Bar Kokhba*, 15. See also Yeivin, *Milḥemet Bar Kokhva*, 131.

37. Yadin's preface to Avramsky, *Bar Kokhva Nesi Yisrael*, 3.

38. On the ambiguity concerning the liberation of Jerusalem, see Isaac and Oppenheimer, "The Revolt of Bar Kokhba," 54–55. However, the liberation is presented as a fact in Yadin, *Bar Kokhba*, 18, and in the public school textbook narratives, such as Ariel, Blich, and Persky, *Mikra'ot Yisrael le-Khita Bet*, 389, and *Mikra'ot Yisrael le-Khita Ḥet*, 511; Natan Persky, ed., *Mikra'ot Yisrael Ḥadashot le-Khita Bet* (The new Israel's reader: Textbook for the second grade) (Tel Aviv: Masada, 1975), 405.

39. See Almog, *Zionism and History*, 110.

40. Yadin, *Bar Kokhba*, 21.

41. Yisrael Eldad, *Pulmus ha-Ḥurban u-Lekaḥav* (The controversy on the destruction and its lessons) (Jerusalem: Van Leer Foundation, 1982), 9–10, 70.

42. Palestinian Talmud, *Ta'anit* 4:8. For similar versions, see Babylonian Talmud, *Gittin* 58a and *Ekha Rabba* 2:5. For a comparison of the different versions, see Yeivin, *Milḥemet Bar Kokhva*, 153–66.

43. Marks, *The Image of Bar Kokhba*, 181–83.

44. Yadin, *Bar Kokhba*, 15. Hereafter pages are given in the text.

45. Amos Elon, *The Israelis: Founders and Sons* (New York: Bantam, 1971), 365.

46. In addition to these soldiers' participation, army officers gave useful advice to Yadin. For example, an Israeli general visiting the site suggested using mine detectors to find more coins (86).

47. Eldad, *Pulmus ha-Ḥurban u-Lekaḥav*, 4–5.

Chapter 5: The Fall of Masada

1. Josephus, *The Wars of the Jews*, book 7.8.3, in *Complete Works*, trans. W. Whiston (Grand Rapids, Michigan: Kregel, 1960), 599. Hereafter pages are given in the text.

2. Masada, according to Josephus, was also the first fortress to fall into the hands of Jewish rebels in A.D. 66. The group who took Masada, led by Menaḥem ben Yehuda the Galilean, later proceeded to Jerusalem and opened the revolt with the aid of arms captured there. When Menaḥem was later murdered by opponents to his "tyrant" rule, a small group of his followers, led by his relative, Yair ben Elazar, escaped to Masada; Josephus, *Wars of the Jews*, 2.8.6–9, pp. 491–92. On the Romans' later conquest of Herodium and Macherus, see ibid, 7.6, pp. 595–97.

3. Josephus provides a detailed account of the Roman siege in *Wars of the Jews*, 7.8.5, p. 600. See also Yoḥanan Aharoni, *Metsada* (Masada) (Tel Aviv: Ma'arkhot, 1963), 16.

4. Josephus describes how he hid in a cave with 40 other Jewish men after the fall of Jotapata. When the others insisted on dying free rather than surrender to the Romans, Josephus persuaded them to draw lots to kill each other in a manner similar to his description of the later Masada episode. Josephus himself escaped death when he remained one of the last two men alive, having persuaded the other survivor to surrender to the Romans; *Wars of the Jews*, 3.8, pp. 514–16.

5. The site of Masada is mentioned only in passing in Strabonis's *Geographica* and Pliny's *Natural History*, which were written in the first century B.C. and the first century A.D., respectively; see M. Avi-Yona, N. Avigad, Y. Aharoni, I. Dunayevsky, and S. Gutman, "Metsada: Seker Arkhe'ologi bi-Shenot 1955–56" (Masada: Archeological survey and excavations, 1955–56), *Israel Exploration Journal* 7 (1957): 9.

6. *Encyclopaedia Judaica* 10:254–55; Yosef Braslavsky, "Aḥarit Metsada ve-Ikvoteiha" (Masada's end and its traces), *Mi-Bifnim* (January 1942): 4–5; Henry Thackeray, *Josephus: The Man and the Historian* (New York: Ktav, 1960), 2, 20.

7. *The Book of Jossipon*, providing a chronicle of Jewish history up to the destruction of the Second Temple, appeared in numerous editions during the Middle Ages and the early modern period; David Flusser, introduction to *Sefer Yosifon* (The book of Jossipon) (Jerusalem: Merkaz Zalman Shazar, 1978), 10–51.

8. See *Sefer Yosifon*, ed. David Flusser (Jerusalem: Mosad Bialik, 1978), 1: 430–31. In his introduction to *Sefer Yosifon* (see note 7), Flusser notes that Jossipon relied on the Hegesippus, a Latin adaptation of *The Wars of the Jews* from the fourth century. Since the language of the Hegesippus was not always clear, Jossipon's version must reflect his understanding of the ending of this episode.

9. A rare example of a rendition of Josephus's version of the end appears in Samuel Usque, *Consolation of the Tribulations of Israel* (1552), trans. Martin A. Cohen (Philadelphia: Jewish Publication Society, 1965), 56. But Usque's book, written in Portuguese, enjoyed only limited circulation and therefore did not have a great influence on Jewish historiography.

10. In analyzing the more radical forms of martyrdom of Ashkenazi Jewry during the first Crusade, Robert Chazan suggests that, although there is no direct reference to Masada as a symbolic model, Jews must have been familiar with its example through Jossipon's work (*European Jews and the First Crusade*, 149, 327, n. 33). See also Yitzḥak Baer's introduction to A. M. Habermann *Sefer Gezerot Ashkenaz ve-Tsorfat* (The book of persecutions in Germany and France) (Jerusalem:

Ofir, 1971); Shalom Spiegel, *The Last Trial: The Akeda* (New York: Behrman House, 1979), 3–27.

11. On the Hebrew edition of 1862, see Y. N. Simḥoni, translation and introduction to *Yosef ben Matityahu: Toldot Milḥemet ha-Yehudim im ha-Roma'im* (Josephus: The wars of the Jews) (Ramat-Gan: Masada, 1923), 30.

12. Among the 120 people I interviewed, none of those who mentioned Josephus as the historical source raised doubts about the accuracy of his account. See also Baila A. Shargel's comment to this effect in "The Evolution of the Masada Myth," *Judaism* 28 (1979): 359–60.

13. See, for example, the educational brochure for the Israeli army, written by the archeologist Yoḥanan Aharoni (*Metsada*, 11–23), and a mimeographed brochure prepared in the late 1970s for Ra'anana Junior High School students before their trip to Masada (n.d., 4). See also the description of a youth movement ritual at Masada in 1942, *Ba-Mivḥan*, December 27, 1942, reprinted in Yitzhak Kafkafi, ed., *Shenot Ha-Maḥanot Ha-Olim, 1934–1945* (The chronicle of Ha-Maḥanot Ha-Olim) (Tel Aviv: Ha-Kibbutz ha-Me'uḥad, 1985), 333.

14. In 1928 an association of high school students, Masada, was founded in Warsaw by the Revisionist Zionist Organization and the name was also used for a Revisionist youth publication in Israel; Romanian Zionist settlers, members of a Masada group, founded a kibbutz by this name in Palestine in 1937; the Jerusalem scouts chose to name themselves Masada and published a newsletter by this name; and an American Zionist youth organization founded in 1940 was also called Masada.

15. *Encyclopaedia Judaica* 11:1079; Aharoni, *Metsada*, 26–27.

16. See, for example, Braslavsky, "Aḥarit Metsada ve-Ikvoteiha," 3; Yosef Weitz, *Seviv Metsada* (Around Masada) (Jerusalem: Sifriyat Adama, 1963), 4.

17. See, for example, the detailed descriptions of early trips to this region in Mordeckai Na'or, ed., *Yam ha-Melaḥ u-Midbar Yehuda, 1900–1967* (The Dead Sea and the Judaean desert) (Jerusalem: Yad Yitzḥak Ben-Zvi, 1990), 236–57.

18. Such early trips were conducted by the well-known teachers Eliezer Yellin, of the Teachers' Seminary in Jerusalem, and Dr. Borgashov of Gymnasia Hertseliya; Tsvi Ilan, *Li-Metsada be-Ikvot ha-Kana'im* (To Masada in the Zealots' footsteps) (Tel Aviv: Shreberk, 1973), 12; Dr. Baruch Ben-Yehuda, the former principal of Gymnasia Hertseliya, in a telephone interview on June 16, 1979. See also Dan Bitan, "Metsada: Ha-Semel veha-Mitos" (Masada, The symbol and the myth), in Na'or, *Yam ha-Melaḥ u-Midbar Yehuda*, 224–26.

19. During the Arab revolt against the British in the late 1930s, there was a break in this budding youth tradition which resumed in the early 1940s.

20. For a more elaborate discussion of those early trips and the youth's response to the casualties, see chapter 8.

21. Protocols of the meeting of the Board of Directors of the Jewish National Fund, April 17, 1934 (The Zionist Archive, Jerusalem); Weitz, *Seviv Metsada*, 6–12.

22. See Berl Katznelson's speech in the twentieth World Zionist Congress and fifth meeting of the Jewish Agency on August 6, 1937 (the Zionist Federation's

stenographic report, 1937, 74, at the Zionist Archive, Jerusalem); Ilan, *Li-Metsada be-Ikvot ha-Kana'im*, 155; Yosef Braslavi, *Yam ha-Melaḥ Saviv-Saviv* (The Dead Sea and its environment), *Ha-Yadata et ha-Aretz?* (Do you know Israel?) (Tel Aviv: Ha-Kibbutz ha-Me'uḥad, 1956), 3:448.

23. Early explorations of youth movement members included specific surveys of the water system and the northern palace as well as early attempts at reconstruction. The findings were published in *Mi-Bifnim*, the publication of the kibbutz movement Ha-Kibbutz Ha-Me'uḥad; see Gutman, *Im Metsada;* Mikha Livne, *Ḥomer Ezer la-Madrikh bi-Metsada* (Instructional materials for the tourist guide to Masada) (Department of Tourism and National Parks Authority, 1966), 64. Although the strategic difficulties of reaching Masada had clearly ruled out the possibility of a major dig prior to the foundation of the state, one cannot avoid the impression that Masada did not attract professional archaeologists at that period; Shmaryahu Gutman's interview on the program "Ha-Meshuga li-Metsada" (The Masada fanatic) was broadcast on Israeli national radio on Jan. 12, 1968. See also Pearlmen, *Zealots of Masada: The Story of a Dig* (New York: Charles Scribner's Sons, 1967) 54–55.

24. Aharoni, *Metsada*, 27.

25. Weitz, *Seviv Metsada*, 16.

26. Yigael Yadin, *Masada: Herod's Fortress and the Zealots' Last Stand* (New York: Random House, 1966), 13–14, 21.

27. On Israelis' love of archeology, see Elon, *Israelis*, 365–75; Neil Asher Silberman, *Between the Past and the Present: Archeology, Ideology, and Nationalism in the Modern Middle East* (New York: Holt, 1989), 123–36. For an example of earlier use of Israeli volunteers, see Avi-Yona et al., "Seker arche'ologi," 4. The scale of volunteers' participation exceeded previous experiences and made it possible to complete an enormous project within a relatively short time.

28. Yadin, *Masada*, 13. Hereafter pages are given in the text.

29. Yigael Yadin in "Tsuk Metsada" (The Masada cliff), a program on Israeli national radio, September 9, 1963.

30. See Baila A. Shargel's analysis of Yadin's stand in "Evolution of the Masada Myth," 364–65. For a similar approach to the Zealots' remains, see Livne, *Ḥomer Ezer la-Madrikh bi-Metsada*, 13.

31. See Silberman, *Between the Past and the Present*, on the interrelations among archaeology, ideology, and nationalism, and Michael Herzfeld's analysis of the contribution of archeology to Greek nationalism in *Ours Once More.*

32. Yadin's *Masada* and Moshe Pearlman's *Zealots of Masada* focus on the excavation itself. Other texts that include the story and/or pictures of the excavation are Ilan, *Li-Metsada be-Ikvot ha-Kana'im*, 63–66, 84–85; *Masada* (New York: The Jewish Theological Seminary and the Jewish Museum, 1967), 19–33. See also the flyer on Masada, produced by the Education Department of the Jewish National Fund (London, n.d.).

33. On the role of relics in providing a symbolic bridge, see Lowenthal, *Past Is a Foreign Country*, 248.

34. Yigael Yadin in the program "Yesh She'elot" (Questions), broadcast on Israeli national radio on April 27, 1966.

35. Shmaryahu Gutman's introduction to Ilan, *Li-Metsada be-Ikvot ha-Kana'im*, 3.

36. Gutman, *Im Metsada*, 144.

37. Shraga Gafni, *Tehilat Metsada* (The glory of Masada) (Tel Aviv: Amiḥai, 1970), 47. Out of 93 pages, 57 pages are devoted to the war and only 11 pages to Elazar's speeches and the mass suicide.

38. Yosef Klausner, *Jesus of Nazareth* (New York: Macmillan, 1925), 204.

39. Braslavsky, "Aḥarit Metsada ve-Ikvoteiha," 3.

40. Uri Brener, *Le-Tsava Yehudi Atsma'i* (For an independent Jewish army) (Efal: Yad Tabenkin, 1985), 387, mentions Masada and Tel Ḥai as two "educational models" for the Palmaḥ underground during 1944–45.

41. The theme of continuity between Masada and the past also appeared in nationalist poems calling for a national revival. See, for example, Yitzḥak Lamdan's description of "Yosef the Galilean" (i.e., Trumpeldor) as the carrier of the promise of Masada's renewal; *Masada* (Tel Aviv: Hedim, 1927; reprinted Tel Aviv: Dvir, 1972), English translation by Leon I. Yudkin, in *Isaac Lamdan: A Study in Twentieth-Century Hebrew Poetry* (Ithaca: Cornell University Press, 1971). See also D. Frankel, "Uri, Yehuda" (Wake up, Judaea) in *Metsada* (Jerusalem: Hitagdut ha-Setudentim ha-Revisionistim, 1933), 21.

42. Dina Porat, *Hanhaga be-Milkud: Ha-Yishuv Nokhaḥ ha-Sho'a, 1942–1945* (An entangled leadership: The Yishuv and the Holocaust) (Tel Aviv: Am Oved, 1986), 44–59; Tom Segev, *Ha-Milion ha-Shevi'i: Ha-Yisra'elim veha-Sho'a* (The seventh million: The Israelis and the Holocaust) (Jerusalem: Keter, 1991), 59–71.

43. Ibid., 37; Yechiam Weitz, "The Yishuv's Self-Image and the Reality of the Holocaust," *Jerusalem Quarterly* 48 (Fall 1988): 75–78.

44. Yitzḥak Gruenbaum's statement in the Jewish Agency Executive meeting of June 30, 1942, quoted in Uri Brener, *Nokhaḥ Iyum ha-Pelisha ha-Germanit le-Eretz Yisrael, 1940–1942* (In face of the threat of a German invasion of Palestine), 2d ed. (Efal: Yad Tabenkin, 1984), 106.

45. See Porat, *Hanhaga be-Milkud*, 27, 45, 56, 61–65. Gruenbaum was a famous Zionist Polish Jew who had served as a member of the Polish parliament, the Sejm, before he immigrated to Palestine. Porat's study shows that Gruenbaum was slow in responding to the information received from Europe and skeptical about it even when it was confirmed by various sources and eyewitness accounts.

46. Yitzḥak Tabenkin, *Devarim* (Efal: Yad Tabenkin, 1974), 3:88–90, reprinted in Brener, *Nokhaḥ Iyum ha-Pelisha ha-Germanit*, 132.

47. David Ben-Gurion's public speech for the Eleventh of Adar, 1943, was published as "Tsav Tel Ḥai" (The Tel Ḥai legacy), *Kuntres* 1, no. 381 (1943): 3–8.

48. Porat argues that one should distinguish between the leaders' strong anti-Diaspora statements in public during the 1930s and early 1940s, which were part of accepted Zionist discourse, and their own feelings of kinship and concern, which they expressed for themselves; *Hanhaga be-Milkud*, 437. This distinction between

public and private discourse is highly significant and perhaps the best evidence for the ideological climate of the period.

49. Firer, *Sokhnim shel ha-Ḥinukh ha-Tsiyoni*, 92–98; Elboim-Dror, *Ha-Ḥinukh ha-Ivri be-Eretz Yisrael*, 2:337–38, 380–82.

50. Ben-Tsiyon Dinur, ed., *Sefer Toldot ha-Hagana* (The history of defense) (Tel Aviv: Ma'arkhot, 1956), I, 2:387. As it appears in Uri Brener's study, the plan to defend the Yishuv vis-à-vis the Nazis may have been better known as *tokhnit ha-tsafon* (the northern plan) or the "Jewish Tubruk"; *Nokhaḥ Iyum ha-Pelisha ha-Germanit*, 141, 148, 156. But it is clear that in discussing the Yishuv's strategies, Masada was on the mind of those involved (e.g., ibid., 106, 154).

51. A meeting of the central leadership of Ha-Maḥanot Ha-Olim youth movement, April 2–3, 1943, quoted in Ben-Eliezer, "Tsva'iyut, Status, ve-Politika," 210.

52. See also Binyamin Kedar, "Tasbikh Metsada" (The Masada complex), *Ha-Aretz*, April 22, 1973, 16; Liebman and Don-Yeḥiya, *Civil Religion in Israel*, 150.

53. This poem was reprinted in a mimeographed brochure that a public high school in Ra'anana prepared for its celebration of a collective bar mitzvah at Masada and was used in 1976.

54. Yitzḥak Gruenbaum, meeting of the Jewish Agency Executive, June 30, 1942, reprinted in Brener, *Nokhaḥ Iyum ha-Pelisha ha-Germanit*, 106. On the leaders' critical attitude toward the Jewish victims in Europe during the war, see also Segev, *Ha-Milion ha-Shevi'i*, 85–98.

55. Liebman and Don-Yeḥiya, *Civil Religion in Israel*, 43, 150.

56. The people of Macherus negotiated with the Romans before the latter turned on Masada; see Josephus, *Wars of the Jews*, 7.6.4, p. 596.

57. Yosef Klausner, "Metsada" (Masada), in *La-No'ar Series* 62 (Tel Aviv: Omanut, 1937), 29–31; Braslavsky, "Aḥarit Metsada ve-Ikvoteiha," 3; Yigael Yadin, preface to Mikha Livne and Ze'ev Meshel, *Metsada* (Masada) (Tel Aviv: National Parks Authority, n.d.), 2; Gafni, *Tehilat Metsada* 76, 91.

58. Dinur, *Sefer Toldot ha-Hagana*, I, 2:387, emphasis added.

59. Marie Syrkin, "The Paradox of Masada," *Midstream* 19 (October 1973): 67.

60. As David G. Roskies points out, Lamdan's *Masada* was incorporated into a Warsaw anthology of 1940 (ed. Yitzḥak Zuckerman and Eliyohu Gutkovsky) and was a major source of inspiration for the uprising of the Warsaw Ghetto; Roskies, *The Literature of Destruction: Jewish Responses to Catastrophe* (Philadelphia: Jewish Publication Society, 1988), 358; Lucy S. Dawidowicz, *The Wars against the Jews, 1933–1945* (New York: Bantam, 1975), 424–25. On the expression "Masada of Warsaw" see Ḥayim Lazar-Litai's book by this title, *Metsada shel Varsha* (Tel Aviv: Makhon Jabotinsky, 1963).

61. Dawidowicz, *War against the Jews*, 425; Porat, *Hanhaga be-Milkud*, 435.

62. See also Shmu'el Avramsky's comments on this selective representation in "Milḥemet ha-Ḥerut shel Metsada" (Masada's war of liberation), *Maḥanayim* 87 (1963): 18.

63. Arye Carmon, "Holocaust Teaching in Israel," *Shoah* (Fall–Winter 1982–83): 22; Liebman and Don-Yeḥiya, *Civil Religion in Israel*, 258, n. 74.

64. Firer, *Sokhnim shel ha-Ḥinukh ha-Tsiyoni,* 70–91.

65. On Yad Va-Shem and its scope, see the official brochure, *Yad Va-Shem: Martyrs' and Heroes Remembrance Authority* (Jerusalem: Yad Va-Shem Authority, 1976). For the 1979 law see *Divrei ha-Knesset* (The Knesset protocols), May 12 and 18, 1953; August 19, 1953; March 10, 1959; April 8, 1959. For further analysis of the meaning of Yom ha-Sho'a (Holocaust day), see Young, "When a Day Remembers"; Liebman and Don-Yeḥiya, *Civil Religion in Israel,* 100–107.

66. See Weitz, "The Yishuv's Self-image and the Reality of the Holocaust," 78–79; for examples of such references in Hebrew textbooks, see Firer, *Sokhnim shel ha-Ḥinukh ha-Tsiyoni,* 81.

Hebrew Literature and Education

1. See chapter 2.

2. See Elboim-Dror, *Ha-Ḥinukh ha-Ivri be-Eretz Yisrael,* 1:159, 242–45. More than half of the students in the new Hebrew school in Jaffa (1906) were sent by their parents to Palestine to receive Hebrew education.

3. Ibid., 1:208–24, 240.

4. Ibid., 1:61, 202.

5. *Encyclopaedia Judaica* 9:930; Elboim-Dror, *Ha-Ḥinukh ha-Ivri be-Eretz Yisrael,* 1:309–50, 368, 372.

6. Shapiro, *Ilit Lelo Mamshikhim,* 73–77; Elboim-Dror, *Ha-Ḥinukh ha-Ivri be-Eretz Yisrael,* 1:189–92, 366.

7. Even-Zohar, "Emergence of Native Hebrew Culture in Palestine," 167–84; Harshav, *Language in Time of Revolution,* 133–80.

8. Ofek, *Sifrut ha-Yeladim ha-Ivrit,* 2:344–45, 352–53, and passim; Elboim-Dror, *Ha-Ḥinukh ha-Ivri be-Eretz Yisrael,* 1:192–95, 367, and vol. 2 passim; see also Firer, *Sokhnim shel ha-Ḥinukh ha-Tsiyoni,* 19 and passim; Tsili Dolev-Gandelman, "The Symbolic Inscription of Zionist Ideology in the Space of Eretz Israel: Why the Native Israeli Is Called *Tsabar,*" in Harvey E. Goldberg, ed., *Judaism Viewed from Within and Without* (Albany: State University of New York, 1987), 261–64.

9. On the role of schools in propagating national ideology, see Louis Althusser, "Ideology and Ideological State Apparatuses," in *Lenin and Philosophy and Other Essays* (New York: Monthly Review Press, 1971), 155–58.

10. Yehuda Grazovsky (later Gur), quoted in Elboim-Dror, *Ha-Ḥinukh ha-Ivri be-Eretz Yisrael,* 1:153, and see 195–96. For similar statements see Shapiro, *Ilit Lelo Mamshikhim,* 82.

11. It is important to note that the Israeli student is assigned to a class of peers who study together in an assigned classroom and advance as one social group from one grade to another. The emphasis on *gibush* (social cohesion) is still a major concern of the *meḥanekh* (the homeroom teacher) today. See Tamar Katriel, "*Gibush:* The Crystallization Metaphor in Israeli Cultural Semantics," in *Communal Webs:*

Communication, Culture, and Acculturation in Contemporary Israel (Albany: University of New York Press, 1991), 11–34.

12. See Na'or, *Tenuot ha-No'ar 1920–1960.*

13. Horowitz and Lissak, *Mi-Yishuv li-Medina*, 191–94; S. N. Eisenstadt, *Israeli Society* (New York: Basic Books, 1967), 231–47.

14. Shapiro, *Ilit Lelo Mamshikhim*, 80–89; Firer, *Sokhnim shel ha-Ḥinukh ha-Tsiyoni*, 92–126, 156–63; Elboim-Dror, *Ha-Ḥinukh ha-Ivri be-Eretz Yisrael*, 1: 359–96; Yoram Ben-Gal, *Moledet ve-Ge'ographia be-Me'a Shenot Ḥinukh Tsiyoni* (*Moledet* and geography in a hundred years of Zionist education) (Tel Aviv: Am Oved, 1993).

15. Ofek, *Sifrut ha-Yeladim ha-Ivrit*, 2:495–501; Zohar Shavit, *Ha-Ḥayim ha-Sifrutiyim be-Eretz Yisrael, 1910–1933* (The literary life in Eretz Israel) (Tel Aviv: Ha-Kibbutz ha-Me'uḥad, 1982), 34–40; Miron, *Im lo Tiheye Yerushalayim*, 114–15.

16. Ofek, *Sifrut ha-Yeladim ha-Ivrit*, 2:464.

17. Shaked, *Ha-Siporet ha-Ivrit*, 3:219; Ofek, *Sifrut ha-Yeladim ha-Ivrit*, 2: 463–501.

18. Elboim-Dror, *Ha-Ḥinukh ha-Ivri be-Eretz Yisrael*, 1:6, 309–10; Shapiro, *Ilit Lelo Mamshikhim*, 67–72.

19. Miron, *Im lo Tiheye Yerushalayim*, 41–47; Ḥever, "Shivḥei Amal u-Fulmus Politi," 116–57.

20. On the relations among literature, ideology, and politics in Russia, see Clark, *Soviet Novel.* On the impact of the Russian literature on Hebrew national culture, see Miron, *Im lo Tiheye Yerushalayim*, 14; Dimitry Segal, "Ha-Sifrut veha-Tarbut ha-Rusit be-Sugiyat Hivatsruta shel Tenu'at ha-Shiḥrur ha-Yehudit" (The impact of Russian literature and culture on the emergence of the Jewish liberation movement), in Ginosar, *Ha-Sifrut ha-Ivrit u-Tenu'at ha-Avoda*, 12.

21. See, for example, George L. Mosse, *Fallen Soldiers*, 21, on the German poets' contribution to the German national cause; see also Peter Uwe Hohendahl, *Building a National Literature: The Case of Germany, 1830–1870* (Ithaca: Cornell University Press, 1989); Herzfeld, *Ours Once More.*

22. Shaked, *Ha-Siporet ha-Ivrit*, 3:244.

23. Shapiro, *Ilit Lelo Mamshikhim*, 75–76.

24. See Clark, *Soviet Novel.* On the realist-collectivist trend of writers of the "Palmaḥ generation," see Dan Miron, *Arba Panim ba-Sifrut ha-Ivrit Bat Yameinu* (Four facets of contemporary Hebrew writing), revised edition (Jerusalem: Schocken, 1975), 332–48; Shaked, *Ha-Siporet ha-Ivrit*, 3:218; Nurit Gertz, *Ḥirbat Ḥiz'a veha-Boker shele-Moḥorat* (Generation shift in literary history) (Tel Aviv: Ha-Kibbutz ha-Me'uḥad, 1983), 9–18, 111–37.

25. Ya'akov Ḥurgin, *Shalshelet ha-Gevura* (Heroic chain) (Tel Aviv: Amiḥai, 1946).

26. Firer observes that only by the later Yishuv period (1930–48) history text-books fully represented the Zionist view of Jewish history (*Sokhnim shel ha-Ḥinukh ha-Tsiyoni*, 183–84). On the comparative role of literature and history in the Hebrew education of the earlier Yishuv period, see Firer's discussion on pages 92–126,

156–63; and Elboim-Dror, *Ha-Ḥinukh ha-Ivri be-Eretz Yisrael,* 1:383; Shapiro, *Ilit Lelo Mamshikhim,* 80–89.

Chapter 6: The Arm, the Plow, and the Gun

1. Yosef Klausner, "Al Kedushat ha-Aretz" (On the sanctification of the country), *Ha-Aretz,* March 21, 1921, 2.

2. Snir, "Trumpeldor," 5–6.

3. Y. Ya'ari-Polskin, *Ḥolmim ve-Loḥamim* (Dreamers and fighters) (Jaffa: Gissin, 1922), 296; David Tidhar, *Entsiklopedia le-Ḥalutsei ha-Yishuv u-Vonav* (Encyclopedia of Israeli pioneers) (Tel Aviv: Sifriyat Rishonim, 1950), 4:1591.

4. On the transformation of historical figures to legendary heroes, see Orrin E. Klapp, *Symbolic Leaders: Public Dramas and Public Men* (Chicago: Aldine, 1964), 32–42, 60; Kent L. Steckmesser, *The Western Hero in History and Legend* (Norman: University of Oklahoma Press, 1965), 53; Michael Owens Jones, "(PC + CB) × SD(R + I + E) = Hero," *New York Folklore Quarterly* 28 (1971): 245.

5. Laskov, *Trumpeldor,* 14–20, 28.

6. Liebman and Don-Yeḥiya, *Civil Religion in Israel,* 45.

7. The emphasis on the hero's total commitment to a transcendent ideal is found cross-culturally. See, for example, Horace P. Beck, "The Making of the Popular Legendary Hero," in Wayland D. Hand, ed., *American Folk Legend* (Berkeley: University of California Press, 1971), 1932; Bruce Rosenberg, *Custer and the Epic of Defeat* (University Park: Pennsylvania State University Press, 1974), 240. A famous American example of a similar patriotic saying is Nathan Hale's declaration, "I only regret that I have but one life to lose for my country." Trumpeldor's own last words echo the famous Roman saying, "Dulce et decorum est pro patria mori."

8. *Le-Yom Tel Ḥai: Ḥoveret Ezer la-Ganenet* (For Tel Ḥai Day: Reader for the nursery school teacher) (Tel Aviv: Histadrut, 1943), 10.

9. Ibid., 3.

10. See, for example, the poems by Levin Kipnis, "Ari ha-Even: Agada" (The stone lion: A legend) (1943), in ibid., 23; Shlomo Skolsky, "Ha-Ari: Agada" (The lion: A legend) (1945), in *Ha-Ari ha-Gelili, 1920–1945* (The Galilean lion) (Tel Aviv: Betar, 1945), 2. See also the plays by Y. Naḥmani, "Agadat ha-Galil" (The legend of Galilee) (n.d.), and S. Elifaz, "Agadat ha-Galil" (n.d.), both in Gratz Education Library, Tel Aviv, Trumpeldor/Tel Ḥai files.

11. *Ha-Aretz,* March 5, 1920, 1. The analogy to the ancient heroes appeared often in the prestate era in speeches and writing. See, for example, Nordau, "Ha-Kapitan Trumpeldor," 50; Snir, "Trumpeldor"; Ben-Gurion, "Tsav Tel Ḥai," 3–8. It also appeared in literary works, such as S. Shalom, "Aḥ, Bne ha-Galil" (Brother, build Galilee), in Harari, ed., *Mo'adim le-Simḥa,* 284; Shim'oni, "Le-Trumpeldor," 2:226–27; D. Frankel, "Uri, Devora" (Wake up, Debora), in *Ha-Ari ha-Gelili,* 2. This theme is part of the image of Trumpeldor perpetuated by

educational materials to date; see also Rivka Bakalash, "Mitos Trumpeldor 'Adam, Dam, Adama' be-Vet ha-Sefer ha-Yesodi" (The Trumpeldor myth "man, blood, earth" in the elementary school), master's thesis, Ben-Gurion University of the Negev, 1988.

12. The poem's words are, "Once there was an ancient hero who broke down cliffs, who lifted rocks; an 'enigmatic hero' was he, with a single arm only" (Avraham Breudes, "Ba-Galil" [In Galilee] [1932], reprinted in *Shir le-Ḥag* (Songs for the holidays) (Tel Aviv: Emunim, 1955), 18.

13. Naḥmani, "Agadat ha-Galil."

14. *Le-Yom Tel Ḥai: Ḥoveret Ezer*, 11.

15. *Dror* (newsletter of Ha-Gymnasia ha-Realit Balfour), no. 5 (11th of Adar, 1935): 11 (Aviezer Yellin Archive for Education, Tel Aviv University, file 3.147/2). I would like to thank Nili Arie for bringing this text to my attention.

16. *Ha-Aretz*, March 5, 1920, 1.

17. Almost the same text appears in Ariel, Blich, and Persky, *Mikra'ot Yisrael le-Khita Bet;* and in the revised edition by Persky, *Mikra'ot Yisrael Ḥadashot le-Khita Bet*, 238. The following text is quoted from the latter source.

18. Uriel Ofek, *Gibor Ḥida* (The enigmatic hero) (Tel Aviv: Shreberk, 1975), 37–38.

19. Ibid., 12. This description of Trumpeldor's attitude is supported by a story that Trumpeldor himself wrote, "Wertheimer," in which he glorifies a new recruit's transformation from an exilic, observant Jew to a secular man and a courageous soldier in the Zion Mule Corps. The story was published posthumously in *Ha-Aretz*, March 21, 1921, 2–3. On Trumpeldor's encounter with traditional Jews see also Dov Rabin, "Yosef Trumpeldor ve-Sipurei Peretz" (Yosef Trumpeldor and Peretz's stories), in *Ha-Po'el ha-Tsa'ir*, March 20, 1962.

20. A program on the history of songs for Tel Ḥai Day, broadcast on Israeli national radio, March 16, 1967. The Hebrew words were composed in 1920 by Abba Ḥushi (who later became the mayor of Ḥaifa). It should be noted, however, that borrowing a non-Jewish melody was not unusual in eastern European Jewish culture or among the Socialist Zionists in Palestine.

21. Anda Amir, "Be-Yom Yod-Alef ba-Adar" (On the Eleventh of Adar), reprinted in *Le-Yom Tel Ḥai: Ḥoveret Ezer*, 27 (the Hebrew verses rhyme). See also Shalom, "Aḥ, Bne ha-Galil."

22. Bela Bar'am. "Yosef ha-Gelili" (Yosef the Galilean), in *Le-Yom Tel Ḥai: Ḥoveret Ezer*, 22.

23. Simon Halkin, *Modern Hebrew Literature: Trends and Values* (New York: Schocken, 1970), 41–43.

24. See, for example, "The Lord is my shepherd," Psalms 23 : 1.

25. Fania Bergstein, "Rigvei ha-Galil" (The soil of Galilee), in *Ḥaruzim Adumim* (Red beads) (Tel Aviv: Ha-Kibbutz ha-Me'uḥad, 1955), 164–70.

26. For discussion of the symbolism of the poppy in relation to World War I, see Paul Fussell, *The Great War and Modern Memory* (New York: Oxford University Press, 1975), 246–49.

27. Sha'ul Tchernichovsky in his poem "Ha-Adam Eino Ela" (Man is not but), reprinted in *Shirim*, 466–69.

28. Shalom Spiegel, *The Last Trial.*

29. See note 17.

30. Avraham Breudes, "Yosef ha-Gelili" (Yosef the Galilean), in *Le-Yom Tel Ḥai: Ḥoveret Ezer*, 24; the Hebrew verses rhyme.

31. H. Tehar-Lev, *Kol mihe-Harim* (A voice from the mountains) (Jerusalem: Sifriyat Adama, 1959).

32. Naḥmani, "Agadat ha-Galil"; S. Meltzer, "Ba-Galil ha-Elyon" (In Upper Galilee), in *Le-Yom Tel Ḥai: Ḥoveret Ezer*, 5; Sara Levy, "Ba-Galil" (In Galilee), ibid., 26.

33. Kipnis, "Yosef Gibor Yisrael" (Yosef, the hero of Israel), in Y. Levinton, Levin Kipnis, and A. Buchner, eds., *Sefer ha-Kita Bet* (Reader for the second grade) (Tel Aviv: Dvir, 1971).

34. Kipnis, "Ari ha-Even," 23–24. For further discussion of Bar Kokhba's lion, see chapter 7.

35. Naḥmani, "Agadat ha-Galil."

36. This image is based on the biblical verse of Nehemiah 4:11.

37. See, for example, Laskov, *Trumpeldor*, 84; an interview with Tanḥum Tanfilov, in "Ha-Adam Yosef Trumpeldor" (The man—Yosef Trumpeldor) broadcast on Israeli national radio on June 6, 1965. See also the tale of how Trumpeldor's extraordinary power and resourcefulness helped him plow the fields and overcome a wild cow with one arm only (Israel Folktales Archives, tale no. 12588).

38. Avraham Breudes's famous poem "Ba-Galil" includes the verse: "Hayo haya gibor hida / ve-Lo zero'a yeḥida" (Once there was an enigmatic hero / Who had only one arm). Note that the Hebrew verse rhymes.

39. Levin Kipnis, "Ha-Yad ha-Ḥazaka" (The strong arm), in A. Buchner, Y. Levinton, and L. Kipnis, eds., *Sefer ha-Kita Zayin* (Reader for the seventh grade) (Tel Aviv: Dvir, 1965), 362–64.

40. Shimon Shor, "Al Kivro shel Yosef ha-Gelili" (On the tomb of Yosef the Galilean), *Ḥaverenu* (the Taḥkemoni School newsletter) (Adar 2, 1924): 1, Aviezer Yellin Archives, file 4.145.

41. The museum, Bet Yosef, was established in Kibbutz Tel Yosef, which is named after the dead hero. According to a recent article, the director of the Tel Ḥai Museum claimed that the appropriate place for Trumpeldor's artificial arm is in his museum. See Batya Feldman, "Ha-Ḥavera Tamar lo Ozevet et ha-Yad shel Trumpeldor" (Comrade Tamar does not leave Trumpeldor's arm), *Ḥadashot*, April 4, 1991, 8–10. I would like to thank Tamar Katriel for bringing this article to my attention.

42. *Le-Yom Tel Ḥai, Yod Alef ba-Adar: Ḥomrei Hadrakha le-Morim be-Vatei ha-Sefer ha-Mamlakhtiyim* (For Tel Ḥai Day, the Eleventh of Adar: Educational materials for public schools teachers) (Jerusalem: Ministry of Education, 1967).

43. *Le-Yom Tel Ḥai: Ḥoveret Ezer*, 3.

44. Ibid., 13.

45. Ibid.; Hebrew verses rhyme.

46. *Ḥaverenu*, Adar 1924, 1.

47. See, for example, Ḥanoch Bartov, *Shel Mi Ata Yeled?* (Whose child are you?) (Tel Aviv: Am Oved, 1970), 241; Amalya Kahana-Carmon, *Ve-Yare'aḥ be-Emek Ayalon* (And moon in the valley of Ayalon) (Tel Aviv: Ha-Kibbutz ha-Me'uḥad, 1971), 176.

48. Within Jewish tradition the Hebrew term *agada* was first used in reference to the nonlegalistic texts in the talmudic-midrashic literature, which served primarily for teaching ethical and moral principles. Later, *agada* referred also to historical-biographical texts related to postbiblical rabbis. Although these tales are not historically accurate, they are presented as true accounts; *Encyclopaedia Judaica* 2: 354–55; Yosef Heinemann, *Agadot ve-Toldoteihen* (Agada and its development) (Jerusalem: Keter, 1974), 11–12; Dan Ben-Amos, "Generic Distinctions in the Aggadah," in F. Talmage, ed., *Studies in Jewish Folklore* (Cambridge, Mass.: Association for Jewish Studies, 1980), 52; Emanuel Bin-Gorion, *Shevilei ha-Agada* (The paths of the legend) (Jerusalem: Bialik Institute, 1970), 33–35, 40–44.

49. Yosef Dan, *Ha-Sipur ha-Ivri bi-Yemei ha-Beinayim* (The Hebrew story in the Middle Ages) (Jerusalem: Keter, 1974), 25.

50. See Liebman and Don-Yeḥiya, *Civil Religion in Israel.*

Chapter 7: Bar Kokhba, the Bonfire, and the Lion

1. Eric Hobsbawm and T. Ranger, eds., *The Invention of Tradition* (Cambridge: Cambridge University Press, 1983).

2. "When you enter the land that I am giving to you and you reap its harvest, you shall bring the first sheaf of your harvest to the priest . . . And from the day on which you bring the sheaf of elevation offering—the day after the Sabbath—you shall count off seven weeks" (Leviticus 23:10, 15; see also Deuteronomy 16:9).

3. On the mourning practices and their diversity see Solomon Ganzfried, ed., *Code of Jewish Law* (New York: Hebrew Publishing Co., 1961), 3:52–53; "Omer," *Encyclopaedia Judaica* 12:1385–86; Levinsky, *Sefer ha-Mo'adim*, 7:333–34; Mordekhai Ha-Cohen, "Lag ba-Omer: Mekorot, Halakhot, Minhagim" (Lag ba-Omer: Sources, laws, customs), *Maḥanayim* 56 (1961): 20–28.

4. Babylonian Talmud, *Yebamot* 62b.

5. Rabbi Menaḥem Ha-Meiri in his commentary to *Yebamot* 62b, *Beit ha-Beḥira.* See Levinsky, *Sefer ha-Mo'adim*, 6:342–43; *Encyclopaedia Judaica* 12:1387.

6. *Ha-Entsiklopedia ha-Ivrit* (The Hebrew encyclopedia) (Jerusalem: Encyclopaedias Publishing Company, 1971), 21:178.

7. Whether the mourning customs stop at that point or are resumed following Lag ba-Omer vary across the different Jewish communities. See Avraham Ben-Ya'akov, *Yalkut Minhagim: Mi-Minhagei Shivtei Yisrael* (An anthology of Jewish communities' customs) (Jerusalem: Ha-Madpis ha-Memshalti, 1967); Ha-Cohen, "Lag ba-Omer," 20–31; Levinsky, *Sefer ha-Mo'adim*, 6:360–70.

8. Menaḥem Ha-Cohen, "Ḥetz va-Keshet be-Lag ba-Omer," (Bow and arrows on Lag ba-Omer) *Maḥanayim* 26 (1961): 38–40.

9. Lou H. Silberman, "The Sefira Season: A Study in Folklore," *Hebrew Union College Annual* 22 (1942): 222–25; Theodor H. Gaster, *Festivals of the Jewish Year*, 3d ed., (New York: William Sloane Associates, 1974), 52–53; Julian Moregenstern, "La ba-Omer: Its Origin and Import," *Hebrew Union College Annual* 29 (1968): 81–90.

10. *Encyclopaedia Judaica* 10:1357.

11. Note that in Hebrew the word for bow and for rainbow is exactly the same. On the explanations regarding the mystical traditions, see Levinsky, *Sefer ha-Mo'adim*, 6:345–53, 359, 361–66, 408–41; Meir Benayahu, "Hitnahagut Mekubalei Tsefat be-Meron" (The behavior of the Safed Kabbalists in Meron), *Sefunot* 6 (1962): 24–34; Betsalel Landau, ed., *Masa Meron* (The Meron journey) (Jerusalem: Usha, 1966).

12. See *Encyclopaedia Judaica* 12:1388; Levinsky, *Sefer ha-Mo'adim*, 6:340–42.

13. This interpretation was raised by the scholar Naḥman Krokhmal in the first half of the nineteenth century. J. Derenbourg, "Le 33e Jour de l'Omer," *Revue des Études Juives* 29 (1894): 149; Ha-Cohen, "Lag ba-Omer," 30.

14. Levinsky, *Sefer ha-Mo'adim*, 6:353–54.

15. *Lag ba-Omer: Ḥoveret la-Talmid* (Lag ba-Omer: A student's work guide) (Jerusalem: Ministry of Education and Culture, Curriculum Planning Department, 1987), 22.

16. See, for example, B. Avivi and A. Keren-Tal, eds., *Mo'adim le-Simḥa* (Happy holidays) (Jerusalem: Kiryat Sefer, 1943), 3–9; Levin Kipnis and Yemima Tchernovitch, eds., *Gan Gani* (My nursery school) (1947; Tel Aviv: Bronfman, 1978), 113–14; Levinsky, *Sefer ha-Mo'adim*, 6:341.

17. This view was supported by a remark made by the prominent medieval Jewish philosopher Maimonides, that Rabbi Akiba was *nose kelim* (armor-bearer) of the king Bar Koziba, in his commentary on laws concerning kings, *Hilkhot Melakhim*, 11:3.

18. Ariel, Blich, and Persky, *Mikra'ot Yisrael le-Khita Bet*, 339; Persky, *Mikra'ot Israel Ḥadashot le-Khita Bet*, 404. Note that in Kipnis and Tchernovitch, *Gan Gani*, and in Z. Ariel, Z. Vilensky, and N. Persky, eds., *Alfoni: Mikra'a le-Khita Alef* (Reader for the first grade) (Tel Aviv: Masada, 1968) Rabbi Akiba is not mentioned at all. See also L. Kipnis, A. Buchner and Y. Levinton, eds., *Sefer ha-Kita Gimel* (Reader for the third grade) (Tel Aviv: Dvir, 1962), and Arye Ḥorshi, *Ḥagim vi-Yemei Zikaron la-Talmid* (Holidays and memorial days for the student) (Tel Aviv: Bronfman, 1974), 185–89.

19. B. Yoel, "Ḥag ha-Mered" (The holiday of the revolt), *Ha-Aretz* (Lag ba-Omer Eve 1927), reprinted in Z. Y. Yaffe and Y. Spivak, eds., *Medura* (Bonfire) (Jerusalem: Keren Kayemet le-Yisrael, 1929), 6–7.

20. Levinsky, *Sefer ha-Mo'adim*, 6:480; Yaffe and Spivak, *Medura*, 111–26. Note also that later the Israel Defense Forces established a tradition of shooting contests on Lag ba-Omer.

21. *Lag ba-Omer: Ḥoveret la-Talmid*, 24.

22. This information is based on the *Lag ba-Omer* tales I found at the Israel Folktales Archives at Ḥaifa University in 1987.

23. Avraham Goldfaden's *Bar Kokhba: Der zuhn Fun dem Shtern* (Bar Kokhba, the son of star: An enlightened melodrama in rhymes) was published in 1887 in Yiddish (see *Encyclopaedia Judaica* 7:716) and in 1908 in New York by the Hebrew Publishing Company. The play was translated into Hebrew by B. Yedidya, and excerpts were reprinted in the Lag ba-Omer anthology for children, edited by Yaffe and Spivak, *Medura*, 84–85.

24. Arye Ḥorshi, *Ḥagim vi-Yemei Zikaron la-Talmid*, 198. See also Levinsky, *Sefer ha-Mo'adim*, 6:478.

25. Persky, *Mikra'ot Israel Ḥadashot le-Khita Bet*, 404. See also Kipnis, *Mo'adei Yisrael*, 16. Ariel, Blich, and Persky, *Mikra'ot Yisrael ke-Khita Bet*, 339; Kipnis and Tchernovitch, *Gan Gani*, 13. Another, though less common, interpretation of the custom of kindling bonfires suggests that the Romans prohibited the kindling of fires because they knew that the rebels used them for communication; therefore bonfires have become a symbol of resistance; Ha-Cohen, "Lag ba-Omer," 38.

26. These reports are reprinted in Yaffe and Spivak, *Medura*, 112–13.

27. See, for example, Yaffe and Spivak, *Medura;* Dalya Talmi, ed., *Leket Shirei Lag ba-Omer* (An anthology of Lag ba-Omer songs) (Tel Aviv: Kiryat ha-Ḥinukh, n.d.); Bornstein-Lazar, *Lag ba-Omer*, 18–24, 34–54.

28. See, for example, the two humorous pieces on this phenomenon by Ephra'im Kishon, "Ḥag ha-Mayim" (The water holiday) in *Ba-Aḥad ha-Amashim* (One of yester days) (Tel Aviv: Tversky, 1963), 159; Yonatan Gefen, "Ha-Mekoshesheth ha-Ketana" (The little gatherer), *Ma'ariv*, May 2, 1975. On the competitive nature of wood gathering, see also Ḥorshi, *Ḥagim vi-Yemei Zikaron la-Talmid*, 198.

29. On the custom of burning a Haman effigy on Purim, see Ḥayyim Schauss, *The Jewish Festivals: History and Observance* (New York: Schocken, 1962), 267. On the custom of burning Hitler's effigy during World War II, see Levinsky, *Sefer ha-Mo'adim*, 6:478. During the *Hilula* celebration on Mount Meron, participants burn clothes immersed in oil, a custom that was disapproved by some religious authorities; see Shmu'el Ḥagai, "Ha-Hadlaka veha-Halakha" (The bonfire and the religious law) *Maḥanayim* 56 (1961): 34–37.

30. Lipovetsky, *Yosef Trumpeldor;* Poznansky, *Me-Ḥayei Yosef Trumpeldor;* Ben-Ari and Kena'ani, *Yosef Trumpeldor;* Laskov, *Trumpeldor.*

31. Kipnis wrote hundreds of short stories, poems, songs, and plays for young children and was editor of numerous children's books. See Tidhar, *Entsikopedia le-Ḥalutsei ha-Yishuv u-Vonav*, 5:2103–5; Ofek, *Sifrut ha-Yeladim ha-Ivrit*, 2:342–52.

32. See, for example, Kipnis and Tchernovitch, *Gan Gani*, 114. This song is still among the first ones that Israeli children learn around the celebration of Lag ba-Omer. See Telma Elyagon and Rafi Pesaḥzon, eds., *Elef Zemer ve-Od Zemer* (The Israeli sing-along) (Ramat Gan: Kinneret, 1985), 4:231.

33. Note that the Hebrew verses rhyme and that the italicized words are repeated twice. The melody for the song was composed by Mordekhai Ze'ira, who,

like Kipnis himself, contributed to the making of many Israeli folk songs. The first publication of this song was in *Gilyonot* (an anthology of stories and songs for the nursery school), ed. Levin Kipnis (Tel Aviv: Association for Nursery School teachers, 1929), 59–62. I would like to thank Meir Noy, who established an archive of Jewish and Israeli folk songs, for this information.

34. We can assume that Kipnis read Levner's work on Bar Kokhba and borrowed the theme of Bar Kokhba and the lion. Levner published Kipnis's first works in his children's magazine *Ha-Peraḥim* and encouraged Kipnis to pursue his career as a writer; Tidhar, *Entsiklopedia le-Ḥalutsei ha-Yishuv u-Vonav*, 5:2103–5. Levner's work on Bar Kokhba, which was first published in *Ha-Ḥayim veha-Teva* in 1905, was reissued as a book, *Bar Kokhva: Sipur Histori mi-Yemei Harisot Betar* (Bar Kokhba: A historical novel on the destruction of Betar) (Warsaw: Barkai, 1923) and again in Israel in 1950.

35. Levner, *Bar Kokhva*, 42.

36. Ibid., 47.

37. Israel Benjamin Levner, "Bar Kokhva veha-Arye" (Bar Kokhba and the lion), in Avivi and Keren-Tal, *Mo'adim le-Simḥa*, 3–6.

38. Levner, *Bar Kokhva*, 54, 82, 105, 116.

39. Kipnis's story is published in two versions (short and long) according to the age of the targeted readers. For the full text of the story, see "Kefirei Arayot" (The lions) in his *Mo'adei Yisrael*, 33–42; for the shorter version see Ariel, Vilensky, and Persky, *Alfoni*, and Ariel, Blich, and Persky, *Mikra'ot Yisrael le-Khita Bet.*

40. Kipnis, "Kefirei Arayot," 38.

41. Kipnis also makes an overt analogy between Bar Kokhba and the lion in the description of their earlier encounters: both like wandering alone at night in the mountains, both shake their hair/mane; and both "roar" to communicate to the other.

42. Shraga Gafni, *Mered Bar Kokhva* (The Bar Kokhba revolt) (Tel Aviv: Amiḥai, 1976), 12. Hereafter pages are given in the text.

43. The image of Bar Kokhba riding his lion also appears in Sha'ul Tchernichovsky's earlier poem "Betara."

44. Kipnis, "Ari ha-Even," 23–24.

45. Kipnis, *Yigal Asher Yigal*, 17–28. The story title uses the double meaning of *Yigal* as both a first name and the future tense of the verb "to redeem" implying that the child will be the redeemer.

46. Ya'akov Ḥurgin, "Ha-Lavi shel Bar Kokhva" (Bar Kokhba's lion), in *Shalshelet ha-Gevura*, 32–41.

47. Bornstein, "Menusato shel Ḥetz ha-Zahav," 7–13.

48. Ḥurgin, "Ha-Lavi shel Bar Kokhva," 33.

49. Bar Kokhba's victory over the lion is thus analogous to Lord Raglan's theme of "victory over a king and/or giant, dragon, or wild beast"; *The Hero: A Study in Tradition, Myth, and Drama* (1936; New York: Meridian Books, 1979), 174. Similarly, the older legend about the snake who killed Bar Kokhba fits Raglan's theme of a hero who loses favor with God, is defeated in the war, and encounters a mys-

terious death. See also Efron, "Milḥemet Bar Kokhba le-Or ha-Masoret ha-Talmudit," 63–64.

50. For Samson's encounter with the lion, see Judges 14:5–6; for David's confrontation with it, see I Samuel 17:35. For cross-cultural analogues, see motif B16.2.3. in Stith Thompson, *Motif Index of Folk Literature* (Bloomington: Indiana University Press, 1976).

51. For the description of Samson breaking his chains, see Judges 15:14, 16: 8–9, 12. Bar Kokhba's performance of a similar act is depicted in Kipnis, "Kefirei Arayot," 38; Gafni, *Mered Bar Kokhva*, 32.

52. For Samson's prayer to God, see Judges 16:28; for Bar Kokhba's prayer to God, see Levner, *Bar Kokhva*, 45.

53. See also Yair Zakovitch, *Ḥayei Shimshon: Nitu'aḥ Sifruti Bikorti* (The life of Samson: A critical-literary analysis) (Jerusalem: Magnes, 1982), 91–92.

54. Gafni, *Mered Bar Kokhva*, 39–47.

55. Thompson, *Motif Index of Folk Literature*, B251.2.11, and B771.2.1.

56. Kipnis, "Bar Kokhva veha-Arye," 341; and "Kefirei Arayot," 42; Gafni, *Mered Bar Kokhva*, 53.

57. See "Ariel" (tale no. 286) in Mikha Yosef Bin-Gorion, *Mimekor Yisrael: Classic Jewish Folktales* (Bloomington: Indiana University Press, 1976), I:513–15. The Israel Folktales Archive has a few versions of this highly popular story recorded from the folk traditions of different Jewish groups. See, for example, IFA 12043, "Ariel," told by Leon Margi from Tangier; IFA 13537, "Rabbi Alfasi veha-Shayara" (Rabbi Alfasi and the convoy), excerpted from Boas Hadad, *Sefer Jerba ha-Yehudit* (The book of Jewish Jerba) (Jerusalem, 1944), 46–47; IFA 12385, "Rabbi Rokhev al Arye" (A rabbi riding a lion), told by Avraham Ataya from Tunisia. This tale was also known among eastern European Jews. For example, in her biography of Berl Katznelson, Anita Shapira refers to it as the first tale relating to the Land of Israel that he read as a child; *Berl: Biographia* (Tel Aviv: Am Oved, 1981), I:21.

58. Israel Folktales Archive, IFA 4040, "Bizkhut Elisha ben Ya'ish Ba'al ha-Mofet" (By virtue of Elish Ya'ish, the miracle maker), told by Ḥayim Aflalu from Morocco. Similarly, a pious Jew who defied the Inquisition's prohibition on studying Torah was spared by six hungry lions when thrown into their den. The king made the Jew his advisor and abolished the prohibition; IFA 10275, "Yisrael de la Rosa be-Gov ha-Arayot" (Yisrael de la Rosa in the lion's den), told by Rabbi Yom Tov Matsli'aḥ from Saloniki, Greece. Another tale describes how a big lion who was starved for three days did not harm the revered Yemenite rabbi, Shalom Shabazi, and hence the king realized that Shabazi was indeed a holy man; IFA 17285, "Rabbi Shalom Shabazi," told by Yeḥiel Dan from Yemen.

59. The only exception among the versions examined here is Gafni's story, in which the impressed Roman emperor grants Bar Kokhba freedom. This modification, like the allusions to Bar Kokhba's religiosity mentioned above, may indicate the growing integration of traditional Jewish and Zionist values in Israeli culture.

60. I heard this story from an elderly museum guide of Ha-Shomer Museum (January 3, 1988) who had heard it from his own parents of the founders' genera-

tion. A similar story is quoted in Walter Laqueur, *Toldot ha-Tsiyonut* (A history of Zionism) (Jerusalem: Schocken, 1975), 194.

61. At another level, one can interpret the Heilperin story as a parody of the new genre of Hebrew heroic tales to which the Bar Kokhba lore belongs: the display of courage and readiness for self-sacrifice vis-à-vis a tame circus lion creates an ironic framework for the desired ideological message of Heilperin's public display. It is difficult to tell if this ironic twist was perceived during the prestate period. It is not surprising, however, that today—according to the museum guide who told me the story—young Israelis improvise humorous interpretations of why the lion refused to devour Heilperin, much in line with the recent humorous lore about Trumpeldor I discuss in chapter 9.

62. Yadin, *Bar Kokhba*, 134.

63. Avramsky, *Bar Kokhva Nesi Yisrael*, 207.

64. Yehuda Dvir, *Bar Kokhva: Ha-Ish veha-Mashi'aḥ* (Bar Kokhba: The man and the messiah) (Jerusalem: Kiryat Sefer, 1964), 107. In line with his thesis about Bar Kokhba's association with a messianic sect, Dvir suggests that the lion represents the messianic hopes associated with Bar Kokhba and supports it with Bar Kokhba's presumed relation to the House of David.

Chapter 8: The Rock and the Vow

1. Yitzḥak Lamdan, *Masada* (1927; Tel Aviv: Dvir, 1972). All quotes are from the English translation by Leon I. Yudkin, in *Isaac Lamdan*, 199–234.

2. See the discussion of Josephus's historical narrative in chapter 5.

3. Tamara Blaushild, "Aliyata u-Nefilata shel ha-Po'ema Masada le-Yitzḥak Lamdan" (The rise and fall of Yitzḥak Lamdan's poem) (master's thesis, Department of Hebrew Literature, Tel Aviv University, 1985), 20.

4. Lamdan mentions Elazar ben Yair only briefly: "Ascend, chain of dance! Never again shall Masada fall! . . . Let us ascend! The son of Yair shall again appear. He is not dead, not dead!" Yudkin, *Issac Lamdan*, 215.

5. For example, Shlomo Tsemaḥ criticized *Masada* sharply as a glorification of despair; *Ha-Po'el ha-Tsa'ir* 26–27 (April 15, 1927): 43; the poet Avraham Shlonsky wrote a negative review of this work, "Im Kri'at *Masada*" (Reading *Masada*), in the literary magazine *Ketuvim*, December 31, 1926, 4. For further discussion of responses to Masada, see Schwartz, Zerubavel, and Barnett, "Recovery of Masada"; for a detailed survey of all these sources, see Blaushild, "Aliyata u-Nefilata shel ha-Po'ema Masada."

6. Lamdan founded the literary journal *Gilyonot*, which, unlike most literary forums of the period, was a nonpartisan publication, and used his editorial column to express his views. See his public statements on the writer's role and the contribution of literature to the national cause in "Teshuva la-Sho'alim" (In response to those who question) in *Gilyonot* 1, no. 1 (1933): 1–2, and "Reshimot" (Notes) in *Moznayim* 26 (1930): 11–12.

7. *Masada* has gone through eleven editions since its publication in 1927. For a detailed review of the references to it in various literatures, see the appendixes to Blaushild, "Aliyata u-Nefilata shel ha-Po'ema Masada," 86–100. None of Lamdan's other works enjoyed the great popularity of *Masada;* Ḥaya Hoffman, "Ha-Af Al Pi Khen ha-Breneri be-Shirat Yitzḥak Lamdan" (Brener's "nevertheless" in the poetry of Yitzḥak Lamdan), in Ginosar, *Ha-Sifrut ha-Ivrit,* 159.

8. For some of the earlier observations on the role of Lamdan's *Masada* in promoting the myth, see Lewis, *History,* 8; Robert Alter, "The Masada Complex," *Commentary* 56 (June 1973): 22; Kedar, "Tasbikh Metsada," 16; Schwartz, Zerubavel, and Barnett, "Recovery of Masada," 147–64.

9. Blaushild, "Aliyata u-Nefilata shel ha-Po'ema Masada," 21.

10. Baruch Kurtzweil, "Ha-Toda'a ha-Historit be-Shirei Yitzḥak Lamdan" (The historical consciousness in the poetry of Yitzḥak Lamdan), in *Bein Ḥazon le-Vein Absurd* (Between vision and absurdity) (Tel Aviv: Schocken, 1966), 100–109.

11. For an early observation about this connection, see Mordekhai Ovadyahu, "Meshorer ha-Tekufa" (The poet of his time), *Ha-Po'el ha-Tsa'ir* 10 (1949): 15.

12. See Schwartz, Zerubavel, and Barnett, "Recovery of Masada," 154.

13. Blaushild, "Aliyata u-Nefilata shel ha-Po'ema Masada," 38.

14. Schwartz, Zerubavel, and Barnett, "Recovery of Masada," 158–61.

15. On the phenomenon of suicide see Elon, *Israelis,* 144. On the Zionist settlers' psychological difficulties see Brakha Ḥabas, *Sefer ha-Aliya ha-Sheniya* (The book of the Second Aliya) (Tel Aviv: Am Oved, 1947), 534–58; Elboim-Dror, *Ha-Ḥinukh ha-Ivri be-Eretz Yisrael,* 1:379–80.

16. "In 1926, 56 people left Palestine for every 100 who entered. In 1927, every 100 newcomers were offset by 187 emigrants. In 1928, the emigration-immigration ratio was 99.5: one person left the country for every person who arrived" (Schwartz, Zerubavel, and Barnett, "Recovery of Masada," 156). More broadly, it is estimated that among members of the Second Aliya emigration reached 90%; Dan Giladi, "Kalkala ve-Ḥevra bi-Tekufat ha-Aliya ha-Sheniya" (Economy and society during the Second Aliya period), in Mordekhai Na'or, ed., *Ha-Aliya ha-Sheniya, 1903–1904* (The Second Aliya, 1903–1904) (Jerusalem: Yad Yitzḥak Ben-Zvi, 1984), 5.

17. Hoffman, "Ha-Af Al Pi Khen ha-Breneri," 163–72.

18. See chapter 5, note 18.

19. In a symbolic contrast to the Hebrew concepts *moledet* and *yediat ha-aretz,* relating to the study of the history and geography of Israel, the study of other parts of the world is labeled *ge'ographia* (geography), a Hebrew derivative of Greek. For a comprehensive study on the development of these subjects in Hebrew education, see Ben-Gal, *Moledet ve-Ge'ographia.*

20. Elboim-Dror, *Ha-Ḥinukh ha-Ivri be-Eretz Yisrael,* 1:389, 2:346; Na'or, *Tenu'ot ha-No'ar,* 246–56; Ben-Eliezer, "Tsva'iyut, Status, ve-Politika," 255–56.

21. Drawing on the biblical meaning of the verb "to know," implying sexual intercourse, "knowing the land" also has sexual connotations. See Meron Benvenisti, *Conflicts and Contradictions* (New York: Villard, 1986), 19.

22. Braslavsky, "Aḥarit Metsada ve-Ikvoteiha," 3; Weitz, *Seviv Metsada,* 4.

23. In 1934, after a student had been killed during a trip, Gymnasia Hertseliya

stopped its trips to the Dead Sea and Masada; interview with Dr. Baruch Ben Yehuda on June 16, 1979. See also Bitan, "Metsada," 224. Trips were altogether stopped during the Arab revolt against the British (1936–39), due to the rising political tensions.

24. Gutman, *Im Metsada*, 8; Kafkafi, *Shenot Ha-Maḥanot Ha-Olim*, 333–34; Bitan, "Metsada," 226–27; Na'or, *Yam ha-Melaḥ u-Midbar Yehuda*, 238–41, 275.

25. See, for example, the various accounts in Na'or, *Yam ha-Melaḥ u-Midbar Yehuda*, 236–75.

26. Shmaryahu Gutman in ibid., 238.

27. Gutman in an interview on the radio program "Shmaryahu Gutman: Ha-Meshuga li-Metsada" (Shmaryahu Gutman: The Masada Fanatic), broadcast on Israeli national radio on January 12, 1968.

28. Rafi Tahon, who reached Masada around the same time, tells how they brought wine with them, thinking that they would feel euphoric. But when they actually reached the summit, hot and thirsty and with no water, they realized how inappropriate the wine was, and they soon continued on their way down; Na'or, *Yam ha-Melaḥ u-Midbar Yehuda*, 254.

29. Azaria Alon estimates the number of casualties in those trips at around twenty-five youth; "Me Haya Midbar Yehuda Avurenu?" (What did the Judaean desert mean to us?), in Na'or, *Yam ha-Melaḥ u-Midbar Yehuda*, 271; Pearlman, *The Zealots of Masada*, 60.

30. N., "Ken, Lelo Takhlit" (Indeed, for no purpose) *Ba-Maḥane* 59 (May 1, 1942): 11; Ben-Avoya, "Ha-Omnam Lelo Takhlit?" (Is it really for no purpose?) *Ba-Maḥane* 60 (June 5, 1942): 10. See also Ben-Eliezer, "Tsva'iyut, Status, ve-Politika," 225.

31. *Ki Alinu li-Metsada* (For we climbed up to Masada) (Tel Aviv: Histadrut Ha-Shomer Ha-Tsa'ir be-Eretz Yisrael, 1942), 13.

32. Victor Turner points out that Christian pilgrimages often contain symbols and metaphors of death that allude to the ideal of self-sacrifice embodied in Jesus Christ and the early martyrs. The representation of death (which sometimes becomes real) highlights the symbolic role of the pilgrimage as a rite of passage. The analogy to this early Hebrew pilgrimage to Masada is indeed striking; Victor W. Turner, *Process, Performance, and Pilgrimage: A Study in Comparative Symbology* (New Delhi: Concept, 1979).

33. Gutman on the radio program "Ha-Meshuga li-Metsada."

34. See Rafi Tahon's account in Na'or, *Yam ha-Melaḥ u-Midbar Yehuda*, 246.

35. Na'or, *Tenu'ot ha-No'ar*, 246–56; Benvenisti, *Conflicts and Contradictions*, 22.

36. Na'or, *Tenu'ot ha-No'ar*, 240.

37. Turner, *Ritual Process*.

38. The three pilgrimage holidays were also called *regalim*, the plural form of the word *regel* (foot).

39. See Weitz, *Seviv Metsada*, 4.

40. See also Benvenisti, *Conflicts and Contradictions*, 35.

41. As noted above, the subtitle of the Hebrew edition of Yadin's book on the Masada excavation is "In Those Days at This Time," a phrase borrowed from the

Ḥanukka prayer. Shmaryahu Gutman signed the prefaces to his *Im Metsada* and to Ilan's *Li-Metsada be-Ikvot-ha-Kana'im* on Ḥanukka Eve, as did Yadin in his preface to Livne and Meshel, *Metsada.*

42. P. E. Lapide, "Masada," *Jewish Heritage* 6 (Spring 1964): 29.

43. During the late prestate period, another term that implies "going up," *ha'apala,* designated clandestine Jewish immigration to Palestine in defiance of the British restriction.

44. The song "El Rosh ha-Har" (words by Levin Kipnis) is included in a recent collection of "best beloved Israeli songs" in the Israeli sing-along tradition (Elyagon and Pesaḥzon, *Elef Zemer ve-Od Zemer,* 2 : 143). The Hebrew verb used in the song is *ha'apilu* of the same root as the word *ha'apala.*

45. See also Gurevitch and Aran, "Al ha-Makom," 31.

46. See, for example, the description of the commemorative rituals at Masada in *Ba-Mivḥan,* December 27, 1942, reprinted in Kafkafi, *Shenot Ha-Maḥanot Ha-Olim,* 333.

47. See Elias Canetti for an analysis of the symbolic use of fire in *Crowds and Power* (New York: Viking Press, 1966). For a symbolic analysis of the rhetoric of fire inscriptions in Israeli youth culture, see Katriel, *Communal Webs,* 51–70.

48. *Ha-Yom ha-Ze* (radio news magazine), July 7, 1969.

49. In 1982 the State of Israel gave a similar official burial to bones identified as the ancient soldiers of the Bar Kokhba revolt of A.D. 132–35. For the analysis of this ritual see Myron J. Aronoff, "Establishing Authority: The Memorialization of Jabotinsky and the Burial of the Bar Kokhba Bones in Israel under the Likud," in *The Frailty of Authority; Political Anthropology Series* 5 (New Brunswick: Transaction, 1986), 105–30, and the discussion in chapter 10.

50. On the commemoration of the Unknown Soldier, see Mosse, *Fallen Soldiers;* Anderson, *Imagined Communities,* 17.

51. On the centrality of the moral-historical injunction to remember in Jewish culture, see Yerushalmi's *Zakhor.*

52. According to Yadin, this tradition began soon after the foundation of the state; introduction to Livne and Meshel, *Metsada,* 3. Recently, however, the Armored Corps moved the ritual from Masada to Latrun, a site on the way to Jerusalem associated with the attempt to break the siege on Jerusalem during the War of Independence.

53. See, for example, Beno Rotenberg, *Metsada* (Masada) (Tel Aviv: Levin Epstein, 1963), 11; Ilan, *Li-Metsada be-Ikvot ha-Kana'im,* 106; Pearlman, *Zealots of Masada,* 40; Yadin, *Masada,* 200.

54. Bob Baseman, *Masada: Pictorial Guide and Souvenir* (Palphot, n.d.).

55. Mikha Livne, *Ma'oz Aḥaron: Ha-Sipur shel Metsada va-Anasheiha* (The last fortress: The story of Masada and its people) (Ministry of Defense, 1986), 214; English translation by Yael Chaver was also published by the Ministry of Defense in 1986.

56. Similar opinions about the cable car were voiced in the radio program "Yesh She'elot" (Questions) on this issue on April 27, 1966.

57. See Eric Cohen, "Tourism as Play," *Religion* 15 (1985): 291–304.

58. Yehuda Almog, one of the promoters of the site of Masada, opposed the installation of a cable car; "Yoman ha-Shavu'a" (The weekly magazine on Israeli national radio, July 28, 1962). He was quoted as saying, "I, on principle, will climb up the Masada until my very last day and will not use all kinds of *machindalakh* [machines] which they installed there"; *Mi-Ḥayeinu* (a publication of the Kibbutz Bet Yosef), March 15, 1973. Similarly, a woman I interviewed who sharply criticized the cable car, referred to it as "facilities," inserting the English word into her Hebrew speech.

59. Livne, *Ḥomer Ezer la-Madrikh bi-Metsada*, 92.

60. H. Bat-Ḥaim, "Bar Mitzvah on Masada," *Hadassah Magazine* 48 (April 1967): 10. As these group ceremonies became more popular, they ceased to be newsworthy.

61. A teacher in a school that began subscribing to the bar mitzvah tradition at Masada explained to me that parents and students preferred Masada over the Western Wall because the former called for a "real trip," overnight camping, and a more dramatic and exciting setting than the latter. While during the late 1970s and early 1980s it appeared that the appeal of Masada was declining in comparison to that of the Western Wall, the Intifada may have reinforced Masada's attractiveness for security reasons.

62. Yigael Yadin on the radio program "Yesh She'elot," April 27, 1966.

63. This development is linked to the emergence of the "tragic commemorative narrative" discussed in chapter 11.

64. See also Edward M. Bruner's and Phyllis Gorfain's discussion of the touristic narration of Masada in their "Dialogic Narration and the Paradoxes of Masada," in Stuart Plattner and Edward M. Bruner, eds., *Text, Play, and Story: The Construction and Reconstruction of Self and Society* (Washington, DC: American Ethnological Society, 1984), 72–73.

65. On the impact of tourism through "commodization" and "sacralization" of tradition, see Dean MacCannell, *The Tourist: A New Theory of the Leisure Class* (New York: Schocken, 1976), 43–48; Davydd J. Greenwood, "Culture by the Pound: An Anthropological Perspective on Tourism as Cultural Commodization," in Valene L. Smith, ed., *Hosts and Guests: The Anthropology of Tourism* (Philadelphia: University of Pennsylvania Press, 1977), 129–38. See also Mosse's comment about the trivialization of battlefields transformed from sites of pilgrimage to tourist attraction; *Fallen Soldiers*, 153–55.

66. See also Dan Ben-Amos's letter of March 6, 1983 to Edward M. Bruner and Phyllis Gorfain, reprinted in their "Dialogic Narration," 77.

67. On "staged authenticity" see MacCannell, *Tourist*, 91–107. On the distinction between "ritual" and "spectacle," see John J. MacAloon, "Olympic Games and the Theory of Spectacle in Modern Societies," in *Rites, Drama, Festival, Spectacle: Rehearsals toward a Theory of Cultural Performance* (Philadelphia: Institute for the Study of Human Issues, 1984), 241–80.

68. The ceremony was reported on Israeli national television, December 19, 1971, and on Israeli national radio, December 7, 1972.

69. "Eru'im be-Misgeret Tsiyun Shenat ha-Sheloshim la-Medina" (Events

marking the thirtieth anniversary of the State of Israel), *Ha-Aretz*, weekend supplement, October 23, 1978, 32.

70. Lewis, *History*, 3–41; E. R. Chamberlin, *Preserving the Past* (London: J. M. Dent & Sons, 1979), 18–27.

71. See, for example, Ronit Vardi, "Metsada" (Masada), *Yediot Aḥronot*, October 14, 1988, 1; Yigal Tomarkin, "Ma Bein Mahler ve-Har ha-Shulḥan be-S.A." (How does Mahler relate to the mountain), *Ha-Aretz*, weekend supplement, October 7, 1988, 23.

72. Ḥayim Breude, "Metsada Nafla Shenit" (Masada fell again), *Yediot Aḥronot*, April 8, 1991.

73. Livne, *Ma'oz Aḥaron*, 214; my translation of the Hebrew text.

74. Greenwood, "Culture by the Pound," 129–38.

Calendars and Sites as Commemorative Loci

1. On the importance of locus for the creation of memory, see Frances A. Yates, *The Art of Memory* (Chicago: University of Chicago Press, 1966), 2–7.

2. The association of Masada with Ḥanukka is important for those who make the youth pilgrimage to Masada during this holiday vacation. But this pilgrimage is not central to the Ḥanukka commemorative tradition in Israeli culture as experienced by the society at large.

3. Yadin, *Ha-Ḥipusim Aḥar Bar Kokhva*, 27. My translation of the Hebrew text. It is interesting to note that the English version of this paragraph differs significantly from the original Hebrew text quoted here.

4. Gafni, *Mered Bar Kokhva*, 85.

5. Ibid.

6. The recent outpouring of literature commemorating the five hundredth anniversary of Columbus's landing in the Americas provides another example of the primary role of literature in the commemoration of the past.

Chapter 9: Tel Ḥai and the Meaning of Pioneering

1. For example, Thompson, *Political Mythology of Apartheid;* Nurit Gertz, "Social Myths in Literary and Political Texts," *Poetics Today* 7 (1986): 621–39; Tamar Katriel and Aliza Shenhar, "Tower and Stockade: A Study in Israeli Settlement Symbolism," *Quarterly Journal of Speech* 76, no. 4 (1990): 359–80; Roger Friedland and Richard Hecht, "The Politics of Sacred Place: Jerusalem's Temple Mount/*al-haram al-sharif*," in Jamie Scott and Paul Simpson-Housley, eds., *Sacred Places and Profane Places: Essays in the Geographies of Judaism, Christianity, and Islam* (New York: Greenwood, 1991); Van Der Veer, "Ayodhya and Somnath," 85–109.

2. The Labor movement itself also suffered from internal tensions between moderates and militants during the 1930s and 1940s. See Anita Shapira, "Ha-

Viku'aḥ be-tokh Mapai al ha-Shimush be-Alimut, 1932–1935" (The debate in Mapai on the use of violence), *ha-Tsiyonut* 5 (1978): 141–81; Yigal Elam, *Ha-Hagana* (The Hagana organization) (Tel Aviv: Zmora & Bitan, 1979), 90–100, 117–59; Ben-Eliezer, "Tsva'iyut, Status, ve-Politika."

3. Laskov, *Trumpeldor*, 232–33; Rogel, *Tel Ḥai*, 50–70.

4. Katznelson, "Anshei Tel Ḥai be-Motam uve-Ḥayeihem"; on Jabotinsky's position see also Ben-Yeruḥam, *Sefer Betar*, 1:42 n. 8; Yosef Nedava, "Jabotinsky u-Farashat Tel Ḥai" (Jabotinsky and the Tel Ḥai affair), *Ha-Uma* 16 (September 1978): 370.

5. Ze'ev Jabotinsky, "Bein ha-Shishi la-Aḥad Asar" (Between the sixth and the eleventh [of Adar]), *Ha-Am*, June 6, 1931, reprinted in *Ketavim: Ba-Sa'ar* (Collected works: The storm) (Jerusalem: Ari Jabotinsky, 1953), 265–71.

6. Ze'ev Jabotinsky, "Mi-Yomani" (From my diary), *Ha-Am*, July 14, 1931, 2.

7. Eliyahu Golomb, *Rashei Perakim le-Toldot Haganat ha-Yishuv* (An outline of the history of the Yishuv's defense) (Jerusalem: Kav le-Kav, 1947), 77.

8. Liebman and Don-Yeḥiya, *Civil Religion in Israel*, 60–61; Ya'akov Shavit, *Me-Rov li-Medina*, 53.

9. Jabotinsky, "Kaddish," 104.

10. Aba Aḥime'ir, "Mi-Tel Ḥai li-Ve'er Tuvia," *Do'ar ha-Yom*, March 11, 1930; reprinted in *Brit ha-Biryonim* (The Biryonim Association) (Tel Aviv: Ha-Va'ad le-Hotsa'at Kitvei Aḥime'ir, 1972), 174.

11. Ya'akov Goldstein and Ya'akov Shavit also suggest that the Revisionists' reconstruction of Trumpeldor's heroic image was modeled after the famous Polish national hero Pilsudski; "Yosef Trumpeldor ki-Demut Mofet, veha-Viku'aḥ al 'Shayekhuto' ha-Tenu'atit" (Yosef Trumpeldor as a model and the controversy about his political affiliation), *Kivunim* 12 (1981): 18–19.

12. See, for example, Ze'ev Jabotinsky, "Al Trumpeldor veha-Ein Davar Shelo" (Trumpeldor and his "never mind"), in *Yosef Trumpeldor: Ḥai Shanim le-Moto*, 53–55; *Ha-Ari ha-Gelili* (Tel Aviv: Betar, 1945), 14.

13. Jabotinsky, "Al Trumpeldor," 54; and again, in *Sipur Yamai* (Autobiography) (Jerusalem: Ari Jabotinsky, 1947), 205–6. Jabotinsky emphasizes that Trumpeldor's *ḥalutz* (pioneer) is "neither a 'landlord' nor a peasant . . . neither a guard, nor even a common worker"—terms that were central to the Socialist ideology. It is interesting to note that, when Jabotinsky first directed public attention to Trumpeldor's "never mind" a few days after the hero's death, he offered a different interpretation, stressing his power of determination, resilience, and humbleness; "Tel Ḥai," *Ha-Aretz*, March 8, 1920, 1.

14. Goldstein and Shavit, "Trumpeldor," 16; Ya'akov Shavit, *Me-Rov li-Medina*, 266–68.

15. This image of the pioneer, based on Neḥemia 4:11, was popular among the early Jewish settlers. The Hagana and Palmaḥ undergrounds, which were affiliated with the Labor movement, continued to emphasize the double commitment to work and defense as represented in this image.

16. *Le-Yom Tel Ḥai: Ḥoveret Ezer*, 7.

17. Katznelson, "Anshei Tel Ḥai."

18. *Zekhor Yemei Tel Ḥai,* 20; *Tel Ḥai: Yalkut* (Tel Ḥai: An anthology) (Tel Aviv: Histadrut, 1934), 165; *Magen va-Shelaḥ: Sheloshim Shana la-Haganat Tel Ḥai* (The shield and the weapon: Thirtieth anniversary of the defense of Tel Ḥai) (Tel Aviv: Histadrut, 1934), 14; see also Goldstein and Shavit, "Trumpeldor," 11–15.

19. Eliezer Smally, "Ha-Maḥresha" (The plow), reprinted in Harari, *Mo'adim le-Simḥa,* 288–90.

20. It is interesting to compare this story's representation of the value of the plow with a similar statement by members of Ha-Shomer that articulated their feeling that "none of us will desert the plow as long as he lives"; Yisrael Giladi, quoted in Gorni, "Ha-Yesod ha-Romanti," 64.

21. Sara Levy, "Ba-Galil."

22. Avraham Breudes, "Hu Lo Met" (He is not dead), in Harari, *Mo'adim le-Simḥa,* 283.

23. Eliezer Smally, "Ha-Degel" (The flag), reprinted in *Ḥoveret la-Madrikh le-Ḥodesh Adar* (Guidelines for the counselor for the month of Adar) (Tel Aviv: Betar, 1979), 47–50.

24. Ofek, *Sifrut ha-Yeladim ha-Ivrit,* 2:463–67.

25. Ḥayim Yosef Brener, "Le-Yom ha-Zikaron" (For the memorial day), *Kuntres* 72 (March 21, 1921): 3; Ze'ev Jabotinsky, "Shir Asirei Ako" (The song of the Acre Prisoners), 1920; reprinted in *Shirim* (Poems) (Jerusalem: Ari Jabotinsky, 1947), 187; and Jabotinsky in a later poem "Shir Tel Ḥai" (The song of Tel Ḥai), 1927; reprinted in *Shirim,* 197–98. On Jabotinsky's early attitude to the Socialist settlers, see Ya'akov Shavit, *Me-Rov li-Medina,* 27, 144.

26. Slutsky, *Mavo le-Toldot Tenu'at ha-Avoda ha-Yisraelit,* 234–35; Laskov, *Trumpeldor,* 54–58.

27. Trumpeldor's "Kol Kore" (A public call) was published in the two major publications of the Labor movement—*Ha-Po'el ha-Tsa'ir,* December 19, 1919, and *Kuntres,* December 30, 1919. On the impact of this public call, see Laskov, *Trumpeldor,* 196–205.

28. Laskov, *Trumpeldor,* 192; *Ha-Aretz* and *Do'ar ha-Yom,* March 8, 1920.

29. Trumpeldor, letter to a friend, November 29, 1911, reprinted in *Tel Ḥai: Yalkut,* 161–69. It is not surprising that the Labor movement was the one to quote this letter that defends its position.

30. Myron J. Aronoff suggests that these ideological disputes actually contributed to the crystallization and legitimation of the Zionist discourse; "Myths, Symbols, and Rituals of the Emerging State," in Laurence J. Silberstein, ed., *New Perspectives on Israeli History: The Early Years of the State* (New York: New York University Press, 1991), 186.

31. See, for example, Levin Kipnis, A. Buchner, and Y. Levinton, *Sefer ha-Kita Gimel;* Ariel, Vilensky, and Persky, *Alfoni: Mikra'a le-Khita Alef;* Persky, *Mikra'ot Yisrael Ḥadashot le-Khita Bet;* see also *Le-Yom Tel Ḥai, Yod Alef ba-Adar.*

32. Among the 120 people I interviewed in the late 1970s, only a handful mentioned Betar in conjunction with Tel Ḥai, and all of them (except for one student)

were older people who remembered the Revisionist-Socialist conflict from their own youth.

33. From the manifesto of a new literary magazine, *Likrat* (1952), quoted by Gershon Shaked in *Gal Ḥadash ba-Siporet ha-Ivrit* (A new wave in Hebrew fiction) (Tel Aviv: Sifriyat ha-Po'alim, 1974), 17. See also Shapiro, *Ilit Lelo Mamshikhim*, 128–41.

34. Liebman and Don-Yeḥiya, *Civil Religion in Israel*, 81–122.

35. Various works by Avraham B. Yehoshua, Amos Oz, Aharon Megged, Yitzḥak Ben-Ner, Ya'akov Shabtai, Amalya Kahana-Carmon, Ruth Almog, and others have portrayed images of alienated, self-doubting Israelis. For further discussion of this development, see Shaked, *Gal Ḥadash;* Gertz, *Ḥirbat Hiz'a veha-Boker shele-Moḥorat;* Miron, *Im lo Tiheye Yerushalayim;* Yael S. Feldman, "Zionism on the Analyst Couch in Contemporary Israeli Literature," *Tikkun* 2 (November–December 1987): 31–34, 91–96; Yael Zerubavel, "The 'Wandering Israeli' in Contemporary Israeli Literature," *Contemporary Jewry* 7 (1986): 127–40. On a parallel development in Israeli film, see Ella Shoḥat, *Israeli Cinema: East/West and the Politics of Representation* (Austin: University of Texas Press, 1989).

36. Aharon Megged, *Ha-Ḥai al ha-Met* (Tel Aviv: Am Oved, 1965), 63; English translation by Misha Louvish, *Living on the Dead* (New York: McCall, 1970), 67–68.

37. S. Yizhar, *Yemei Tsiklag* (The days of Tsiklag), 3d ed. (Tel Aviv: Am Oved, 1959), 1021–22.

38. Yesha'ayahu Ben-Porat et al. *Ha-Meḥdal* (The Oversight) (Tel Aviv: Hotsa'a Meyuḥedet, 1974), 293.

39. See, for example, Tamar Meroz, "Trumpeldor Basar va-Dam" (Trumpeldor of flesh and blood), *Ha-Aretz*, weekend magazine, March 20, 1970, 12; Laskov, *Trumpeldor*, 248; Ram Evron, "Tov Lamut be'ad Artsenu?" (Is it good to die for our country?), *Davar*, weekend magazine, March 24, 1972, 22. Dan Almagor gave wide publicity to these doubts in his programs on this subject in the Israeli media, followed by two articles, "Ma be-Emet Amar Trumpeldor?" (What did Trumpeldor really say?), *Yediot Aḥronot*, weekend magazine, March 16, 1979; and "Milim Aḥronot al Trumpeldor" (Last words about Trumpeldor), *Yediot Aḥronot*, April 13, 1979.

40. The informants who defied the authenticity of Trumpeldor's last words were mostly adults educated in Israel as opposed to new immigrants who knew little (or nothing) of the myth of Tel Ḥai, and children, who tend to accept the textbook version they learn at school.

41. References to the hero's last words appeared in several Hebrew newspapers (*Do'ar ha-Yom* and *Ha-Aretz*, March 8, 1920; *Ha-Po'el ha-Tsa'ir* and *Kuntres* 29, March 12, 1920) and in private communications following the battle of Tel Ḥai (Rogel, *Tel Ḥai*, 190, 195 n. 45; Laskov, *Trumpeldor*, 248). According to Laskov, Trumpeldor's wording may have been slightly different: "Never mind, it is worth dying for the homeland."

42. Nedava, "Jabotinsky u-Farashat Tel Ḥai," 373, n. 17; Yosef Nedava, "Bein Historia le-Mitos" (Between history and myth), *Yediot Aḥronot*, July 6, 1979, 23;

Menachem Begin in an interview, quoted by Elḥanan Oren, "Moreshet ve-Shorasheiha: Tel Ḥai—Mitos ve-Emet" (A legacy and its roots: Tel Ḥai—Myth and truth), *Shorashim* 2 (1980): 153–80.

43. Uri Brener, "Tenu'at ha-Po'alim be-Mivḥan Tel Ḥai" (The Labor Movement Tested in Tel Ḥai), in *Lekaḥ Tel Ḥai: Ha-Hityashvut u-Gevul ha-Tsafon* (The lesson of Tel Ḥai: Settlement and the northern border) (Efal: Yad Tabenkin and Ha-Kibbutz ha-Me'uḥad, 1980), 16–19; B. Reptor, "Beineinu le-Vein Jabotinsky" (Between us and Jabotinsky), ibid, 26–29.

44. Rogel, *Tel Ḥai*, 14–15, 233–44; and introduction to *Lekaḥ Tel Ḥai*, n.p.; see also Elam, *Ha-Hagana*, 19.

45. Jabotinsky, "Tel Ḥai"; Klausner, "Hem Naflu Ḥalalim."

46. See, for example, Ben-Gurion, "Zsav Tel Ḥai," 3–4; Aharon Megged, ed., *Masekhet ha-Hagana* (The story of the Hagana) (Tel Aviv: Irgun Ḥavrei ha-Hagana, 1966), 9.

47. Persky, *Mikra'ot Yisrael Ḥadashot*, 239; see also Sara Ben-Ḥanan, ed. *Ze Sifrenu, Sefer Sheni* (This is our book: Reader for the second grade) (Jerusalem: Marcus, 1971), 224; Ariel, Vilensky, and Persky, *Alfoni*, 52; *Zekhor Yemei Tel Ḥai*, 22–23.

48. *Encyclopaedia Judaica* 9:683.

49. The strategy of *ḥoma u-migdal* produced sixty new Jewish settlements in Palestine during the Arab revolt of the late 1930s and continued during the 1940s. On Tel Ḥai's inspiration for this settlement movement, see Rogel, *Tel Ḥai*, 224–25; Elḥanan Oren, *Hityashvut bi-Shenot Ma'avak, 1936–1947* (Settlement and struggle) (Jerusalem: Yad Yitzḥak Ben-Zvi, 1978), 49, 93, 159, 178; and "Moreshet ve-Shorasheiha," 154–56, 159–64.

50. Oren, "Moreshet Tel Ḥai" (The legacy of Tel Ḥai), in *Lekaḥ Tel Ḥai*, 11.

51. Anita Shapira, "Ha-Tsiyonut veha-Ko'aḥ" (Zionism and power), in *Halikha al Kav ha-Ofek*, 69–70; Elam, *Ha-Hagana*, 22, 80–81.

52. Rogel, *Tel Ḥai*, 17, 19.

53. On Gush Emunim and its ideology, see Kevin Avruch, "Traditionalizing Israeli Nationalism: The Development of Gush Emunim," *Political Psychology* 1, no. 1 (1979): 47–57; Myron J. Aronoff, "The Revitalization of Political Culture: Gush Emunim," in *Israeli Visions and Divisions: Cultural Change and Political Conflict* (New Brunswick: Transaction, 1989), 69–91; Dani Rubenstein, *Mi la-Adonai Elai: Gush Emunim* (On the Lord's side: Gush Emunim) (Tel Aviv: Ha-Kibbutz ha-Me'uḥad, 1982), 126–30; Ehud Sprinzak, "The Iceberg Model of Political Extremism," in David Newman, ed. *The Impact of Gush Emunim* (London: Croom Helm, 1985), 30–31; Ian S. Lustick, *For the Land the Lord: Jewish Fundamentalism in Israel* (New York: Council on Foreign Relations, 1988), 42–71; Gideon Aran, "Jewish Zionist Fundamentalists: 'The Bloc of the Faithful' in Israel," in Martin E. Marty and R. Scott Appleby, eds. *Fundamentalism Observed* (American Academy of the Arts and Sciences; Chicago: University of Chicago Press, 1991), 265–344; Robert Paine, "Jewish Ontologies of Time and Political Legitimation in Israel" in Henry J. Rutz, ed., *The Politics of Time* (Washington D.C.: American Ethnological Society, 1992), 150–70.

54. Rubenstein, *Mi la-Adonai Elai*, 128.

55. Yisrael Epstein, ed., *Shenei Mo'adim: Yod Alef ba-Adar, Semel ha-Yahadut ha-Mitḥadeshet; Purim, Semel ha-Yahadut ha-Galutit* (Two holidays: The Eleventh of Adar, symbol of Jewish renewal; Purim, symbol of exilic Judaism) (Warsaw: Betar, 1937).

56. See, for example, Levy Itzḥak Ha-Yerushalmi, "Ha-Maḥresha veha-Ḥerev o ha-Ḥerev veha-Maḥresha" (The plow and the sword or the sword and the plow), *Ma'ariv (Yamim ve-Leilot)*, September 22, 1978, 8–9; Ruth Bundi, "Mi-Tel Ḥai ve-Ad Yameinu" (Since Tel Ḥai until today), *Davar*, weekend magazine, March 23, 1979, 8. Amos Elon remarked that one of the vocal promoters of the new settlements may have "lost his hope to turn [Prime Minister] Begin into Trumpeldor of the 1970s"; "Ba-Ḥazara meha-Kor be-Einayim Mefukaḥot" (Back from the cold with open eyes), *Ha-Aretz*, October 6, 1978, 13; see also Yoram Ben-Porat, "Ha-Daḥpor veha-Emuna" (The bulldozer and faith), *Ha-Aretz*, June 17, 1979, 9.

57. Tsvi Shilo'aḥ, "Mi-Tel Ḥai ve-Ad Ne'ot Sinai" (From Tel Ḥai to Ne'ot Sinai), *Yediot Aḥronot*, April 10, 1979, 17.

58. Elliott Oring, *Israeli Humor: The Content and Structure of the Chizbat of the Palmaḥ* (Albany: State University of New York Press, 1981), 129–30.

59. This *chizbat*, recorded by Dan Ben-Amotz and Ḥayim Ḥefer, was translated and published in Oring's collection; ibid., 126–28.

60. On the *schlemiel* as a folk and literary type, see Ruth R. Wisse, *The Schlemiel as a Modern Hero* (Chicago: University of Chicago Press, 1971). See also Irving Howe and Eliezer Greenberg, eds. *A Treasury of Yiddish Stories* (New York: Schocken, 1973), 614–27.

61. This *chizbat* was published by Puchu, a writer of the Palmaḥ generation, in the youth magazine *Mashehu* in its Purim issue, March 1988. There is no indication whether this *chizbat* originated in the 1940s or is a new composition written in the spirit of the older Palmaḥ lore. I would like to thank Tamar Katriel for bringing this text to my attention.

62. This caricature by Danny Kerman was originally published in *Dvar ha-Shavua* and was reprinted in *Yediot Aḥronot* with Almagor's article "Milim Aḥronot al Trumpeldor," April 13, 1979.

63. A more recent piece in *Yediot Aḥronot* (August 9, 1991) entitled "Ma Kara la-Arye?" (What happened to the lion?) notes that one of the veteran members of Kfar Giladi observed that the teeth fell out of the lion's mouth, and suggests that it may be an attribute of its old age that also "represents what is happening to the Labor movement."

64. In Hebrew, "Trumpeldor haya gibor / kol ha-yom haya gibor / be-yad aḥat ba-maḥresha / be-yad sheniya haya gibor." In other versions, the word *amputee* (*gidem*) replaces *hero* in the last line ("with his other hand he was an amputee") or replaces the word *hero* in all lines. Still another version has the second line as "all day long he was a peasant."

65. The colloquial use of the Hebrew word *zayin* (weapon) as a reference to penis makes this sexual allusion more explicit.

66. The melodies I heard used with this song-joke include "Bar Kokhba veha-

Arye" (Bar Kokhba and the lion), the traditional Ḥanukka hymn "Ma'oz Tsur Yeshu'ati" (Mighty rock of my salvation), and the folk song "El ha-Ḥoresh ha-Karov" (To the nearby forest).

67. A white license plate indicates that a car has been purchased at a considerable discount which the Israeli government provides to new immigrants and disabled persons.

68. One joke is based on the Hebrew expression "to take an example from someone" (meaning "to follow someone's example"): "Q: Why did Trumpeldor have only one arm? A: Because they took [cut off] an example from him [*ki lakḥu mimenu dugma*]." Another joke states that Trumpeldor contributed "the finger of Galilee" (Israel's northern tip prior to 1967) from his amputated hand, thus providing a literary meaning to the myth's claim regarding Israel's debt to the defense of Tel Ḥai for its control over the northern Galilee.

69. Danny Kerman et al., *Davar Akher Legamre* (Utterly different) (Tel Aviv: Am Oved, 1988), 126.

70. See, for example, Reḥavam Ze'evi's article on the importance of the *aḥarai* (follow me) doctrine for the Israel Defense Forces in *Ba-Maḥane*, December 18, 1969, 10–11.

71. See Ya'akov Ha-Elyon's moving account of his personal experiences in the rehabilitation ward after the Six-Day War. He describes the macabre humor of the patients as they argued which was worse, to be a "Trumpeldor" or a "crippled pilot," after the title of a Russian novel about a pilot who continued to fly even after his leg was amputated; *Regel Shel Buba* (A doll's leg) (Tel Aviv: Am Oved, 1973), 181.

72. The cartoon was published by B. Michael et al., *Zoo Eretz Zoo?* (This land is a zoo), 2d ed. (Jerusalem: Domino Press, 1982), 162–63. The educational text it targets is quoted from a textbook that was widely used by the secular public schools until the late 1970s. See Ariel, Blich, and Persky, *Mikra'ot Yisrael le-Khita Bet*, 252–53.

73. Brian Sutton-Smith, "Shut Up and Keep Digging: The Cruel Joke Series," *Midwest Folklore* 10 (1960): 11–22; Roger D. Abrahams, "Ghastly Commands: The Cruel Joke Revisited," *Midwest Folklore* 11 (1961): 235–46; Alan Dundes, *Cracking Jokes: Studies of Sick Humor Cycles and Stereotypes* (Berkeley: Ten Speed Press, 1987), 15–18.

74. See, for example, the resemblance between the masturbation joke quoted above and the following Keller joke: "Why does Helen Keller masturbate with only one hand? So she can moan with the other" (Mac E. Barrick, "The Helen Keller Joke Cycle," *Journal of American Folklore* 93 [1980]: 448, joke 19).

75. M. M. Bakhtin, *Rabelais and His World* (1965; English translation by Helene Iswolsky, Bloomington: Indiana University Press, 1984), 317–18.

76. The government's claim that the offensive in Lebanon was vital for Israel's security was widely questioned when it developed into a war in which civilians were also hurt. Although official announcements refer to this war by its official name—*Mivtsa Shelom ha-Galil* (Operation Peace of Galilee)—emphasizing its de-

fensive character, this name did not catch on, and Israelis commonly refer to it as the Lebanon War.

77. Israelis refer to this kind of jokes as *bediḥot zeva'a* (ghastly jokes), a term analogous to sick or cruel humor.

78. This piece "Me'a va-Aḥad Ra'ayonot le-Kishut Ḥalal ha-Limud o ha-Kita" (One hundred and one ideas for decorating the teaching space or the classroom) was published in *Davar Aḥer* no. 153, the satirical supplement of the daily newspaper *Davar*, September 13, 1986. The Hebrew title uses a pun—*ḥalal*—implying both "classroom space" and "a dead body."

79. "Ma Lamadeta ba-Gan ha-Yom?" (What did you learn in the nursery school today?), lyrics by Ḥayim Ḥefer (1964); reprinted in Amnon Birman, ed. *Be-Etsem, Ad ha-Etsem: Mi-Mivḥar ha-Satira ha-Yisra'elit* (Under the skin: Selected Israeli satires) (Jerusalem: Keter, 1988), 230–31.

80. The movie, directed by Renen Schorr, was shown in the 1987 Jerusalem Film Festival.

81. The following song repertoire is quoted from B. Michael, "Mi-Zemirot Eretz ha-Arazim" (From the songs of Lebanon), *Ha-Aretz*, December 31, 1983; Aliza Shenhar, "Liheyot Sham: Shirei Meḥa'a shel Ḥayalim bi-Levanon" (To be there: Protest songs by soldiers during the Lebanon War), *Ḥetz* 1 (April 1989): 34–43.

82. The original song was translated into Hebrew and has become part of Israeli folksong repertoire.

83. See Shenhar, "Liheyot Sham," 39–40.

84. A. J. Obrdlik, "Gallows Humor: A Sociological Phenomenon," *American Journal of Sociology* 47 (1942): 709–16. See Dundes, *Cracking Jokes*, 10, on sick humor during the Vietnam War. Emmanuel Ringelblum kept a record of Jewish gallows humor during the Holocaust; *Notes from the Warsaw Ghetto: The Journal of Emmanuel Ringelblum*, ed. Jacob Sloan (New York: Schocken, 1974), 22, 49, 65, 68.

85. The joke refers to stories about Nazis' practice of making soap from their victims' bodies. See Ephra'im Davidson, *Seḥok Pinu: Otsar le-Humor ve-Satira ba-Sifrut ha-Ivrit me-Reshita ve-Ad Yameinu* (Our Humor: An anthology of humor and satire in Hebrew literature from its beginning until today) (Ḥulon: Biblos, 1972), 482.

86. Amos Kenan, "Hitbahamut" (Bestialization), *Yediot Aḥronot*, June 2, 1989, 17.

87. Yael S. Feldman, "'Identification with the Aggressor' or the 'Victim's Complex'?: Holocaust and Ideology in Israeli Theater," *Modern Judaism* 9 (1989): 165–78; Sidra DeKoven Ezraḥi, "Revisioning the Past: The Changing Legacy of the Holocaust in Hebrew Literature," *Salmagundi*, no. 68–69 (Fall 1985–Winter 1986): 269–70.

88. Bakhtin, *Rabelais and His World*, 153–54. On the issue of symbolic inversion and transgression, see Barbara Babcock, *The Reversible World: Symbolic Inversion in Art and Society* (Ithaca: Cornell University Press, 1978); Peter Stallybrass and Allon

White, *The Politics and Poetics of Transgression* (Ithaca: Cornell University Press, 1986), 1–26.

89. In that regard, Israeli griping behavior functions as a similar behavior pattern. See Katriel, "*Kiturim:* The Griping Mode in Israeli Social Discourse," in *Communal Webs*, 35–49.

Chapter 10: The Bar Kokhba Revolt and the Meaning of Defeat

1. Yehoshafat Harkabi, *Be-Tokef ha-Metsi'ut* (Facing reality) (Jerusalem: Van Leer Foundation, 1981); and *Ḥazon, Lo Fantazia: Likḥei Mered bar Kokhva ve-Re'al-ism Medini be-Yameinu* (Vision, no fantasy: Realism in international relations) (Jerusalem: Domino Press, 1982), English translation by Max Ticktin, *The Bar Kokhba Syndrome* (Chappaqua, NY: Rossel Books, 1983).

2. Harkabi, *Be-Tokef ha-Metsi'ut*, 1–7. The following references are to this publication, but Harkabi repeated these points in his expanded version of the following year.

3. Harkabi, *Bar Kokhba Syndrome*, 105.

4. Ibid., 107.

5. Ibid., 165–86.

6. Perhaps the most famous example is the Prophet Nathan's use of a parable in order to rebuke King David for his immoral conduct when he desired Batsheba and sent her husband to his death at the battlefield; II Samuel 12:1–4.

7. Harkabi, *Ḥazon, Lo Fantazia*, 136.

8. Harkabi, *Bar Kokhba Syndrome*, 104.

9. Harkabi, *Ḥazon, Lo Fantazia*, 17.

10. Oppenheimer, *Mered Bar-Kokhva.*

11. Eldad, *Pulmus ha-Ḥurban u-Lekaḥav*, and David Roke'aḥ, "Iyun Histori" (Historical discussion), published in the same volume (Jerusalem: Van Leer Foundation, 1982), 89–122.

12. Aharon Oppenheimer and Uriel Rappoport, eds., *Mered Bar-Kokhva: Meḥkarim Ḥadashim* (The Bar Kokhba revolt: A new approach) (Jerusalem: Yad Yitḥak Ben-Zvi, 1984).

13. "For Israelis, Bar Kokhba Isn't Ancient History," *New York Times*, January 31, 1982, 22E.

14. Ḥagai Eshet, quoted in ibid.

15. Israeli historian Ya'akov Shavit rejects the idea that the Bar Kokhba revolt carries any symbolic political value to contemporary Israelis: No one would seriously claim today, he argues, that a national rebellion that ended in destruction and two thousand years of exile would shape or even influence anyone's political views; "Mered Bar-Kokhva: Ha-Omnam Mofet?" (The Bar Kokhba revolt: Is it a model?), *Yediot Aḥronot*, literary supplement, June 11, 1982. The response to Harkabi's position nonetheless seems to disprove Shavit's view. See also Jonathan Frankel, "Bar Kokhba and All That," *Dissent* 31 (Spring 1984): 194.

16. Harkabi, *Bar Kokhba Syndrome*, 104.

17. Eldad, *Pulmus ha-Ḥurban u-Lekaḥav*, 76–82.

18. See Tsvi Lavi, "Bar Kokhva: Yigael Yadin Meshiv li-Yehoshafat Harkabi" (Bar Kokhba: Yigael Yadin responds to Yehoshafat Harkabi), *Ma'ariv*, October 17, 1980, 14; Eldad, *Pulmus ha-Ḥurban u-Lekaḥav*, 17.

19. For Roke'aḥ's rebuttal see "Iyun Histori," 89–122. According to him the rebels saw their death in the war as martyrdom because during a period of political persecution the laws of Kiddush ha-Shem require a Jew to die for lesser prohibitions than the three major ones, idolatry, adultery, and murder.

20. Ibid., 121.

21. See Yadin's statements in Lavi, "Bar Kokhva," 14; Ya'akov Shavit, "Mered Bar-Kokhva."

22. Harkabi, *Bar Kokhba Syndrome*, 118.

23. Eldad, *Pulmus ha-Ḥurban u-Lekaḥav*, 59, 71–72; note his anachronistic use of the term *porshim* (i.e., dissidents, a term that members of the Labor movement used in reference to the Revisionists during the prestate conflict between them) to suggest an analogy between the Revisionists and the ancient fighters for freedom (p. 29).

24. Lavi, "Bar Kokhva"; Eldad, *Pulmus ha-Ḥurban u-Lekaḥav*, 58–62. See also Yoram Beck, "Meridat ha-Ru'aḥ ba-Ḥomer" (The spirit's revolt against matter), *Ha-Aretz*, literary supplement, July 31, 1981; Itamar Kahalani, "Analogiot she-Einan bi-Mekoman" (Inappropriate analogies), letter to the editor, *Ha-Aretz*, June 14, 1981.

25. Eldad, *Pulmus ha-Ḥurban u-Lekaḥav*, 8. To further show what they regarded as the absurdity of Harkabi's view, his critics argued that if one were to pursue his line of thinking, one would have to glorify Marshal Pétain for surrendering to the Germans in order to save Paris from destruction; Eldad, *Pulmus ha-Ḥurban u-Lekaḥav*, 44; Beck, "Meridat ha-Ru'aḥ ba-Ḥomer." This accusation was answered by one of Harkabi's supporters: "How can one compare generations of Jewish leadership with this despicable collaborator? Is anyone who is not prepared to hit his head against the wall a traitor?" Magen Broshi, "Mered Bar-Kokhva u-Lekaḥav" (The Bar Kokhba revolt and its lessons), *Ha-Aretz*, literary supplement, August 28, 1981, 18–19.

26. Yadin, quoted by Lavi, "Bar Kokhva." See also Roke'aḥ, "Iyun Histori," 122.

27. Eldad, *Pulmus ha-Ḥurban u-Lekaḥav*, 83.

28. Ibid.

29. Lavi, "Bar Kokhva."

30. Broshi, "Mered Bar-Kokhva u-Lekaḥav," 19. See also Amos Elon, "Ha-Tiḥyena ha-Atsamot ha-Ele?" (Will these bones be revived?), *Ha-Aretz*, May 14, 1982, 14.

31. Ibid.

32. Harkabi, *Bar Kokhba Syndrome*, 111.

33. For a more detailed analysis of the political developments leading to the state funeral and its social meaning, see Aronoff, "Establishing Authority," 105–30.

34. According to Aronoff, Begin accepted this proposal despite its earlier rejec-

tion by the chair of the Ministerial Committee on Symbols and Ceremonies, a Liberal minister in Begin's cabinet; ibid., 117.

35. See Elon, "Ha-Tiḥyeina ha-Atsamot ha-Ele?"; Ilan Peleg, *Begin's Foreign Policy, 1977–1983, and Israel's Move to the Right* (New York: Greenwood Press, 1987), 78–81. Eldad's response to Harkabi articulated, as we saw earlier, the desire to defend the Betarist political views in this connection, while also trying to show that Bar Kokhba was not a partisan symbol.

36. Aronoff points out that this strategy also underlay the celebration of Jabotinsky's one-hundredth birthday celebrations in 1980–81; "Establishing Authority," 110–16.

37. Aronoff indicates that the Ministry of Defense and the Ministry of Education and Culture received instructions to emphasize this theme and the Bar Kokhba revolt; ibid., 118.

38. Ibid., 120.

39. Yehoshua Praver, "Ir David, Kever Yisrael" (David's City, a Jewish grave), *Ma'ariv*, August 28, 1981, 20; Aronoff, "Establishing Authority," 117; Yosef Shavit, "Ha-Rav Goren" (Rabbi Goren), *Yediot Aḥronot*, August 28, 1981, 8.

40. Shavit, "Ha-Rav Goren."

41. Aronoff, "Establishing Authority," 117.

42. "Goren Finds Burial Site for Bar Kokhba's Men," *Jerusalem Post*, international edition, November 8–14, 1981, 8.

43. "Goren Plans to Search Caves for More Bones," *Jerusalem Post*, international edition, November 8–14, 1981, 5.

44. "Chief Rabbi 'Copter Adventure," *Jerusalem Post*, international edition, November 22–28, 1981, 6.

45. "Goren Finds Burial Site."

46. Goren later said he did not touch or take any of the bones he saw there, and the director of the Antiquities Division was reported to have stated that just entering an archaeological site is not a violation of the law; "Chief Rabbi 'Copter Adventure."

47. *Ha-Aretz*, May 7, 1982, 3.

48. "Goren Finds Burial Site," 8.

49. Aronoff, "Establishing Authority," 117; *Ha-Aretz*, December 12, 1981, 5.

50. According to the claim of an identified archaeologist, the bones that Aharoni found in the Cave of Horrors near Naḥal Ḥever, first classified as the remains of Bar Kokhba men, were later diagnosed as Chalcolithic. Since the bones that Yadin found were similar, they too must be from the Chalcolithic period (4000–3000 B.C.E.). The same person argued that if these were Jews, the relatives would have buried the bones according to Jewish custom and would not have collected them in baskets, losing many pieces. See "The Bones May Be 5000 Years Old," *Jerusalem Post*, international edition, November 15–21, 1981, 6; *Ha-Aretz*, May 7, 1982, 3.

51. Shavit, "Ha-Rav Goren," 8; "Bones May Be 5,000 Years Old," 6.

52. The anthropologist who examined the remains of nineteen people Yadin

unearthed in 1960 said that only three are adult males and the majority are children under six; see "Goren Finds Burial Site." The bones were accordingly separated into three caskets: women's, children's, men's; Aronoff, "Establishing Authority," 118.

53. On the army's involvement in the preparations for the burial, see *Ha-Aretz*, May 7, 1982, 3. See also Aronoff's detailed description of the funeral in "Establishing Authority," 118–19: the caskets were carried by military chaplains, and the army's chief chaplain and the head of the chaplaincy for burials recited prayers. The chief of staff and a number of generals were among the select audience.

54. Aronoff, "Establishing Authority," 119.

55. Elon, "Ha-Tiḥyena ha-Atsamot ha-Ele?" 14. The reference to "our glorious fathers" calls to mind the famous title of Moshe Shamir's historical novel on the Hasmonean dynasty—*Aḥai Giborei ha-Tehila* (My glorious brothers). That Shamir became a political activist supporting the Jewish settlement of the West Bank may not be incidental to Begin's choice of this allusion.

56. Aronoff, "Establishing Authority," 120–21.

57. *Ha-Aretz*, international edition, May 7, 1982, 3, 10. The National Park Authority's opposition was suppressed by the prime minister's office and the office of the minister of agriculture, under whose jurisdiction it operates, arguing that the cabinet approved the national ceremony.

58. Aronoff, "Establishing Authority," 119. See also Elon, "Ha-Tiḥyena ha-Atsamot ha-Ele?"

59. Ya'akov Tsur, a Labor representative, in the Knesset Education Committee meeting, as reported in "Chief Rabbi 'Copter Adventure." See also *Ha-Aretz*, international edition, May 7, 1982, 3.

60. Elon, "Ha-Tiḥyena ha-Atsamot ha-Ele?" See also Ya'akov Shavit's reference to the indifferent or contemptuous responses to the ceremony ("Mered Bar Kokhva"). Aronoff describes a group of demonstrators, dressed like Romans, who protested against the ceremony, "You're making a laughing stock out of history!" "Establishing Authority," 119.

61. On the religious controversy over Masada, see chapter 11.

62. "Goren Finds Burial Site."

Chapter 11: Masada and the Meaning of Death

1. For a recent study of Israelis' views of their Jewish identity and their changing attitude toward the Holocaust, see Yair Auron, *Zehut Yehudit Yisra'elit* (Jewish Israeli identity) (Tel Aviv: Sifriyat ha-Po'alim, 1993). On the sanctification of life in the Holocaust as an important value, see Sha'ul Esh, "Kiddush ha-Ḥayim be-Tokh ha-Ḥurban" (The sanctification of life during the Holocaust), in Yisrael Gutman and Rivia Rotkirkhen, eds. *Sho'at Yehudei Eiropa* (The Holocaust of European Jews) (Jerusalem: Yad Va-Shem, 1973), 255–68; Yisrael Gutman, "Kiddush ha-Shem ve-

Kiddush ha-Ḥayim" (Martyrdom and the sanctification of life), *Yalkut Moreshet* 24 (October 1977): 7–22.

2. For an example of the new trend of interpretation of heroism in the Holocaust, see *Informational Guidelines to the Commander* (April 1980), quoted in Liebman and Don-Yeḥiya, *Civil Religion in Israel*, 178; and Young, "When a Day Remembers."

3. This is also reflected in special programs for Yom ha-Sho'a veha-Gevura that include an international quiz on Jewish heroism during World War II, broadcast live on Israeli television; Young, "When a Day Remembers," 65.

4. Avraham B. Yehoshua, "Bein Metsada le-Jabel Ataka" (Between Masada and Jabel Ataka), 1973, reprinted in *Ha-Kir veha-Har* (The wall and the mountain) (Tel Aviv: Zmora & Bitan, 1989), 31.

5. The concept of "defeated heroism" (*ha-gevura ha-yehudit ha-menutsaḥat*) was used by Berl Katznelson in his introduction to Heilperin's *Sefer ha-Gevura*. Significantly, the story of Masada opens this anthology, which focuses mostly on Exile. As noted earlier, the publication of this anthology was motivated by the desire to modify the Hebrew youth's highly negative view of Exile.

6. Liebman and Don-Yeḥiya argue that this view is central to the new Israeli civil religion and is manifested in the prominent place of the Holocaust in it; *Civil Religion in Israel*, 142–44. See also Gertz, "The Few against the Many," 94–104.

7. For discussion of the tension between the acknowledged and the unconscious responses to Lamdan's *Masada*, see Schwartz, Zerubavel, and Barnett, "Recovery of Masada," 158–61.

8. See also discussion in chapter 5.

9. Yadin, *Masada*, 15. See also the discussion of Josephus's position in a popular book, *Metsada shel Yosef ben Matityahu* (Josephus's Masada) by Avino'am Heimi (Ramat Gan: Masada, 1976), 7–9.

10. See Thackeray, *Josephus*, 41; Menaḥem Luz, "Ne'um ha-Mishne shel Elazar bi-Metsada ve-Kli'arkhus Ish Soli" (Clearchus of Soli as a source of Elazar's Deuterosis) in Rappoport, *Yosef ben Matityahu*, 79–81; Menaḥem Stern, "Darko Shel Yosef ben Matityahu bi-Khetivat ha-Historia" (Josephus's approach to historical writing), in *Historyonim ve-Askolot Historiyot* (Historians and historical schools) (Jerusalem: Ha-Ḥevra ha-Historit ha-Yisra'elit, 2d ed., 1977), 22–28.

11. Trude Weiss-Rosmarin, "Masada and Yavne," *Jewish Spectator* 31 (November 1966): 4–7; idem, "Masada, Josephus, and Yadin," *Jewish Spectator* 32 (October 1967): 28, 30–32; idem, "Reflections on Leadership," *Jewish Spectator* 33 (March 1968): 2–5; idem, "Masada Revisited," *Jewish Spectator* 34 (December 1969): 3–5, 29.

12. Mary E. Smallwood, *The Jews under the Romans' Rule* (Leiden: E. J. Brill, 1976), 338. Clearly, this argument does not explain why Josephus did not refrain from reporting the Romans' revenge on the Jewish rebels in other cases.

13. On Josephus's sources see Thackeray, *Josephus*, 45; Broshi, "Meheimanuto shel Yosef ben Matityahu," 21–27.

14. Yisrael L. Levin, "Ha-Kana'im be-Sof Tekufat Bayit Sheni ki-Ve'aya His-

toriografit" (The Zealots at the end of the Second Temple period as a historiographic problem), *Katedra* 1 (1977): 40–41; Yehuda Rosenthal, "Ha-Kana'im ba-Masoret ha-Yehudit: Shetei Megamot" (The Zealots in Jewish tradition: Two approaches), *Katedra* 1 (1977): 58. Both Levin and Rosenthal suggest that there is a pronounced pro-Zealot trend in Israeli scholarship while criticism of the Zealots tends to be voiced out of Israel.

15. Solomon Zeitlin, "The Sicarii and Masada," *Jewish Quarterly Review* 57 (April 1967): 263; and "The Slavonic Josephus and the Dead Sea Scrolls: An Exposé of Recent Fairy Tales," *Jewish Quarterly Review* 58 (January 1968): 198; Sidney B. Hoenig, "The Sicarii in Masada: Glory or Infamy?" *Tradition* 11 (Spring 1970): 6–11; and "The Historic Masada and the Halakha," *Tradition* 13 (Fall 1972): 101–3. See also Morton Smith, "Zealots and the Sicarii: Their Origins and Relations," *Harvard Theological Review* 64 (January 1971): 1–19; Richard A. Horsley, "Josephus and the Bandits," *Journal for the Study of Judaism* 10 (July 1979): 37–63; Arye Kasher, ed., *Ha-Mered ha-Gadol: Ha-Sibot veha-Nesibot li-Fritsato* (The Great Jewish Revolt: Its causes and circumstances) (Jerusalem: Merkaz Zalman Shazar, 1983), 299–388.

16. For example, Josephus describes a Sicarii raid on Ein Gedi in which they killed seven hundred people, mostly women and children, when they knew that neither the Roman forces nor the Jews in Jerusalem would intervene; *Wars of the Jews*, 4.7.2, p. 537.

17. Hoenig, "Historic Masada and the Halakha," 112; and "Sicarii in Masada," 14–17.

18. Solomon Zeitlin, "Masada and the Sicarii: The Occupants of Masada," *Jewish Quarterly Review* 55 (April 1965): 313; and "Sicarii and Masada," 255–56; Hoenig, "Sicarii in Masada," 24; and "Historic Masada and the Halakha," 109. See also Yehuda Rosenthal, "Al Metsada ve-Giboreiha" (On Masada and its heroes), *Ha-Do'ar* 47, no. 38 (September 20, 1968): 693–95; and "Teshuva la-Masig" (A reply to a critic), *Ha-Do'ar* 48, no. 3 (November 15, 1968): 44.

19. Shubert Spero, "In Defense of the Defenders of Masada," *Tradition* 11 (Spring 1970): 31–43; and "A Letter to the Editor: The Defenders of Masada," *Tradition* 13 (Fall 1971): 136–38; Re'uven Gordis, "Al Gevuratam shel Meginei Metsada" (On the heroism of the Masada heroes), *Ha-Do'ar* 37, no. 40 (October 25, 1968): 756–57; Ḥaim Orlan, "Od al Metsada ve-Giboreiha" (More on Masada and its heroes), *Ha-Do'ar* 37, no. 40 (October 25, 1968): 755–56; idem, "Be-Shulei ha-Diyunim veha-Iyunim al Metsada" (In the margins of the discussion and the study of Masada), *Ha-Do'ar* 48, no. 7 (December 13, 1968): 102–3; idem, "Metsada: Ha-Perek ha-Histori she-Kofim Aleinu Kivyakhol . . ." (Masada: The chapter that is seemingly forced upon us), *Ha-Do'ar* 48, no. 18 (February 28, 1969): 277–78; Louis I. Rabinowitz, "The Masada Martyrs according to the Halakha," *Tradition* 11 (Fall 1970): 31–37.

20. Orlan, "Be-Shulei ha-Diyunim veha-Iyunim al Metsada," 102.

21. Yigael Yadin, interview with Nathan Yanai, *Ba-Maḥane*, March 18, 1969.

22. Yadin, *Masada*, 15. See also Broshi, "Meheimanuto shel Yosef ben Ma-

tityahu," 21–22. For criticism of Yadin's approach, see Alter, "Masada Complex," 21–22; Shargel, "Evolution of the Masada Myth," 364–65; Pierre Vidal-Naquet, *Les Juifs, la mémoire et le présent* (Paris: Librairie François Maspero, 1981), 43–59.

23. Weiss-Rosmarin, "Masada and Yavne," 6.

24. Hoenig, "Sicarii in Masada," 8–9. See also Rosenthal, "Al Metsada ve-Giboreiha," 693–95; Leo Gutman, "Masada and the Talmud: A Letter," *Tradition* 10 (Fall 1969): 98–99.

25. The story of Yoḥanan ben Zakkai appears in a few texts, including *Avot de-Rabbi Natan* 4:22–24 (1st version), 6:19 (2d version); *Ekha Rabba* 1:31; Babylonian Talmud, *Gittin* 56:1–2. For a comparative analysis of these versions, see Alon, *Meḥkarim be-Toldot Yisrael,* 1:219–52.

26. Weiss-Rosmarin, "Masada and Yavne," 7.

27. Kedar, "Tasbikh Metsada," 16; see also Lewis, *History,* 102.

28. Rabinowitz, "Masada Martyrs," 34–37; Spero, "In Defense of the Defenders of Masada," 31–43. See also an earlier statement by the Israeli historian Gedalyahu Alon to this effect in *Meḥkarim be-Toldot Yisrael,* 1:269.

29. Yosef Klausner, *Historia shel ha-Bayit ha-Sheni* (History of the Second Temple) (Jerusalem: Aḥiasaf, 1951), 5:289.

30. Rotenberg, *Masada,* 46. See also Louis Finkelstein's position in "Masada and Its Heroes," in *Masada* (New York: Jewish Theological Seminary of New York and the Jewish Museum, 1967), 12–15.

31. The prohibition of suicide is based on the interpretation of the biblical verse "But for your own life-blood I will require a reckoning"; Genesis 9:5. On the sanctions against suicide, see Ganzfried, *Code of Jewish Law,* book 4, 108–9; "Suicide," *Encyclopaedia Judaica* 15:489–90.

32. On the history of the concept of Kiddush ha-Shem, see Itamar Grunwald, "Kiddush ha-Shem: Beruro shel Musag" (Kiddush ha-Shem: The clarification of the concept), *Molad* 1 (1967): 476–84. On the development of the laws of martyrdom see Shlomo Goren, "Mitsvat Kiddush ha-Shem le-Or ha-Halakha" (The commandment of Kiddush ha-Shem in Jewish law), *Maḥanayim* 41 (1960): 7–15; "On Kiddush ha-Shem and Ḥillul ha-Shem" (On the sanctification and the desecration of God's name), *Encyclopaedia Judaica* 10:977–81. Note especially the discussion on the ambiguity about the obligation to die for Kiddush ha-Shem when forced to commit a minor transgression in private.

33. For these arguments by Masada's critics, see Weiss-Rosmarin, "Masada and Yavne," 6–7; Hoenig, "Sicarii in Masada," 17–18; Bernard Heller, "Masada and the Talmud," *Tradition* 10 (Winter 1968): 33.

34. Weiss-Rosmarin, "Masada and Yavne," 7; Heller, "Masada and the Talmud," 34; Hoenig, "Sicarii in Masada," 19–21; D. Frimer, "Masada in Light of the Halakha," *Tradition* 12 (Summer 1971): 33; Kedar, "Tasbikh Metsada," 16.

35. Rabinowitz, "Masada Martyrs," 34–37.

36. Ibid., 33–34.

37. For King Saul's death, see I Samuel 31:4–6. On the analogy with Masada, see Zvi Kolitz, "Masada: Suicide or Murder?" *Tradition* 12 (1971): 23–25; Frimer,

"Masada," 28–34; Shlomo Goren, "Gevurat Metsada le-Or ha-Halakha" (The heroism of Masada in view of the Jewish law), *Maḥanayim* 67 (1963): 7–12.

38. Goren published his interpretation in "Gevurat Metsada le-Or la-Halakha," 12. Goren's position, published as early as 1960 in the Orthodox American Hebrew magazine *Or ha-Mizraḥ*, drew sharp criticism as violating the spirit of Jewish law from another Israeli rabbi, Moshe Tsvi Neria; "'Hit'abdut Lada'at': Giborei Metsada le-Or ha-Halakha" (Suicide: The Masada heroes in view of the Jewish law), *Or ha-Mizraḥ* 8 (January 1961): 8–12. See also the discussion of Goren's position in Frimer, "Masada," 27–39.

39. For recent studies of martyrdom narratives of the Crusades period, see Ivan G. Marcus, "From Politics to Martyrdom: Shifting Paradigms in the Hebrew Narratives of the 1096 Crusade Riots," *Prooftexts* 2, no. 1 (1982): 40–52; Chazan, *European Jews and the First Crusade*. For examples of the use of those cases in support of Masada, see Frimer, "Masada," 29; Spero, "In Defense of the Defenders of Masada," 39–40; Kolitz, "Masada: Suicide or Murder?" 24.

40. Ya'akov Katz, "Bein 1096 le-1648/49" (Between 1096 and 1648/49), in S. Ettinger, S. W. Baron, B. Dinur, and I. Halpern, eds., *Sefer ha-Yovel le-Yitzḥak F. Baer* (Yitzḥak Baer: Jubilee book) (Jerusalem: Historical Society of Israel, 1960), 332; Shimon Huberband, *Kiddush ha-Shem: Ketavim mi-Yemei ha-Sho'a* (Kiddush ha-Shem: Writings from the days of the Holocaust), ed. Naḥman Blumental and Yosef Kermish (Tel Aviv: Zakhor, 1969); Pesach Schindler, "The Holocaust and Kiddush ha-Shem in Hassidic Thought," *Tradition* 13, no. 4/14, no. 1 (1973): 88–104; Yosef Gotferstein, "Kiddush ha-Shem be-Mahalakh ha-Dorot ve-Yiḥudo bi-Tekufat ha-Sho'a" (Kiddush ha-Shem during the Holocaust and its distinction during the period of the Holocaust), in *Ha-Amida ha-Yehudit bi-Tekufat ha-Sho'a* (Jerusalem: Yad Va-Shem, 1970), 359–84.

41. Heller, "Masada and the Talmud," 33.

42. Kolitz, "Masada: Suicide or Murder?" 5. Note, however, that Goren, who applied the Masada precedent to situations when a soldier in captivity fears torture or betrayal, recommended killing oneself over killing each other to avoid the prohibition of "thou shall not murder" ("Gevurat Metsada le-Or ha-Halakha," 11).

43. Josephus, *Wars of the Jews*, 7.9, p. 603.

44. Zeitlin, "Sicarii and Masada," 262.

45. Hoenig, "Sicarii in Masada," 15.

46. Kedar, "Tasbikh Metsada," 16. See also Raphael Rotenstein, "Ha-Mitos ha-Matrid" (The disturbing myth), *Ha-Aretz*, April 20, 1973, 16; Rosenthal, "Teshuva la-Masig," 44.

47. Jossipon, *Sefer Yosifon*, 1:430–31.

48. Most of those who objected to the suicide on this ground were students and parents associated with the general public schools who more clearly subscribe to the secular Hebrew values, including the idea of fighting to the very end. A few of the students from a religious public school voiced similar criticism, but none of their parents did.

49. Stewart Alsop, "The Masada Complex," *Newsweek*, July 12, 1971, 92.

50. Stewart Alsop, "Again, the Masada Complex," *Newsweek*, March 19, 1973, 104.

51. Michael Elizur, letter to the editor, *Newsweek*, April 16, 1973, 10–11.

52. *Ha-Aretz*, April 29, 1973, quoted in Daniel Bar-Tal, "The Masada Syndrome: A Case of Central Belief," Discussion Paper 3 (Tel Aviv: International Center for Peace in the Middle East, 1983) 11. Moshe Dayan, then the Minister of Defense, referred to the Masada complex in a public speech at the site of Masada in which he reviewed Israel's suffering from acts of terrorism of the Palestinian organization, Black September. The speech, made on Jan. 11, 1978, was broadcast on the news magazine, "Ha-Yom ha-Ze" (Today) on Israeli national radio.

53. Ya'akov Reuel, "Sisco and the Masada Complex," *Jerusalem Post Weekly*, August 3, 1971, 9; Kedar, "Tasbikh Matsada"; Dan Margalit and Matti Golan, "Ha-Mimshal bi-Fe'ula" (The administration in action), *Ha-Aretz*, April 27, 1973, 13; Alter, "Masada Complex," 19–24; Syrkin, "Paradox of Masada," 66–70.

54. Tsemaḥ, "Masada."

55. Chaim Weizmann, in a speech at the twenty-second World Zionist Congress, quoted in Abba Eban, *An Autobiography* (New York: Random House, 1977), 68; see also Laqueur, *Toldot ha-Tsiyonut*, 451.

56. On Ben-Gurion's growing distance from Masada during the early state period, see Liebman and Don-Yeḥiya, *Civil Religion in Israel*, 99–100.

57. Jay Y. Gonen, *Psychohistory of Zionism* (New York: Mason Charter, 1975), 213–36.

58. Bar-Tal, "Masada Syndrome."

59. Kedar, "Tasbikh Metsada." Kedar expanded his critique of the Masada myth in the English version of his earlier Hebrew article, "Masada: The Myth and the Complex," *Jerusalem Quarterly* 24 (Summer 1982): 57–63.

60. Lewis, *History*, 102. See also Alsop's statement that "beyond the horizon, it may be that Israel is creating its own Masada" ("Again, the Masada Complex") and Robert Alter's poignant remarks on this issue in "Masada Complex."

61. I disagree here with Shargel's suggestion in "Evolution of the Masada Myth," 367–71, that the perception of Masada as a "complex" represents a new phase of the myth but rather see it as one of the expressions of its recent development. In my own interviews in the late 1970s, only two informants referred to the Masada complex, and both were academic Israelis who had lived abroad for a few years.

62. Peleg, *Begin's Foreign Policy*, 51–93; Lustick, *For the Land and the Lord*, 72–90; Rubenstein, *Mi la-Adonai Elai*, 44, 128.

Conclusion: History, Memory, and Invented Tradition

1. Northrop Frye points out that mythical structures ("mythoi") shape the writing of fiction; *Anatomy of Criticism* (Princeton: Princeton University Press, 1957), 162–239. Hayden White modifies his argument as he applies it to historical narratives; *Tropics of Discourse*, 61–62. His analysis of the impact of such structures

(which he calls "pre-generic plot structures") on the shaping of historical narrative rings more forcefully in the case of the commemorative narrative.

2. Gerald Prince, *Narratology: The Form and Function of Narrative* (Berlin: Mouton, 1982), 151–53. Barbara Herrnstein Smith defines narrative integrity as "the property of a system of which the parts are more obviously related to each other than to anything outside the system"; *Poetic Closure: A Study of How Poems End* (Chicago: University of Chicago Press, 1968), 23–24.

3. Yerushalmi, *Zakhor*, 40.

4. Yerushalmi points out the Jewish custom of adding later events to the commemorative framework of an existing holiday rather than adding a new day of remembrance to the holiday cycle; ibid., 46–52.

5. On the centrality of the myth of the few against many in Israeli culture and its literary and political expressions, see Gertz, "The Few against the Many," 94–104, and "Social Myths in Literary and Political Texts," 621–39.

6. The traditional commemoration of the giving of the Torah on Mount Sinai at Shavuot is overshadowed by the evocation of the ancient ritual of donating first fruits to the Temple; Passover is celebrated as the Spring Holiday, Sukkot as the Harvest Festival, and the minor holiday of Tu bi-Shevat as the Holiday of the Trees. This commemorative trend was most pronounced during the prestate and early-state periods. See Liebman and Don-Yeḥiya, *Civil Religion in Israel*, 49–53.

7. See ibid., 54; Elihu Katz and Michael Gurevitch, *Tarbut ha-Penai be-Yisrael* (Leisure culture in Israel) (Tel Aviv: Am Oved, 1973), 298–300.

8. Zerubavel, "Holiday Cycle and the Commemoration of the Past," 111–18. See also Gertz, "The Few against the Many," 94–104.

9. Avraham Breudes, "Uve-Khol Et uve-Khol Zeman" (At any time), in *Shir le-Ḥag* (Song for the holiday) (Tel Aviv: Emunim, 1955), 21.

10. Children's confusion about holiday stories has generated a whole body of teachers' folklore. The well-known satirist Ephra'im Kishon wrote a piece on this subject, "Nes Pesaḥ" (The miracle of Passover), in *Ba-Aḥad ha-Amashim* (Tel Aviv: Tversky, 1963), 227, and several informants referred to similar satires and a recording by the Israeli comedian Rivka Mikha'eli. Aronoff quotes an Israeli child's question that reveals the cultural expectation that these holiday commemorations create. After listing several holidays commemorating conflicts, she says, "Daddy, tell me—who were our enemies on Tu bi-Shevat [the holiday celebrating the new year for the trees]?" Aronoff, "Myths, Symbols, and Rituals," 185.

11. Don Handelman and Elihu Katz, "State Ceremonies of Israel: Remembrance Day and Independence Day," in Don Handelman, *Models and Mirrors: Towards an Anthropology of Public Events* (Cambridge: Cambridge University Press, 1990), 191–233; Young, "When a Day Remembers," 54–75; see also Chaim Schatzker's discussion of the teaching of the Holocaust within the context of the holiday cycle as compared to history curriculum; "The Holocaust in Israeli Education," *International Journal of Political Education* 5 (1982): 75–82.

12. See Rogel's concluding remarks in *Lekaḥ Tel Hai*, 47; Harkabi, *The Bar Kokhba Syndrome*, 104.

13. Note, however, Biale's remarks about a similar ambiguity in the interpreta-

tion of the outcome of the Maccabean revolt; *Power and Powerlessness in Jewish History*, 19–21.

14. See Yehoshafat Harkabi's critique, discussed in chapter 10, on the danger of focusing on short-term military victories without considering their long-term political implications.

15. Smith, *Poetic Closure*, 117. See also Frank Kermode, *The Sense of an Ending: Studies in the Theory of Fiction* (New York: Oxford University Press, 1967), 7, 35–36; Edward Said, *Beginnings: Intention and Method* (New York: Columbia University Press, 1985).

16. Mink, "Narrative Form as a Cognitive Instrument," 145–47.

17. Maurice Halbwachs, in *Collective Memory*, 54, remarks that events are recognized as important in retrospect; see also White, *Content of the Form*, 21; Said, *Beginnings*, 29.

18. White, *Tropics of Discourse*, 98. Dan Sperber and Deidre Wilson point out that people first establish the message that they wish to articulate and only then choose the context that would maximize its relevance; *Relevance: Communication and Cognition* (Cambridge: Harvard University Press, 1986), 142.

19. Kermode, *Sense of an Ending*, 45.

20. Prince, *Narratology*, 156.

21. William Labov, "The Transformation of Experience in Narrative Syntax," in *Language in the Inner City* (Philadelphia: University of Pennsylvania Press, 1972), 365–66. See also Smith, *Poetic Closure*, 120.

22. See, for example, Alain Robbe-Grillet's novels and essay *Pour un nouveau roman* (Paris: Les Editions de Minuit, 1963); English translation by Richard Howard, *For a New Novel: Essays on Fiction* (New York: Grove Press, 1965); and Philip Stevick, ed., *Antistory: An Anthology of Experimental Fiction* (New York: Free Press, 1971).

23. Ariel, Blich, and Persky, *Mikra'ot Yisrael le-Khita Bet*, reprinted in a later edition by Persky, *Mikra'ot Israel Ḥadashot le-Khita Bet*, 238–39; see also Ariel, Vilensky, and Persky, *Alfoni*, 52.

24. *Le-Yom Tel Ḥai: Ḥoveret Ezer*, 23.

25. Persky, *Mikra'ot Israel Ḥadashot le-Khita Bet*, 404. See also an earlier version in Ariel, Blich, and Persky, *Mikra'ot Yisrael le-Khita Bet*, 339; Kipnis, *Mo'adei Yisrael*, vol. 3, appendix.

26. If the retreat is considered part of the event, one can indeed refer to it as "the fall of Tel Ḥai" and define the outcome of this battle as "the first major armed victory of Arabs over the Jews in post-war Palestine"; Neil Caplan, *Palestinian Jewry and the Arab Question 1917–1925* (London: Frank Cass, 1978), 52.

27. See Eviatar Zerubavel's discussion of "mental gaps" and "mental quantum leaps" in *Fine Line*, 21–32.

28. *Ha-Hagana*, 37–38. See also Dinur, *Sefer Toldot ha-Hagana*, 1:584–85; Ḥorshi, *Ḥagim vi-Yemei Zikaron la-Talmid*, 97–98.

29. Eliezer Smally, "Yom Tel Ḥai" (Tel Ḥai Day), in *Benei ha-Yore* (The first rain's offsprings) (Tel Aviv: Haskala la-Am, 1937), 140–41.

30. Persky, *Mikra'ot Yisral Ḥadashot*, 239. See also *Le-yom Tel Ḥai: Ḥoveret Ezer*, 23.

31. Gafni, *Tehilat Metsada*, 83.

32. Quoted in Rotenberg, *Metsada*, 11.

33. Benedict Anderson states that nationalism created a secular transformation of death into continuity; *Imagined Communities*, 19. See also Bellah, "Civil Religion in America," 168–86, esp. 176–79; Warner, *The Living and the Dead*, 255–79; Mosse, *Fallen Soldiers*, 70–80; Connerton, *How Societies Remember*, 42–43.

34. H. Hubert and M. Mauss, *Sacrifice: Its Nature and Function* (Chicago: University of Chicago Press, 1964), 278.

35. "We are not the descendants of the Masada people," an Israeli journalist recently wrote, "because they all died. We are the descendants of those who compromised"; Yehonatan Gefen, "Huzremu Koḥot" (Forces were sent), *Ma'ariv* (*Sofshavu'a*), July 30, 1993. I would like to thank Dan Ben-Amos for bringing this quote to my attention.

36. For the discussion of "loss of character," see Klapp, *Symbolic Leaders*, 215. As an Israeli journalist put it, "It is difficult to identify with a 'monument' whose only attributes are a few daring, patriotic statements"; Evron, "Tov Lamut be'ad Artsenu?" 22.

37. The advertisement for Laskov's biography of Trumpeldor, published in *Ma'ariv*, February 25, 1972, reads as follows: "The first authoritative biography of a wonderman: a soldier and an officer, an agricultural worker and a leader (and by training, a dentist and a lawyer). This is the story of the loves and the separations, the achievements and the failures of a historical leader who became a legend."

38. From Laskov's personal files (emphasis added). On the desire to discover the real man behind the legend, see also Tamar Meroz, "Trumpeldor Basar va-Dam" and Evron, "Tov Lamut be'ad Artsenu?" The sheer surprise of discovering the real human being behind the masking legend was also articulated in a letter of General Meir Zore'a ("Zaro") to Shulamit Laskov, March 28, 1972, which was published in *Yediot Aḥronot*, May 10, 1972: "At the beginning I wondered what was your point in dealing with 'worn-out coins' [platitudes]. [But] your treatment of the facts presents . . . not a unidimensional hero made of paper, but a solid, three-dimensional figure, alive and active . . . For me, Yosef Trumpeldor now leaves the field of childhood platitudes and enters the sphere of remarkable marvels."

39. Linda Dégh, "The 'Belief Legend' in Modern Society: Form, Function, and Relationship to Other Genres," in Wayland D. Hand, ed., *American Folk Legend* (Berkeley: University of California Press, 1971), 55–68; and Linda Dégh and A. Vázsonyi. "Legend and Belief," *Genre* 4 (September 1971): 281–304, reprinted in Dan Ben-Amos, ed., *Folklore Genres* (Austin: University of Texas Press, 1976), 93–123.

BIBLIOGRAPHY

Abrahams, Roger D. "Ghastly Commands: The Cruel Joke Revisited." *Midwest Folklore* 11 (1961): 235–46.

Aḥad Ha-Am. "Teḥiyat ha-Ru'aḥ" (Spiritual revival), in *Kol Kitvei Aḥad Ha-Am* (Ahad Ha-Am's collected works). Tel Aviv: Dvir, 1956, 173–86.

Aharoni, Yoḥanan. *Metsada* (Masada). Tel Aviv: Ma'arkhot, 1963.

Aḥime'ir, Aba. "Mi-Tel Ḥai li-Ve'er Tuvia" (From Tel Ḥai to Be'er Tuvia). *Do'ar ha-Yom*, March 11, 1930; reprinted in *Brit ha-Biryonim* (The Biryonim Association). Tel Aviv: Ha-Va'ad le-Hotsa'at Kitvei Aḥime'ir, 1972, 173–75.

A. L. "Le-Zekher Aḥai she-Naflu ba-Galil" (In memory of my brothers who fell in Galilee). *Ha-Po'el ha-Tsa'ir*, March 26, 1920, 17.

Almagor, Dan. "Ma be-Emet Amar Trumpeldor?" (What did Trumpeldor really say?) *Yediot Aḥronot*, weekend magazine, March 16, 1979.

———. "Milim Aḥronot al Trumpeldor" (Last words about Trumpeldor). *Yediot Aḥronot*, April 13, 1979.

Almog, Shmuel. *Zionism and History: The Rise of a New Jewish Consciousness*. New York: St. Martin's, 1987.

Alon, Azaria. "Me Haya Midbar Yehuda Avurenu?" (What did the Judaean desert mean to us?), in Mordekhai Na'or, ed., *Yam ha-Melaḥ u-Midbar Yehuda 1900–1967*. (The Dead Sea and the Judaean desert). Jerusalem: Yad Yitzḥak Ben-Zvi, 1990, 270–75.

Alon, Gedalyahu. *Meḥkarim be-Toldot Yisrael bi-Yemei Bayit Sheni uvi-Tekufat ha-Mishna veha-Talmud* (Studies in Jewish history of the Second Temple, the Mishnaic, and the Talmudic periods). Tel Aviv: Ha-Kibbutz ha-Me'uḥad, 1967.

Alsop, Stewart, "The Masada Complex." *Newsweek*, July 12, 1971, 92.

———. "Again, the Masada Complex." *Newsweek*, March 19, 1973, 104.

Alter, Robert, "The Masada Complex." *Commentary* 56 (June 1973): 19–24.

———. *The Invention of Hebrew Prose: Modern Fiction and the Language of Realism*. Seattle: University of Washington Press, 1988.

Althusser, Louis. "Ideology and Ideological State Apparatuses," in *Lenin and Philosophy and Other Essays*. New York: Monthly Review Press, 1971, 127–86.

Amir, Anda. "Be-Yom Yod-Alef ba-Adar" (On the Eleventh of Adar), in *Le-Yom Tel Ḥai: Ḥoveret Ezer la-Ganenet* (For Tel Ḥai Day: A reader for the nursery school teacher). Tel Aviv: Histadrut, 1943, 27.

Anderson, Benedict. *Imagined Communities: Reflections on the Origin and Spread of Nationalism*. London: Verso, 1983.

Aran, Gideon. "Jewish Zionist Fundamentalists: 'The Bloc of the Faithful' in Israel," in Martin E. Marty and R. Scott Appelby, eds. *Fundamentalism Observed*. American Academy of the Arts and Sciences. Chicago: University of Chicago Press, 1991, 265–344.

Ariel, Z., M. Blich, and N. Persky, eds. *Mikra'ot Yisrael le-Khita Bet* (Israel's reader: Textbook for the second grade). Jerusalem: Masada, 1965.

———. *Mikra'ot Yisrael le-Khita Ḥet* (Israel's reader: Textbook for the eighth grade). Jerusalem: Masada, 1966.

Ariel, Z., Z. Vilensky, and N. Persky, eds. *Alfoni: Mikra'a le-Khita Alef* (Reader for the first grade). Tel Aviv: Masada, 1968.

Aronoff, Myron J. *The Frailty of Authority*. Political Anthropology Series, vol. 5. New Brunswick: Transaction, 1986.

———. "The Revitalization of Political Culture: Gush Emunim," in *Israeli Visions and Divisions: Cultural Change and Political Conflict*. New Brunswick: Transaction, 1989, 69–91.

———. "Myths, Symbols, and Rituals of the Emerging State," in Laurence J. Silberstein, ed. *New Perspectives on Israeli History: The Early Years of the State*. New York: New York University Press, 1991, 175–92.

Auron, Yair. *Zehut Yehudit Yisra'elit* (Jewish Israeli identity). Tel Aviv: Sifriyat ha-Po'alim, 1993.

Avivi, B., and A. Keren-Tal, eds. *Mo'adim le-Simḥa* (Happy holidays). Jerusalem: Kiryat Sefer, 1943.

Avi-Yona, M., N. Avigad, Y. Aharoni, I. Dunayevsky, and S. Gutman. "Metsada: Seker Arkhe'ologi bi-Shenot 1955–56" (Masada: Archeological survey and excavation) *Israel Exploration Journal* 7 (1957): 9–16.

Avramsky, Shmu'el. *Bar Kokhva Nesi Yisrael* (Bar Kokhba the leader of Israel). Tel Aviv: Masada, 1961.

———. "Milḥemet ha-Ḥerut shel Metsada" (Masada's war of liberation). *Maḥanayim* 87 (1963): 16–23.

Avruch, Kevin. "Traditionalizing Israeli Nationalism: The Development of Gush Emunim," *Political Psychology* 1, no. 1 (1979): 47–57.

Babcock, Barbara. *The Reversible World: Symbolic Inversion in Art and Society*. Ithaca: Cornell University Press, 1978.

Baer, Yitzhak F. *Galut*. New York: Schocken, 1947.

———. Introduction, A. M. Habermann. *Sefer Gezerot Ashkenaz ve-Tsorfat* (The book of persecutions in Germany and France). Jerusalem: Ofir, 1971.

Bakalash, Rivka. "Mitos Trumpeldor 'Adam, Dam, Adama' be-Vet ha-Sefer ha-Yesodi" (The Trumpeldor myth "man, blood, earth" in the elementary school). Master's thesis, Ben-Gurion University of the Negev, 1988.

Bakhtin, M. M. *Rabelais and His World*, 1965; English translation by Helene Iswolsky, Bloomington: Indiana University Press, 1984.

Bar'am, Bela. "Yosef ha-Gelili" (Yosef the Galilean), in *Le-Yom Tel Ḥai: Ḥoveret Ezer la-Ganenet* (For Tel Ḥai Day: A reader for the nursery school teacher). Tel Aviv: Histadrut, 1943, 20–22.

Barrick, Mac E. "The Helen Keller Joke Cycle." *Journal of American Folklore* 93 (1980): 441–49.

Bar-Tal, Daniel. "The Masada Syndrome: A Case of Central Belief." Discussion Paper 3. Tel Aviv: International Center for Peace in the Middle East, 1983.

Bartov, Ḥanoch. *Shel Mi Ata Yeled?* (Whose child are you?) Tel Aviv: Am Oved, 1970.

Baseman, Bob. *Masada: Pictorial Guide and Souvenir.* Palphot, n.d.

Bat-Ḥaim, H. "Bar Mitzvah on Masada." *Hadassah Magazine* 48 (April 1967): 10.

Beck, Horace P. "The Making of the Popular Legendary Hero," in Wayland D. Hand, ed., *American Folk Legend.* Berkeley: University of California Press, 1971, 121–32.

Beck, Yoram. "Meridat ha-Ru'aḥ ba-Ḥomer" (The spirit's revolt against matter). *Ha-Aretz*, literary supplement, July 31, 1981.

Becker, Carl L. "What Are Historical Facts?" in Phil L. Snyder, ed. *Detachment and the Writing of History: Essays and Letters of Carl L. Becker.* Ithaca: Cornell University Press, 1958, 41–64.

Bellah, Robert N. "Civil Religion in America." *Daedalus* (Winter 1967): 1–21; reprinted in *Beyond Belief: Essays on Religion in a Post-traditional World.* New York: Harper & Row, 1970, 168–86.

Ben-Amos, Dan. "Generic Distinctions in the Aggadah," in F. Talmage, ed. *Studies in Jewish Folklore.* Cambridge, Mass: Association for Jewish Studies, 1980, 45–71.

Ben-Ari, N., and E. Kena'ani, eds. *Yosef Trumpeldor: Po'alo u-Tekufato/Yosef Trumpeldor: His Life and His Times* (Hebrew and English). Tel Aviv: Mif'alei Tarbut ve-Ḥinukh, 1970.

Ben-Avoya. "Ha-Omnam Lelo Takhlit?" (Is it really for no purpose?) *Ba-Maḥane* 60 (June 5, 1942): 10.

Benayahu, Meir. "Hitnahagut Mekubalei Tsefat be-Meron" (The behavior of the Safed Kabbalists in Meron). *Sefunot* 6 (1962): 9–41.

Ben-Eliezer, Uri. "Tsva'iyut, Status, ve-Politika: Dor Yelidei ha-Aretz veha-Hanhaga ba-Asor she-Kadam la-Hakamat ha-Medina" (Militarism, status, and politics: The generation of Israeli-born and the Yishuv's leadership). Ph.D. diss., Tel Aviv University, 1988.

Ben-Gal, Yoram. *Moledet ve-Ge'ographia be-Me'a Shenot Ḥinukh Tsiyoni* (*Moledet* and geography in a hundred years of Zionist education). Tel Aviv: Am Oved, 1993.

Ben-Gurion, David. "Tsav Tel Ḥai" (The Tel Ḥai legacy) *Kuntres* 1, no. 381 (1943): 3–8.

———. *Medinat Yisrael ha-Meḥudeshet* (The renewed state of Israel). Tel Aviv: Am Oved, 1969.

Ben-Ḥanan, Sara, ed. *Ze Sifrenu, Sefer Sheni* (This is our book: Reader for the second grade). Jerusalem: Marcus, 1971.

Ben-Porat, Yesha'ayahu et al. *Ha-Meḥdal* (The oversight). Tel Aviv: Hotsa'a Meyuḥedet, 1974.

Ben-Porat, Yoram. "Ha-Daḥpor veha-Emuna" (The bulldozer and faith). *Ha-Aretz*, June 17, 1979, 9.

Benvenisti, Meron. *Conflicts and Contradictions*. New York: Villard, 1986.

Ben-Ya'akov, Avraham. *Yalkut Minhagim: Mi-Minhagei Shivtei Yisrael* (An anthology of Jewish communities' customs). Jerusalem: Ha-Madpis ha-Memshalti, 1967.

Ben-Yeruḥam, C., ed. *Sefer Betar: Korot u-Mekorot* (The book of Betar: History and sources). Jerusalem: Betar, 1969.

Ben-Zvi, Rachel Yana'it. *Anu Olim* (We climb up). Tel Aviv: Am Oved, 1962.

Berdiczewski [Bin-Gorion], Mikha Yosef. *Ba-Derekh*. Lipsia: Shtibl, 1922.

Bergman, Shmu'el Hugo. "Ha-No'ar ha-Yisraeli ve-Yahadut ha-Tefutsot" (Israeli youth and the Jews of the Dispersion). *Maḥanayim* 66 (1962): 22–23.

Bergstein, Fania. "Rigvei ha-Galil" (The soil of Galilee), in *Ḥaruzim Adumim* (Red beads). Tel Aviv: Ha-Kibbutz ha-Me'uḥad, 1955, 164–70.

Bhabha, Homi K. "DissemiNation: Time, Narrative, and the Margins of the Modern Nation," in Homi K. Bhabha, ed., *Nation and Narration*. London: Routledge, 1990, 290–322.

Biale, David. *Power and Powerlessness in Jewish History*. New York: Schocken, 1986.

Bialik, Ḥayim Naḥman. *Shirim* (Poems). Tel Aviv: Dvir, 1966.

———. *Selected Poems: Bialik*, English translation by Ruth Nevo. Tel Aviv: Dvir, 1981.

Bin-Gorion, Emanuel. *Shevilei ha-Agada* (The paths of the legend). Jerusalem: Bialik Institute, 1970.

Bin-Gorion [Berdiczewski], Mikha Yosef. *Mimekor Yisrael: Classic Jewish Folktales*. Bloomington: Indiana University Press, 1976.

Bitan, Dan. "Metsada: Ha-Semel veha-Mitos" (Masada: The symbol and the myth), in Mordekhai Na'or, ed. *Yam ha-Melaḥ u-Midbar Yehuda 1900–1967* (The Dead Sea and the Judaean Desert). Jerusalem: Yad Yitzḥak Ben-Zvi, 1990, 221–35.

Blaushild, Tamara. "Aliyata u-Nefilata shel ha-Po'ema Masada le-Yitzḥak Lamdan" (The rise and fall of Yitzḥak Lamdan's poem). Master's thesis, Department of Hebrew Literature, Tel Aviv University, 1985.

Bornstein, Tamar. "Menusato shel Ḥets ha-Zahav" (The escape of the golden arrow), in *Sipurai ha-Ahuvim* (My beloved tales). Tel Aviv: Zelkovitz, 1960, 7–13.

Bornstein-Lazar, Tamar. *Lag ba-Omer*. Revivim, n.d.

Braslavi [Braslavsky], Yosef. *Yam ha-Melaḥ Saviv-Saviv* (The Dead Sea and its environment); *Ha-Yadata et ha-Aretz?* (Do you know Israel?) *Series*, vol. 3. Tel Aviv: Ha-Kibbutz ha-Me'uḥad, 1956.

———. "Milḥama ve-Hitgonenut shel Yehudei Eretz Yisrael ad Mas'ei ha-Tselav" (War and defense of Palestinian Jews until the Crusades). *Maḥanayim* 41 (Ḥanukka 1960): 57–68.

Braslavsky, Yosef. "Aḥarit Metsada ve-Ikvoteiha" (Masada's end and its traces). *Mi-Bifnim* (January 1942): 3–24.

Brener, Uri. "Tenu'at ha-Po'alim be-Mivḥan Tel Ḥai" (The Labor movement Tested in Tel Ḥai), in *Lekaḥ Tel Ḥai: Ha-Hityashvut u-Gevul ha-Tsafon* (The lesson of Tel Ḥai: Settlement and the northern border). Efal: Yad Tabenkin and Ha-Kibbutz ha-Me'uḥad, 1980, 16–19.

———. ed. *Nokhaḥ Iyum ha-Pelisha ha-Germanit le-Eretz Yisrael, 1940–1942* (In the face of the threat of a German invasion of Palestine). Efal: Yad Tabenkin, 2d edition, 1984.

———. *Le-Tsava Yehudi Atsma'i* (For an independent Jewish army). Efal: Yad Tabenkin, 1985.

Brener, Yosef Ḥayim. "Tel Ḥai." *Ha-Adama* 1 (March 1920), reprinted in G. Rivlin, ed., *Moreshet Tel Ḥai* (Tel Ḥai's legacy). Tel Aviv: Ma'arakhot, 1947, 131–33.

———. "Le-Yom ha-Zikaron" (For the memorial day). *Kuntres* 72, March 21, 1921, 3.

Breude, Ḥayim. "Metsada Nafla Shenit" (Masada fell again). *Yediot Aḥronot*, April 8, 1991.

Breudes, Avraham. *Shir le-Ḥag* (Song for the holiday). Tel Aviv: Emunim, 1955.

———. "Hu Lo Met" (He is not dead), reprinted in Ḥayim Harari, ed. *Mo'adim le-Simḥa* (Festivals and holidays). Tel Aviv: Omanut, 1941, 283.

———. "Yosef ha-Gelili" (Yosef the Galilean), in *Le-Yom Tel Ḥai: Ḥoveret Ezer la-Ganenet* (For Tel Ḥai Day: A reader for the nursery school teacher). Tel Aviv: Histadrut, 1943, 24.

Broshi, Magen. "Mered Bar-Kokhva u-Lekaḥav" (The Bar Kokhba revolt and its lessons). *Ha-Aretz*, literary supplement, August 28, 1981, 18–19.

———. "Meheimanuto shel Yosef ben Matityahu" (The credibility of Josephus), in Uriel Rappoport, ed., *Yosef ben Matityahu: Historyon shel Eretz Yisrael ba-Tekufa ha-Helenistit veha-Romit* (Josephus Flavius: Historian of Eretz Israel in the Hellenistic-Roman period). Jerusalem: Yad Yitzḥak Ben-Zvi, 1982, 21–27.

Bruner, Edward M. and Phyllis Gorfain, "Dialogic Narration and the Paradoxes of Masada," in Stuart Plattner and Edward M. Bruner, eds. *Text, Play, and Story: The Construction and Reconstruction of Self and Society*. Washington, DC: American Ethnological Society, 1984.

Buchner, A., Y. Levinton, and L. Kipnis, eds. *Sefer ha-Kita Zayin* (Reader for the seventh grade). Tel Aviv: Dvir, 1965.

Bundi, Ruth. "Mi-Tel Ḥai ve-Ad Yameinu" (Since Tel Ḥai until today). *Davar*, weekend magazine, March 23, 1979, 8.

Cahan, Ya'akov. *Kitvei Ya'akov Cahan* (Ya'akov Cahan: Collected works). Tel Aviv: Hotsa'at Va'ad ha-Yovel, 1948.

Canetti, Elias. *Crowds and Power*. New York: Viking Press, 1966.

Caplan, Neil. *Palestinian Jewry and the Arab Question, 1917–1925*. London: Frank Cass, 1978.

Carmon, Arye. "Holocaust Teaching in Israel." *Shoah* (Fall–Winter 1982–83): 22–25.

Carr, E. H. *What Is History?* New York: Penguin Books, 1971.

Chamberlin, E. R. *Preserving the Past*. London: J. M. Dent & Sons, 1979.

Chazan, Robert. *European Jews and the First Crusade.* Berkeley: University of California Press, 1987.

Chomsky, Ze'ev. *Ha-Lashon ha-Ivrit be-Darkhei Hitpat'ḥuta* (The Hebrew language and its development). Jerusalem: Re'uven Mass, 1967.

Clark, Katerina. *The Soviet Novel: History as Ritual.* Chicago: University of Chicago Press, 1985.

Cohen, Eric. "Tourism as Play." *Religion* 15 (1985): 291–304.

Collingwood, R. G. *The Idea of History.* Oxford: Clarendon, 1946.

Connerton, Paul. *How Societies Remember.* Cambridge: Cambridge University Press, 1989.

Coser, Lewis A. Introduction to *Maurice Halbwachs: On Collective Memory,* edited and translated by Lewis A. Coser. Chicago: University of Chicago Press, 1992.

Dan, Yosef. *Ha-Sipur ha-Ivri bi-Yemei ha-Beinayim* (The Hebrew story in the Middle Ages). Jerusalem: Keter, 1974.

Davidson, Ephra'im. *Seḥok Pinu: Otsar le-Humor ve-Satira ba-Sifrut ha-Ivrit me-Reshita ve-Ad Yameinu* (Our laughter: An anthology of humor and satire in Hebrew literature from its beginning until today). Ḥulon: Biblos, 1972.

Davis, Natalie Zemon, and Randolph Starn. Introduction to a special issue on collective memory and countermemory, *Representations* 26 (Spring 1989): 1–6.

Dawidowicz, Lucy S. *The War against the Jews, 1933–1945.* New York: Bantam, 1975.

Dégh, Linda. "The 'Belief Legend' in Modern Society: Form, Function, and Relationship to Other Genres," in Wayland D. Hand, ed., *American Folk Legend.* Berkeley: University of California Press, 1971, 55–68.

Dégh, Linda, and A. Vázsonyi. "Legend and Belief." *Genre* 4 (September 1971): 281–304; reprinted in Dan Ben-Amos, ed., *Folklore Genres.* Austin: University of Texas Press, 1976, 93–123.

Derenbourg, J. "Le 33e Jour de Omer." *Revue des Études Juives* 29 (1894): 149.

Derr, M. "Min Metsada ve-Ad Ata" (From Masada to the present). *Metsada* (Masada). Jerusalem: Hitagdut ha-Setudentim ha-Revisionistim, 1934, 25.

Dinur, Ben-Tsiyon, ed. *Sefer Toldot ha-Hagana* (The history of defense). Tel Aviv: Ma'arkhot, 1956.

Dio Cassius, *Roman History;* English translation by Earnest Cary. London: Heinemann, Loeb Classical Library, [1925], 1955.

Dolev-Gandelman, Tsili. "The Symbolic Inscription of Zionist Ideology in the Space of Eretz Israel: Why the Native Israeli Is Called *Tsabar,*" in Harvey E. Goldberg, ed. *Judaism Viewed from Within and Without.* Albany: State University of New York, 1987, 257–84.

Dundes, Alan. *Cracking Jokes: Studies of Sick Humor Cycles and Stereotypes.* Berkeley: Ten Speed Press, 1987.

Durkheim, Émile. *The Elementary Forms of the Religious Life,* 1915; English translation by Joseph Ward Swain. New York: Free Press, 1965.

Dvir, Yehuda. *Bar Kokhva: Ha-Ish veha-Mashi'aḥ* (Bar Kokhba: The man and the messiah). Jerusalem: Kiryat Sefer, 1964.

Eban, Abba. *An Autobiography.* New York: Random House, 1977.

Efron, Yehoshua. "Milḥemet Bar Kokhva le-Or ha-Masoret ha-Talmudit ha-Eretz Yisra'elit ke-Neged ha-Bavlit" (Bar Kokhba in the light of the Palestinian and Babylonian Talmudic traditions), in Aharon Oppenheimer and Uriel Rappoport, eds. *Mered Bar-Kokhva: Meḥkarim Ḥadashim.* (The Bar Kokhba revolt: A new approach). Jerusalem: Yad Yitzḥak Ben-Zvi, 1984, 47–105.

Eisen, Arnold M. *Galut: Modern Jewish Reflection on Homelessness and Homecoming.* Bloomington: Indiana University Press, 1986.

Eisenstadt, N. *Israeli Society.* New York: Basic Books, 1967.

Elam, Yigal. *Ha-Hagana.* (The Hagana organization). Tel Aviv: Zmora & Bitan, 1979.

Elboim-Dror, Rachel. *Ha-Ḥinukh ha-Ivri be-Eretz Yisrael* (Hebrew education in Palestine), vol. 1:1854–1914; vol. 2:1914–1920. Jerusalem: Yad Yitzḥak Ben-Zvi, 1986 & 1990.

Eldad, Yisrael. *Pulmus ha-Ḥurban u-Lekaḥav* (The controversy on the destruction and its lessons). Jerusalem: Van Leer Foundation, 1982.

Eliade, Mircea. *Myth and Reality.* New York: Harper & Row, 1963.

Elon, Amos. *The Israelis: Founders and Sons.* New York: Bantam, 1971.

———. "Ba-Ḥazara meha-Kor be-Einayim Mefukaḥot" (Back from the cold with open eyes). *Ha-Aretz,* October 6, 1978, 13.

———. "Ha-Tiḥyena ha-Atsamot ha-Ele?" (Will these bones be revived?). *Ha-Aretz,* May 14, 1982, 14.

Elyagon, Telma, and Rafi Pesaḥzon, eds. *Elef Zemer ve-Od Zemer* (The Israeli singalong). Ramat-Gan: Kinneret, 1981–85.

Epstein, Yisrael, ed. *Shenei Mo'adim: Yod Alef ba-Adar, Semel ha-Yahadut ha-Mitḥadeshet; Purim, Semel ha-Yahadut ha-Galutit* (Two holidays: The Eleventh of Adar, symbol of Jewish renewal; Purim, symbol of exilic Judaism). Warsaw: Betar, 1937.

Esh, Sha'ul. "Kiddush ha-Ḥayim be-Tokh ha-Ḥurban," (The sanctification of life during the Holocaust), in Yisrael Gutman and Rivia Rotkirkhen, eds. *Sho'at Yehudei Eiropa* (The Holocaust of European Jews). Jerusalem: Yad Va-Shem, 1973, 255–68.

Eusebius, *Ecclesiastical History.* English translation by Kirsopp Lako. London: Heinemann, Loeb Classical Library, [1926], 1975.

Even-Zohar, Itamar. "The Emergence of Native Hebrew Culture in Palestine, 1882–1948." *Studies in Zionism* 4 (1981): 167–84.

Evron, Ram. "Tov Lamut be'ad Artsenu?" (Is it good to die for our country?). *Davar,* weekend magazine, March 24, 1972, 22.

Ezraḥi, Sidra DeKoven. "Revisioning the Past: The Changing Legacy of the Holocaust in Hebrew Literature," *Salmagundi,* no. 68–69 (Fall 1985–Winter 1986): 245–70.

Feldman, Batya. "Ha-Ḥavera Tamar lo Ozevet et ha-Yad shel Trumpeldor" (Comrade Tamar does not leave Trumpeldor's arm). *Ḥadashot,* April 4, 1991, 8–10.

Feldman, Yael S. "Zionism on the Analyst Couch in Contemporary Israeli Literature," *Tikkun* 2 (November–December 1987): 31–34, 91–96.

———. " 'Identification with the Aggressor' or the 'Victim's Complex'?: Holocaust and Ideology in Israeli Theater," *Modern Judaism* 9 (1989): 165–78.

Felman, Ya'akov. "Terumato shel Eliezer Ben-Yehuda li-Teḥiyata shel ha-Lashon ha-Ivrit" (Eliezer Ben-Yehuda's contribution to the revival of the Hebrew language). *Katedra* 2 (1976): 83–95.

Finkelstein, Louis. "Masada and Its Heroes," in *Masada.* New York: The Jewish Theological Seminary and the Jewish Museum, 1967, 12–15.

Firer, Ruth. *Sokhnim shel ha-Ḥinukh ha-Tsiyoni* (The agents of Zionist education). Ḥaifa: Ḥaifa University Press; and Tel Aviv: Sifriyat ha-Po'alim, 1985.

Flusser, David, ed. and Introduction to *Sefer Yosifon* (The book of Jossipon). Jerusalem: Merkaz Zalman Shazar, 1978.

Foucault, Michel. *Language, Counter-memory, Practice: Selected Essays and Interviews.* Translated and edited by Donald F. Bouchard. Ithaca: Cornell University Press, 1977.

Frankel, D. "Uri, Yehuda" (Wake up, Judaea), in *Metsada* (Masada). Jerusalem: Hitagdut ha-Setudentim ha-Revisionistim, 1933, 21.

———. "Uri, Devora" (Wake up, Deborah), in *Ha-Ari ha-Gelili, 1920–1945.* Tel Aviv: Betar, 1945, 2.

Frankel, Jonathan. "Bar Kokhba and All That." *Dissent* 31 (Spring 1984): 192–202.

———. "The 'Yizkor' Book of 1911: A note on National Myths in the Second Aliya," in *Religion, Ideology, and Nationalism in Europe and America: Essays Presented in Honor of Yehoshua Arieli.* Jerusalem: Historical Society of Israel and Zalman Shazar Center for Jewish History, 1986.

Friedland, Roger, and Richard Hecht. "The Politics of Sacred Place: Jerusalem's Temple Mount/*al-haram al-sharif,*" in Jamie Scott and Paul Simpson-Housley, eds., *Sacred Places and Profane Places: Essays in the Geographies of Judaism, Christianity, and Islam.* New York: Greenwood, 1991.

Friedman, Menaḥem. *Ḥevra va-Dat: Ha-Ortodoxia ha-Lo Tsiyonit be-Eretz Yisrael, 1918–1936* (Society and religion: The non-Zionist orthodoxy in Palestine). Jerusalem: Yad Yitzḥak Ben-Zvi, 1978.

Frimer, D. "Masada in Light of the Halakha." *Tradition* 12 (Summer 1971): 27–43.

Frye, Northrop. *Anatomy of Criticism.* Princeton: Princeton University Press, 1957.

Funkenstein, Amos. *Tadmit ve-Toda'a Historit ba-Yahadut uvi-Sevivata ha-Tarbutit* (Perceptions of Jewish history from Antiquity to the present). Tel Aviv: Am Oved, 1991.

Fussell, Paul. *The Great War and Modern Memory.* New York: Oxford University Press, 1975.

Gafni, Shraga. *Tehilat Metsada* (The glory of Masada). Tel Aviv: Amiḥai, 1970.

———. *Mered Bar Kokhva* (The Bar Kokhba revolt). Tel Aviv: Amiḥai, 1976.

Ganzfried, Solomon, ed. *Code of Jewish Law.* New York: Hebrew Publishing Company, 1961.

Gaster, Theodor H. *Festivals of the Jewish Year.* New York: William Sloane Associates, 3rd edition, 1974.

Gefen, Yonatan. "Ha-Mekosheshet ha-Ketana" (The little gatherer). *Ma'ariv*, May 2, 1975.

———. "Huzremu Koḥot" (Forces were sent), *Ma'ariv (Sofshavu'a)*, July 30, 1993.

Genette, Gerald. *Narrative Discourse: An Essay in Method*. Ithaca: Cornell University Press, 1980.

Gertz, Nurit. *Ḥirbat Ḥiz'a veha-Boker shele-Moḥorat* (Generation shift in literary history). Tel Aviv: ha-Kibbutz ha-Me'uḥad, 1983.

———. "The Few against the Many." *Jerusalem Quarterly* 30 (1984): 94–104.

———. "Social Myths in Literary and Political Texts." *Poetics Today* 7 (1986): 621–39.

———. *Nekudot Tatspit: Tarbut ve-Ḥevra be-Yisrael*. (Perspectives on culture and society in Israel). Tel Aviv: Ha-Universita ha-Petuḥa, 1988.

Giladi, Dan. "Kalkala ve-Ḥevra bi-Tekufat ha-Aliya ha-Sheniya" [Economy and society during the Second Aliya period"], in Mordekhai Na'or, ed. *Ha-Aliya ha-Sheniya, 1903–1904* (The Second Aliya, 1903–1904). Jerusalem: Yad Yitzḥak Ben-Zvi, 1984, 4–25.

Gillis, John R., ed. *Commemorations: The Politics of National Identity*. Princeton: Princeton University Press, 1994.

Gilnert, Lewis, ed. *Hebrew in Ashkenaz: A Language in Exile*. New York: Oxford University Press, 1993.

Goldfaden, Avraham. *Bar Kokhba: Der Zuhn Fun dem Shtern: A Musikalishe Melodrama in Raymen* (Bar Kokhba, the son of star: An enlightened melodrama in rhymes). New York: Hebrew Publishing Company, 1908.

Goldstein, Ya'akov, and Ya'akov Shavit. "Yosef Trumpeldor ki-Demut Mofet, veha-Viku'aḥ al 'Shayekhuto' ha-Tenu'atit" (Yosef Trumpeldor as a model and the controversy about his political affiliation). *Kivunim* 12 (1981): 9–21.

Golomb, Eliyahu. *Rashei Perakim le-Toldot Haganat ha-Yishuv* (An outline of the history of the Yishuv's defense). Jerusalem: Kav le-Kav, 1947.

Gonen, Jay Y. *Psychohistory of Zionism*. New York: Mason Charter, 1975.

Gordis, Re'uven. "Al Gevuratam shel Meginei Metsada" (On the heroism of the Masada heroes). *Ha-Do'ar* 37 (no. 40), October 25, 1968, 756–57.

Goren, Shlomo. "Mitsvat Kiddush ha-Shem le-Or ha-Halakha" (The commandment of Kiddush ha-Shem in Jewish law). *Maḥanayim* 41 (1960): 7–15.

———. "Gevurat Metsada le-Or ha-Halakha" (The heroism of Masada in view of the Jewish law). *Maḥanayim* 67 (1963): 7–12.

Gorni, Yosef. "Ha-Yesod ha-Romanti ba-Idi'ologia shel ha-Aliya ha-Sheniya" (The romantic element in the ideology of the Second Aliya). *Assufot* 10 (1966): 55–75.

———. "Yaḥasa shel Mifleget Po'alei Tsiyon be-Eretz Yisrael la-Gola bi-Tekufat ha-Aliya ha-Sheniya" (The attitude of "Poalei Zion" of Palestine to Exile during the Second Aliya), in *ha-Tsiyonut* 2 (1971): 74–89.

Gotferstein, Yosef. "Kiddush ha-Shem be-Mahalakh ha-Dorot ve-Yiḥudo bi-Tekufat ha-Sho'a" (Kiddush ha-Shem during the Holocaust and its distinction during the period of the Holocaust), in *Ha-Amida ha-Yehudit bi-Tekufat ha-Sho'a*. Jerusalem: Yad Va-Shem, 1970, 359–84.

Greenwood, Davydd J. "Culture by the Pound: An Anthropological Perspective on Tourism as Cultural Commodization," in Valene L. Smith, ed. *Hosts and Guests: The Anthropology of Tourism*. Philadelphia: University of Pennsylvania Press, 1977, 129–38.

Grunwald, Itamar. "Kiddush ha-Shem: Beruro shel Musag" (Kiddush ha-Shem: The clarification of the concept) *Molad* 1 (1967): 476–84.

Gurevich, Zali, and Gideon Aran. "Al ha-Makom" (About the place). *Alpayim* 4 (1991): 9–44.

Gutman, Leo. "Masada and the Talmud: A Letter." *Tradition* 10 (Fall 1969): 98–99.

Gutman, Shmaryahu. *Im Metsada* (With Masada). Tel Aviv: Ha-Kibbutz ha-Me'uḥad, 1964.

Gutman, Yisrael. "Kiddush ha-Shem ve-Kiddush ha-Ḥayim" (Martyrdom and the sanctification of life). *Yalkut Moreshet* 24 (October 1977): 7–22.

Ha-Ari ha-Gelili, 1920–1945 (The Galilean lion, 1920–1945). Tel Aviv: Betar, 1945.

Ḥabas, Brakha, ed. *Sefer ha-Aliya ha-Sheniya* (The book of the Second Aliya). Tel Aviv: Am Oved, 1947.

Ha-Cohen, Menaḥem. "Ḥetz va-Keshet be-Lag ba-Omer" (Bow and arrows on Lag ba-Omer) *Maḥanayim* 26 (1961): 38–40.

Ha-Cohen, Mordekhai. "Lag ba-Omer: Mekorot, Halakhot, Minhagim" (Lag ba-Omer: Sources, laws, customs). *Maḥanayim* 56 (1961): 20–31.

Ḥadash. "Mi-Saviv: Al Mot Loḥem" (From around: The death of a warrior). *Ha-Po'el ha-Tsa'ir*, March 12, 1920, 26.

Ha-Elyon, Ya'akov. *Regel Shel Buba* (A doll's leg). Tel Aviv: Am Oved, 1973.

Ḥagai, Shmu'el. "Ha-Hadlaka veha-Halakha" (The bonfire and the religious law) *Maḥanayim* 56 (1961): 34–37.

Ha-Hagana (The defense). Israel Defense Forces, Education Headquarters, 4th edition, 1975.

Halbwachs, Maurice. *La Mémoire collective*, 1950; English translation by F. J. and V. Y. Ditter, *The Collective Memory*. New York: Harper & Row, 1980.

Halkin, Shmu'el. *Bar Kokhba: Dramatisher Poeme* (Bar Kokhba: A dramatic poem). Moscow: Emes, 1939.

Halkin, Simon. *Modern Hebrew Literature: Trends and Values*. New York: Schocken, 1970.

Halpern, Ben. *The Idea of the Jewish State*. Cambridge: Harvard University Press, 1961.

Handelman, Don, and Elihu Katz. "State Ceremonies of Israel: Remembrance Day and Independence Day," in Don Handelman, *Models and Mirrors: Towards an Anthropology of Public Events*. Cambridge: Cambridge University Press, 1990, 191–233.

Handler, Richard. *Nationalism and the Politics of Culture in Quebec*. Madison: University of Wisconsin Press, 1988.

Harari, Ḥayim, ed. *Mo'adim le-Simḥa* (Festivals and holidays). Tel Aviv: Omanut, 1941.

Harkabi, Yehoshafat. *Be-Tokef ha-Metsi'ut* (Facing reality). Jerusalem: Van Leer Foundation, 1981.

———. *Ḥazon, Lo Fantazia: Likḥei Mered Bar Kokhva ve-Re'alism Medini be-Yameinu* (Vision, no fantasy: Realism in international relations). Jerusalem: Domino Press, 1982; English translation by Max Ticktin, *The Bar Kokhba Syndrome.* Chappaqua, NY: Rossel Books, 1983.

Harshav, Benjamin. *Language in Time of Revolution.* Berkeley: University of California Press, 1993.

Hartman, Geoffrey H. "Public Memory and Modern Experience," *Yale Journal of Criticism* 6 (1993): 239–47.

Ha-Yerushalmi, Levy Itzḥak. "Ha-Maḥresha veha-Ḥerev o ha-Ḥerev veha-Maḥresha" (The plow and the sword or the sword and the plow) *Ma'ariv (Yamim ve-Leilot)*, September 22, 1978, 8–9.

Hazaz, Ḥayim. "Ha-Derasha" (The sermon), 1942; reprinted in *Avanim Rot'ḥot* (Seething stones). Tel Aviv: Am Oved, 1970, 219–37; English translation by Ben Halpern in Robert Alter, ed. *Modern Hebrew Literature.* New York: Behrman House, 1975, 271–87.

Ḥefer, Ḥayim. "Ma Lamadeta ba-Gan ha-Yom?" (What did you learn in the nursery school today?), 1964; reprinted in Amnon Birman, ed. *Be-Etsem, ad ha-Etsem: Mi-Mivḥar ha-Satira ha-Yisra'elit* (Under the skin: Selected Israeli satire). Jerusalem: Keter, 1988, 230–31.

Heilperin, Yisrael, ed. *Sefer ha-Gevura: Antologia Historit Sifrutit* (The book of heroism: A historical literary anthology). Tel Aviv: Am Oved, 1941.

Heimi, Avino'am. *Metsada shel Yosef ben Matityahu* (Josephus's Masada). Ramat Gan: Masada, 1976.

Heinemann, Yosef. *Agadot ve-Toldoteihen* (Agada and its development). Jerusalem: Keter, 1974.

Heller, Bernard. "Masada and the Talmud." *Tradition* 10 (Winter 1968): 31–34.

Herman, Simon N. *Jewish Identity: A Social Psychological Perspective.* Beverly Hills: Sage Publications, 1977.

Hertzberg, Arthur, ed. *The Zionist Idea: A Historical Analysis and Reader.* New York: Meridian Books, 1960.

Herzfeld, Michael. *Ours Once More: Folklore, Ideology, and the Making of Modern Greece.* New York: Pella, 1986.

Herzog, Ḥana. "Ha-Musagim 'Yishuv Yashan' ve-'Yishuv Ḥadash' be-He'ara Sotsiologit" (The concepts of 'old Yishuv' and 'new Yishuv' from a sociological perspective). *Katedra* 32 (July 1984): 99–108.

Ḥever, Ḥanan. "Shivḥei Amal u-Fulmus Politi" (The praise of labor and a political controversy), in Pinḥas Ginosar, ed. *Ha-Sifrut ha-Ivrit u-Tenu'at ha-Avoda* (Hebrew literature and the Labor movement). Be'er Sheba: Ben-Gurion University Press, 1989, 116–57.

Hobsbawm, E., and T. Ranger, eds. *The Invention of Tradition.* Cambridge: Cambridge University Press, 1983.

Hoenig, Sidney B. "The Sicarii in Masada: Glory or Infamy?" *Tradition* 11 (Spring 1970): 5–30.

———. "The Historic Masada and the Halakha." *Tradition* 13 (Fall 1972): 100–115.

Hoffman, Ḥaya. "Ha-Af Al Pi Khen ha-Breneri be-Shirat Yitzḥak Lamdan" (Brener's 'nevertheless' in the poetry of Yitzḥak Lamdan), in Pinḥas Ginosar, ed. *Ha-Sifrut ha-Ivrit u-Tenu'at ha-Avoda* (Hebrew literature and the Labor movement). Be'er Sheba: Ben-Gurion University Press, 1989, 158–77.

Hohendahl, Peter Uwe. *Building a National Literature: The Case of Germany, 1830–1870.* Ithaca: Cornell University Press, 1989.

Horowitz, Dan, and Moshe Lissak. *Mi-Yishuv li-Medina* (The origins of Israeli polity). Tel Aviv: Am Oved, 1977.

Ḥorshi, Arye. *Ḥagim vi-Yemei Zikaron la-Talmid* (Holidays and memorial days for the student). Tel Aviv: Bronfman, 1974.

Horsley, Richard A. "Josephus and the Bandits." *Journal for the Study of Judaism* 10 (July 1979): 37–63.

Howe, Irving, and Eliezer Greenberg, eds. *A Treasury of Yiddish Stories.* New York: Schocken, 1973.

Huberband, Shimon. *Kiddush ha-Shem: Ketavim mi-Yemei ha-Sho'a* (Kiddush ha-Shem: Writings from the days of the Holocaust), edited by Naḥman Blumental and Yosef Kermish. Tel Aviv: Zakhor, 1969.

Hubert, H., and M. Mauss. *Sacrifice: Its Nature and Function.* Chicago: University of Chicago Press, 1964.

Ḥurgin, Ya'akov. *Shalshelet ha-Gevura* (Heroic chain). Tel Aviv: Amiḥai, 1946.

Hutton, Patrick H. "Collective Memory and Collective Mentalities: The Halbwachs-Ariès Connection," *Historical Reflections/Réflexions Historiques* 15, no. 2 (1988): 311–22.

———. *History as an Art of Memory.* Hanover, N.H.: University Press of New England, 1993.

Ibn Daud, Avraham. *Sefer ha-Kabala* (The book of tradition), edited by Gerson D. Cohen. Philadelphia: Jewish Publication Society, 1967.

Ilan, Tsvi. *Li-Metsada be-Ikvot ha-Kana'im* (To Masada in the Zealots' footsteps). Tel Aviv: Shreberk, 1973.

Isaac, Benjamin, and Aharon Oppenheimer. "The Revolt of Bar Kokhba: Ideology and Modern Scholarship," *Journal of Jewish Studies* 36, no. 1 (1985): 33–60.

Ish-Shalom, Michael. "Anu Ḥotrim le-Atid" (We strive for the future). *Metsada* (Masada). Jerusalem: Hitagdut ha-Setudentim ha-Revisionistim, 1934, 13.

Jabotinsky, Ze'ev [Vladimir]. "Tel Ḥai." *Ha-Aretz,* March 8, 1920, 1.

———. "Kaddish" (Prayer for the dead), 1928; reprinted in *Ketavim: Zikhronot Ben Dori* (Collected works: Memoirs of my generation). Tel Aviv: Ari Jabotinsky, 1947, 103–9.

———. "Bein ha-Shishi la-Aḥad Asar" (Between the sixth and the eleventh [of Adar]). *Ha-Am,* June 6, 1931; reprinted in *Ketavim: Ba-Sa'ar* (Collected works: The storm). Jerusalem: Ari Jabotinsky, 1953, 265–71.

———. "Mi-Yomani" (From my diary.) *Ha-Am*, July 14, 1931, 2.

———. "Al Trumpeldor veha-Ein Davar Shelo" (Trumpeldor and his "never mind"), in *Yosef Trumpeldor: Ḥai Shanim le-Moto* (Yosef Trumpeldor: Eighteenth anniversary of his death). Tel Aviv: Keren Tel Ḥai, 1938, 53–55.

———. *Shirim* (Poems). Jerusalem: Ari Jabotinsky, 1947.

———. *Sipur Yamai* (Autobiography). Jerusalem: Ari Jabotinsky, 1947.

Jones, Michael Owens. "(PC + CB) × SD(R + I + E) = Hero." *New York Folklore Quarterly* 28 (1971): 243–60.

Josephus. *Complete Works.* translated by W. Whiston (Grand Rapids, Michigan: Kregel, 1960; Hebrew translation by Y. N. Simḥoni, *Yosef ben Matityahu: Toldot Milḥemet ha-Yehudim im ha-Roma'im.* Ramat-Gan: Masada, 1923.

Jossipon. *Sefer Yosifon* (The book of Jossipon), edited by David Flusser. Jerusalem: Bialik Institute, 1978.

Kafkafi, Yitzḥak, ed. *Shenot Ha-Maḥanot Ha-Olim, 1934–1945* (The chronicle of Maḥanot Ha-Olim). Tel Aviv: Ha-Kibbutz ha-Me'uḥad, 1985.

Kahana-Carmon, Amalya. *Ve-Yare'aḥ be-Emek Ayalon* (And moon in the valley of Ayalon). Tel Aviv: Ha-Kibbutz ha-Me'uḥad, 1971.

Kammen, Michael. *Mystic Chords of Memory.* New York: Knopf, 1991.

Kapferer, Bruce. *Legends of People, Myths of State: Violence, Intolerance, and Political Culture in Sri Lanka and Australia.* Washington, DC: Smithsonian Institution Press, 1988.

Kasher, Arye, ed. *Ha-Mered ha-Gadol: Ha-Sibot veha-Nesibot li-Fritsato* (The Great Jewish Revolt: Its causes and circumstances). Jerusalem: Merkaz Zalman Shazar, 1983.

Katriel, Tamar. *Communal Webs: Communication, Culture, and Acculturation in Contemporary Israel.* Albany: State University of New York Press, 1991.

———. "Remaking a Place: Cultural Productions in an Israeli Pioneering Museum." *History and Memory* 5 (Fall/Winter 1993): 104–35.

Katriel, Tamar, and Aliza Shenhar. "Tower and Stockade: A Study in Israeli Settlement Symbolism." *Quarterly Journal of Speech* 76, no. 4 (1990): 359–80.

Katz, Elihu, and Michael Gurevitch. *Tarbut ha-Penai be-Yisrael* (Leisure culture in Israel). Tel Aviv: Am Oved, 1973.

Katz, Ya'akov. "Bein 1096 le-1648/49" (Between 1096 and 1648/49), in S. Ettinger, S. W. Baron, B. Dinur, and I. Halpern, eds. *Sefer ha-Yovel le-Yitzḥak F. Baer* (Yitzḥak Baer: Jubilee book) Jerusalem: Historical Society of Israel, 1960, 318–37.

Katznelson, Berl. "Anshei Tel Ḥai be-Motam uve-Ḥayeihem" (The Tel Ḥai people in their death and their lives). *Davar*, March 23, 1929.

———. Introduction to Yisrael Heilperin, ed., *Sefer ha-Gevura: Antologia Historit Sifrutit* (The book of heroism: A historical literary anthology). Tel Aviv: Am Oved, 1941, 9–12.

Kedar, Binyamin Z. "Tasbikh Metsada" (The Masada complex). *Ha-Aretz*, April 22, 1973, 16; English version, "Masada: The Myth and the Complex." *Jerusalem Quarterly* 24 (Summer 1982): 57–63.

Kenan, Amos. "Hitbahamut" (Bestialization). *Yediot Aḥronot* June 2, 1989, 17.

Kerman, Danny, et al. *Davar Akher Legamre* (Utterly different). Tel Aviv: Am Oved, 1988.

Kermode, Frank. *The Sense of an Ending: Studies in the Theory of Fiction.* New York: Oxford University Press, 1967.

Ki Alinu li-Metsada (For we climbed up Masada). Tel Aviv: Histadrut Ha-Shomer Ha-Tsa'ir be-Eretz Yisrael, 1942.

Kipnis, Levin. "Ari ha-Even: Agada" (The stone lion: a legend), in *Le-Yom Tel Ḥai: Ḥoveret Ezer la-Ganenet* (For Tel Ḥai Day: A reader for nursery school teachers). Tel Aviv: Histadrut, 1943, 23–24.

———. "Bar Kokhva veha-Arye" (Bar Kokhba and the lion), in *Gilyonot.* Tel Aviv: Association for Nursery School Teachers, 1929, 59–62; reprinted in Levin Kipnis and Yemima Tchernovitch, eds. *Gan Gani* (My nursery school), 1947; Tel Aviv: Bronfman, 1978, 114.

———. "Ha-Yad ha-Ḥazaka" (The strong arm), in A. Buchner, Y. Levinton, and L. Kipnis, eds. *Sefer ha-Kita Zayin* (Reader for the seventh grade). Tel Aviv: Dvir, 1965, 362–64.

———. "Yosef Gibor Yisrael" (Yosef, the hero of Israel), in Y. Levinton, L. Kipnis, and A. Buchner, eds. *Sefer ha-Kita Bet* (Reader for the second grade). Tel Aviv: Dvir, 1971.

———. *Mo'adei Yisrael: Lag ba-Omer* (Israel's holidays: Lag ba-Omer). Tel Aviv: Samuel Simson, 1974.

Kipnis, Levin, A. Buchner, and Y. Levinton, eds. *Sefer ha-Kita Gimel* (Reader for the third grade). Tel Aviv: Dvir, 1962.

Kipnis, Levin, and Yemima Tchernovitch, eds. *Gan Gani* (My nursery school). 1947; Tel Aviv: Bronfman, 1978.

Kishon, Ephra'im. *Ba-Aḥad ha-Amashim* (One of yester days). Tel Aviv: Tversky, 1963.

Klapp, Orrin E. *Symbolic Leaders: Public Dramas and Public Men.* Chicago: Aldine, 1964.

Klausner, Shm'uel. "Ha-Ivri he-Ḥadash" (The new Hebrew Man). *Zemanim,* nos. 323, 325, 329, 330 (September–October), 1954.

Klausner, Yosef. "Hem Naflu Ḥalalim" (They are dead). *Ha-Aretz,* March 9, 1920, 2.

———. "Al Kedushat ha-Aretz" (On the sanctification of the country). *Ha-Aretz,* March 21, 1921, 2.

———. *Jesus of Nazareth.* New York: Macmillan, 1925.

———. "Metsada" (Masada). *La-No'ar Series* no. 62. Tel Aviv: Omanut, 1937.

———. *Historia shel ha-Bayit ha-Sheni* (History of the Second Temple). Jerusalem: Aḥiasaf, 1951.

Kni'el, Yehoshua. *Hemshekh u-Temura: ha-Yishuv ha-Yashan veha-Yishuv he-Ḥadash bi-Tekufat ha-Aliya ha-Rishona veha-Sheniya* (Continuity and change: The old and new Yishuv during the First and Second Aliyas). Jerusalem: Yad Yitzḥak Ben-Zvi, 1982.

Kohn, Hans. *The Idea of Nationalism.* New York: Macmillan, 1944.

Kolitz, Zvi. "Masada: Suicide or Murder?" *Tradition* 12 (Summer 1971): 5–25.

Kurtzweil, Baruch. "Ha-Toda'a ha-Historit be-Shirei Yitzḥak Lamdan" (The historical consciousness in the poetry of Yitzḥak Lamdan), in *Bein Ḥazon le-Vein Absurd* (Between vision and absurdity). Tel Aviv: Schocken, 1966, 100–109.

Labov, William. "The Transformation of Experience in Narrative Syntax," in *Language in the Inner City.* Philadelphia: University of Pennsylvania Press, 1972, 354–96.

Lag ba-Omer: Ḥoveret la-Talmid (Lag ba-Omer: A student's work guide). Jerusalem: Ministry of Education and Culture, 1987.

Lamdan, Yitzḥak. *Masada.* Tel Aviv: Hedim, 1927; reprinted, Tel Aviv: Dvir, 1972; English translation by Leon I. Yudkin, in *Isaac Lamdan: A Study in Twentieth-Century Hebrew Poetry.* Ithaca: Cornell University Press, 1971, 199–234.

———. "Reshimot" (Notes), in *Moznayim* 26 (1930): 11–12.

———. "Teshuva la-Sho'alim" (In response to those who question), in *Gilyonot* 1, no. 1 (1933): 1–2.

Landau, Betsalel, ed. *Masa Meron* (The Meron journey). Jerusalem: Usha, 1966.

Landau, Judah Leo. *Bar Kokhva: Shir Ḥezyon Tuga ba-Ḥamesh Ma'arakhot* (Bar Kokhba: A tragic poem consisting of five scenes). Lvov: Druck von Anna Waidowicz, 1884.

Lapide, P. E. "Masada." *Jewish Heritage* 6 (Spring 1964): 28–29.

Laqueur, Walter. *Toldot ha-Tsiyonut* (A history of Zionism). Jerusalem: Schocken, 1975.

Laskov, Shulamit. *Trumpeldor: Sipur Ḥayav* (Trumpeldor: A biography). Ḥaifa: Shikmona, 1972.

Lavi, Tsvi. "Bar Kokhva: Yigael Yadin Meshiv li-Yehoshafat Harkabi" (Bar Kokhba: Yigael Yadin responds to Yehoshafat Harkabi). *Ma'ariv,* October 17, 1980, 14.

Lazar-Litai, Ḥayim. *Metsada shel Varsha* (Masada of Warsaw). Tel Aviv: Makhon Jabotinsky, 1963.

Leach, Edmund. *Political Systems of Highland Burma.* Boston: Beacon Press, 1954.

Lehmann, Meir Marcus. *Rabbi Akiva: Sipur Histori* (Rabbi Akiba: A historical novel), 1896; reprinted Tel Aviv: Netsaḥ, 1954.

Lekaḥ Tel Ḥai: Hityashvut u-Gevul ha-Tsafon (The lesson of Tel Ḥai: Settlement and the northern border). Efal: Yad Tabenkin and Ha-Kibbutz ha-Me'uḥad, 1980.

Levin, Yisrael L. "Ha-Kana'im be-Sof Tekufat Bayit Sheni ki-Ve'aya Historiografit" (The Zealots at the end of the Second Temple period as a historiographic problem). *Katedra* 1 (1977): 39–60.

Levinsky, Yom Tov, ed. *Sefer ha-Mo'adim* (The book of holidays). Tel Aviv: Dvir, 1955.

Levinson, Avraham. "Gevurat Yisrael" (Jewish heroism), in *Magen va-Shelaḥ: Sheloshim Shana la-Haganat Tel Ḥai* (The shield and the weapon: Thirtieth anniversary of the defense of Tel Ḥai). Tel Aviv: Histadrut, 1950, 79–89.

Lévi-Strauss, Claude. *La Pensée sauvage,* 1962; English translation, *The Savage Mind.* Chicago: University of Chicago Press, 1970.

Levner, Israel Benjamin. *Bar Kokhva: Sipur Histori mi-Yemei Harisot Betar* (Bar Kokhba: a historical novel on the destruction of Betar). Warsaw: Barkai, 1923.

———. "Bar Kokhva veha-Arye" (Bar Kokhba and the lion), in B. Avivi and A. Keren-Tal, eds. *Mo'adim le-Simḥa: Lag ba-Omer.* Jerusalem: Kiryat Sefer, 1943, 3–6.

Levy, Sara. "Ba-Galil" (In Galilee), in *Le-Yom Tel Ḥai: Ḥoveret Ezer la-Ganenet* (For Tel Ḥai Day: Reader for the nursery school teacher). Tel Aviv: Histadrut, 1943, 26.

Lewis, Bernard. *History: Remembered, Recovered, Invented.* Princeton: Princeton University Press, 1975.

Le-Yom Tel Ḥai: Ḥoveret Ezer la-Ganenet (For Tel Ḥai Day: Reader for the nursery school teacher). Tel Aviv: Histadrut, 1943.

Le-Yom Tel Ḥai, Yod Alef ba-Adar: Ḥomrei Hadrakha le-Morim be-Vatei ha-Sefer Tikhoniyim (For Tel Ḥai Day, the Eleventh of Adar: Instructional materials for teachers in high schools). Jerusalem: Ministry of Education, 1967.

Liebman, Charles, and Eliezer Don-Yeḥiya. *Civil Religion in Israel.* Berkeley: University of California Press, 1983.

Lipovetsky, Pesaḥ [Ben-Amram]. *Yosef Trumpeldor: Ishiyuto, Ḥayav, Pe'ulotav* (Yosef Trumpeldor: His personality, life, activities). Kovna: Semel, 1924.

Lipsitz, George. *Time Passages: Collective Memory and American Popular Culture.* Minneapolis: University of Minnesota Press, 1989.

Livne, Mikha. *Ḥomer Ezer la-Madrikh bi-Metsada* (Instructional materials for the tourist guide to Masada). Department of Tourism and National Parks Authority, 1966.

———. *Ma'oz Aḥaron: Ha-Sipur shel Metsada va-Anasheiha* (The last fortress: The story of Masada and its people). Ministry of Defense, 1986; English translation by Yael Chaver, Ministry of Defense, 1986.

Livne, Mikha, and Ze'ev Meshel. *Metsada* (Masada). Tel Aviv: National Parks Authority, n.d.

Lowenthal, David. *The Past Is a Foreign Country.* Cambridge: Cambridge University Press, 1985.

Lustick, Ian S. *For the Land and the Lord: Jewish Fundamentalism in Israel.* New York: Council on Foreign Relations, 1988.

Luz, Ehud. *Makbilim Nifgashim: Dat u-Le'umiyut ba-Tenu'a ha-Tsiyonit be-Mizraḥ Eiropa be-Reshita, 1882–1904* (Religion and nationalism in the early Zionist movement, 1882–1904). Tel Aviv: Am Oved, 1985.

Luz, Menaḥem. "Ne'um ha-Mishne shel Elazar bi-Metsada ve-Kli'arkhus Ish Soli" (Clearchus of Soli as a source of Elazar's Deuterosis), in Uriel Rappoport, ed. *Yosef ben Matityahu: Historyon shel Eretz Yisrael ba-Tekufa ha-Helenistic veha-Romit* (Josephus Flavius: historian of Eretz Israel in the Hellinistic-Roman period). Jerusalem: Yad Yitzḥak Ben-Zvi, 1982, 79–90.

Lyotard, Jean François. *The Post-modernist Condition: A Report on Knowledge;* English translation by Geoff Bennington and Brian Massunmi. Minneapolis: University of Minnesota Press, 1984.

MacAloon, John J. "Olympic Games and the Theory of Spectacle in Modern Societies," in *Rites, Drama, Festival, Spectacle: Rehearsals toward a Theory of Cultural Performance.* Philadelphia: Institute for the Study of Human Issues, 1984, 241–80.

MacCannell, Dean. *The Tourist: A New Theory of the Leisure Class.* New York: Schocken, 1976.

Magen va-Shelaḥ: Sheloshim Shana la-Haganat Tel Ḥai (The shield and the weapon: Thirtieth anniversary of the defense of Tel Ḥai). Tel Aviv: Histadrut, 1950.

Marcus, Ivan G. "From Politics to Martyrdom: Shifting Paradigms in the Hebrew Narratives of the 1096 Crusade Riots." *Prooftexts* 2, no. 1 (1982): 40–52.

Margalit, Dan, and Matti Golan, "Ha-Mimshal bi-Fe'ula" (The administration in action), *Ha-Aretz,* April 27, 1973, 13.

Marks, Richard G. *The Image of Bar Kokhba in Traditional Jewish Literature: False Messiah and National Hero.* University Park, PA: Pennsylvania State Press, 1993.

Masada. New York: Jewish Theological Seminary and the Jewish Museum, 1967.

Masekhet Gevura le-Yom ha-Hagana, Yod Alef ba-Adar (The story of heroism for the Defense Day, the Eleventh of Adar). Israel Defense Forces, 1949.

"Me'a va-Aḥad Ra'ayonot le-Kishut Ḥalal ha-Limud o ha-Kita" (One hundred and one ideas for decorating the teaching space or the classroom), *Davar Aḥer* no. 153, September 13, 1986.

Megged, Aharon. *Ha-Ḥai al ha-Met.* Tel Aviv: Am Oved, 1965; English translation by Misha Louvish, *Living on the Dead.* New York: McCall, 1970.

———, ed. *Masekhet ha-Hagana* (The story of the Hagana). Tel Aviv: Irgun Ḥavrei ha-Hagana, 1966.

Meltzer, S. "Ba-Galil ha-Elyon" (In Upper Galilee), in *Le-Yom Tel Ḥai: Ḥoveet Ezer la-Ganenet* (For Tel Ḥai Day: a Reader for the Nursery School Teacher). Tel Aviv: Histadrut, 1943, 5.

Meroz, Tamar. "Trumpeldor Basar va-Dam" (Trumpeldor of flesh and blood). *Ha-Aretz,* Weekend Magazine, March 20, 1970, 12–14.

Michael, B. "Mi-Zemirot Eretz ha-Arazim" (From the songs of Lebanon). *Ha-Aretz,* December 31, 1983.

Michael, B., et al. *Zoo Eretz Zoo?* (This land is a zoo). Jerusalem: Domino Press, 2nd edition, 1982.

Mink, Louis O. "Narrative Form as a Cognitive Instrument," in Robert H. Canary and Henry Kozicki, eds. *The Writing of History: Literary Form and Historical Understanding.* Madison: University of Wisconsin Press, 1978, 129–49.

Mintz, Alan. *Ḥurban: Responses to Catastrophe in Hebrew Literature.* New York: Columbia University Press, 1984.

Miron, Dan. *Arba Panim ba-Sifrut ha-Ivrit Bat Yameinu* (Four facets of contemporary Hebrew writing). Jerusalem: Schocken, 1975.

———. *Im lo Tiheye Yerushalayim: Ha-Sifrut ha-Ivrit be-Heksher Tarbuti-Politi* (If there is no Jerusalem: Essays on Hebrew writing in a cultural-political context). Tel Aviv: Ha-Kibbutz ha-Me'uḥad, 1987.

Mishori, Elik. "Leida me-Ḥadash shel Omanut Ivrit" (The rebirth of a Hebrew art), in Nurit Gertz, ed. *Nekudot Tatspit: Tarbut ve-Ḥevra be-Yisrael* (Perspectives on culture and society in Israel). Tel Aviv: Ha-Universita ha-Petuḥa, 1988, 175–94.

Morag, Shlomo. "Ha-Ivrit ha-Ḥadasha be-Hitgabshuta: Lashon be-Aspaklaria shel Ḥevra" (The shaping of modern Hebrew: Language in a social mirror). *Katedra* 55 (1990): 70–92.

Moregenstern, Julian. "La ba-Omer: Its Origin and Import." *Hebrew Union College Annual* 29 (1968): 81–90.

Morrison, Toni. *Beloved.* New York: Knopf, 1987.

Mosse, George L. *Fallen Soldiers: Reshaping the Memory of the World Wars.* New York: Oxford University Press, 1990.

N., "Ken, Lelo Takhlit" (Indeed, for no purpose) *Ba-Maḥane* 59 (May 1, 1942): 11.

Na'or, Mordekhai, ed. *Tenu'ot ha-No'ar 1920–1960* (Youth movements, 1920–1960). Jerusalem: Yad Yitzḥak Ben-Zvi, 1989.

———, ed. *Yam ha-Melaḥ u-Midbar Yehuda 1900–1967* (The Dead Sea and the Judaean desert 1900–1967). Jerusalem: Yad Yitzḥak Ben-Zvi, 1990.

Nedava, Yosef. *Sefer Olei ha-Gardom* (The book of the executed). Tel Aviv: Shelaḥ, 1952.

———. "Jabotinsky u-Farashat Tel Ḥai" (Jabotinsky and the Tel Ḥai affair). *Ha-Uma* 16 (September 1978): 366–73.

———. "Bein Historia le-Mitos" (Between history and myth). *Yediot Aḥronot*, July 6, 1979, 23.

Neria, Moshe Tsvi. "'Hit'abdut Lada'at': Giborei Metsada le-Or ha-Halakha" (Suicide: The Masada heroes in view of the Jewish law). *Or ha-Mizraḥ* 8 (January 1961): 8–12.

Nora, Pierre (sous la direction de). *Les Lieux de mémoire.* Vol. 1. *La République.* Paris: Gallimard, 1984.

———. "Between Memory and History: Les Lieux de Mémoire." *Representations* 26 (1989): 7–25.

Nordau, Max. "Ha-Kapitan Trumpeldor: Divrei Hesped" (Captain Trumpeldor: An obituary), 1920; reprinted in *Yosef Trumpeldor: Ḥai Shanim le-Moto* (Yosef Trumpeldor: Eighteenth anniversary of his death). Tel Aviv: Keren Tel Ḥai, 1938, 50.

Noy, Dov. "Gevurat Yisrael ba-Maḥteret" (The underground Jewish heroism). *Maḥanayim* 52 (1961): 122–28.

Obrdlik, A. J. "Gallows Humor: A Sociological Phenomenon." *American Journal of Sociology* 47 (1942): 709–16.

Ofek, Uriel. *Gibor Ḥida* (The enigmatic hero). Tel Aviv: Shreberk, 1975.

———. *Sifrut ha-Yeladim ha-Ivrit, 1900–1948* (Hebrew children's literature, 1900–1948). Tel Aviv: Dvir, 1988.

Ofrat, Gideon. *Adama, Adam, Dam: Mitos he-Ḥalutz u-Fulḥan ha-Adama be-Maḥazot ha-Hityashvut* (Land, man, blood: The myth of the pioneer and the ritual of earth in Eretz Israel settlement drama). Tel Aviv: Gome, 1980.

Oppenheimer, Aharon, ed. *Mered Bar-Kokhva* (The Bar Kokhba revolt). Jerusalem: Merkaz Zalman Shazar, 1980.

Oppenheimer, Aharon, and Uriel Rappoport, eds. *Mered Bar-Kokhva: Meḥkarim Ḥadashim* (The Bar Kokhba revolt: A new approach). Jerusalem: Yad Yitzhak Ben-Zvi, 1984.

Oren, Elḥanan. *Hityashvut bi-Shenot Ma'avak, 1936–1947* (Settlement and struggle, 1936–1947). Jerusalem: Yad Yitzḥak Ben-Zvi, 1978.

———. "Moreshet Tel Ḥai" (The legacy of Tel Ḥai), in *Lekaḥ Tel Ḥai: Ha-Hityashvut u-Gevul ha-Tsafon* (The lesson of Tel Ḥai: Settlement and the northern border). Efal: Yad Tabenkin and Ha-Kibbutz ha-Me'uḥad, 1980, 5–13.

———. "Moreshet ve-Shorasheiha: Tel Ḥai—Mitos ve-Emet" (A legacy and its roots: Tel Ḥai—myth and truth). *Shorashim* 2 (1980): 153–80.

Oring, Elliott. *Israeli Humor: The Content and Structure of the Chizbat of the Palmah*. Albany: State University of New York Press, 1981.

Orlan, Ḥayim. "Od al Metsada ve-Giboreiha" (More on Masada and its heroes). *Ha-Do'ar*, 37 (no. 40), October 25, 1968, 755–56.

———. "Be-Shulei ha-Diyunim veha-Iyunim al Metsada" (In the margins of the discussion and the study of Masada). *Ha-Do'ar* 48 (no. 7), December 13, 102–103.

———. "Metsada: Ha-Perek ha-Histori she-Kofim Aleinu Kivyakhol . . ." (Masada: The chapter that is seemingly forced upon us). *Ha-Do'ar* 48 (no. 18), February 28, 1969, 277–78.

Ovadyahu, Mordekhai. "Meshorer ha-Tekufa" (The poet of his time). *Ha-Po'el ha-Tsa'ir* 10 (1949): 15.

Paine, Robert. "Masada: A History of Memory." Paper presented at the annual meeting of the Canadian Historical Association, Kenigston, 1988.

———. "Jewish Ontologies of Time and Political Legitimation in Israel" in Henry J. Rutz, ed. *The Politics of Time*. Washington D.C.: American Ethnological Society, 1992, 150–70.

Pearlman, Moshe. *The Zealots of Masada: The Story of a Dig*. New York: Charles Scribner's Sons, 1967.

Peleg, Ilan. *Begin's Foreign Policy, 1977–1983, and Israel's Move to the Right*. New York: Greenwood Press, 1987.

Persky, Nathan, ed. *Mikra'ot Yisrael Ḥadashot le-Khita Bet* (The new Israel's reader: Textbook for the second grade). Tel Aviv: Masada, 1975.

Pinsky, David. *Meshiḥim: Dramen* (Messiahs: Dramas). 1928: translated into Hebrew as *Meshiḥim: Dramot*. Tel Aviv: Am Oved, 1952.

Porat, Dina. *Hanhaga be-Milkud: Ha-Yishuv Nokhaḥ ha-Sho'a, 1942–1945* (An entangled leadership: The Yishuv and the Holocaust). Tel Aviv: Am Oved, 1986.

Poznansky, Menaḥem, ed. *Me-Ḥayei Yosef Trumpeldor* (On Yosef Trumpeldor's life). Tel Aviv: Am Oved, 1953.

Praver, Yehoshua. "Ir David, Kever Yisrael" (David's City, a Jewish grave), *Ma'ariv*, August 28, 1981, 20.

Prince, Gerald. *Narratology: The Form and Function of Narrative*. Berlin: Mouton, 1982.

Puchu. "Chizbat: Trumpeldor al ha-Gilbo'a" (Trumpeldor on the Gilbo'a). *Mashehu*, Purim issue, March 1988.

Rabin, Dov. "Yosef Trumpeldor ve-Sipurei Peretz" (Yosef Trumpeldor and Peretz's stories), in *Ha-Po'el ha-Tsa'ir*, March 20, 1962.

Rabinovitch, A. Z. "Hirhurim" (Reflections). *Kuntres* 72, March 15, 1921.

Rabinowitz, Louis I. "The Masada Martyrs according to the Halakha." *Tradition* 11 (Fall 1970): 31–37.

Raglan, Lord. *The Hero: A Study in Tradition, Myth, and Drama*, 1936; New York: Meridian, 1979.

Reptor, B. "Beineinu le-Vein Jabotinsky" (Between us and Jabotinsky), in *Lekaḥ Tel Ḥai: Ha-Hityashvut u-Gevul ha-Tsafon* (The lesson of Tel Ḥai: Settlement and the northern border). Yad Tabenkin and Ha-Kibbutz ha-Me'uḥad, 1980, 26–29.

Reuel, Ya'akov. "Sisco and the Masada Complex," *Jerusalem Post Weekly*, August 3, 1971, 9.

Ringelblum, Emmanuel. *Notes from the Warsaw Ghetto: The Journal of Emmanuel Ringelblum*, edited by Jacob Sloan. New York: Schocken, 1974.

Robbe-Grillet, Alain. *Pour un nouveau roman.* Paris: Les Editions de Minuit, 1963; English translation by Richard Howard, *For a New Novel: Essays on Fiction.* New York: Grove Press, 1965.

Rogel, Nakdimon. *Tel Ḥai: Ḥazit Lelo Oref* (Tel Ḥai: A front without rear). Tel Aviv: Yariv-Hadar, 1979.

———. "Lekaḥ Tel Ḥai" (The lesson of Tel Ḥai), in *Lekaḥ Tel Ḥai: Ha-Hityashvut u-Gevul ha-Tsafon* (The lesson of Tel Ḥai: Settlement and the northern border). Yad Tabenkin and Ha-Kibbutz ha-Me'uḥad, 1980, n.p.

Roke'aḥ, David. "Iyun Histori" (Historical discussion), in *Pulmus ha-Ḥurban u-Lekaḥav* (The controversy on the destruction and its lessons). Jerusalem: Van Leer Foundation, 1982, 89–122.

Rosenberg, Bruce. *Custer and the Epic of Defeat.* University Park: Pennsylvania State University Press, 1974.

Rosenthal, Yehuda. "Al Metsada ve-Giboreiha" (On Masada and its heroes). *Ha-Do'ar* 47 (no. 38), September 20, 1968, 693–95.

———. "Teshuva la-Masig" (A reply to a critic). *Ha-Do'ar* 48 (no. 3), November 15, 1968, 44–45.

———. "Ha-Kana'im ba-Masoret ha-Yehudit: Shetei Megamot" (The Zealots in Jewish tradition: Two approaches). *Katedra* 1 (1977): 58.

Roskies, David G., ed. *The Literature of Destruction: Jewish Responses to Catastrophe.* Philadelphia: Jewish Publication Society, 1988.

Rotenberg, Beno. *Metsada* (Masada). Tel Aviv: Levin Epstein, 1963.

Rotenstein, Raphael. "Ha-Mitos ha-Matrid" (The disturbing myth), *Ha-Aretz*, April 20, 1973, 16.

Rubenstein, Dani. *Mi la-Adonai Elai: Gush Emunim* (On the Lord's side: Gush Emunim). Tel Aviv: Ha-Kibbutz ha-Me'uḥad, 1982.

Rubinstein, Amnon. *Liheyot Am Ḥofshi* (To be a free people). Tel Aviv: Schocken, 1977.

Said, Edward W. *Beginnings: Intention and Method.* New York: Columbia University Press, 1985.

Schatzker, Chaim. "The Holocaust in Israeli Education." *International Journal of Political Education* 5 (1982): 75–82.

Schauss, Hayyim. *The Jewish Festivals: History and Observance.* New York: Schocken, 1962.

Schindler, Pesach. "The Holocaust and Kiddush ha-Shem in Hassidic Thought." *Tradition* 13 (no. 4)–14 (no. 1), (1973): 88–104.

Schudson, Michael. "The Present in the Past versus the Past in the Present." *Communication* 11 (1989): 105–13.

Schwartz, Barry. "The Social Context of Commemoration: A Study in Collective Memory." *Social Forces* 61 (1982): 374–402.

Schwartz, Barry, Yael Zerubavel, and Bernice Barnett, "The Recovery of Masada: A Study in Collective Memory." *Sociological Quarterly* 27, no. 2 (1986): 147–64.

Schweid, Eliezer. *Mi-Yahadut le-Tsiyonut, mi-Tsiyonut le-Yahadut* (Between Judaism and Zionism). Jerusalem: Ha-Sifriya ha-Tsiyonit, 1983.

Segal, Dimitry. "Ha-Sifrut veha-Tarbut ha-Rusit be-Sugiyat Hivatsruta shel Tenu'at ha-Shiḥrur ha-Yehudit" (The impact of Russian literature and culture on the emergence of the Jewish liberation movement), in Pinḥas Ginosar, ed. *Ha-Sifrut ha-Ivrit u-Tenu'at ha-Avoda* (Hebrew literature and the Labor movement). Be'er Sheba: Ben-Gurion University Press, 1989, 1–16.

Segev, Tom. *Ha-Milion ha-Shevi'i: Ha-Yisra'elim veha-Sho'a* (The seventh million: The Israelis and the Holocaust). Jerusalem: Keter, 1991.

Shaked, Gershon. *Gal Ḥadash ba-Siporet ha-Ivrit* (A new wave in Hebrew fiction). Tel Aviv: Sifriyat ha-Po'alim, 1974.

———. *Ha-Siporet ha-Ivrit, 1880–1980* (Hebrew narrative fiction, *1880–1980*). Vol. 3. Tel Aviv: Ha-Kibbutz ha-Me'uḥad and Keter, 1988.

Shalom, S. "Aḥ, Bne ha-Galil" (Brother, build Galilee), in Ḥayim Harari, ed. *Mo'adim le-Simḥa* (Festivals and holidays). Tel Aviv: Omanut, 1941, 284.

Shapira, Anita. "Ha-Viku'aḥ be-tokh Mapai al ha-Shimush be-Alimut, 1932–1935" (The debate in Mapai on the use of violence), ha-*Tsiyonut* 5 (1978): 141–81.

———. *Berl: Biographia* (Berl: A biography). Tel Aviv: Am Oved, 1981.

———. *Halikha al Kav ha-Ofek* (Visions in conflict). Tel Aviv: Am Oved, 1988.

Shapira, Avhaham. *Aharon David Gordon u-Mekorotav ba-Ḥasidut uva-Kabala* (A. D. Gordon and his roots in Hasidism and Kabbala). Tel Aviv: Am Oved, forthcoming.

Shapiro, Yonathan. *Ilit Lelo Mamshikhim* (An elite without successors). Tel Aviv: Sifriyat ha-Po'alim, 1984.

Shargel, Baila A. "The Evolution of the Masada Myth." *Judaism* 28 (1979): 357–71.

Shavit, Ya'akov. "Mered Bar Kokhva: Ha-Omnam Mofet?" (The Bar Kokhba revolt: Is it a model?). *Yediot Aḥronot*, literary supplement, June 11, 1982.

———. *Me-Rov li-Medina: Ha-Tenu'a ha-Revisionistit, ha-Tokhnit ha-Hityashvutit, veha-Ra'ayon ha-Ḥevrati, 1925–1935* (Revisionism in Zionism: The Revisionist movement, the plan for colonizatory regime and social ideas). Tel Aviv: Hadar, 1983.

———. *Ha-Mitologiot shel ha-Yamin* (The mythologies of the Zionist Right). Kfar Saba: Bet Berl, 1986.

———. *Me-Ivri ad Kena'ani* (From Hebrew to Canaanite). Jerusalem: Domino Press, 1984.

Shavit, Yosef. "Ha-Rav Goren" (Rabbi Goren). *Yediot Aḥronot*, August 28, 1981, 8.

Shavit, Zohar. *Ha-Ḥayim ha-Sifruitiyim be-Eretz Yisrael, 1910–1933* (The literary life in Eretz Israel, 1910–1933). Tel Aviv: Ha-Kibbutz ha-Me'uḥad, 1982.

Shenhar, Aliza. "Liheyot Sham: Shirei Meḥa'a shel Ḥayalim bi-Levanon" (To be there: Protest songs by soldiers during the Lebanon War). *Ḥetz* 1 (April 1989): 34–43.

Shilo'aḥ, Tsvi. "Mi-Tel Ḥai ve-Ad Ne'ot Sinai" (From Tel Ḥai to Ne'ot Sinai). *Yediot Aḥronot*, April 10, 1979, 17.

Shils, Edward. *Center and Periphery: Essays in Macrosociology*. Chicago: University of Chicago Press, 1975.

Shim'oni, David. "Le-Trumpeldor" (To Trumpeldor), 1929; reprinted in *Shirim* (Poems). Tel Aviv: Masada, 1954, 2:226–27.

Shi'urim be-Historia le-Veit ha-Sefer ha-Mamlakhti (Lessons in history for the public schools). Jerusalem: Ministry of Education, Center for Curriculum Development, 1987.

Shlonsky, Avraham. "Im Kri'at *Masada*" [Reading *Masada*). *Ketuvim*, December 31, 1926, 4.

———. "Amal" (Labor), 1927; reprinted in *The Penguin Book of Hebrew Verse*, translated and edited by T. Carmi. Harmondsworth: Penguin, 1981, 534.

Shoḥat, Ella. *Israeli Cinema: East/West and the Politics of Representation*. Austin: University of Texas Press, 1989.

Shulman, Kalman. *Harisot Betar* (The ruins of Betar). Vilna, 1900.

Silberman, Lou H. "The Sefira Season: A Study in Folklore." *Hebrew Union College Annual* 22 (1942): 222–25.

Silberman, Neil Asher. *Between the Past and the Present: Archaeology, Ideology, and Nationalism in the Modern Middle East*. New York: Holt, 1989.

Silverman, Carol. "Reconstructing Folklore: Media and Cultural Policy in Eastern Europe." *Communication* 11 (1989): 141–60.

Simḥoni, Y. N., trans. Introduction, *Yosef ben Matityahu: Toldot Milḥemet ha-Yehudim im ha-Roma'im* (Josephus: The wars of the Jews). Ramat-Gan: Masada, 1923.

Skolsky, Shlomo. "Ha-Ari: Agada" (The lion: A legend), in *Ha-Ari ha-Gelili, 1920–1945* (The Galilean lion). Tel Aviv: Betar, 1945, 2.

Slutsky, Yehuda. *Mavo le-Toldot Tenu'at ha-Avoda ha-Yisra'elit* (Introduction to the history of the Labor movement in Israel). Tel Aviv: Am Oved, 1973.

Smallwood, Mary E. *The Jews under the Romans' Rule*. Leiden: E. J. Brill, 1976.

Smally, Eliezer. *Anshei Bereshit* (The people of Genesis). Tel Aviv: Shtibel, 1933.

———. "Yom Tel Ḥai" (Tel Ḥai Day), in *Benei ha-Yore* (The first rain's offsprings). Tel Aviv: Haskala la-Am, 1937, 130–41.

———. "ha-Maḥresha" (The plow), in Ḥayim Harari, ed. *Mo'adim le-Simḥa* (Festivals and holidays). Tel Aviv: Omanut, 1941, 288–90.

———. "Ha-Degel" (The flag), reprinted in *Ḥoveret la-Madrikh le-Ḥodesh Adar* (Guidelines for the counselor for the month of Adar). Tel Aviv: Betar, 1979, 47–50.

Smilansky, Moshe. "Makom Kadosh" (A holy place). *Ha-Aretz*, March 14, 1920, 1.

Smith, Barbara Herrnstein. *Poetic Closure: A Study of How Poems End*. Chicago: University of Chicago Press, 1968.

Smith, Morton. "Zealots and the Sicarii: Their Origins and Relations," *Harvard Theological Review* 64 (January 1971): 1–19.

Snir. "Trumpeldor." *Kuntres*, no. 208 (March 6, 1925): 5–6.

Sperber, Dan and Deidre Wilson. *Relevance: Communication and Cognition*. Cambridge: Harvard University Press, 1986.

Spero, Shubert. "In Defense of the Defenders of Masada." *Tradition* 11 (Spring 1970): 31–43.

———. "A Letter to the Editor: The Defenders of Masada." *Tradition* 13 (Fall 1971): 136–38.

Spiegel, Shalom. *The Last Trial: The Akeda*. New York: Behrman House, 1979.

Sprinzak, Ehud. "The Iceberg Model of Political Extremism," in David Newman, ed. *The Impact of Gush Emunim*. London: Croom Helm, 1985, 27–45.

Stallybrass, Peter, and Allon White. *The Politics and Poetics of Transgression*. Ithaca: Cornell University Press, 1986.

Steckmesser, Kent L. *The Western Hero in History and Legend*. Norman: University of Oklahoma Press, 1965.

Stern, Menaḥem. "Darko Shel Yosef ben Matityahu bi-Khetivat ha-Historia" (Josephus's approach to historical writing), in *Historyonim ve-Askolot Hitoriyot* (Historians and historical schools), Jerusalem: Ha-Ḥevra ha-Historit ha-Yisra'elit, 1977, 2d edition, 22–28.

Stevick, Philip, ed. *Anti-story: An Anthology of Experimental Fiction*. New York: Free Press, 1971.

Sutton-Smith, Brian. "Shut Up and Keep Digging: the Cruel Joke Series." *Midwest Folklore* 10 (1960): 11–22.

Syrkin, Marie. "The Paradox of Masada." *Midstream* 19 (October 1973): 66–70.

Talmi, Dalya, ed. *Leket Shirei Lag ba-Omer* (An anthology of Lag ba-Omer songs). Tel Aviv: Kiryat ha-Ḥinukh, n.d.

Tchernichovsky, Sha'ul. *Shirim* (Poems). Jerusalem: Schocken, 1959.

———. *Kitvei Tchernichovsky* (Tchernichovsky: Collected works). Tel Aviv: Hotsa'at Va'ad ha-Yovel, 1932.

Tehar-Lev, H. *Kol mihe-Harim* (A voice from the mountains). Jerusalem: Sifriyat Adama, 1959.

Tel Ḥai: Yalkut (Tel Hai: An anthology). Tel Aviv: Histadrut, 1934.

Terdiman, Richard. "Deconstructing Memory: On representing the Past and Theorizing Culture in France since the Revolution." *Diacritics* 15 (Winter 1985): 13–36.

Thackeray, Henry. *Josephus: The Man and the Historian*. New York: Ktav, 1960.

Thompson, Leonard. *The Political Mythology of Apartheid.* New Haven: Yale University Press, 1985.

Thompson, Stith. *Motif Index of Folk Literature.* Bloomington: Indiana University Press, 1976.

Tidhar, David. *Entsiklopedia le-Ḥalutsei ha-Yishuv u-Vonav* (Encyclopaedia of Israeli pioneers). Tel Aviv: Sifriyat Rishonim, 1950.

Tomarkin, Yigal. "Ma Bein Mahler ve-Har ha-Shulḥan be-S.A." (How does Mahler relate to the mountain), *Ha-Aretz,* weekend supplement, October 7, 1988, 23.

Trumpeldor, Yosef. "Wertheimer." *Ha-Aretz,* March 21, 1921, 2–3.

Tsemaḥ, Shlomo. "*Masada:* Yitzḥak Lamdan." *Ha-Po'el ha-Tsa'ir* nos. 26–27, April 15, 1927, 43.

Tudor, Henry. *Political Myth.* New York: Praeger, 1972.

Turner, Victor W. *The Ritual Process: Structure and Anti-Structure.* Harmondsworth, Middlesex: Penguin Books, 1974.

———. *Process, Performance, and Pilgrimage: A Study in Comparative Symbology.* New Delhi: Concept, 1979.

Usque, Samuel. *Consolation for the Tribulations of Israel,* 1552; English translation by Martin A. Cohen. Philadelphia: Jewish Publication Society, 1965.

Van Der Veer, Peter. "Ayodhya and Somnath: Eternal Shrines, Contested Histories." *Social Research* 59, no. 1 (1992): 85–109.

Van Gennep, Arnold. *The Rites of Passage.* 1908; Chicago: University of Chicago Press, 1960.

Vardi, Ronit. "Metsada" (Masada). *Yediot Aḥronot,* October 14, 1988, 1.

Vidal-Naquet, Pierre. *Les Juifs, la mémoire, et le présent.* Paris: Librairie François Maspero, 1981.

Vital, David. *The Origins of Zionism.* Oxford: Oxford University Press, 1975.

Walzer, Michael. *Exodus and Revolution.* New York: Basic Books, 1985.

Warner, W. Lloyd. *The Living and the Dead: A Study in the Symbolic Life of Americans.* Yankee City series, vol. 5. New Haven: Yale University Press, 1959.

Weiss-Rosmarin, Trude. "Masada and Yavne." *Jewish Spectator* 31 (November 1966): 4–7.

———. "Masada, Josephus, and Yadin." *Jewish Spectator* 32 (October 1967): 28, 30–32.

———. "Reflections on Leadership." *Jewish Spectator* 33 (March 1968): 2–5.

———. "Masada Revisited." *Jewish Spectator* 34 (December 1969): 3–5, 29.

Weitz, Yechiam. "The Yishuv's Self-Image and the Reality of the Holocaust." *Jerusalem Quarterly* 48 (Fall 1988): 73–87.

Weitz, Yosef. *Seviv Metsada* (Around Masada). Jerusalem: Sifriyat Adama, 1963.

White, Hayden. *Tropics of Discourse: Essays in Cultural Criticism.* Baltimore: Johns Hopkins University Press, 1978.

———. *The Content of the Form: Narrative Discourse and Historical Representation.* Baltimore: Johns Hopkins University Press, 1987.

Wilson, William A. *Folklore and Nationalism in Modern Finland.* Bloomington: Indiana University Press, 1976.

Wisse, Ruth R. *The Shlemiel as a Modern Hero.* Chicago: University of Chicago Press, 1971.

Ya'ari-Polskin, Y. *Ḥolmim ve-Loḥamim* (Dreamers and fighters). Jaffa: Gissin, 1922.

Yad Va-Shem: Martyrs' and Heroes Remembrance Authority. Jerusalem: Yad Va-Shem Authority, 1976.

Yadin, Yigael. *Masada: Herod's Fortress and the Zealots' Last Stand.* New York: Random House, 1966.

———. *Ha-Ḥipusim aḥar Bar-Kokhva* (In search of Bar Kokhba). Jerusalem: Weinfeld & Nicholson, 1971; English edition, *Bar-Kokhba: The Rediscovery of the Legendary Hero of the Second Jewish Revolt Against Rome.* Jerusalem: Weinfeld & Nicholson, 1971.

Yaffe, Z. Y., and Y. Spivak, eds. *Medura* (Bonfire). Jerusalem: Keren Kayemet le-Yisrael, 1929.

Yates, Frances A. *The Art of Memory.* Chicago: University of Chicago Press, 1966.

Yehoshua, Avraham B. "Bein Metsada le-Jabel Ataka" (Between Masada and Jabel Ataka), 1973; reprinted in *Ha-Kir veha-Har* (The wall and the mountain). Tel Aviv: Zmora & Bitan, 1989, 29–31.

———. *Bi-Zekhut ha-Normaliyut* (Between right and right). Tel Aviv: Schocken, 1980.

Yeivin, Shmu'el. *Milḥemet Bar Kokhva* (The Bar Kokhba war). Jerusalem: Mosad Bialik, 1957.

Yerushalmi, Yosef Hayim. *Zakhor: Jewish History and Jewish Memory.* Seattle: University of Washington Press, 1982.

Yizhar, S. *Yemei Tsiklag* (The days of Tsiklag). Tel Aviv: Am Oved, 3rd edition, 1959.

Young, James E. "When a Day Remembers: A Performative History of Yom Hashoah." *History and Memory* 2, no. 3 (1990): 54–75.

Zakovitch, Yair. *Ḥayei Shimshon: Nitu'aḥ Sifruti Bikorti* (The life of Samson: A critical-literary analysis). Jerusalem: Magnes, 1982.

Ze'evi, Reḥavam. "Aḥarai" (Follow me). *Ba-Maḥane*, December 18, 1969, 10–11.

Zeitlin, Solomon. "Masada and the Sicarii: The Occupants of Masada." *Jewish Quarterly Review* 55 (April 1965): 299–317.

———. "The Sicarii and Masada." *Jewish Quarterly Review* 57 (April 1967): 251–70.

———. "The Slavonic Josephus and the Dead Sea Scrolls: An Exposé of Recent Fairy Tales." *Jewish Quarterly Review* 58 (January 1968): 173–203.

Zekhor Yemei Tel Ḥai (Remember the days of Tel Ḥai). Tel Aviv: Teachers Council for the Jewish National Fund, 1960.

Zerubavel, Eviatar. *Hidden Rhythms: Schedules and Calendars in Social Life.* Chicago: University of Chicago Press, 1981.

———. "Easter and Passover: On Calendars and Group Identity." *American Sociological Review* 47 (1982): 284–89.

———. *The Seven Day Circle: The History and Meaning of the Week.* New York: Free Press, 1985.

———. *The Fine Line: Making Distinctions in Everyday Life.* New York: Free Press, 1991.

———. *Terra Cognita: The Mental Discovery of America.* New Brunswick: Rutgers University Press, 1992.

Zerubavel, Yael. "The Last Stand: On the Transformation of Symbols in Modern Israeli Culture." Ph.D. diss., University of Pennsylvania. Ann Arbor, MI: University Microfilms, 1980.

———. "The Holiday Cycle and the Commemoration of the Past: Folklore, History, and Education," in *Proceedings of the Ninth World Congress of Jewish Studies.* Jerusalem: World Union of Jewish Studies, 1986, 4:111–18.

———. "The 'Wandering Israeli' in Contemporary Israeli Literature," *Contemporary Jewry* 7 (1986): 127–40.

———. "New Beginning, Old Past: The Collective Memory of Pioneering in Israeli Culture," in Laurence J. Silberstein, ed. *New Perspectives on Israeli History: The Early Years of the State.* New York University Press, 193–215.

———. "The Politics of Interpretation: Tel Ḥai in Israeli Collective Memory." *Association for Jewish Studies Review* 16, nos. 1–2 (1992): 133–60.

———. "The Historical, the Legendary, and the Incredible: Invented Tradition and Collective Memory in Israel," in John R. Gillis, ed. *Commemorations: The Politics of National Identity.* Princeton: Princeton University Press, 1994, 105–23; Hebrew translation in David Oḥana and Robert Wistrich, ed. *Mitos ve-Historia.* Van Leer Institute and Ha-Kibbutz ha-Me'uḥad, forthcoming.

———. "The 'Death of Memory' and the Memory of Death: Masada and the Holocaust as Historical Metaphors." *Representations* 45 (Winter 1994): 72–100; Hebrew translation in *Alpayim* 10 (Fall 1994): 42–67.

Zielberscheid, Ya'akov, and Arie Pialkov, eds. *Tel Ḥai: Kibbutz Hakhshara be-Folin* (Kibbutz Tel Ḥai in Poland). Tel Aviv: Ha-Kibbutz ha-Me'uḥad, 1979.

Zrubavel [Gilad], ed. *Moreshet Gevura* (The heroic heritage). Tel Aviv: Ma'arkhot, 1947.

———, ed. *Sefer ha-Palmaḥ* (The Palmaḥ book). Tel Aviv: Ha-Kibbutz ha-Me'uḥad, 1963.

INDEX

Aaron, 218
Abraham, 88
agada. See legend
Aḥad Ha-Am, 30, 244 n. 5, 245 n. 18
Aharoni, Yoḥanan, 188, 189
Aḥime'ir, Aba, 152
akeda (the binding of Isaac), 90
Akiba (ben Yosef), Rabbi, 52, 255 n. 21
  and Bar Kokhba, 25, 49–51, 53, 98–99, 202, 224
  and Lag ba-Omer, 97, 99, 140, 269 n. 18
aliya la-regel. See pilgrimage
Almog, Shmuel, 21
Alsop, Stewart, 209, 294 n. 60
Anderson, Benedict, 214
Antiquity, 115, 231
  end of, 34, 194. *See also* Bar Kokhba revolt; Masada, the fall of
  and Hebrew language, 2, 29, 31–32, 250 n. 73
  and National Revival, 31–36, 58–59, 66, 68, 70–72, 85–88, 102, 126, 129–30, 179–85, 194–95, 203, 209, 217, 222
  embodies nationhood, 16, 22–26, 31–36, 215, 217, 247 n. 40
  ancient revolts, 23–25, 36, 46, 53, 63, 72–73, 111–12, 215
  See also archeology; Zionist master commemorative narrative
Arab-Israeli conflict, 39–41, 44, 148–49, 151, 173, 194, 235, 254 n. 38
  See also Palestinian-Israeli conflict
archeology
  and Bar Kokhba revolt, 30, 56–59, 113, 178, 185–89
  and Masada, 63–68, 120, 122, 129–33, 139, 178, 196, 207, 211–12, 236, 260 nn. 23, 32
  and nationalism, 57–59, 65–66, 68, 129–33, 135, 186–87, 189, 260 nn. 27, 31
  conflict with rabbinical authorities, 186–89, 288 n. 46
Aronoff, Myron, 190
autobiographical memory, 4, 103, 162, 198, 234–35, 239 n. 4
Avraham B., Yehoshua, 194
Avramsky, Shmu'el, 113

Bakhtin, 173
Bar Giora, Shimon, 23, 202
  organization, 36
Bar Kokhba, Shimon, 19, 23, 86, 95, 221, 224
  "legendary" image, 50–54, 96, 99, 103–10, 141, 236
  negative image, 50–51, 54, 103, 179, 255 n. 10